COMPREHENSIVE REVIEW GUIDE for HEALTH INFORMATION

RHIA & RHIT Exam Prep

CARLA TYSON-HOWARD, EdD, MHA, RHIA
Chair, Health Information Technology Department
Houston Community College

SHIRLYN C. THOMAS, MEd, RHIA
Executive Director, Holistic Community Development Corporation
Adjunct Instructor, Health Information Technology Department
Houston Community College

JONES AND BARTLETT PUBLISHERS
Sudbury, Massachusetts
BOSTON   TORONTO   LONDON   SINGAPORE

World Headquarters

Jones and Bartlett Publishers	Jones and Bartlett Publishers	Jones and Bartlett Publishers
40 Tall Pine Drive	Canada	International
Sudbury, MA 01776	6339 Ormindale Way	Barb House, Barb Mews
978-443-5000	Mississauga, Ontario L5V 1J2	London W6 7PA
info@jbpub.com	Canada	United Kingdom
www.jbpub.com		

Jones and Bartlett's books and products are available through most bookstores and online booksellers. To contact Jones and Bartlett Publishers directly, call 800-832-0034, fax 978-443-8000, or visit our website www.jbpub.com.

Substantial discounts on bulk quantities of Jones and Bartlett's publications are available to corporations, professional associations, and other qualified organizations. For details and specific discount information, contact the special sales department at Jones and Bartlett via the above contact information or send an email to specialsales@jbpub.com.

Production Credits

Publisher: David Cella
Editorial Assistant: Maro Asadoorian
Production Manager: Julie Champagne Bolduc
Production Assistant: Jessica Steele Newfell
Associate Marketing Manager: Lisa Gordon
Manufacturing and Inventory Control Supervisor: Amy Bacus
Composition: Cape Cod Compositors, Inc.
Cover Design: Brian Moore
Cover Image: © Photodisc
Printing and Binding: Courier Stoughton
Cover Printing: Courier Stoughton

Library of Congress Cataloging-in-Publication Data

Tyson-Howard, Carla.
    Comprehensive review guide for health information : RHIA & RHIT exam prep / Carla Tyson-Howard, Shirlyn C. Thomas.
        p. ; cm.
    Includes bibliographical references.
    ISBN 978-0-7637-5661-1 (pbk. : alk. paper)
    1. Medical records—Management—Examinations, questions, etc.   2. Information resources management—Examinations, questions, etc.   I. Thomas, Shirlyn C.   II. Title.
    [DNLM: 1. Forms and Records Control—organization & administration—Examination Questions.   2. Information Management—Examination Questions.   3. Medical Records—Examination Questions. W 18.2 T994c 2009]
    RA976.T97 2009
    651.5'04261076—dc22
                    2008028936

6048

Printed in the United States of America
12 11 10 09 08   10 9 8 7 6 5 4 3 2 1

Contents

Contents

CHAPTER 4

Health Care Statistics, Research, and Epidemiology   121

CHAPTER 5

Quality Management and Performance Improvement   163

CHAPTER 6

Information Technology and Systems   223

About the Authors

Carla Tyson-Howard, EdD, MHA, RHIA
Chair, Health Information Technology Department
Houston Community College
Houston, Texas

Shirlyn C. Thomas, MEd, RHIA
Executive Director, Holistic Community Development Corporation (CDC)
Galveston, Texas
Adjunct Instructor, Health Information Technology Department
Houston Community College
Houston, Texas

CONTRIBUTING AUTHORS

Casandra Johnson, RHIT, CCS
(Chapter 8: Clinical Classification Systems)
Health Information Manager
Park Plaza Hospital
Houston, Texas

Bunmi Ogunleye, MSHEd, CHES, RHIA
(Chapter 5: Quality Management and Performance Improvement)
Health Information Manager
Harris County Hospital District
Adjunct Instructor, Houston Community and North Harris Montgomery Junior Colleges
Houston, Texas

Irma Rodriguez, MEd, RHIA, CCS
(Chapter 2: Health Data Management and Health Services Organization and Delivery)
Chair, Health Information Technology Department
South Texas College
McAllen, Texas

Acknowledgments

I am grateful to G-d for giving me the idea, inspiration, and energy to co-develop this review guide with my sister-partner, Shirlyn Thomas. It is a labor of love to my students and health information students around the world. I hope that this review guide brings clarity and focus to your studies and exam preparation.

I express gratitude to my mentors, Linda Johnson and Tella Williams, for guiding me in the health information field. Thank you also to Debora Butts for reviewing and providing input on the text while under construction. I thank the co-authors for sharing their knowledge, wisdom, and expertise. I acknowledge Houston Community College for supporting faculty in the use of technology to make the teaching and learning process easier.

In memory of my father, Carl, I thank him and my mother, Odell Tyson, for instilling in me the importance of education. Thanks to my sister, Cassandra Tyson, and my friend Elizabeth Hoover for countless hours of reviewing and referencing material.

Finally, I acknowledge my handsome husband, John Howard, whose encouragement and endless love is priceless.

—*Carla Tyson-Howard*

No one is or becomes without the help of others. I would like to express my sincere gratitude to the others in my life who have contributed in various ways to make this product a living instrument to help others.

To God and my Lord and Savior, for creating me in your image and your likeness and for equipping me with all that was needed to complete your idea.

To Carla, for being a conduit of the idea and allowing me to share a part of making the lives of others better and for being one of my greatest teachers.

To my mother, who has given me a genetic transfer of determination and tenacity.

To my wonderful and precious husband, who became whatever I needed in the toughest parts of the process and is always a source of strength.

To my children, LaToya, T.K., and Trae, who are my inspirations and whose faces I reflect on when the going gets tough.

To my sisters, Deborah and Kim, who are parts of the foundation on which I stand. Thanks for your never-ending support.

—*Shirlyn Thomas*

Introduction

PRODUCT INSTRUCTION

Congratulations on your choice to use the *Comprehensive Review Guide for Health Information: RHIA and RHIT Exam Prep*. It is an invaluable resource for navigating through school and preparing for the national exams. This comprehensive review of health information is designed to assist students in passing the national examination for Registered Health Information Administrators (RHIA) and Registered Health Information Technicians (RHIT) and with navigating through coursework. This product was created to meet the needs of the basic learning styles, which include audio (hearing) learners, visual (seeing) learners, and tactile (experience) learners. Keep in mind, this review series is not to teach or introduce new information, but to highlight major areas of study that you have learned or are learning during your coursework.

This unique product contains all the components needed for a comprehensive strategy for test success. The book is divided into sections by knowledge clusters and contains over 600 test questions. Each of the eight sections is divided into a review of the subject area, application of knowledge (short answer, fill in the blank, and matching questions), and test of knowledge (50 multiple-choice questions). Answers and references are provided for the test of knowledge. To assure maximum strength of your knowledge, answers for the application of knowledge are not provided (except in the clinical classification systems section). If you do not know these answers, you must reread the review section or reference your text books. The book ends with a 200-question, 4.5-hour mock exam. The audio-review content provides a personal tutor of the knowledge clusters. The audio content will tutor you with some of the questions in the health data management, statistics, coding, and management sections. Look for the ♪ sign to indicate the questions reviewed in the audio portion.

All test questions have been created utilizing the Domains and Subdomains structure dictated by the American Health Information Management Association. To maximize this learning tool, we recommend the following:

1. Review the content areas in the review section of the book. Begin with your challenging areas first (visual learning).
2. Listen to the audio review series while reviewing the focused content area of study (audio learning).

3. Complete the workbook exercises related to the content area of study (tactile learning).
4. Evaluate your comprehension of the content area by taking the "Test Your Knowledge" exam on the relevant content area.
5. Repeat this process until you have completed all of the content areas.
6. After completion of all areas of content in the review book section, audio, and workbook, take the mock examination. The mock exam in this review consists of 200 questions, and you will have 4.5 hours to complete it. To make it easier for you to determine your areas of strengths and those requiring additional study, the test is divided by competencies. You will need your calculator to perform mathematical computations. You also will need your ICD-9-CM and CPT books to answer the coding questions. When you take the actual RHIA and RHIT exams, you will not need coding books to take either exam. All information that will be needed to answer a coding question will be included in the body of the question. The question will include the code itself, narrative, and any other relevant information from the code books.
7. Repeat steps 1 through 4 for areas of weakness as indicated by the mock exam results.
8. Continue to reinforce learning by listening to the audio review series while exercising, driving, cooking, or even falling asleep.

In addition, utilize your textbooks to provide more support for challenging areas. Remember the steps in your study process (Figure 1-1). Information about the exams may change. Be sure you consult with the American Health Information Management Association (AHIMA) to obtain the latest information. Their website is www.ahima.org.

The RHIA and RHIT national exams of the AHIMA are based on an explicit set of competencies. The 4-hour, 180-question RHIA examination consists of 160 scored questions and 20 pretest questions. The 3.5-hour RHIT exam consists of 150 questions (130 scored questions and 20 pretest questions). The competency domains and the number of questions on the exams are listed for each. The levels (RE = Recall, AP = Application, AN = Analysis) refer to the levels of learning for the RHIA and RHIT Exam competencies per the national body, AHIMA.

Review →	Practice →	Test →	Review →	Reinforce
↓	↓	↓	↓	↓
Review book content and audio review series	Workbook content	Take the test-your-knowledge exams	After mock exam, identify areas to review again	Review audio series

Figure 1-1 Study Process Steps

RHIA Examination: Competency Statements	RE	AP	AN	T
Domain 1: Health Data Management				*40*
Subdomain A. Health Data Structure, Content and Standards	2	6	5	
1. Manage health data: Data elements (plan, design, monitor, verify, interpret)				
2. Manage health data: Data sets (plan, design, monitor, verify, interpret)				
3. Manage health data: Data bases (plan, design, monitor, verify, interpret)				
4. Assure that documentation in the health record supports the diagnosis and reflects the progress, clinical findings, and discharge status				
5. Maintain processes, policies, and procedures to assure the accuracy and integrity of health data				
6. Clinical vocabularies and terminologies used in the organization's health information systems (evaluate, select, monitor, verify, interpret)				
7. Abbreviation usage in the organization's health information system (plan, select, monitor)				
Subdomain B. Health Care Information Requirements and Standards	2	5	4	
1. Develop organization-wide health-record documentation guidelines				
2. Maintain organizational compliance with health care information regulations and standards (such as documentation, retention, reporting)				
3. Interpret, communicate, and apply current laws and accreditation, licensure, and certification standards related to health information initiatives at the national, state, local, and facility levels				
4. Ensure organizational survey readiness regarding health care information for accreditation, licensing, and/or certification processes				
Subdomain C. Clinical Classification Systems	2	6	0	
1. Select electronic applications for clinical classification and coding				
2. Implement and manage applications and processes for clinical classification and coding				

(continues)

RHIA Examination: Competency Statements *(continued)*

	RE	AP	AN	*T*
3. Validate coding accuracy, using clinical information found in the health record				
4. Assign diagnosis and procedure codes				
Subdomain D. Reimbursement Methodologies	2	3	3	
1. Manage the use of clinical data required in reimbursement systems and prospective payment systems (PPS) in health care delivery				
2. Manage organization's revenue cycle, including chargemaster, claims management, and finance decision support (plan, design, monitor, verify, interpret)				
3. Implement and manage processes for compliance and reporting (such as National Correct Coding Initiative; Local Medical Review Policies [LMRP]; Medicare Code Editor [MCE]; Resource Based Relative Value Scale [RBRVS]; Outpatient Code Editor [OCE])				
Domain 2: Health Statistics, Biomedical Research and Quality Management				*16*
Subdomain A. Health Care Statistics and Research	0	4	4	
1. Manage databases (plan and/or select, design, abstract, monitor, verify, interpret)				
2. Analyze and present data for quality management, utilization management, risk management, and other patient-care-related studies				
Subdomain B. Quality Assessment and Performance Improvement	0	4	4	
1. Facility-wide quality management and performance improvement programs (monitor and report)				
2. Provide data for health care decision making, including quality, safety, and effectiveness of health care (assess data needs, design data collection process, coordinate data collection, collect data, interpret data, report information)				
Domain 3: Health Services Organization and Delivery				*32*
Subdomain A. Health Care Statistics and Research	3	8	5	
1. Analyze and respond to the information needs of internal and external customers throughout the continuum of health care services				

RHIA Examination: Competency Statements *(continued)*

	RE	AP	AN	*T*
Subdomain B. Health Care Privacy and Confidentiality, and Legal and Ethical Issues	3	8	5	
1. Coordinate the implementation of legal and regulatory requirements related to the health information infrastructure regarding health care privacy and confidentiality issues				
2. Manage access, disclosure, and use of personal health information				
3. Organization-wide confidentiality policies and procedures (develop, implement, maintain)				
4. Health care privacy training programs (develop, implement, maintain)				
5. Investigate and mitigate health care privacy issues/problems				
Domain 4: Information Technology and Systems				*32*
Subdomain A. Information and Communication Technologies	2	5	1	
1. Implement and manage use of technology applications to ensure data collection, storage, analysis, and reporting of information				
2. End-user hardware and software applications to enhance health information documentation (plan, select, implement)				
Subdomain B. Data, Information, and File Structure	1	2	2	
1. Database architecture to meet organizational needs, including data dictionary, data modeling, data warehousing (plan, design, implement, monitor, verify)				
2. Apply data, communications, and functional standards to achieve interoperability of health care information systems such as HL7, ASTM (plan, design, implement, monitor, verify)				
Subdomain C. Data Storage and Retrieval	2	2	2	
1. Apply data/record storage principles and techniques, including paper based, hybrid (paper with any other medium), electronic				
2. Query and report from databases using data-mining techniques				
3. Design and generate routine and custom reports				
Subdomain D. Data Security	2	2	1	
1. Security measures to safeguard protected health information (PHI) (plan, design, implement, monitor, enforce)				
2. Protect data integrity and validity using software or hardware technology				

(continues)

RHIA Examination: Competency Statements *(continued)*

	RE	AP	AN	*T*
Subdomain E. Health Care Information Systems	2	4	2	
1. Evaluate and recommend clinical, administrative, and specialty service applications				
2. Health Information Management (HIM) departmental applications such as transcription, chart management, encoder (plan, workflow design, application design, select, test, implement, monitor functionality, evaluate multiple aspects, including goal attainment, return on investment (ROI), support, system administrator)				
3. Organization-wide information systems (plan, workflow design, application design, select, test, implement, monitor functionality, evaluate goal attainment including ROI, support, system administrator)				
Domain 5: Organizational and Management				*40*
Subdomain A. Human Resources Management	3	6	3	
1. Manage human resources such as staff recruitment, supervision, retention, counseling, disciplinary action				
2. Ensure compliance with employment laws				
3. Training programs, including staff orientation, continuing education, systems (develop, implement, maintain)				
4. Productivity standards for health information functions (develop, implement, maintain, feedback to staff)				
5. Benchmarking for HIM departments, such as staffing and productivity (develop, implement, maintain, feedback)				
6. Perform job analyses				
7. Develop job descriptions				
8. Develop, motivate, and support work teams				
Subdomain B. Financial and Resource Management	3	6	3	
1. Prepare and monitor budgets				
2. Prepare and monitor contracts				
3. Conduct cost-benefit analysis to justify resource needs				
Subdomain C. Strategic Planning and Organizational Development	2	2	2	
1. Develop strategic and operational plans for facility-wide health information management				
2. Facilitate team building, negotiation, and change management				

RHIA Examination: Competency Statements *(continued)*

	RE	AP	AN	*T*
Subdomain D. Project and Operations Management	2	5	3	
1. Implement and evaluate process engineering to ensure efficient workflow and appropriate outcomes				
2. Implement project management techniques to achieve project goals				
3. Ensure compliance with relevant HIM service regulations and accreditation standards				
4. Identify and implement HIM best practices				
5. Resolve customer complaints				
Total Number of Examination Items	33	78	49	*160*

RHIT Examination: Competency Statements

	RE	AP	AN	*T*
Domain 1: Health Data Management				*39*
Subdomain A. Health Data Structure, Content and Standards	2	2	4	
1. Collect and maintain data sets and databases				
2. Conduct qualitative analysis to assure that documentation in the health record supports the diagnosis and reflects the progress, clinical findings, and discharge status				
3. Apply clinical vocabularies and terminologies used in the organization's health information systems				
4. Comply with national patient safety goals as related to abbreviation usage				
5. Verify timeliness, completeness, accuracy, and appropriateness of data and data sources (e.g., patient care, management, billing reports, and/or databases)				
Subdomain B. Health Care Information Requirements and Standards	2	4	3	
1. Monitor the accuracy and completeness of the health record as defined by organizational policy, external regulations, and standards				
2. Perform analysis of health records to evaluate compliance with regulations and standards:				
a. Quantitative analysis				
b. Qualitative analysis				

(continues)

RHIT Examination: Competency Statements *(continued)*

	RE	AP	AN	T
3. Apply policies and procedures to assure organizational compliance with regulations and standards				
Subdomain C. Clinical Classification Systems	2	12	0	
1. Use and monitor applications and work processes to support clinical classification and coding				
2. Apply diagnosis/procedure codes using ICD-9-CM				
3. Apply procedure codes using CPT/HCPCS				
4. Ensure accuracy of diagnostic/procedural groupings (e.g., APC, DRG, IPS)				
5. Adhere to current regulations and established guidelines in code assignment				
6. Validate coding accuracy using clinical information found in the health record				
7. Identify discrepancies between coded data and supporting documentation				
Subdomain D. Reimbursement Methodologies	2	4	2	
1. Apply policies and procedures for the use of clinical data required in reimbursement and prospective payment systems (PPS) in health care delivery (e.g., APC, DRG, RVU, RBRVS)				
2. Support accurate revenue cycle through:				
a. Coding				
3. Use established guidelines to comply with reimbursement and reporting requirements (e.g., National Correct Coding Initiative [NCCI], local medical review policies [LMRP])				
Domain 2: Health Statistics, Biomedical Research and Quality Management				16
Subdomain A. Health Care Statistics and Research	1	4	2	
1. Abstract and maintain data for clinical indices/databases/registries				
2. Collect, organize, and present data for:				
a. Administrative purposes				
b. Financial purposes				
c. Performance improvement programs				
d. Quality management				
Subdomain B. Quality Assessment and Performance Improvement	1	4	4	
1. Participate in facility-wide quality assessment program				
2. Present data in verbal and written forms				

RHIT Examination: Competency Statements *(continued)*	RE	AP	AN	*T*
Domain 3: Health Services Organization and Delivery				*22*
Subdomain A. Health Care Delivery Systems	3	5	1	
1. Comply with accreditation, licensure, and certification standards from government (national, state, and local levels) and private organizations (e.g., The Joint Commission [TJC])				
2. Apply policies and procedures to comply with the changing regulations among various payment systems for health care services such as Centers for Medicare and Medicaid Services (CMS), managed care				
3. Differentiate the roles of various providers and disciplines throughout the continuum of health care and respond to their information needs				
4. Understand the role of various providers and disciplines throughout the continuum of health care services				
Subdomain B. Health Care Compliance, Confidentiality, Ethical, Legal, and Privacy Issues	2	7	4	
1. Implement the legal and regulatory requirements related to health information				
2. Apply regulatory policies and procedures for access and disclosure of PHI				
3. Maintain user access logs/systems to track access to and disclosure of patient-identifiable data				
4. Identify and report privacy issues/problems				
5. Demonstrate and promote legal and ethical standards of practice				
6. Report compliance issues according to organizational policy				
7. Collaborate with staff to prepare the organization for accreditation, licensing, and/or certification surveys				
8. Implement health record documentation guidelines and provide education to staff				
Domain 4: Information Technology and Systems				*33*
Subdomain A. Information and Communication Technologies	5	4	0	
1. Use technology, including hardware and software, to ensure data collection, storage, analysis, retrieval, and reporting of information				
2. Use common software applications (e.g., spreadsheets, databases, presentation, e-mail) in the execution of work processes				

(continues)

RHIT Examination: Competency Statements *(continued)*				
	RE	**AP**	**AN**	*T*
3. Use specialized software in the completion of HIM processes (e.g., chart management, coding, release of information)				
4. Apply policies and procedures for the use of networks, including intranet and Internet applications to facilitate the electronic health record (EHR), personal health record (PHR), public health, and other administrative applications				
5. Protect data integrity using software or hardware technology (data should be complete, accurate, consistent, and current)				
Subdomain B. Data, Storage and Retrieval	4	5	1	
1. Use appropriate electronic or imaging technology for data/record storage				
2. Maintain integrity of patient numbering and filing systems				
3. Design forms, graphical user interfaces, and other health record documentation tools				
4. Maintain integrity of master patient/client index/enterprise master patient index (EMPI)				
5. Query and generate reports using appropriate software				
6. Design and generate reports using appropriate software				
7. Coordinate, use, and maintain archival and retrieval systems for patient information (e.g., in multiple formats)				
Subdomain C. Data Security	2	3	3	
1. Apply confidentiality and security measures to PHI				
2. Apply departmental and organizational data and information system security policies				
3. Use and summarize data compiled from audit trail				
Subdomain D. Health Care Information Systems	1	3	2	
1. Collect and report data on incomplete records and timeliness of record completion				
2. Maintain filing and retrieval systems for health records				
Domain 5: Organizational Resources				20
Subdomain A. Human Resources	3	5	6	
1. Apply the fundamentals of team leadership				
2. Develop and/or contribute to:				
a. Strategic plans, goals, and objectives for areas of responsibility				
b. Job descriptions				

RHIT Examination: Competency Statements *(continued)*

	RE	AP	AN	T
3. Develop and/or conduct performance appraisals				
4. Participate in intradepartmental and interdepartmental teams/committees				
5. Develop and implement staff orientation and training programs				
6. Provide consultation, education, and training to users of health information				
a. Internal users (e.g., health care providers, administrators)				
7. Assess, monitor, and report				
a. Quality standards				
b. Productivity standards				
8. Perform staffing analysis to determine adequate coverage				
9. Prioritize job functions and activities				
10. Use quality improvement tools and techniques to assess, report, and improve processes				
11. Promote positive customer relations				
12. Apply the principles of ergonomics in work process design				
13. Comply with local, state, and federal regulations regarding labor relations				
Subdomain B. Financial and Physical Resources	1	3	2	
1. Determine and monitor resources to meet workload needs, including staff, equipment, and supplies				
2. Make recommendations for items to include in budgets				
3. Monitor coding and revenue cycle processes				
4. Recommend cost-saving and efficient means of achieving work processes and goals				
Total Number of Examination Items	31	65	34	*130*

STUDY TIPS

You are either navigating your way through your HIM program or preparing to take your national RHIA or RHIT exam. Either way, the *Comprehensive Review Guide for Health Information: RHIA and RHIT Exam Prep* is an excellent tool in your arsenal for success. Because everyone is different and our learning styles vary, different methods work for different people. The following are only suggestions for improving your current study techniques to help launch your achievement in the field of HIM.

1. **Make a study schedule.** Use a calendar to plan the days and times to study specific courses or subject areas. Space out your studying; review class materials at least several times a week, focusing on one topic at a time.
2. **Set a standard place to study** such as your office, library, kitchen table, or wherever is comfortable and conducive for focused and concentrated learning. Make sure you have adequate lighting and that you are not distracted by noises.
3. **Place all of your study material in front of you:** lecture notes, course textbooks, study guides, and any other relevant material.
4. **Use the audio portion of this product to maximize your learning.** Listen to it as you drive, ride the bus, jog, cook, or even nap. Use it to walk you through some of the computation.
5. **Take notes** and write down a summary of the important ideas as you read through your study material. Make notes in your books. There is nothing wrong with writing in your books; they are your books.
6. **Take short breaks frequently.** Your memory retains the information that you study at the beginning and the end better than what you study in the middle.
7. **Make sure that you understand the material well.** Do not just read through the material and try to memorize everything. Use the review guide to test your knowledge. Make an exam for yourself and answer the questions. The more times you test yourself, the more you increase your chance of scoring higher on your exam.
8. **Use the review guide** to review the main information of the knowledge clusters quickly. You also may use the review guide to rewrite the main ideas, information, and formulas to reinforce your comprehension of the material. This may make it easier to retain the key concepts that will be on the test.
9. If you choose to study in a group, **only study with others who are serious** about the test. Study groups are not social gatherings for happy hour. At the end of the predetermined study period you may want to end with snacks and fellowship. However, the latter is not the main purpose of coming together; stay focused.
10. **Listen to the audio portion of the review guide at a low volume as you study.** You also may listen to relaxing music at a low volume to relieve some of the boredom of studying.
11. **Try listening to the audio portion of this review guide as you nap.** Do not study later than the time you usually go to sleep; you may fall asleep or be tempted to go to sleep. Instead, try studying in the afternoon or early evening. If you are a morning person, try studying in the morning.

TEST-TAKING TIPS

Studying is only a part of getting good results on your exam. You also have to master test taking so that you will score the most points.

1. Familiarize yourself with the AHIMA knowledge clusters. Know what is expected for you to know and master. Read the candidate application book and know what is allowed in the testing center and take the resources you will need with you.
2. Many colleges and state and local associations offer review sessions for mastering the national exams. Go to the reviews and incorporate the testing hints that are relevant to you. Take careful notes and ask questions about items you may be confused about.
3. Do not try to cram the night before the exam. You have studied hard and have retained as much information as you possibly can. Get at least eight hours of sleep the night before the exam.
4. Eat before the exam. You will need the energy that having food in your stomach will provide, and it will help you stay focused on the task at hand. Avoid heavy foods that can make you groggy.
5. Use your alarm clock to assure that you do not oversleep for the exam. Try to show up at least 15 minutes before the test will start. Use this time to acquaint yourself with bathroom and water fountain locations. This also is a good time to pray or meditate and calm yourself.
6. Time is of the essence. Whether you are taking a test in class or the national RHIA or RHIT exams, you have a limited amount of time. Schedule your time accordingly. If you notice yourself spending too much time on one question, come back to it later if you have time. Pace yourself.
7. The RHIA and RHIT are multiple choice test. Multiple-choice test-taking tips include the following:
   a. Read the question before you look at the answer.
   b. Try to come up with the answer in your head before looking at the possible answers. This will cut down the distractions of the choices given.
   c. Eliminate answers you know are not correct.
   d. Read all the choices before choosing your answer.
   e. There is no guessing penalty, so always take an educated guess if you do not know the answer.
   f. Do not keep changing your answer. Usually your first choice is the right one unless you misread the question.
8. Keep a positive attitude throughout the whole test and try to stay relaxed; if you start to feel nervous, take 10 deep breaths and relax.
9. When you are finished and if you have time left, look over your test and make sure that you have answered all the questions. Only change an answer if you misread or misinterpreted the question, because your first answer is usually the correct one.

It is our hope that this product helps you to achieve your goal of becoming a credentialed professional in the field of health information. Good studying to you and may your success be great!

Health Data Management and Health Services Organization and Delivery

1. Definition, Purpose, Uses, and Users of the Health Record
   a. Health Record Defined
      i. Also referred to as the medical record, patient record, resident record, or client record
      ii. Identifies the patient, the diagnosis, treatments rendered, and documentation of all results
      iii. Used as a documentation tool for continuous patient care
      iv. Serves as a communication tool for health care professionals
      v. Serves as a data and information collection tool for all health care services
      vi. Combination of discrete data elements and narrative in various media, including paper, electronic, voice, images, and waveforms
      vii. Electronic health record
         1. Health care information managed by electronic system(s) used to capture, transmit, receive, store, retrieve, link, and manipulate multimedia data
   b. Purpose of Health Record
      i. Primary source of health data and information for the health care industry
      ii. Created as a direct byproduct of health care delivered in a health setting and is the legal documentation of care provided by the health care professionals
      iii. A valuable source of aggregate data for research and program evaluation
      iv. Health care reimbursement
   c. Uses of Patient Record
      i. Documenting health care services provided to an individual in order to support ongoing communication and decision making among health care providers
         1. Planning and managing diagnostic, therapeutic, and nursing services
      ii. Establishing a record of health care services provided to an individual that can be used as evidence in legal proceedings
         1. Protects the legal interest of the patient, health care provider, and health care organization

      iii. Assessing the efficiency and effectiveness of the health care services provided

          1. Evaluating the adequacy and appropriateness of care

      iv. Documenting health care services provided in order to support reimbursement claims that are submitted to payers

      v. Supplying data and information that support the strategic planning, administrative decision making, and research activities as well as support the public policy development related to health care (regulations, legislation, and accreditation standards)

  d. Five Unique Roles of a Patient's Health Record

      i. A record of the patient's health status and the health services provided over time

      ii. Provides a method for clinical communication and care planning among the individual health care practitioners serving the patient

      iii. Serves as the legal document describing the health care services provided

      iv. A source of data for clinical, health services, and outcomes research

      v. Serves as a major resource for health care practitioner education

  e. Users of Patient Record and Health Data

      i. Patient

      ii. Health care practitioners

      iii. Health care providers and administrators

      iv. Third-party payers

      v. Utilization managers

      vi. Quality of care committees

      vii. Accrediting, licensing, and certifying agencies

      viii. Governmental agencies

      ix. Attorneys and the courts in the judicial process

      x. Planners and policy developers

      xi. Educators and trainers

      xii. Researchers and epidemiologists

      xiii. Media reporters

2. **Format of the Health Record**

  a. Source-Oriented Health Record

      i. Documents are organized into sections according to the practitioners and departments that provide treatment.

          1. Example

             a. Laboratory records are grouped together, radiology records are grouped together, clinical notes are grouped together, and so on.

  b. Problem-Oriented Health Record

      i. Developed by Dr. Lawrence Weed in the 1960s, in response to the lack of clarity of the patient's problems in the source-oriented record

      ii. Divided into four parts

          1. Database

          2. Problem list

          3. Initial plan

          4. Progress notes (SOAP)

             a. **S**ubjective

               i. Patient states the problem to health care provider.

            b. **O**bjective

               i. What the practitioner identifies

            c. **A**ssessment

               i. Combines the subjective and objective to make a conclusion

   d. Plan

     i. The approach to be taken to resolve the patient's problem

  c. Integrated Health Records

    i. Documentation from various sources is intermingled and organized in strict chronological or reverse chronological order.

    ii. Advantage is that it is easy to follow the course of the patient's diagnosis and treatment.

    iii. Disadvantage is that the format makes it difficult to compare similar information.

3. **Basic Principles of Health Record Documentation**

  a. General Documentation Guidelines of the American Health Information Management Association (AHIMA)

    i. Uniformity of both the content and format of the health record

    ii. Organized systematically to facilitate data retrieval and compilation

    iii. Only authorized individuals should be allowed to document in the record.

    iv. Policies must identify which individuals may receive and transcribe verbal physician's orders.

    v. Documentation should occur when the services were rendered.

    vi. Entries should identify authors clearly.

    vii. Individuals making entries should use only abbreviations and symbols approved by the organization and/or medical staff.

    viii. All entries in the record should be permanent.

    ix. Error correction for paper-based records

     1. Never obliterate errors; original entry should remain legible, and corrections should be entered in chronological order.

     2. Draw a single line in ink through the incorrect entry. Print "error" or "correction" at the top of the entry along with a legal signature or initials, date, time, reason for change, and the title and discipline of the individual making the correction. Add correct information to the entry.

     3. Late entries should be labeled as such.

    x. Any corrections on information added to the record by the health care provider from verbal corrections from the patient should be inserted as an addendum or a separate note with no changes in the original entries in record.

    xi. Health information department should develop, implement, and evaluate policies and procedures related to the quantitative and qualitative analysis of the health record.

  b. Common Time Frames for Completion of Health Record Documents

    i. History and physical: within 24 hours of admission

    ii. Operative report: immediately following surgery

    iii. Verbal orders: cosigned within 24 hours

    iv. Discharge summary: immediately after discharge of patient

  c. The Joint Commission (TJC, formerly the Joint Commission on Accreditation of Healthcare Organizations, or JCAHO) Type I Recommendation

    i. Too many delinquent records may cause the hospital to receive a Type I Recommendation, which must be resolved in order to retain accreditation.

    ii. Guidelines that indicate a Type I Recommendation

     1. The number of delinquent records is greater than 50% of the average number of discharged patients per quarter, over the previous 12 months.

    2. All medical records must have a history documented within 24 hours.

    3. All medical records, including a surgery, must have an immediate postoperative note documented, and the operative report must be dictated immediately after surgery.

4. **Content of the Acute Care Health Record**

    a. Administrative Data (includes demographic and financial information as well as various consent and authorization forms related to the provision of care and the handling of confidential patient information)

        i. Registration record

        ii. Consent to treatment

        iii. Consent to release information

        iv. Consent to special procedures

        v. Advanced directives

        vi. Patient rights acknowledgment

        vii. Property and valuables list

        viii. Birth and death certificates

    b. Clinical Data (documents the patient's medical condition, diagnosis, and treatment as well as the health care services provided)

        i. Medical history and review of systems

        ii. Physical examination

        iii. Interdisciplinary patient care plan

        iv. Physician's orders

        v. Progress notes (clinical observations)

        vi. Reports and results of diagnostic and therapeutic procedures

        vii. Consultation reports

        viii. Discharge and interval summary that includes final instructions given to patient upon discharge

        ix. Operative data

            1. Anesthesia report

            2. Recovery room record

            3. Operative report

            4. Pathology report

        x. Obstetric data

            1. Antepartum record

            2. Labor and delivery record

            3. Postpartum record

        xi. Neonatal data

            1. Birth history

            2. Neonatal identification

            3. Neonatal physical examination

            4. Neonate progress notes

        xii. Nursing data

            1. Nursing notes

            2. Graphic sheet

            3. Medication sheet

            4. Special care units

        xiii. Ancillary data

            1. Electrocardiographic reports

            2. Laboratory reports

            3. Radiology and imaging reports

            4. Radiation therapy

            5. Therapeutic services

      6. Case management and social service record
      7. Patient and family teaching and participation
      8. Discharge and follow-up plan
5. Record Content for Alternative Health Care Sites
  a. Ambulatory Care
     i. Patient data items
     ii. Patient care provider data items
     iii. Encounter data items
  b. Emergency Room
     i. Identification
     ii. History of the present disease or injury
     iii. Physical findings and vital signs
     iv. Laboratory and radiology reports if needed
     v. Diagnosis
     vi. Treatment
     vii. Disposition of the case
  c. Long-Term Care
     i. Socio-demographic information
     ii. Database
     iii. Patient care plans
     iv. Ancillary reports
     v. Activities of facility-community living
     vi. Correspondence and third-party information
  d. Home Health Care
     i. Initial database
       1. Diagnoses and problems
       2. History and physical condition
       3. Current medication and treatment
       4. Activity limitations
       5. Dietary information
       6. Suitability of residence
     ii. Plan of treatment contains
       1. Identified patient problems and needs
       2. Goals and objectives for patient care
       3. Services provided, including type, frequency, and duration
       4. Plan implementation
     iii. Progress notes
     iv. Discharge summary
     v. Consent forms
     vi. Service agreement
  e. Hospice Care
     i. Initial database
     ii. Interdisciplinary team documentation
     iii. Ongoing documentation
     iv. Discharge/transfer record
     v. Bereavement record
     vi. Consents
  f. Mental Health Care
     i. Identification/face sheet
     ii. Evaluation for admission
     iii. Problem-asset list
     iv. Comprehensive evaluation
     v. Periodic summaries

      vi. Transfer and/or discharge summary

      vii. Death summary

      viii. History and physical examination

      ix. Consultations

      x. Diagnostic tests, including X-rays or other operations or procedures

      xi. Physician orders

      xii. Record of medication administered

      xiii. Progress notes

      xiv. Flow sheets

      xv. Electroshock observations documentation

      xvi. Seizures

      xvii. Issues related to infectious disease control

      xviii. Legal and administrative

      xix. Previous admissions

  g. Rehabilitative Care

      i. Identification data

      ii. Pertinent history

      iii. Disability diagnosis, rehabilitation problems, goals, and prognosis

      iv. Assessments

      v. Ancillary reports

      vi. Program manager information

      vii. Decision-making information

      viii. Evaluations

      ix. Staff conferences reports

      x. Program plans

      xi. Progress notes

      xii. Relative correspondence

      xiii. Release forms

      xiv. Discharge report

      xv. Follow-up report

6. **Data Quality Monitoring**

  a. The accuracy of data depends on the manual or computer information system design for collecting, recording, storing, processing, accessing, and displaying data, as well as the ability and follow-through of the individuals involved in each phase of the activities.

      i. Systems should be developed to ensure the accuracy and timeliness of documentation at the point of care, to monitor output, and to take appropriate correction action when needed.

      ii. Health information technicians may perform a quality improvement (QI) study to evaluate data quality of paper or computerized patient records; the study may assess the presence of reports and authentications as well as the quality of the information documented in the entries.

  b. Quantitative Analysis Ensures

      i. Patient identification on the front and back of every paper form or on every screen is correct.

      ii. All necessary authorizations or consents are present and signed or authenticated by the patient or legal representative.

      iii. Documented principal diagnosis on discharge, secondary diagnoses, and procedures are present in the appropriate form or location within the record.

      iv. Discharge summary is present when required, and authenticated.

    v. History and physical report are present, documented within the time frame required by appropriate regulations, and authenticated as appropriate.

    vi. When a consultation request appears in the listing of physician or practitioner orders, a consultation report is present and authenticated.

    vii. All diagnostic tests ordered by the physician or practitioner are present and are authenticated by comparing physician orders, financial bill, and the test reports documented in the patient's health record.

    viii. An admitting progress note, a discharge progress note, and an appropriate number of notes documented by physicians or clinicians throughout the patient's care process are present.

    ix. Each physician or practitioner order entered into the record is authenticated.

        1. Admitting and discharge physician or practitioner orders are present.

        2. Orders are present for all consultations, diagnostic tests, and procedures, when these reports are found in the record.

    x. Operative, procedure, or therapy reports are present and authenticated, when orders, consent forms, or other documentation in the record indicates they were performed.

    xi. A pathology report is present and authenticated when the operative report indicates that tissue was removed.

    xii. Preoperative, operative, and postoperative anesthesia reports are present and authenticated.

    xiii. Nursing or ancillary health professionals' reports and notes are present and authenticated.

    xiv. Reports required for patients treated in specialized units are present and authenticated.

    xv. Preliminary and final autopsy reports on patients who have expired at the facility are present and authenticated.

c. Qualitative Analysis Involves Checks

    i. Review for obvious documentation inconsistencies related to diagnoses found on admission forms, physical examination, operative and pathology reports, care plans, and discharge summary.

    ii. Analyze the record to determine whether documentation written by various health care providers for one patient reflects consistency.

    iii. Compare the patient's pharmacy drug profile with the medication administration record to determine consistency.

    iv. Review an inpatient record to determine whether it reflects the general location of the patient at all times or whether serious time gaps exist.

    v. Determine whether the patient record reflects the progression of care, including the symptoms, diagnoses, tests, treatments, reasons for the treatments, results, patient education, location of patient after discharge, and follow-up plans.

    vi. Interview the patient and/or family.

        1. Review recorded patient demographic information and medical history with the patient several hours or days after admission to determine completeness and accuracy.

        2. A patient may be too physically ill or mentally confused at admission or the family may be too preoccupied with the patient to provide valid data.

      vii. Compare written instructions to the patient that are documented in the record with the patient's or family's understanding of those instructions.

      viii. Review for other documentation as determined by the facility.

    d. AHIMA-Identified Characteristics of Data Quality

      i. Accuracy: data are the correct values and are valid.

      ii. Accessibility: data items should be easily obtainable and legal to collect.

      iii. Comprehensiveness

        1. All required data items are included.

        2. The entire scope of the data is collected and intentional limitations are documented.

      iv. Consistency: the value of the data should be reliable and consistent across applications.

      v. Currency

        1. Data should be up to date.

        2. A datum value is up to date if it is current for a specific point in time.

        3. It is outdated if it was current at some preceding time yet incorrect at a later time.

      vi. Definition

        1. Clear definitions should be provided so that current and future data users will know what the data mean.

        2. Each data element should have clear meaning and accepted values.

      vii. Granularity: the attributes and values of data should be defined at the correct level of detail.

      viii. Precision: data values should be just large enough to support the application or process. To collect data precise enough for application, acceptable values or value ranges for each data item must be defined (e.g., values for sex should be limited to male, female, or unknown).

      ix. Relevance: the data are meaningful to the performance of the process or application for which they are collected.

      x. Timeliness: determined by how the data are being used and their context

7. Forms Design

    a. Well-designed and controlled forms or computer views (information on screens) are important to reduce errors and recopying of data and to increase efficiency.

    b. Forms team (view team, forms committee) is charged to work on administrative and patient information applications and become involved in the selection of data collection technology.

      i. Forms team forwards its patient-related recommendations to the clinical information committee for approval, and its administrative recommendations follow the organizational chain of command.

      ii. Team members include

        1. Health information management

        2. Information systems

        3. Materials management

        4. Patient care services

        5. Quality improvement

        6. Others as need

c. General Forms Design Principles
    i. Need of users
        1. Forms should be designed to meet needs of all users (patients, health care providers, government agencies, health care facility staff).
    ii. Purpose of form or view
        1. Standardize, identify, and instruct, facilitate documentation and decision making, and promote consistency in data collection, reporting, and interpretation.
        2. Identify patients and practitioners and instruct them step by step in what data items to gather, where to obtain them, and how to record them.
        3. Good instructions that facilitate complete and accurate documentation should be provided for forms.
    iii. Selection and sequencing of items
        1. Construct a list or grid of required data to ensure the collection of all required data and elimination of unnecessary items.
        2. Flow should be logical and take into consideration the order of data collection or transfer.
        3. Numbering items makes references to both items and written instructions on completion of forms faster and easier.
    iv. Standard terminology, abbreviations, and format
        1. Words, numbers, and abbreviations should be standardized.
        2. A master format or template should be developed by the forms team or committee.
    v. Instructions
        1. Instructions should briefly identify who should complete the data items and provide guidance to the user of the form.
        2. Computer views typically provide this information on introductory screens and as needed throughout data entry.
    vi. Simplification
        1. Forms or views should be created only when there is an established need that is not being met by an existing form.
        2. All forms or views are documented and available.
    vii. Paper forms design
        1. Header and footer
        2. Introduction and instructions
        3. Body and close
        4. Other production considerations
            a. Only approved forms should be used in the health care record.
            b. There should be a master for each paper form and all copies should be made from the original or master.
            c. Using standardized paper size (8.5 by 11) keeps cost low and facilitates copying and filing.
            d. Multipart forms may require carbon sheets or NCR paper.
            e. Duplicating methods include in-house and commercial printing.
    viii. Computer-view or screen-format design considerations
        1. Needs of user
        2. Purpose of view
        3. Selection and sequencing of essential data items
        4. Standardization of terminology, abbreviations, and formats
        5. Provision of instructions

      6. Attention to simplification

      7. Views require the development of menus of alternatives and screen or window formats that may include spots to touch with a finger or light pen

    ix. Online system interfaces make it possible to

      1. Organize the data entry fields in logical format

      2. Include field edits

      3. Include passwords to add, delete, or modify data

      4. Allow simultaneous entry or updating in many tables at one time

      5. Include brief instructions on the screens or provide more lengthy help screens

      6. Make the screens attractive through the use of color, lines, and borders

      7. Use default values in a field to eliminate the need to key repeated data

      8. Allow automatic sequential numbering

      9. Show data on the screen from a different table when the key field is entered (e.g., for the Master Patient Patient Index (MPI), where the doctor's number, name, address, etc. can automatically appear on the screen)

      10. Develop or customize menus or submenus to add, delete, or change data

8. Health Care Data Sets and Databases

  a. The purpose of a minimum data set (MDS) is to promote comparability and compatibility of data by using standard data items with uniform definitions.

  b. The National Committee on Vital and Health Statistics has promulgated data sets that have influenced both the conditions of participation and claim forms on which Medicare and Medicaid data sets are based.

  c. Data sets facilitate uniformity in collection and analytical techniques of hospital data.

    i. Uniform Hospital Discharge Data Set (UHDDS): uniform collection of data on inpatients

    ii. Uniform Ambulatory Core Data Set (UACDS): improve ability to compare data in ambulatory care settings.

    iii. Minimum Data Set (MDS) for Long-Term Care (LTC) and Resident Assessment Instrument (RAI): comprehensive functional assessment of long-term care patients

    iv. Outcome and Assessment Information Set (OASIS): comprehensive assessment for adult home care patient and forms the basis for measuring patient outcomes

    v. Uniform Clinical Data Set (UCDS): data collection utilized by peer review organizations to determine the quality of patient care

9. Data Quality and Technology

  a. Electronic Health Record (EHR) or Computer-Based Patient Record (CPR)

    i. CPR defined by Institute of Medicine (IOM) as a record that resides in a system specifically designed to support users by providing accessibility to complete and accurate data, alerts, reminders, clinical decision support systems, links to medical knowledge, and other aids.

      1. 2003 core functionalities

        a. Health information and data

        b. Results management

           c. Order entry management

           d. Decision support

           e. Electronic communication and connectivity

           f. Patient support

           g. Administrative processes

           h. Reporting and population health management

       ii. The EHR has the ability to capture data from multiple electronic sources and is the primary source of information at the point of care.

       iii. Information is maintained online indefinitely, immediately retrievable, and continuously backed up.

   b. Data Versus Information

       i. Data

           1. A collection of elements on a given subject

           2. Raw facts and figures expressed in text, numbers, symbols, and images

           3. Facts, ideas, or concepts that can be captured, communicated, and processed, either manually or electronically

       ii. Information

           1. Data that have been processed into meaningful form, either manually or by computer, in order to make them valuable to the user

           2. Adds to a representation and tells the recipient something that was not known before

   c. Database Structure and Model

       i. Data model: a plan or pattern for an information system, including the database structure, known as a conceptual model, and the translation of the concept to the computer, known as the physical model

       ii. Entities: persons, locations, things, or concepts about which data can be collected and stored

       iii. Attribute: describes an entity or distinct characteristic about it

       iv. Relationship: associations between entities

       v. Character, field, record, and file

           1. Character: collection of bits make up a byte; a byte is a character such as a number, letter, or symbol.

           2. Field: made up of several characters such as name, age, or gender

           3. Record: made up of a series of fields about one person or thing

           4. File

               a. Made up of fields (columns) and records (rows) about an entity such as a patient

               b. Table is another word for file or entity

       vi. Database models

           1. Relational model

           2. Hierarchical model

           3. Network model

           4. Object-oriented model

   d. Data Quality and Computer Systems

       i. Edits, rules, or validation checks are added to the database, along with a message to be displayed when the data do not satisfy the condition.

           1. Checks look at the who, what, when, where, and why of transactions.

      2. Transaction is an event that takes place during the routine course of business.
- **a.** Event validation
- **b.** Transaction validation
- **c.** Sequence checks
- **d.** Batch tools
- **e.** Audit trail
- **f.** Duplicate processing
- **g.** Format checks
- **h.** Reasonableness checks
- **i.** Check digits

  ii. Data characteristics
1. Validity
2. Reliability
3. Completeness
4. Recognizability
5. Timeliness
6. Relevance
7. Accessibility
8. Security
9. Legality

e. Architecture
- **i.** Open system: hardware, software, transmission, media, and database industry standards allow different computer vendor systems to communicate to each other.
- **ii.** Closed system: communication is possible only on one vendor's system.
- **iii.** Hardware
  1. Physical equipment that makes up computers and computer systems
  2. Mainframes, minicomputers, microcomputers
- **iv.** Electronic data-entry technology
  1. Keyed-entry devices
     - **a.** Keyboard and mouse
     - **b.** Light pen
     - **c.** Touch-sensitive screen
     - **d.** Graphics tablet
  2. Portable and hand-held terminals
     - **a.** Point-of-care applications are well-suited to this technology.
  3. Scanned entry
     - **a.** Optical scanners
     - **b.** Bar code readers
     - **c.** Optical character readers
     - **d.** Mark-sense readers
     - **e.** Magnetic-ink character readers
  4. Other entry devices
     - **a.** Magnetic strips
     - **b.** Voice recognition
     - **c.** Biomedical devices
     - **d.** Electronic data interchange
- **v.** Output
  1. Terminal or workstation
  2. Printers

       vi. Software
1. Operating systems software
2. Application software
   f. Communications Technology
       i. Local area network (LAN): multiple devices connected via communications media and located in a small geographical area
       ii. Wide area network (WAN): a computer network that connects separate institutions across a large geographical area
       iii. Internet
1. Similar to a WAN in that it serves multiple users and connects with various communication channels, but structure is different
2. Consists of thousands of loosely connected network servers (LANs and WANs), and no single group is responsible for it
3. Web-based health care information systems make it possible for health care workers to search for and quickly find huge amounts of information on virtually any health-related topic
       iv. Intranet
1. Private network that has its servers located inside a firewall

10. Data Access and Retention
   a. Assignment of Health Record Identification and Numbering
       i. Alphabetic identification: the patient's name identifies the patient's record.
       ii. Numeric identification
1. Serial numbering: a new number is assigned to the patient for each new encounter at the facility.
2. Unit numbering: the patient retains the same number for every encounter at the facility.
3. Serial-unit numbering: a new number is assigned to the patient for each new encounter at the facility, but the former records are brought forward and filed under the new number.
   b. Filing Equipment
       i. Filing cabinets
       ii. Open-shelf files (least expensive option)
       iii. Motorized revolving units
       iv. Compressible units
   c. Space Management
       i. Centralized filing: records filed in one location
       ii. Decentralized filing: records filed in multiple locations
   d. Filing Methodologies
       i. Alphabetic filing starts with last names and then includes first name and middle initial (see Table 2-1).
       ii. Straight numeric filing: filing charts in sequential order; the records start with the chart with lowest number value and end with the chart with highest number value.
       iii. Terminal digit filing
1. Numeric filing is divided into three parts.
2. It is read from right to left instead of left to right (see Table 2-2).
   e. Calculating Storage Requirements
       i. Consider filing system, numbering system, filing equipment, average size of individual records, volume of patients, and the number of readmissions
       ii. Example: A hospital has 6000 discharges per year, uses the TDO unit numbering filing system, with open shelves. The open shelves have

Table 2-1 Alphabetic Filing Records

Last	First	Middle
Burns	Linda	Cooper
James	Annie	
James	Kiesha	
James	Kiesha	T.
Ramirez	Juan	
Zen	Lee	M.

8 shelves per unit that are 36 inches wide with 34 inches of actual filing space. The average record is 3 inches thick. The hospital requires 18,000 inches (6000 discharges at 3 inches each) of filing space. Each open shelf unit has 272 linear filing inches available (8 shelves with 34 inches each). Therefore, the hospital needs 67 open shelf units (18,000 inches divided by 272 filing inches per unit). Although 18,000 divided by 272 is 66.17, the hospital cannot purchase a fraction of a unit; therefore, they must purchase 67 units to file 6000 records.

  f. Health Record Retrieval

      i. Audit filing area periodically to assure files are in order and all records are accounted for

      ii. Requested records are located, checked out, and tracked.

         1. Calculating retrieval rate

            a. Statistics are maintained to determine the accuracy, quantity, and quality of the filing and retrieval system.

            b. The ratio of the number of records located to the number of records requested

Table 2-2 Illustration of Terminal Digit Filing (TDO)

	←		
Record 1	15	35	86
Record 2	16	35	86
Record 3	00	36	86
Record 4	01	00	87
	Tertiary Digits	**Secondary Digits**	**Primary Digits**

This table indicates how to read records (charts) in Terminal Digital Filing (TDO). The arrow illustrates that the numbers on the record are read from right to left. In filing or retrieving records, follow these steps:

1. Go to the primary section (terminal section). In the case of records 1, 2, and 3, the section is 86. In the case of record 4, the section is 87.
2. Within the primary digits, go to the subdivision of the secondary digits. In records 1 and 2, this is 35. In record 3, it is 36. In record 4, it is 0.
3. Lastly, go to the subdivision of the tertiary digits. Record 1 is subdivision 15, record 2 is subdivision 16, record 3 is subdivision 00, and record 4 is subdivision 01.

        c. Example: The ambulatory care clinic requested 9043 records during the month of March. The filing area retrieved 9039 of the requested records. Therefore, the department had a 99.96 percent retrieval rate ([9039/9043] × 100).

    g. Record Retention

      i. State statutes and regulations

        1. Statute of limitations

          a. Varies by state and determines the period of time in which a legal action can be brought against a facility

          b. It begins at the time of the event, or at the age of majority if the patient was treated as a minor.

          c. Retention schedule

            i. The American Hospital Association recommends retaining records for a minimum of 10 years.

            ii. If minor, 10 years past age of majority

      ii. Facility closure

        1. If the facility is sold to health care provider, the record is an asset of the sale.

        2. If the buyer is not a health care provider, the record is not to be sold, but other arrangements should be made.

        3. The state department of health may assume responsibility for the records.

      iii. Disasters such as fires, broken water pipes, blocked drains, malfunctioning equipment, environmental storms and floods

    h. Image-Based Records Storage

      i. Magnetic disk

      ii. Optical disk platters

      iii. Optical scanning (Paper, X-rays, MRIs, or microfilm are scanned and converted into a computer-readable digital format.)

      iv. Jukebox device

      v. Micrographics

        1. Creating miniature pictures on film

        2. Microfilm, roll, jacket, microfiche

        3. Computer-assisted retrieval of microfilm

          a. Scanner

          b. Optical character recognition

11. Secondary Health Information Data Sources

    a. Indexes

      i. Listing or arrangement of data in a designated order; contains special types of information

      ii. Purpose is to assist in the location of desired information

      iii. Master patient index (MPI)

        1. Identifies all patients admitted to a health care facility for treatment, along with their identifying information

        2. Also referred to as master person index, master population index, master name file, enterprise-wide master person or patient index, regional master patient index, and master patient database

      iv. Number index: chronological list of patient's identification numbers issued to patients

      v. Physician index: provides every physician with a list of identifying medical cases

    vi. Disease index: list of diseases and conditions according to the classification system used in the facility

    vii. Procedure or operation index: list of surgical and procedural codes

b. Registries

    i. Created to monitor various diseases and health problems with different goals and objectives

    ii. Each register serves a different purpose or is maintained for different outcomes (goals). As with the index outline, the register is identified and its purpose follows.

    iii. Admission and discharge register: kept permanently and in chronological order

    iv. Operating room register

        1. Maintained for 10 years

        2. Provides statistical data for caseload analysis and administrative reports

    v. Births and deaths registers: provide accessible information about births and deaths

    vi. Emergency room register: monitors the patients who enter the emergency room for services

    vii. Cancer or tumor registry

        1. System that monitors all types of cancer diagnosed or treated in an institution

        2. Database components

            a. Reference date: beginning date of data collection

            b. Case eligibility: cases that meet the eligibility criteria for inclusion into the database

            c. Patient eligibility: inpatients and outpatients diagnosed and/or treated for cancer who are eligible for inclusion in the database

            d. Patient index: permanent alphabetic file that identifies patients who have been entered into the registry database

            e. Case finding: method for locating and identifying every reportable case in the database

            f. Accession register

                i. List of numbers assigned by the facility to the patient

                ii. First two digits of accession number indicate the year when patient was eligible and added to the registry (Table 2-3)

            g. Abstracting: preparation of a brief summary on the patient

            h. Coding: code assigned to cancer diagnosis

Table 2-3 Accession Register

Accession Number	Patient's Name	Primary	Site	Date of Diagnosis
xx-0001/00	Smith, Robert	Liver	C22	01/02/xx
xx-0002/02	Williams, Joe	Colon	C18	01/03/xx
xx-0245/02	Chavez, Juan	Lung	C34	01/03/xx
xx-0004/01	Cruz, Tom	Prostate	C61	01/04/xx
xx-0004/02	Cruz, Tom	Colon	C18	01/04/xx

          i. Staging: recording the extent of the spread of the disease for every case entered into the registry database

          j. Primary site file: permanent file that contains an abstract of every primary neoplasm site for each patient

      3. Quality control: process of ensuring the completeness, accuracy, and timeliness of the data collected

      4. American College of Surgeons requires annual lifetime follow-up of the patient

      5. Patient information is confidential and protected from unauthorized access

      6. Use of cancer registry data

          a. Annual report

          b. Quality outcome and improvement

          c. Administrative reports

          d. Cancer conferences

          e. Marketing

          f. Request log or file

      7. Staffing includes certified tumor registrar (CTR)

      8. Cancer committee

          a. Policymaking body that meets at least quarterly

          b. Responsible for planning, initiating, stimulating, and assessing all cancer-related activities in the institution

   viii. Other registry subjects

      1. National and state cancer registries

      2. HIV/AIDS

      3. Birth defects

      4. Diabetes

      5. Implant

      6. Organ

      7. Trauma

12. Health Information Management Organizations and Professionals

   a. Health Care Information and Management Systems Society (HIMSS) provides leadership in health care for the management of technology and management systems.

      i. Certified Professional in Health Information Management Systems (CPHIMS)

      ii. Certified in Health Care Security (CHS)

   b. International Federation of Health Record Organizations (IFHRO) supports national associations and health record professionals to improve health records.

   c. International Medical Informatics Association (IMIA) promotes informatics in health care and biomedical research.

   d. National Cancer Registrars Association (NCRA) supports quality cancer data management.

      i. Certified Tumor Registrar (CTR)

   e. American Medical Informatics Association (AMIA) supports information technology professionals to improve health care.

   f. American Association for Medical Transcription (AAMT) is the largest association for medical transcription.

   g. College of Healthcare Information Management Executives (CHIME) serves needs of health care chief information officers and advocates for more effective use of information management in health care.

h. American Health Information Management Association (AHIMA)
    i. Association for HIM practitioners
    ii. This association sets guidelines and standards for patient records and health information systems.
        1. Accreditation of education programs
          a. AHIMA accredits coding certificate programs.
          b. Commission on Accreditation of Health Information and Informatics Management (CAHIIM) accredits professional education programs at the associate, baccalaureate, and post-baccalaureate certificate levels at college and universities across the nation.
        2. Certification and registration programs
          a. Processes whereby the public can be assured that certified individuals have met or maintain a level of competency required to deliver quality health information
            i. Registered health information administrator (RHIA) has achieved a baccalaureate in HIM with 30 hours of continuing education within a two-year cycle.
            ii. Registered health information technician (RHIT) has achieved an associate degree in HIM with 20 hours of continuing education within a two-year cycle.
            iii. Certified coding specialist (CCS) must complete a formal self assessment process annually to maintain credentialed status.
            iv. Certified coding specialist-physician (CCS-P) must complete a formal self-assessment process annually to maintain credentialed status.
            v. Certified coding associate (CCA)
            vi. Certified in health care privacy and security (CHPS) designation signifies advanced competency in designing, implementing, and administering comprehensive privacy and security protection programs.

13. **Health Services Organization and Delivery**
    a. Definitions
        i. Accreditation
          1. The professional organizations such as TJC and the AOA regulate and review the standards of health care organization.
        ii. Alternative delivery systems: health care provided by methods other than the traditional inpatient care, including home health, ambulatory, hospice, and other types of health care
        iii. Care: the management of, responsibility for, or attention to the safety and well-being of another person or other persons
        iv. Client: individual who is receiving professional services
        v. Inpatient: patient who is receiving health care services such as room, board, and continuous nursing service in a hospital
        vi. Health: defined by World Health Organization as a person who is in a state of complete physical, mental, and social well-being
        vii. Health care services: services such as hospital, ambulatory care, home setting, or other health-related services
        viii. Health information management (HIM): a health profession that is responsible for the uses of health information, accuracy, and protection of clinical information

    ix. Hill-Burton Act: legislation enacted in 1946 that provided funding for the construction of hospitals and other health care facilities

    x. Hospital: health care institution with an organized medical and professional staff and with inpatient beds available around the clock whose primary function is to provide inpatient medical, nursing, and other health-related services to patients for both surgical and non-surgical conditions and that usually provides some outpatient services, particularly emergency care

    xi. Hospital inpatient: a patient who stays in the hospital overnight and is provided room, board, and nursing service in a unit or area of the hospital

    xii. Hospital patient: a patient who receives or is utilizing health care services for which the hospital is liable or held accountable

    xiii. Outpatient: patient who is receiving ambulatory care services in a hospital or hospital-based clinic or department

    xiv. Patient: individual who is receiving health care services

    xv. Payer: individual or organization who pays for health care services

    xvi. Primary patient record: health care professionals use this record to review the patient data or documents.

    xvii. Provider: any entity that provides health care services to patients, such as a hospital or clinic

    xviii. Resident: a patient who resides in a long-term care facility.

    xix. Secondary patient record: a record used for selected data elements to aid in research conducted by clinical and non-clinical people

b. Historical Development

    i. People who are ill have always gone to people with reputations as healers.

    ii. Earliest written health record dates back to 2700 B.C. and is from an Egyptian physician and dentist.

    iii. Greek medicine became the forerunner of modern medicine 2500 years ago.

    iv. The concept of hospital is rooted in medieval Christendom, when religious orders cared for the sick.

    v. Term *hospital* originated in fifth century, from the Latin word *hospitium*.

    vi. During Middle Ages, the hospitium evolved from a Christian tradition of offering weary travelers a place to rest (called hospice); such places were funded by the churches and wealthy individuals.

    vii. Cortez founded the first permanent hospital in North America in 1554, which was the Jesus of Nazareth Hospital in Mexico.

    viii. First school in America dedicated to training physicians was founded in 1765 in Philadelphia.

    ix. To assure the quality of American medical education, the American Medical Association (AMA) was formed in 1847.

    x. The American Hospital Association (AHA) was established in 1848 to promote public welfare by providing better health care in hospitals.

    xi. In late 19th century, state governments established mental institutions for the confinement of the mentally ill rather than housing them in prisons and poorhouses.

    xii. In mid 1800s, plantation owners in Hawaii, mining companies in Pennsylvania and Minnesota, and lumber companies tried to attract and keep immigrant workers by offering medical care to the workers.

xiii. In early 1900s, hospitals were funded by private beneficiaries, endowments, and donations.
  1. Hospitals viewed as boarding houses for poor and sick.
  2. Private sector had little interest in serving the population as a whole, assuming that the local government would pay for the poor.
  3. Physicians did not do history and physicals on the patients and seldom documented diagnoses, care, and treatment.

xiv. Between 1870s and 1920s, the number of American hospitals increased from fewer than 200 to more than 6000.
  1. Private benevolence was responsible for establishing hundreds of new hospitals that were not interested in providing care to the poor.
  2. By 1910, there were as many hospitals per 1000 population as there are today.
  3. Not all of the population was being served.
  4. Hospitals operated on the principle that the more expensive the care, the more valuable the service, which resulted in the escalation of health care cost.

xv. The Flexner Report of 1910 identified serious problems and inconsistencies in medical education.
  1. This resulted in the closing of many proprietary schools.
  2. Remaining schools underwent curriculum revision.
  3. AMA initiated accreditation process for medical education.

xvi. In 1913, the American College of Surgeons (ACS) was founded to develop a system of hospital standardization to improve patient care and recognize hospitals that had the highest ideals.
  1. The ACS collected data from the health record to establish standards and improve quality of care.
  2. Upon analysis of the data, the ACS realized that the documentation was inadequate.
  3. In 1917, the ACS established the Hospital Standardization Program, which laid the groundwork for establishing standards of care.
  4. In 1919, the ACS adopted the minimum standards, which identified the standards that were essential for the "proper care and treatment of patients in any hospital."

xvii. Due to the need for more hospitals and high-quality health care that was accessible to all Americans, in 1946 the Hill-Burton Act provided funding for the construction of hospitals and other health care facilities based on state need.

xviii. The early 1950s saw an increase in the number and complexity of hospitals and nonsurgical specialties, which burdened the hospital standardization program.
  1. As a result, the Joint Commission on Accreditation of Hospitals (JCAH) (currently referred to as TJC) was founded in 1952 and adopted the hospital standardization program.

xix. The 1950s experienced an increase in biomedical advances, technology, and patient demand for more health care services.
  1. Medical advances extended life expectancy, which resulted in an increasing elderly population.
  2. Hospitals became more expensive, and the uninsured and underinsured (primarily the poor and elderly) could not access the health care system.
  3. The federal and state government did little to control hospital costs.

xx. In 1965, Congress amended the Social Security Act of 1935, establishing both Title XVIII (Medicare) and Title XIX (Medicaid).

1. Medicare is a federally funded program that provides health insurance for the elderly and certain other groups.

2. Medicaid supports the states in paying for health care for people who are indigent.

xxi. The 1960s saw a proliferation of various health care facilities, including long-term care, psychiatric and substance abuse, and programs for people with developmental disabilities.

1. JCAH redefined standards to reflect the optimal achievable as opposed to minimum acceptable and began to develop standards for various types of health care facilities.

a. In the late 1980s, JCAH changed its name to the Joint Commission on Accreditation of Healthcare Organizations (JCAHO) to reflect its broader scope.

xxii. Occupational Safety and Health Act was passed in 1970, which mandated that employers provide a safe and healthy workplace.

xxiii. In 1977, the AMA founded the Committee on Allied Health Education and Accreditation (CAHEA) for the purpose of accrediting allied health programs, but the Committee was disbanded in 1994.

xxiv. The federal Department of Health, Education and Welfare (HEW) was reorganized in 1980 to become the Department of Health and Human Services (DHHS). It is a federal, cabinet-level department responsible for health issues, including health care and cost, welfare of various populations, occupational safety, and income security plans.

1. DHHS oversees but is not limited to the following: Centers of Disease Control and Prevention (CDC); Food and Drug Administration (FDA); Office of Inspector General; Substance Abuse and Mental Health Services Administration (SAMHSA); National Institutes of Health (NIH); Indian Health Service (IHS); and the Centers of Medicare and Medicaid Services (CMS), formerly the Health Care Financing Administration (HCFA).

xxv. In 1982, the Tax Equity and Fiscal Responsibility Act (TEFRA) established a mechanism for controlling the cost of the Medicare program and set limits on reimbursement and required the development of the prospective payment system.

xxvi. The Consolidated Omnibus Budget Reconciliation Act (COBRA) of 1985, known as the antidumping statute, established criteria for the transfer and discharge of Medicare and Medicaid patients.

xxvii. The Patient Self-Determination Act of 1990 gave patients the right to set advance directives.

xxviii. In 1992, the Computer-Based Patient Record Institute was created for the purpose of developing strategy that supports the development and adoption of the computer-based patient record.

xxix. In 1996, the Health Insurance Portability and Accountability Act (HIPAA) provided for continuity of health coverage and attempted to control fraud and abuse in health care, reduce health care cost, and guarantee the security and privacy of health information.

xxx. The health care delivery system has evolved into a complex system composed of various and multiple types of facilities, providers, payers, and regulators.

1. In 1990s, health care was costly and not accessible to all citizens, yet consumers demanded more and better care.

2. The advances in technology and scientific developments have increased the life expectancy.

3. Alternative medicine includes unconventional therapies that may or may not have been proven to be effective and herbal remedies, massage therapy, natural food diets, acupuncture, and biotherapy.

4. Due to the escalating cost of health care, the rising number of uninsured and underserved in both urban and rural areas, reform of the health care delivery system is ongoing.

    a. Plans for health care reform address issues such as universal coverage, health care cost, and the quality of care provided.

c. Health care occupations licensed by states and/or certified or registered by accrediting agencies include but are not limited to the following

    i. Physicians: Doctor of Medicine (MD) and Doctor of Osteopathy (DO)

    ii. Nurses:

        1. Registered nurse (RN)

        2. Licensed practical nurse (LPN)

        3. Nurse practitioner

        4. Clinical nurse specialist

        5. Certified nurse midwife

        6. Certified nurse anesthetist

    iii. Dentist

    iv. Pharmacist

    v. Podiatrist

    vi. Chiropractor (DC)

    vii. Optometrist (DO)

    viii. Health care administrators

    ix. Allied health personnel

        1. Laboratory technologist and technicians

            a. Radiologic technologist

            b. Nuclear medicine technologist

            c. Histologic technician

            d. Diagnostic medical sonographer

            e. Cytotechnologist

            f. Clinical laboratory technician

            g. Cardiovascular technologist

            h. Ophthalmic laboratory technician

        2. Therapeutic science practitioners

            a. Physical therapist and physical therapist assistant

            b. Occupational therapist and occupational therapist assistant

            c. Speech language pathologist

            d. Physician assistant

            e. Surgeon assistant

            f. Respiratory therapist

            g. Music therapist

            h. Therapeutic recreation specialist

            i. Paramedic

        3. Behavior scientist

            a. Social worker

            b. Rehabilitation counselor

        4. Support services

            a. Health information managers

            b. Dental laboratory technologist

      c. Electroencephalographic technologist

      d. Food service administrator

      e. Surgical technologist

      f. Environmental health technologist

d. Hospitals (may be classified by ownership, population served, number of beds, length of stay, type, patients, or organization)

  i. Ownership

    1. Government (federal, state, or local)

      a. Federally owned hospitals receive funding as well as administrative direction from the branch of the government that owns them.

        i. Native Americans and native Alaskans

        ii. Facilities for active and retired military personnel and their dependents

        iii. Veterans (Department of Veteran Affairs medical centers)

        iv. Merchant marines

      b. State facilities for mental illness, mental retardation, chronic disease, and medical education

      c. County, district, and city hospitals: local facilities established to meet the health care needs of the community that are governed by elected officials

    2. Non-governmental

      a. For-profit

        i. Proprietary

        ii. Private

        iii. Investor

      b. Not-for-profit

        i. Churches and religious orders

        ii. Industries

        iii. Unions

        iv. Fraternal organizations

  ii. Population served (based upon the group to whom services are provided); examples include pediatric, women's, psychiatric, cancer, burn

  iii. Bed size

    1. Total number of inpatient beds with which the facility is equipped and staffed for patient admissions

    2. A facility is licensed by the state for a specific number of beds.

  iv. Length of stay

    1. If average length of stay is less than 30 days, hospital is short-term or acute-care facility.

    2. If average length of stay is more than 30 days, hospital is a long-term-care facility.

  v. Types

    1. General: provides patient with diagnostic and therapeutic services for a variety of medical conditions, including radiographic, clinical, laboratory, and operating room services

    2. Special: provides diagnostic and therapeutic services for patients with a specific medical condition such as diabetes, cancer, burns, sports injuries, or eye injuries or diseases

    3. Rehabilitation and chronic disease: provides diagnostic and therapeutic services to patients who are disabled or handicapped and require restorative and adjustive services

      4. Psychiatric: provides diagnostic and therapeutic services for patients with mental illness, including psychiatric, psychological, and social work services

      5. Critical access hospital (CAH): certified by the state as necessary to residents in the community, or no hospital or other CAH within 35 miles; no more than 25 beds, with an average length of stay of 96 hours

  vi. Patients

      1. Inpatients

      2. Observation patients

      3. Ambulatory care patients

      4. Emergency patients

      5. Newborn patients

  vii. Organization (typical of traditional acute-care facility)

      1. Composition and structure

        a. Governing board

          i. Also called governing body, board of trustees, board of governors, or board of directors

          ii. Has ultimate legal authority and responsibility for the operation of the hospital, including the quality and cost of care

          iii. Functions according to bylaws established by the board, has regular meetings with documented minutes, and has sub-committees (standing and special) that assist in the responsibilities of the board

            1. Standing committees may include executive, finance, medical staff, nominating, personnel, physician recruitment, or long-range planning.

            2. Special committees may be created for specific projects or tasks and are disbanded upon completion.

        b. Administration

          i. Chief executive officer (CEO) is a hospital administrator or president who is selected by the governing board and is the principal administrative official of the health care facility.

          ii. Chief operating officer (COO) is also called the vice president or executive vice president and is an associate administrator who oversees the operation of specific departments.

          iii. Chief information officer (CIO) is responsible for information resources management, which includes design, integration, and implementation of health information systems (administrative, financial, and clinical).

          iv. Chief financial officer (CFO), sometimes called director of finance or fiscal affairs director, directs the financial operations.

        c. Medical staff

          i. Formally organized staff or licensed physicians, and other licensed providers as permitted by law (dentist, podiatrist, midwives)

          ii. Governed by its own bylaws, rules, and regulations, which must be approved by the hospital's governing board

          iii. TJC states the primary responsibility of the medical staff is the quality of the professional services provided by the members with clinical privileges and the responsibility of being accountable to the governing board

iv. Recommends staff appointments and reappointments, delineates clinical privileges and continuing medical education, and maintains a high quality of patient care

v. Medical staff is organized to include officers, committees, and clinical services.

vi. Clinical services include, but not limited to, the following:

1. Medicine (cardiology, dermatology, oncology, pediatrics, psychiatry, radiology)
2. Surgery (anesthesiology, gynecology, obstetrics, orthopedics, urology)

d. Essential services

i. Nursing
ii. Diagnostic radiology
iii. Nuclear medicine
iv. Dietetics
v. Pathology and clinical laboratory
vi. Emergency
vii. Pharmaceutical
viii. Physical rehabilitation
ix. Respiratory care
x. Social services
xi. Other services

1. Pastoral care
2. Ethics
3. Patient representatives (advocates)
4. Patient escort
5. Plant technology
6. Safety management
7. Central supply

xii. Health information management (medical records department)

1. Responsible for management of all paper and electronic patient information
2. Develops and maintains an information system
3. Responsible for the organization, maintenance, production, and dissemination of information, including data security, integrity, and access
4. Functions include transcribing, coding, release of information, retrieving and storing health information, managing databases, and filing information

2. Hierarchical form

a. Historical model for hospitals
b. Individuals at the top have authority that passes downward through a chain of command.

3. Vertical operation

a. The governing board has ultimate authority, followed by the CEO.
b. The organization includes a governing board, administration, medical staff, department directors, supervisors, and numerous subordinates.

4. Matrix organizational scheme

a. Flexible and supports multidimensional organization
b. This scheme supports general managers who focus on managing people and processes, as opposed to strategy and structure.

        c. Horizontal information communication that embraces individual capabilities

        d. Employees have dual responsibilities and may have two or more supervisors, but they have a shared vision that supports the organization as a whole.

    5. Product line management

        a. Hospital may be organized around product line categories, such as obstetrics/gynecology, rehabilitation, or cardiology, as opposed to departments such as nursing, pharmacy, or respiratory therapy.

e. Ambulatory Care

  i. Comprehensive term for all types of health care provided in an outpatient setting

  ii. Patient travels to and from the facility on the same day and is not hospitalized

  iii. Two major types

    1. Freestanding medical centers

      a. Physician solo practices

      b. Partnerships

      c. Group practices

      d. Public health departments

      e. Neighborhood and community health centers (NHCs, CHCs)

        i. Serve the needs of a catchment area (defined geographic area that is served by a health care program, project, or facility)

        ii. Funded by grants, DHHS, local and state health departments

        iii. Services provided at low or no cost to patients

    2. Organized settings (function independently of the physician providing the care)

      a. Hospital-owned clinics

        i. Satellite clinics: clinics located at a distance from the hospital

        ii. Observation units for patients who need assessment and monitoring but do not require admission to hospital

        iii. Outpatient departments

      b. Outpatient departments provide primary or specialized care, including preadmission testing, pediatrics, obstetrics, gynecology, psychiatry, surgery, neonatal care, sports medicine, oncology.

      c. Ambulatory treatment units

      d. Emergency rooms (emergency departments, emergency care areas)

        i. Provide care for urgent, life-threatening, or potentially disabling conditions

        ii. Patients are triaged (rapid assessment to determine urgency and type of care needed).

        iii. Ranked from level I (most comprehensive) to level IV (not required to operate 24 hours a day), based on the center's hours of operation, availability of physicians, nurses, and other trained staff, access to laboratory, radiology surgery, anesthesia, equipment and drugs

        iv. Mortality trauma center

          1. Specialized staff and equipment

          2. Air transport system

    e. Ancillary services

      i. Hospital diagnostic and therapeutic services that are provided to both outpatients and inpatients; exclude room and board

      ii. Hospital is able to charge patients or third parties directly.

    f. Health maintenance organizations (HMOs)

      i. Managed health care that integrates health care delivery with insurance for health care

      ii. Subscribers voluntarily enroll in plan.

      iii. Providers voluntarily agree to participate in plan.

      iv. HMO assumes an explicit contractual responsibility for providing care.

      v. Subscriber to HMO makes a fixed periodic payment that is independent of utilization of health care services.

      vi. HMO bears financial risk.

      vii. Four basic models

        1. Staff

          a. HMO employs salaried physicians to provide care to HMO subscribers.

          b. HMO owns and operates ambulatory care facilities (ancillary services and physician offices).

          c. Inpatient care is under contract with local health care facilities.

        2. Group

          a. HMO contracts with group practices and hospitals to provide care to subscribers

        3. Network

          a. HMO contracts with various providers to treat the HMO clients.

          b. Providers' clients may be HMO subscribers and non-HMO patients.

        4. Independent practice association (IPA)

          a. Legal, separate entity of health care providers that contract with HMO for provision of services and compensation for those services

          b. Patient population is HMO and non-HMO patients.

    g. Surgicenters: freestanding minor surgical facilities

    h. Urgent care centers

      i. Serve patients who need routine care or have minor but urgent health care problems

      ii. Patients may walk in, and appointments are not required.

f. Home Health Care Services

    i. Provision of medical and non-medical care in the home or place of residence to promote, maintain, or restore health or to minimize the effect of disease or disability

    ii. Mainly provide post-acute care and rehabilitation therapies

g. Long-Term Care

    i. Care provided over a long period of time (30 days or more) to patients who have chronic diseases or disabilities

    ii. Care includes personal, social, recreational, dietary, and skilled nursing services.

    iii. Patients are usually referred to as residents.

      iv. Historically, two types of facilities include skilled-nursing facilities (SNFs), which provide a higher level of care to sicker patients, and intermediate-care facilities (ICFs).

        1. In 1987, the Nursing Home Reform Act reduced the differences between the two types of facilities by mandating that ICFs provide the same level of care and staffing as SNFs.

      v. Several types of long-term care facilities

        1. Nursing: comprehensive term that describes nursing care and related services for residents who need medical, nursing, or rehabilitative care; sufficient number of nursing personnel employed on a 24-hour basis to provide care to residents according to the care plan

        2. Independent living: apartments and condominiums that allow residents to live independently; assistance includes dietary, health care, and social services

        3. Domiciliary (residential)

          a. Supervision, room, and board are provided for people who are unable to live independently.

          b. Most residents need assistance with activities of daily living (bathing, dressing, eating).

        4. Life care centers (retirement communities)

          a. Provide living accommodations and meals for a monthly fee

          b. Other services include housekeeping, recreation, health care, laundry, and exercise programs.

        5. Assisted living: offers housing and board with a broad range of personal and supportive care services

      vi. To be certified as a Medicare or Medicaid provider, a nursing facility must comply with the conditions of participation.

      vii. Facility is licensed by state to provide a designated level of care, which may be personal care, room and board, or skilled nursing care.

   h. Hospice Care

      i. Literally means "given to hospitality"

      ii. Provides palliative and supportive care to terminally ill patients and their families, with consideration for their physical, spiritual, social, and economic needs

      iii. Respite care: an intervention in which the focus of care is on giving the caregiver time off while continuing the care of the patient

  i. Adult Day Care

      i. Provides supervision, medical, and psychological care and social activities for older adult clients who reside at home

      ii. Clients either cannot stay alone or prefer social interaction during the day.

      iii. Services include intake assessment, health monitoring, occupational therapy, personal care, transportation, and meals.

  j. Sub-Acute Care

      i. Transitional level of care that may be necessary immediately after the initial phase of an acute illness

      ii. Commonly used with patients who have been hospitalized and are not yet ready for return to long-term care or home care

      iii. May be located in a designated area of the hospital or nursing facility, or provided by a home health agency

k. Mobile Diagnostic Services
  i. Health care services are transported to the patients, especially diagnostic procedures (mammography, magnetic resonance) and preventive services (immunizations, cholesterol screening).
l. Contract Services
  i. Health care organizations contract for services that include food, laundry, waste disposal, transcription, and housekeeping.
m. Multi-Hospital Systems
  i. Health care systems composed of two or more hospitals that are owned, contractually managed, sponsored, or leased by a single organization
  ii. Include acute, sub-acute, long-term, pediatric, rehabilitation, or psychiatric facilities; may provide diagnostic services

14. Regulatory Agencies
  a. Agencies review patient information to provide public assurance that quality health care is being provided and monitored.
  b. Data serve as evidence in assessing compliance with standards of care.
  c. Licensure
    i. Gives legal approval for a person to practice within his or her profession
    ii Gives legal approval for a facility to operate
    iii. Sets minimal standards for a facility to operate
    iv. Virtually every state requires hospitals, sanatoria, nursing homes, and pharmacies be licensed to operate, even though requirements and standards for licensure may vary by state.
    v. Addresses staffing, credentialing, physical aspects of facility, services provided, and review of health records
    vi. Typically reviewed annually
  d. Nongovernmental Agencies
    i. American Association of Ambulatory Health Care (AAAHC)
    ii. AHIMA
      1. Established the *Professional Practice Standards for Health Information Management Services*, which provides a structured model of standards, guidelines, and measures of quality and quantity
    iii. American Medical Association (AMA)
      1. Involved in accreditation of medical schools, residency programs, and some allied health programs
      2. Collaborates with the Committee on Allied Health Education and Accreditation (CAAHEP) in the accreditation of allied health programs
    iv. American Osteopathic Association (AOA)
      1. Bureau of Professional Education accredits osteopathic medical education.
      2. Has a voluntary program that accredits osteopathic hospitals
      3. HHS recognizes accredited hospitals as eligible for receiving Medicare funds.
    v. Commission on Accreditation of Rehabilitation Facilities (CARF)
      1. Accredits rehabilitation facilities
      2. Sets quality standards to improve care, shares aggregate data, identifies competent organizations that provide rehabilitation services, and provides an organized forum in which people served, providers, and others can participate in quality improvement

        vi. Community Health Accreditation Program (CHAP)
1. Accredits home health agencies
2. Subsidiary of the National League for Nursing
3. More emphasis on patient perspectives than on clinical care

        vii. The Joint Commission (TJC, formerly JCAHO)
1. Develops accreditation standards for various types of health care facilities

        viii. National Committee for Quality Assurance (NCQA)
1. Accrediting agency for managed care organizations
2. Mission is to improve quality of patient care and health plan performance in conjunction with managed care plans, purchasers, consumers, and the public.
3. The Health Plan Employer Data and Information Set (HEDIS), a component of the NCQA, is a standardized set of performance measures designed to allow purchasers and consumers to compare the performance of managed care plans.

        ix. National League of Nursing (NLN)
1. Accredits nursing schools from diplomas to doctorate degrees
2. Establishes standards for nursing curriculum

e. Federal Regulatory Agencies

    i. DHHS is the branch of federal government primarily responsible for numerous health care regulatory programs and agencies.
1. Administration for Children and Families administers and funds state grants to support activities that improve the development of children, youth, and families.
2. Administration on Aging (AoA) advocates for older persons.
3. Agency for Healthcare Research and Quality (AHRQ) established by Omnibus Budget Reconciliation Act of 1989; purpose is to produce and disseminate scientific and policy relevant information that improves the quality, reduces cost, and enhances effective health care.
4. Agency for Toxic Substances and Disease Registry (ATSDR) protects workers and the public from exposure to adverse effects of hazardous substances.
5. CDC is concerned with communicable diseases, environmental health, and foreign quarantine activities.
    a. National Center for Health Statistics (NCHS)
        i. Under management of CDC
        ii. Federal government's principal vital and health statistics agency
        iii. Provides data to monitor the nation's health
6. CMS (formerly the Health Care Financing Administration, or HCFA) is responsible for the Medicare and Medicaid programs, with special emphasis on quality and utilization control.
7. FDA is responsible for the safety of foods, drugs, medical devices, cosmetics, and radiation-emitting equipment, and for proper labeling, product information, safety, and efficacy.
8. Health Resources and Services Administration (HRSA) distributes major grant funding to state governments and the private sector, especially funding for community-based health services.
9. IHS is responsible for providing health care through a network of hospitals, health centers, health stations, and schools health

centers, and through contracts with private providers to eligible Native Americans.

10. National Committee on Vital and Health Statistics (NCVHS)
   a. Statutory public advisory body on health data, statistics, and national health information policy
   b. Encourages the evolution of shared, public-private national health information infrastructure that will promote the availability of valid, credible, timely, and comparable health data
   c. Advises on HIPAA
   d. Standardizes health information by formalizing uniform data sets
      i. Data sets promulgated by the NCVHS
         1. UHDDS
         2. UACDS
         3. Minimum Data Set for Long-Term Care (MDS)
         4. OASIS
11. NIH
   a. Major research center composed of numerous departments and divisions
   b. Major source of funding for health-related research
12. Occupational Safety and Health Administration (OSHA)
   a. Created by the Occupational Safety and Health Act of 1970, which mandated that employers provide a safe and healthy work environment
   b. Responsible for developing standards and regulations and conducting inspections and investigations to determine compliance, and proposes corrective actions for noncompliance
13. Office of Inspector General is responsible for conducting and monitoring audits, inspections, and investigations regarding programs or projects sponsored by the DHHS.
14. SAMHSA is concerned with the effective prevention and treatment of addictive and mental disorders.
15. Clinical Vocabularies
   a. Nomenclature
      i. International Standards Organization (ISO) defines nomenclature as a system of clinical terms of preferred terminology.
      ii. Classification and nomenclature often used interchangeably.
   b. Clinical Terminology
      i. Provides for the proper use of clinical words as names or symbols
      ii. Equated with a nomenclature by AHIMA's Coding Policy and Strategy Committee
   c. Clinical Vocabularies
      i. A list or collection of clinical words or phrases, with their meanings
      ii. Used to represent concepts and to communicate these concepts; include symptoms, diagnoses, procedures, and health status
      iii. *Controlled vocabularies* refers to a code or classification system that requires information to be presented using a preestablished term.
      iv. Classification and nomenclature systems
         1. International Classification of Diseases, Ninth Revision Clinical Modification (ICD-9-CM); only used in United States; developed by World Health Organization (WHO) to code and classify diagnoses and procedures

2. International Classification of Diseases, 10th Revision, Clinical Modification contains substantial increases in content over ICD-9-CM.

3. International Classification of Diseases, 10th Revision, Procedural Coding System replaces tabular list of procedures, volume 3 of ICD-9-CM.

4. International Classification of Diseases for Oncology (ICD-O) is used for coding neoplasms in tumor or cancer registries.

5. International Classification on Functioning, Disability, and Health (ICF) is used to describe body functions, structures, activities, and participation.

6. Current Procedural Terminology (CPT) describes medical, surgical, and diagnostic services and was adopted by CMS as level I of the Healthcare Common Procedure Coding System (HCPCS).

7. Healthcare Common Procedure Coding System (HCPCS) is administered by CMS and includes two levels of codes.
   a. Level 1: current procedural terminology (CPT).
   b. Level 2: alphanumeric procedure and modifier codes represent items, supplies, and non-physician services not covered by the CPT codes.
   c. Level 3: were local procedure and modifier codes used prior to 2003. They are no longer used; additional Level 2 codes to compensate for the loss of the Level 3 codes.

8. Diagnostic and Statistical Manual of Mental Diseases (DSM-IV) is a five-axis coding system.

9. Diagnosis Related Groups (DRG) is used to bill for inpatient services rendered.

10. Ambulatory Payment Classification (APC) is used to bill for outpatient services and is based on the grouping procedures by CPT/HCPCS.

11. International Classification of Primary Care (ICPC-2) is a coding classification of primary care.

12. Current Dental Terminology is a national standard for reporting dental services by the federal government under HIPAA and is recognized by third-party payers.

13. Galen Common Reference Model is a computer-based clinical terminology developed in Europe for representing medical concepts.

14. National Drug Codes (NDC) was developed by the FDA as a universal product identifier for drugs used in humans.

15. ABC codes were created by Alternative Link; they describe alternative medicine, nursing, and other integrative health care interventions.

16. **Financing Health Care Services: Reimbursement Methodologies and Systems**
   a. DHHS is the largest purchaser of health care in the United States.
   b. Private prepaid health plans or federal health care programs cover about 85% of Americans.
   c. Prior to prospective payment system (PPS), individuals, insurance companies, and government plans reimbursed providers on a retrospective fee-for-service basis.
   d. Patient Payment Methods
      i. Direct pay (out-of-pocket): patient pays provider directly.

ii. A prepaid health plan (insurance) is considered indirect pay; it is a purchased policy in which the insured may pay a deductible and is protected from loss by the insurer's agreement to reimburse for such loss.

   1. In 1860, the Franklin Health Assurance Company of Massachusetts became the first commercial insurance company in the United States to provide health care coverage.

   2. In 1929, Baylor University Hospital in Dallas, Texas agreed to provide health care services to Dallas schoolteachers, which was the birth of Blue Cross.

   3. In the 1950s, Blue Cross and Blue Shield began to offer major medical insurance coverage for catastrophic illnesses and injuries.

   4. Health care insurance coverage expanded through the 1950s, and more Americans were covered by a major medical plan or indemnity plan (insurance coverage in the form of cash payment).

   5. Types of insurance

     a. Commercial

       i. Private health insurance plans; financed through the insured person's payment of premiums

       ii. Employer-based insurance; group health insurance coverage, in which companies contract with private insurers to provide coverage to employees

     b. Blue Cross Blue Shield

       i. Blue Cross (1929) covered hospital care.

       ii. Blue Shield (1939) covered physician services.

      iii. In 1982, Blue Cross and Blue Shield merged.

        1. First prepaid health care plan in the United States

        2. One of the largest nonprofit insurance companies in the United States

      iv. Offers health insurance to individuals, small businesses, seniors, and large employer groups

      v. Federal employees offered

        1. Preferred provider organizations (PPOs): health care services provided to members at a discounted rate.

        2. Point-of-service plan: subscribers select providers from a network, but allowed to use out-of-network providers at a higher copayment rate.

     c. Government-sponsored health care programs

       i. Medicare (1965)

        1. Title XVIII of the Social Security Act

        2. Part A: hospitalization insurance for those eligible for social security benefits

        3. Part B: voluntary supplemental insurance to help pay for physician services, medical services, and medical and surgical supplies

        4. Part C: Medicare advantage plans run by private companies

          a. Similar to HMOs and PPOs

          b. Provides all of Part A and Part B benefits

          c. Copayments, coinsurance, and deductibles are charged to recipients.

          d. Vision, hearing, dental, wellness, and prescription medications provided at extra cost to beneficiary.

          5. Part D: prescription drug coverage through private insurance companies

       ii. Medicaid (1966)

          1. Title XIX of the Social Security Act

          2. Medical assistance for individuals and families with low incomes

          3. Managed at the state level

       iii. Civilian Health and Medical Program-Veterans Administration (CHAMPVA): provides health care services for dependents and survivors of disabled veterans, survivors of veteran who dies from service-connected conditions, and survivors of military personnel who died in the line of duty

       iv. TRICARE (formerly CHAMPUS): provides coverage for dependents of armed forces personnel and retirees receiving care outside a military treatment facility

       v. Indian Health Service: provides federal health services to American Indians and Alaska natives

      vi. State Children's Health Insurance Program (SCHIP): Title XXI of the Social Security Act provides federal funds to states; these funds allow states to expand existing insurance programs to cover children up to age 19, thus expanding coverage to a greater number of children.

  e. Reimbursement Methodologies

    i. Fee for service

      1. Third-party payers and/or patients issue payments to health care providers based on charges assigned to each service performed for each patient.

       a. Traditional fee-for-service: third-party payers and/or patients pay health care providers after services have been rendered.

       b. Managed fee-for-service: costs are controlled by the managed-care plan's management of members' uses of services; providers are reimbursed by fee schedules.

    ii. Episode of care

      1. Health care plan compensates providers with a lump-sum payment to compensate them for all services delivered to a patient for a specific illness and over a specific period of time.

      2. Also referred to as bundled payments, which cover multiple services and providers

      3. Capitation

       a. Based on per-person premiums instead of itemized for each procedure or service

       b. Calculated on projected cost per patient per month

      4. Global payment

       a. Utilized with procedures that involve professional and technical components (e.g., radiological services)

       b. Lump-sum payments distributed to health care providers and facilities that provided services, equipment, and supplies

      5. Prospective payment

       a. Tax Equity and Fiscal Responsibility Act (1982) modified Medicare's retrospective hospital inpatient payment system to a prospective payment system (PPS).

       b. In 1983, CMS implemented PPS for hospital care provided to Medicare patients.

    c. DRGs is a system used to control Medicare spending; DRG determines payment to facility.

    d. Omnibus Budget Reconciliation Act (1986) mandated CMS to develop a prospective system for hospital-based outpatient services rendered to Medicare beneficiaries.

    e. Effective October 2007, CMS implemented Medicare Severity Diagnosis-Related Groups (MS-DRGs).

       i. Expanded DRGs from 538 to 745

       ii. Revised complications and comorbidities list

       iii. Redistributed cardiac cases into lower-weighted DRGs

       iv. Instituted a 1.2% reduction in overall payments to offset any coding and documentation improvements, which drew the fire of many hospital associations

       v. Payment penalties proposed for complications that occur while a patient is in the hospital

6. Resource-based relative value scale (RBRVS): implemented in 1992 by CMS for reimbursement of physician services of beneficiaries covered under Medicare Part B

7. Medicare SNF PPS

    a. System was mandated by Balanced Budget Act and implemented in 1998.

    b. SNF paid according to a per-diem PPS based on case-mix-adjusted payment rates.

8. Medicare/Medicaid outpatient PPS

    a. Implemented in 2001 with authorization of Balanced Budget Act and applies to the following:

       i. Hospital outpatient services, including partial hospitalization

       ii. Certain Part B services to beneficiaries who have no Part A coverage

       iii. Partial hospitalization services provided by CHCs

       iv. Vaccines, splints, casts, and antigens provided by home health agencies (HHAs) that provide medical and health related services

       v. Vaccines provided by comprehensive outpatient rehabilitation facilities (CORFs)

       vi. Splints, casts, and antigens provided to hospice patients for the treatment of non-terminal illnesses

       vii. CPT/HCPCS codes used to calculate payment

9. Home health PPS

    a. Balanced Budget Act called for development and was implemented in 2001 for covered services to Medicare beneficiaries.

    b. OASIS data set and Home Assessment Validation and Entry (HAVEN) data entry software is used to conduct patient assessments.

    c. Home health resource groups (HHRGs) is the classification system for Home Health PPS.

10. Ambulance fee schedule

    a. Included in 2002 as part of the BBA

    b. Ambulance services are reported using HCPCS codes.

11. Inpatient rehabilitation facility (IRF) PPS

    a. Implemented in 2002 with authorization of BBA

    b. Patient assessment instrument (PAI) completed for all patients.

      c. Inpatient rehabilitation validation and entry (IRVEN) system collects PAI and transmits it to national IRF-PAI database.

        i. Patients are classified into case-mix groups (CMG).

        ii. The CMG relative weight is used to calculate payment.

    12. Long-term care hospitals (LTCHs) PPS: Balanced Budget Refinement Act of 1999, amended by Benefits Improvement Act of 2000, mandated a 2002 implementation of a DRG-based PPS for LTCHs.

    13. Inpatient psychiatric facilities (IPFs): Balanced Budget Refinement Act of 1999 mandated a per-diem PPS that became effective in 2005 and utilizes DRGs.

f. Reimbursement Claims Processing

    i. Patient accounts department is responsible for billing third-party payers, processing accounts receivable, monitoring payments, and verifying insurance.

    ii. Explanation of benefits (EOB) statement is sent to patient to explain services provided, amounts billed, and payments made by health plan.

    iii. Remittance advice (RA) sent to provider to explain payments made by third-party payers.

    iv. Either CMS-1500 (physician office visit) or UB-04 (CMS-1450) (inpatient, outpatient, home health, hospice, long-term care) claim form is submitted to third-party payer for reimbursement.

    v. Medicare carriers process Part B claims for services by physicians and medical suppliers, while Medicare fiscal intermediaries process Part A claims and hospital-based Part B claims for institutional services (Blue Cross and Blue Shield).

    vi. Support processes

      1. Management of fee schedules (MFS)

        a. Third-party payers update fee-for-service fee schedules (list of health care services and procedures using CPT/HCPCS codes) on an annual basis.

        b. Health care providers notify Medicare at the end of each year whether they are willing to participate in program.

        c. Non-participating providers may or may not accept assignment; if assignment is accepted, provider is paid 95% of MFS (5% less than participating providers).

      2. Chargemaster

        a. Also called charge description master (CDM); contains information about health care services and transactions provided to a patient

        b. Allows provider to accurately charge routine services and supplies to the patient

        c. Services, supplies, and procedures included on chargemaster generate reimbursement for approximately 75% of UB-04 claims submitted for outpatient service.

        d. Routinely updated and maintained by representatives from health information management, clinical services, finance, business office/patient financial services, compliance, and information systems

        e. HIM professionals provide expertise concerning CPT codes updates.

      3. Revenue cycle

        a. Assures facility is properly reimbursed for services provided

        b. Major functions include

           i. Admitting, patient-access management

           ii. Case management

           iii. Charge capture

           iv. Health information management

           v. Patient financial services, business office

           vi. Finance

           vii. Compliance

           viii. Information technology

        c. Revenue cycle indicators

           i. Value and volume of discharges

           ii. Number of accounts-receivable days

           iii. Number of bill-hold days

           iv. Percentage and amount of write-offs

           v. Percentage of clean claims

           vi. Percentage of claims returned to providers

           vii. Percentage of denials

           viii. Percentage of accounts missing documents

           ix. Number of query forms

           x. Percentage of late charges

           xi. Percentage of accurate registrations

           xii. Percentage increased point-of-service collections for elective procedures

           xiii. Percentage of increased DRG payments due to improved documentation and coding

      4. Documentation and coding quality

        a. Accurate coding is contingent upon complete, accurate, legible, and timely documentation.

        b. ICD-9-CM and CPT coding drives reimbursement and is a mechanism used to determine utilization of services and the quality of care rendered to patients.

        c. HIPAA authorizes the Office of the Inspector General (OIG) to investigate cases of health care fraud, which includes unnecessary services, upcoding, unbundling, and billing for services not provided.

g. Health Care Reform

    i. Due to increased health care expenditures in mid 1990s, hospitals and practitioners formed alliances, networks, systems, and joint ventures that made them more competitive.

      1. Integrated delivery networks

      2. Health care systems

      3. Health care organizations

    ii. Comprehensive care models offer full range of health care services, including hospitals, primary care physicians, specialty care physicians, and other pertinent health care providers.

      1. Accountable health plans

      2. Coordinated care networks

      3. Community care networks

      4. Integrated health systems

h. HMOs

    i. Oldest of managed health care plans

    ii. Integrates health care delivery with insurance for health care

    i. PPOs

        i. Network of physicians who enter into agreement to provide health care services on a discounted fee schedule

        ii. Patients pay a penalty fee for using nonparticipating physicians.

    j. National Health Insurance

        i. In 1915, the American Association of Labor Legislation drafted model health insurance legislation that was never adopted into law.

        ii. In the 1930s, the Committee on the Cost of Medical Care was formed to address access to medical care; however, their recommendations were not followed.

        iii. In 1939, the Tactical Committee on Medical Care drafted the Wagner National Health Act, which supported a federally funded national health program that the state and local governments would manage; it was not enacted.

        iv. In 1945, President Truman introduced a universal comprehensive national insurance plan that was not adopted into law.

        v. In 1946, Hill-Burton Act initiated health care facility construction program under Title VI of the Public Health Service Act; it provided federal grants for modernizing hospitals, and in return, hospitals would provide free or reduced-cost medical services to those unable to pay.

        vi. In 1965, Title XVIII of the Social Security Act established Medicare, which covered most Americans over age 65.

            1. Overseen by CMS

            2. Health insurance to complement retirement, survivors, and disability insurance benefits

            3. Groups added in 1973 included

                a. Those entitled to Social Security or railroad retirement disability cash benefits for at least 24 months

                b. Most persons with end-stage renal disease

                c. Certain individuals over 65 who were not eligible for paid coverage but elected to pay for Medicare benefits

        vii. In 1966, Title XIX of the Social Security Act established Medicaid.

            1. Overseen by CMS

            2. Health care coverage was added to states' public assistance programs for low-income groups, families with dependent children, aged, and the disabled.

            3. Currently the program covers approximately 40% of indigent population.

PRACTICAL APPLICATION OF YOUR KNOWLEDGE

1. Define the following terms:
   a. Accreditation

   b. Inpatient

   c. Hospital

   d. Outpatient

   e. Patient

   f. Primary patient record

   g. Provider

   h. Resident

   i. Secondary patient record

2. In 1913 the American College of Surgeons was founded. What did it do to improve patient care?

3. What was the result of the Hill-Burton Act of 1946?

4. Describe Title XVIII of the Social Security Act.

5. Describe Title XIX of the Social Security Act.

6. Discuss the following:
   a. DHHS

   b. CMS

   c. TEFRA

   d. COBRA

   e. HIPAA

7. State the various ways that a hospital may be classified.

8. State the responsibilities of the following administrative leaders:

Governing Board	
CEO	
COO	
CIO	
CFO	

9. How is the medical staff managed?

10. Compare the following health care facilities:

Acute-Care	
Ambulatory Care	
Home Health Care	
Hospice	
Long-Term Care	
Urgent Care Center	
Adult Day Care	

11. Discuss the following regulatory agencies:

TJC (formerly JCAHO)	
AAAHC	
AMA	
AoA	
CARF	
CHAP	
NCQA	
NLN	

12. Match the government agency with its mission or purpose.

a. CDC	**e.** IHS	**h.** DHHS
b. NCHS	**f.** OSHA	**i.** AHRQ
c. CMS	**g.** FDA	**j.** ATSDR
d. OIG		

   i. _____ Responsible for numerous health care regulatory programs and encompasses various agencies

   ii. _____ Produces and disseminates relevant scientific and policy information that improves the quality and reduces cost of effective health care

   iii. _____ Protects workers and the public from exposure to adverse effects of hazardous substances

   iv. _____ Concerned with communicable diseases, environmental health, and foreign quarantine activities

   v. _____ Federal government's principal vital and health statistics agency

   vi. _____ Responsible for the safety of foods, drugs, medical devices, cosmetics, and radiation-emitting equipment

   vii. _____ Responsible for Medicare and Medicaid programs

   viii. _____ Responsible for providing health care to Native Americans

   ix. _____ Responsible for developing standards and regulations concerning safe and healthy work environments

   x. _____ Conducts and monitors audits, inspections, and investigations sponsored by DHHS

13. What are the purposes of the health record?

14. Who uses the health record?

15. Distinguish between the source-oriented and the problem-oriented health record.

Source Oriented	Problem Oriented

16. Match the formats of the paper-based medical records:
    a. Source-oriented medical record
    b. Problem-oriented medical record
    c. Integrated medical record
        i. _____ Most common paper-based health record
        ii. _____ Medical record is organized into sections according to treatment and data collection.
        iii. _____ Developed by Dr. Lawrence L. Weed
        iv. _____ Recorded in strict chronological order without any divisions by source
        v. _____ Medical record divided into database, problem list, initial plan, and progress notes
        vi. _____ Progress notes written in SOAP format

17. State general documentation guidelines.

18. Compare the contents of the various health care records:

Acute-Care	
Ambulatory Care	
Emergency Room	
Long-Term Care	
Home Health Care	
Hospice	
Mental Health	

♪ **19.** Calculate the following:

    a. A health information management department currently using 2000 linear filing inches to store medical records plans to purchase new open-shelf filing units. Each of the shelves in a new 6-shelf unit measures 36 linear filing inches. It is estimated that an additional 500 filing inches should be planned to allow for 6-year expansion needs. How many new file-shelving units should be purchased?

    b. Out of 2694 records requested from the health information management department, 2588 were located. What is the record retrieval rate?

    c. A new health information department has purchased 300 units of 6-shelf files and plans to implement a terminal digit filing system. How many shelves should be allocated to each primary number?

    d. A health information management department has a total of 2000 filing inches. When using the unit numbering system, how much shelving space should remain open to allow for expansion?

    e. City General Hospital has been in operation for 20 years. It has 15,000 admissions per year. The health care facility has expanded and will allow for 500 more admissions per year from now on. There are 3000 linear feet of filing space available and half is being used. The facility expects a 35% readmission rate. If a unit numbering filing system is used, how many file folders will be needed for next year?

20. Contrast quantitative and qualitative analysis.

21. Describe the following data sets:

    a. UHDDS

    b. UACDS

c. MDS Long-Term Care and RAI

d. OASIS

e. UCDS

22. What is the difference between a LAN and a WAN?

23. Describe the following indexes and registries:
   a. MPI

   b. Number index

   c. Physician index

   d. Disease index

   e. Procedure index

   f. Admission and discharge register

   g. Operating room register

   h. Birth register

      i. Death register

      j. Emergency room register

      k. Cancer or tumor registry

24. How did TEFRA affect the reimbursement of health care?

25. How has the Balanced Budget Act affected the reimbursement of health care?

26. What are the purposes of the following classification systems?
      a. ICD-9-CM

      b. CPT

      c. HCPCS

      d. ICD-O

      e. APC

      f. DRG

      g. RBRVS

27. Discuss the Chargemaster.

28. Explain the revenue cycle.

29. Mark these statements as True or False.

a. _____ The primary criterion used to evaluate a filing system is the satisfaction of the file clerks.

b. _____ Movable open shelving saves a lot of filing space.

c. _____ In a centralized filing system, record control and security are easier to maintain than in a decentralized system.

d. _____ Color coding of medical record folders assists with the control of misfiles.

e. _____ A hospital with limited filing space should retain all records in hard copy indefinitely.

f. _____ The master patient index is the best source for locating patients with an ICD-9-CM diagnostic code of 250.01.

g. _____ According to the American Health Information Management Association, records of minor patients may be destroyed when the patient reaches the age of majority.

h. _____ In the family numbering system, records are best filed in alphabetical order.

i. _____ Straight numeric filing is a system for filing records in the exact chronological order in which the patients were admitted.

j. _____ The health information manager should develop a retention schedule for the transfer and destruction of medical records, registers, and indexes.

k. _____ If a patient's name cannot be found in the master patient index, then the patient was never admitted in the facility.

l. _____ A Health Maintenance Organization is an entity that combines the provision of health care insurance and the delivery of health care services at predetermined payment rates.

m. _____ A military hospital is a government-owned federal facility.

n. _____ The chief financial officer is responsible for overseeing all accounting and financial affairs of the facility.

o. _____ The attending physician has the major responsibility for assuring a complete and accurate medical record.

p. _____ Non-governmental for-profit proprietary hospitals provide the best overall quality health care.

q. _____ The forms committee often serves as the final approval of forms to be used in the medical record.

r. _____ In order to assure accurate communication, abbreviations should be avoided in the medical record.

s. _____ A certified coding specialist must have a least an associate's degree from an accredited college or university.

t. _____ The Commission on Accreditation of Rehabilitation Facilities accredits facilities that provide rehabilitative care.

u. _____ The terminal-digit filing system has 100 primary filing sections ranging from 00–99.

v. _____ Quantitative and qualitative analysis accomplish the same results for medical record completion.

w. _____ Accreditation by the Joint Commission of Accreditation of Healthcare Organizations is a voluntary process.

x. _____ A final progress note can substitute for a discharge summary for patients who expire within 48 hours of admission.

y. _____ If a physician expires, then his/her incomplete medical records may be filed as is, along with a written explanation.

z. _____ The primary focus of the screen format of computer-based patient records is the end user.

30. Compare the following credentials:
   a. RHIA

   b. RHIT

   c. CCS

   d. CHPS

TEST YOUR KNOWLEDGE

Select the best answer for the questions or incomplete statements.

1. The process by which an organization or agency performs an external review and grants recognition to the program of study or institution that meets certain predetermined standards is called:
   a. standardization.
   b. registration.
   c. formalization.
   d. accreditation.

2. In the following cancer registry accession register, what does the prefix of the patients' accession numbers represent?
   a. Date of accession
   b. Month of accession
   c. Year of accession
   d. Cancer stage

Cancer Registry Accession Register

Account Number	Patient's Name	Primary	Site	Date of Diagnosis
09-0001/00	Cantu, Bobby	Liver	C22	01/08/2009
09-0002/02	Wilson, Joan	Colon	C18	01/08/2009
09-0245/02	Tyler, Kenneth	Lung	C34	01/08/2009
09-0004/01	Mason, Andre	Prostate	C61	01/08/2009
09-0004/02	Mason, Andre	Colon	C18	01/08/2009

3. Dr. Barbette is delinquent, with 10 of her 15 medical records needing to be completed. What is her delinquency rate?
   a. 5%
   b. 10%
   c. 33%
   d. 67%

4. Upon discharge analysis of a patient's record, the analyst does not see a discharge order written by the physician. What can the analyst assume?
   a. The patient expired prior to discharge.
   b. The patient left against medical advice.
   c. The family members requested hospice care.
   d. The patient will continue treatment on an outpatient basis.

5. Which of the following is a secondary record for J. Pratt?
   a. ICD-9-CM code of 650 in the diagnostic index
   b. Emergency room record dated June 6
   c. Mental health record at Houston Honorary Adolescent Center
   d. Admitted and discharged same day with ICD-9-CM code of 650

6. How long should the master patient index be maintained?
   a. 5 years
   b. 10 years
   c. 20 years
   d. Indefinitely

7. The Hill-Burton Act of 1946:
  a. enacted legislation funding the construction of hospitals and other health care facilities.
  b. established the retrospective payment system.
  c. assured the provision of health care for the indigent.
  d. provided health care to Americans 65 years of age and older.

8. Dr. Thomas made an error in recording the progress notes in a patient's medical record. What is the first thing he should do to correct the error?
  a. Remove the page on which he made the error
  b. Tell the nursing staff to ignore the statement
  c. Draw a single line through the error
  d. Obliterate the error and enter correct entry

9. A patient is hospitalized for less than 48 hours. Which of the following is permissible in lieu of a discharge summary?
  a. Discharge order
  b. Final progress note
  c. Discharge diagnosis
  d. Final diagnosis

10. Who is responsible for developing bylaws governing physicians' completion of medical records?
  a. Governing board
  b. Chief of medicine
  c. Chief executive officer
  d. Medical staff

11. Which system avoids assigning a new number for each patient encounter?
  a. Straight numerical
  b. Serial numbering
  c. Unit numbering
  d. Serial-unit numbering

12. By signing a consent for treatment, the patient agrees to:
  a. allow the hospital to release information to his/her insurance company.
  b. treatments and procedures to be performed by health care providers.
  c. take all medications prescribed and dispensed by health care providers.
  d. allow hospital to dispose of property and values in the case of death.

13. Reviewing the record to assure the presence of a discharge summary is referred to as:
  a. legal analysis.
  b. qualitative analysis.
  c. documentation analysis.
  d. quantitative analysis.

14. A major advantage of the source-oriented medical record is the:
  a. speed at which individual sheets can be located.
  b. ease with which health care providers can follow the course of one problem.
  c. strict chronology that keeps episode of care clearly defined by date.
  d. forms are designed to support numbering and tracking of problems.

15. Which of the following would be most beneficial in locating a charged-out medical record?
  a. Outguide
  b. Transfer notice
  c. Requisition slip
  d. Master patient index

16. Which of the following filing systems would be most affected in the event of a divorce?
  a. Family
  b. Unit
  c. Serial
  d. Serial-unit

17. A patient had an appendectomy due to appendicitis. This operative report must be completed when?
   a. Immediately after surgery
   b. Within 24 hours of surgery
   c. Within 48 hours of surgery
   d. Within 15 days of discharge

18. A post-anesthesia note is required when?
   a. Immediately after surgery
   b. Within 24 hours of surgery
   c. Within 48 hours of surgery
   d. Within 15 days of discharge

19. A discharge summary:
   a. may be completed in lieu of a clinical resume.
   b. must be dictated and typed for ease of readability.
   c. is not required for a stay of 48 hours or less.
   d. is not required when death occurs within 48 hours or less.

20. Which of the following is an example of a government agency that has an interest in the standardization of records and data collection?
   a. The Joint Commission
   b. Department of Health and Human Services
   c. American Medical Association
   d. American Health Information Management Association

21. The health record may be used for personal and non-personal reasons. Which is an example of personal use of the health record?
   a. Patient reviews record with provider for understanding of health status.
   b. Health information professional assigns ICD-9-CM codes.
   c. Accrediting agency reviews record to assure quality health care.
   d. Employer reviews health care data to evaluate job injuries.

22. Place the following in terminal digit order: 01-34-54, 01-35-55, 02-05-49, 02-66-48
   a. 01-34-54, 01-35-55, 02-05-49, 02-66-48
   b. 02-05-49, 01-34-54, 01-35-55, 02-66-48
   c. 02-66-48, 02-05-49, 01-35-55, 01-34-54
   d. 02-66-48, 02-05-49, 01-34-54, 01-35-55

23. The condition that is primarily responsible for the patient's admission to the hospital is the _____ diagnosis.
   a. primary
   b. principal
   c. preliminary
   d. discharge

24. Which of the following is not a major hospital classification?
   a. General
   b. Special
   c. Psychiatric
   d. Cardiac

25. Which of the following would the physician include in the discharge summary?
   a. Blood pressure and pulse
   b. Review of systems
   c. Do not resuscitate order
   d. Instructions for future care

26. As the director of health information of a newly established acute care facility, where would you expect to find directives concerning the minimum health record contents?
   a. The Joint Commission
   b. Credentials committee meeting minutes
   c. Medical record committee meeting minutes
   d. Benchmarks from area acute care facilities

27. A health record analyst is reviewing the medical record for authentication of all entries. This process is commonly termed:
   a. qualitative analysis.
   b. quantitative analysis.
   c. closed record review.
   d. point of care review.

28. Information in a tumor registry is collected to:
   a. bill for treatment rendered.
   b. inform patients of their cancer status.
   c. improve patient care.
   d. determine the appropriate cancer stage.

29. LaToya wants to put her health care decisions in writing in the event she has an incurable or irreversible condition and is unable to communicate her wishes. What should she institute?
   a. Advance directive
   b. Executor of her estate
   c. Transfer on death
   d. Legal guardian

30. The automated record tracking system is a database that:
   a. locates misplaced health records.
   b. verifies the requested patient's name and health record number.
   c. stores current and past health record locations.
   d. records dissatisfaction of record requesters with service.

31. A health information technician wants to obtain a chronological list of all patients admitted to the facility during the third quarter with a diagnosis of appendicitis. Which database should the technician utilize?
   a. Accession register
   b. Master patient index
   c. Disease index
   d. Patient register

32. Which application is best suited for bar coding?
   a. Birth certificate registration
   b. Diagnostic and procedural coding
   c. Record tracking/location
   d. Misfiled records

33. During the month of December, there were 3489 discharges with 134 incomplete records. What was the incomplete record rate for the month?
   a. .384%
   b. 3.84%
   c. 26.03%
   d. 38.40%

34. Last month Houston Hospital discharged 517 patients. Each chart is approximately 1.8 inch thick. A shelving unit in the health information department has 7 shelves and each shelf is 36 inches. How many shelving units are needed to store one month of discharged records?
   a. 2.05
   b. 3.00
   c. 3.69
   d. 4.00

35. The arrangement that links health care financing and service delivery and allows payers to exercise significant economic control over how and what services are delivered is referred to as what?
   a. Medicare
   b. Medicaid
   c. Managed care
   d. Fee for service

36. Ellen, a 78-year-old end-stage renal cancer patient, is in need of palliative care. Which facility would best meet her needs?
   a. Skilled nursing facility
   b. Hospice
   c. Rehabilitation facility
   d. Home health care

37. At the close of World War II, the growth in the number of hospitals can be attributed to:
   a. Hill-Burton Act of 1946.
   b. Clinton Health Security Act of 1993.
   c. HIPAA of 1996.
   d. AARP, founded in 1958.

38. Which of the following agencies is concerned with communicable diseases, environmental health, and foreign quarantine activities?
   a. Centers for Medicare and Medicaid Services
   b. National Institutes of Health
   c. Health Resources and Services Administration
   d. Centers for Disease Control and Prevention

39. Which of the following organizations is responsible for developing standards and conducting investigations to determine compliance in matters related to occupational safety and health?
   a. DHHS
   b. CMS
   c. COBRA
   d. OSHA

40. Which act established the Patient Antidumping Law?
   a. HIPAA
   b. TEFRA
   c. COBRA
   d. OSHA

41. When this act was passed, it helped to improve the quality of health care, reduce cost, and enhance the effectiveness of health care.
   a. Health Information Portability and Accountability Act
   b. Tax Equity and Fiscal Responsibility Act
   c. Omnibus Budget Reconciliation Act
   d. Occupational Safety and Health Act

42. This hospital provides care to military personnel and their dependents. How is it classified?
   a. Voluntary
   b. Proprietary
   c. Government
   d. Not for profit

43. Manuel receives surgery in one day and is discharged to home. Where was he treated?
   a. Surgicenter
   b. Satellite clinic
   c. Ancillary department
   d. Observation unit

44. Hospital ownership is either:
   a. proprietary or government.
   b. charitable or government.
   c. stand alone or with clinics.
   d. government or non-government.

45. According to TJC (formerly JCAHO) standards, a hospital is required to:
   a. provide charitable care to the indigent.
   b. promote performance improvement.
   c. employ an RHIA or RHIT.
   d. review and update policies yearly.

46. Warren, a 12-year-old Boy Scout, breaks his leg while hiking with the troop. Which type of facility might Bob's Boy Scout leader take him to for emergent treatment?
   a. Surgicenter
   b. Ambulatory care clinic
   c. Specialty hospital
   d. General hospital

47. Dr. Lewis is retired. Which medical staff membership might he be awarded?
   a. Courtesy
   b. Honorary
   c. Tributary
   d. Consulting

48. The governing board is responsible for setting the overall direction of the hospital. Other responsibilities include all except which of the following?
   a. Selecting TJC standards to uphold
   b. Selecting qualified administrative leadership
   c. Monitoring the quality of care
   d. Establishing bylaws in accordance with license

49. Which of the following is considered a clinical support service?
   a. OB/GYN
   b. Cardiology
   c. Volunteer services
   d. Health information management department

50. Cecile, a 78-year-old female, needs intermittent skilled nursing care. Which facility would best meet her needs?
   a. Skilled nursing facility
   b. Hospice
   c. Rehabilitation facility
   d. Home health care

Health Care Privacy, Confidentiality, Legal, and Ethical Issues

1. **Introduction to the Legal System**
   a. The legal system is the system of principles and processes by which people who live in a society deal with their disputes and problems, seeking to solve or settle them without resort to force. Laws govern the relationships among private individuals, organizations, and government. The legal system is a combination of private and public law.
      i. Private
         1. Also considered civil law
         2. Concerned with the recognition and enforcement of the rights and duties of private individuals and organizations (i.e., patient and health care facility)
         3. Legal issues between private parties are torts and contracts
            a. Tort
               i. An injury or wrong committed against an individual or his property
               ii. In tort action, one party asserts that wrongful conduct on the part of another caused harm and seeks compensation for the harm suffered.
            b. Contract
               i. Concerned with legally enforceable agreements between two or more individuals
               ii. In contract disputes, one party asserts that in failing to fulfill an obligation, the other party breached a contract, and the asserting party seeks either compensation or performance of the obligation as a remedy.
      ii. Public
         1. Deals with the relationships between private parties and the government; consists of criminal law and government regulations
            a. Criminal
               i. Prohibits conduct considered injurious to society as a whole and provides for punishment of those found to have engaged in such conduct
               ii. Crime versus tort
                  1. Crime is an offense against a person or the public at large.
                  2. Tort is a civil wrong against an individual.
            b. Regulations
               i. Multiple government regulations require private individuals and organizations to follow specified courses of action in connection with their activities.

71

        iii. Sources of law
- **1.** Constitution
  - **a.** Supreme law of the land
  - **b.** Establishes the general organization of the federal government, and grants certain powers to and places limits on the three branches of the federal government (executive, legislative, judicial)
  - **c.** Each state has its own constitution.
  - **d.** Each city has its own charter.
- **2.** Statutes
  - **a.** Statutory or codified law refers to written laws or statutes enacted by such bodies as the United States Congress and state and local legislatures.
  - **b.** Constitutional and federal law take precedence over conflicting state laws, and state laws take precedence over conflicting local government rules.
- **3.** Decisions of the court
  - **a.** Common law or uncodified law derived from the common law of England applied to the courts of the United States
  - **b.** Consist of principles that have evolved over time from court decisions resolving controversies
  - **c.** When a case decision is considered to serve as an authority or example for subsequent similar or identical cases, the case is said to have set a legal precedent.
- **4.** Rules of administrative agencies
  - **a.** Legislatures have delegated to administrative agencies the responsibility and power to implement various laws (e.g., DHHS).
  - **b.** The delegated powers include quasi-legislative power to adopt regulations and the quasi-judicial power to decide how the statutes and regulations apply to individual situations.
  - **c.** Legislatures delegate these powers because legislators do not have the time or expertise to address the complex issues involved in some areas that need to be regulated.

b. Branches of the Government (Federal and State)
- **i.** Executive (president or governor)
  - **1.** Enforces and administers the law
  - **2.** United States Constitution invests this power in the President, who is the administrative head of the executive branch.
  - **3.** Oversees various agencies, including DHHS, which manages CMS
- **ii.** Legislative (Congress and state legislatures)
  - **1.** Enacts laws
  - **2.** Creates new legislation, amends or repeals existing legislation
  - **3.** Federal and state levels (except Nebraska, which has only one house) consist of two houses, one composed of senators and the other representatives.
- **iii.** Judicial (U.S. Supreme Court, various state and federal courts)
  - **1.** Responsible for interpreting the law through hearing and resolving disputes in accordance with the law
  - **2.** Three sources of judicial power
    - **a.** Federal courts
      - **i.** Have jurisdiction over
        - **1.** Cases involving questions of federal law
        - **2.** Treaties

    3. Cases concerning maritime matters

    4. Cases that involve two or more states

   ii. Federal court system structure

    1. District courts (trial courts)

    2. Courts of appeal

    3. Supreme Court

  b. State courts

   i. Vary by state but can be divided into four general categories

    1. Trial courts of limited jurisdiction

    2. Trial courts of general jurisdiction

    3. Intermediate appellate courts

    4. Courts of last resort (supreme courts)

  c. Administrative agencies

   i. Empowered by law to make regulations with the force of the law, and can also conduct hearings and take measures to enforce these regulations

   ii. Example: CMS

 3. Each level of government (federal, state) has its own set of courts.

  a. Courts have different jurisdiction based upon geographical area, area of authority, and type of case.

  b. Trial and appellate courts

   i. Trial courts initially hear a case and pass judgment (original jurisdiction).

   ii. Litigants unsatisfied with trial court decisions may appeal their case to appellate courts (court of appeals).

    1. Two types of review (see Table 3-1)

     a. Error correction monitors decisions of lower trial courts for proper application and interpretation of law; does not seek new evidence, but examines records of lower courts for errors.

     b. Sort cases for Supreme Court review

Table 3-1 Federal and State Court Sequences of Appeals

Level of Court	Federal	State
Highest appellate courts	U.S. Supreme Court (may consider appeals from state supreme courts on federal questions)	State supreme courts
Appellate courts	U.S. Court of Appeals	Circuit courts, district courts, and courts of common pleas
Special jurisdiction courts	U.S. Customs, Claims, and Tax	
Trial courts	U.S. District Courts	District, probate, family, criminal courts
Lower local courts (non-jury)		Traffic, police, small claims, Justice of Peace

2. Health Record Requirements and Retention Guidelines
  a. Record Requirements
    i. Federal and state laws and regulations provide guidance as to patient record content, privacy, and security.
    ii. Some state laws and regulations specify that health records must be maintained by health care institutions and that the information must be kept confidential.
    iii. Most state law expressly allows a patient or authorized representative to inspect the health record (typically, a written request must be made and reasonable cost paid).
    iv. State licensing laws usually address at least the minimum content of a health record.
    v. In addition to federal, state, and local laws, numerous nongovernmental agencies specify standards for health care facilities (e.g., TJC).
    vi. TJC, American Osteopathic Association (AOA), Medicare/Medicaid Conditions of Participation (CoP), and other accrediting bodies provide standards for patient recordkeeping.
      1. There should be one record per patient, with the following contents for an inpatient record:
        a. History and physical
        b. Documentation of infections and complications
        c. Consent forms
        d. Notes, reports, ancillary reports
        e. Discharge summary
        f. Final diagnosis
  b. Reporting Requirements
    i. In certain circumstances, federal and state law allows health care organizations to disclose confidential information without the patient's consent.
      1. Child abuse
      2. Abuse of adults and injuries to disabled persons
      3. Abortions
      4. Cancer
      5. Death or injury from use of a medical device
      6. Communicable diseases, including HIV/AIDS, tuberculosis, etc.
      7. Gun shot wounds
    ii. Categories 1–7 do specify what can be reported without the consent of the patient due to state and federal law.
    iii. If a person's diagnosis falls in one of the above categories, it can be reported to the authorities in cases of abuse.
    iv. Anything outside of this cannot be disclosed unless there is the patient's consent.
  c. Retention Guidelines
    i. Forces influencing retention of health information are as follows:
      1. Health care providers' ability to
        a. Render continuing patient care
        b. Conduct education and research
        c. Defend a professional liability action
      2. Storage constraints
      3. Historical value
      4. Research and education
      5. Medium for storing records

       6. New technology

       7. Fiscal concerns

     ii. Retention schedule as recommended by AHIMA (see Table 3-2)

  d. Record Destruction

     i. Instances of health record destruction

       1. In ordinary course of business

       2. Provider's closure

     ii. Institution should have a policy addressing the controlling statute or regulation governing when a health record may be destroyed.

     iii. Records may be destroyed through shredding, burning, or some other means.

     iv. Some states require facility to maintain an abstract of patient data prior to destroying, or may require patient to be notified that his/her record will be destroyed.

     v. Facilities should maintain a permanent, dated, certified log of evidence of patient records that have been destroyed in the ordinary course of business.

3. Confidentiality, Consent, and Security of Health Records

  a. Creation of health record is the responsibility of health care facility and those who provide care to the patient.

  b. Ownership of Health Record

     i. Physical health record is the property of the health care provider, physician, or hospital that maintains it, because it is the health care provider's business record.

     ii. Patients have limited rights to access and control the disclosure of their information.

     iii. The patient and others have an interest in the information contained within the health record.

     iv. The patient and others as authorized have the right to access the information but do not have a right to possess the physical record.

Table 3-2 Record Retention Guidelines

Document	Retention Guideline
Adult patient health record	10 years after the most recent encounter
Minor patient health record	Age of majority plus statute of limitation governing medical malpractice lawsuits
Diagnostic images (e.g., X-rays)	5 years
Disease index	10 years
Fetal heart monitor record	10 years after infant reaches age of majority
Master patient index	Permanently
Operative index	10 years
Physician index	10 years
Register of births	Permanently
Register of deaths	Permanently
Register of surgical procedures	Permanently

c. Confidentiality

    i. Privacy is the right of an individual to be left alone.

    ii. Information derived from a clinical relationship between patients and health care professionals is patient-specific health information.

        1. Health care providers should protect patient-specific health information from disclosure.

    iii. Confidential communication is information given in the belief that it will not be disclosed to another party.

    iv. Confidentiality after death

        1. Patient's personal representative or the executor of the patient's estate may waive privilege.

d. Privileged Communication

    i. Special relationship between patient and health care provider

    ii. Three elements of privileged communication

        1. Relationship between patient and provider

        2. Information must have been acquired through such a relationship.

        3. Information must have some connection with the provider's task of treating the patient.

e. Types of Consent

    i. Do not resuscitate

        1. Tells medical professionals not to perform cardiopulmonary resuscitation (CPR) if the patient's breathing or heartbeat stops

        2. An adult patient may consent to DNR through a health care proxy or durable power of attorney.

    ii. Admission includes generalized consent that documents a patient's consent to receive medical treatment at the facility.

    iii. Release of information is consent for provider to release health care information for the purpose of reimbursement, continuity of care, or other reason, as authorized by the patient or patient's legal representative.

    iv. Informed consent (treatment and surgery)

        1. Process of advising a patient about treatment options and, depending on state laws, the provider may be obligated to disclose a patient's diagnosis, proposed treatment/surgery, reason for treatment/surgery, possible complications, likelihood of success, alternative treatment options, and risks if the patient does not undergo treatment/surgery

        2. Should include an explanation of the risks and benefits of treatment/surgery, alternatives, and evidence that the patient or appropriate legal representative understands and consents to the treatment/surgery

        3. TJC standards require that a patient consent to treatment and that the record contain evidence of consent.

        4. AOA requires a dated, timed, and signed informed consent for surgery on the patient's chart prior to surgery being performed.

        5. Medicare CoP state that all records must contain written patient consent for treatment and procedures specified by the medical staff, or by federal or state law

f. Advance Directive

    i. As part of the Omnibus Budget Reconciliation act of 1990, the U.S. Congress passed the Patient Self-Determination Act. The act required providers participating in the Medicare and Medicaid programs to inform patients of their rights to express written preferences regarding health care decisions to be followed if the patient becomes unable to make or communicate decisions, such as a decision to withdraw life support systems.

    ii. Legal document in which patients provide instructions as to how they want to be treated in the event they become very ill and there is no reasonable hope for recovery

  g. Durable Power of Attorney

    i. Legal document in which patients name someone close to them to make decisions about their health care in the event they become incapacitated

    ii. Also called a health care proxy

  h. Security of Health Records

    i. Organizations must maintain the physical and electronic protection of the integrity, availability, and confidentiality of computer-based information and the resources used to enter, store, process, and communicate it.

    ii. Security of paper-based health records

      1. Maintain secure from unauthorized access

      2. Utilize a tracking system to locate records

      3. Educate personnel on confidentiality of patient information

    iii. Records must be protected from loss, theft, tampering, and destruction.

4. Laws and Regulations Regarding Health Records

  a. Statute of Limitations

    i. Legislatively imposed time constraints that restrict the period of time after the occurrence of an injury during which a legal action must be commenced

    ii. Should a cause of action be initiated later than the time prescribed, the case cannot proceed.

    iii. The statutory period begins when an injury occurs, although in some cases (usually involving foreign objects left in the body during surgery) the statutory period commences when the injured person discovers or should have discovered the injury.

5. Release of Information and Subpoenas

  a. Release of Information

    i. Patient or legal representative may authorize disclosure of patient's health care information unless it would be in the patient's best interest not to have such information disclosed, such as psychiatric information.

    ii. The patient or legal representative controls access by all third parties except those to which the health care institution is required to report information of a medical nature or as otherwise provided by law.

  b. Subpoena

    i. Court order requiring someone to appear in court to give testimony

    ii. Disregarding a subpoena can result in contempt of court.

    iii. Common elements of valid subpoena

      1. Name of court where lawsuit is brought

      2. Names of parties to the lawsuit

      3. Docket number of the case

      4. Date, time, and place of the requested appearance

      5. Specific documents to be produced if a subpoena duces tecum is involved

        a. Subpoena duces is a written order commanding a person to appear, give testimony, and bring all documents (records) described in the subpoena to court.

Table 3-3 Federal Laws and Regulations for Health Information

Legislation	Summary
Drug Abuse and Treatment Act (1972)	Requires drug and alcohol abuse patient records to be kept confidential and not subject to disclosure except as provided by law
Emergency Medical Treatment and Active Labor Act of the Consolidated Omnibus Budget Reconciliation Act (1985)	Hospitals and physicians who participate in the Medicare program must follow certain guidelines for the treatment and transfer of all patients, regardless of patient participation and eligibility for Medicare. Also referred to as antidumping law
Federal Tort Claims Act (1946)	The U.S. government's immunity from tort liability was largely abolished and certain conditions for suits and claims against the U.S. government were established.
Freedom of Information Act (1966)	Individuals can seek access to information without the authorization of the person to whom the information applies when the information is held by a federal agency (except personal records such as medical records).
Health Care Quality Improvement Act (1986)	Established the National Practitioner Data Bank (NPDB), which contains information about practitioner's credentials, including previous medical malpractice payment and adverse action history.
Health Insurance Portability and Privacy Act (1996)	Mandated administrative simplification regulations that govern privacy, security, and electronic transactions standards for health care information

      6. Name and telephone number of attorney who requested the subpoena

      7. Signature, stamp, or seal of the official empowered to issue the subpoena

      8. Witness fees, where provided by law

   iv. Contempt of court

      1. Results when a person fails to obey a subpoena and is punishable by fine or imprisonment

   v. Subpoena ad testificandum

      1. Court order that requires a person to appear in court to testify

   vi. Subpoena duces tecum

      1. Court order that commands a person to come to court and produce whatever documents are named in the order

Table 3-4 Federal and State Legislation Relevant to Health Care and Maintenance of Health Records

Legislation	Summary
Patient Self-Determination Act (1990)	Requires that all health care facilities notify patients age 18 and over that they have the right to have an advance directive placed in their medical record. Facilities must inform patients, in writing, of state laws and facility policies regarding implementation of advance directives. The patient record must document whether the patient has executed an advance directive. Allows a person to: 1. Make decision concerning medical care 2. Accept or refuse treatment 3. Present their request for treatment at time of admission (administrative directive or living will)
Privacy Act (1974)	Gives individuals some control over the information collected about them by the federal government; under this act, people have the right to: 1. Learn what information has been collected about them 2. View and have a copy of that information 3. Maintain limited control over the disclosure of that information to other persons or entities
Occupational Safety and Health Act (1970)	Created the Occupational Safety and Health Administration (OSHA), whose mission is to ensure safe and healthy workplaces
Omnibus Budget Reconciliation Act (1987)	Created the Nursing Home Reform Act, which ensures residents of nursing homes receive quality care, requires provision of certain services, and establishes a residents' bill of rights
Omnibus Budget Reconciliation Act (1990)	Requires reporting of adverse actions to the Centers of Medicare and Medicaid Services (CMS) and to state medical boards and licensing agencies
Tax Equity and Fiscal Responsibility Act (1982)	TEFRA introduced the Peer Review Organization (PRO) program as a component of Medicare law to ensure the quality of care rendered to patients.
Uniform Business Records as Evidence Act (1936)	Stipulates that records can be admitted as evidence in a court of law if they were kept in the ordinary course of business. As of 1995, 46 of the 50 states had adopted it.
Uniform Healthcare Information Act (1985)	Serves as a model for state adoption and provides rules about health information management. As of 1996, only Montana and Washington had enacted this model legislation.

Table 3-5 Landmark Cases

Case	Court Decision
Behringer vs. Medical Center at Princeton (1991)	News of a physician on staff at the hospital where he was treated and diagnosed with AIDS was circulated among staff and patients. Physician sued the hospital for breach of duty to maintain confidentiality of his diagnosis. Court found hospital liable for failure to take reasonable precautions to ensure his information was held confidential.
Darling vs. Charleston Community Community Medical Hospital (1965)	Case dismantled doctrine of charitable immunity. Court held that the governing board has the duty to establish mechanisms for the medical staff to evaluate, counsel, and when necessary, take action against an unreasonable risk of harm to a patient arising from the patient's treatment by a personal physician. Court held that, based on the hospital's obligation to select high-quality physicians to be medical staff members, the hospital may be held liable for a patient's injury caused by a physician who does not meet those standards but was given medical staff membership and privileges.
Griswold vs. Connecticut (1965)	Court ruled that the right to privacy limits governmental authority to regulate contraception, abortion, and other decisions affecting reproduction.
Judge vs. Rockford Memorial Hospital (1958)	Director of nurses wrote a letter to a nurse's professional registry stating that the hospital wanted to discontinue a particular nurse's services because narcotics were disappearing whenever the nurse was on duty. Court found communication to be privileged, because the director of nurses had a legal duty to make the communication in the interests of society. Nurse's claims for damages were denied by the court.
Reisner vs. Regents of the University of California (1995)	Physician failed to warn his patient that she had contracted HIV through a blood transfusion. As a result, the hospital and physician were sued when the patient's sexual partner was exposed to the virus. The court held that the hospital was liable for the physician's failure to warn.

Table 3-5 Landmark Cases *(continued)*	
Case	**Court Decision**
Tarasoff vs. Board of Regents (1976)	Determined that there was a duty to warn an individual against whom the patient has made a credible threat to harm

6. Health Insurance Portability and Accountability Act (HIPAA) of 1996

    a. Goals of HIPAA (see Figure 3-1)

        i. Enacted to improve the portability and continuity of health insurance coverage in the group and individual markets, to combat waste, fraud, and abuse in health insurance and health care delivery, to promote the use of medical savings accounts, to improve access to long-term care services and coverage, to simplify the administration of health insurance, and for other purposes

        ii. Addresses issues related to the portability of health insurance after leaving employment

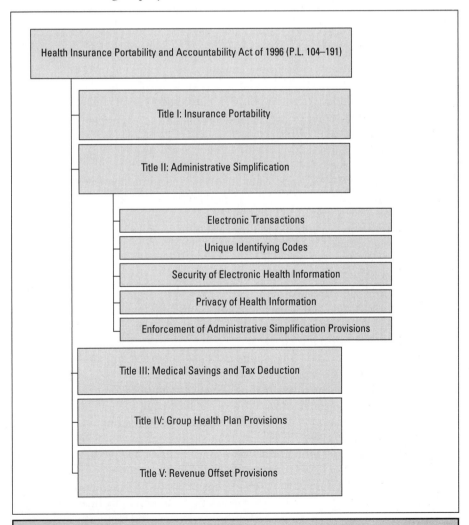

Figure 3-1 Five Portions of HIPAA

   iii. Created the Healthcare Integrity and Protection Data Bank (HIPDB), whose mission is to inform federal agencies about potential quality problems with clinicians, suppliers, and providers of health care services

   iv. Five portions of HIPAA

    1. Insurance portability

    2. Administrative simplification, including

     a. Standardization of electronic formats for transmission of 11 specific electronic transactions

     b. Unique identifying codes for health care providers, health plans, employers, and individuals

     c. Security of electronic health information

     d. Privacy of individually identifiable health information (privacy rule)

     e. Enforcement of the administrative simplification provisions

    3. Medical savings and tax deductions

    4. Group health plan provision

    5. Revenue offset provisions

 b. Administration Simplifications

   i. CMS is responsible for implementing various provisions of HIPAA.

   ii. Requires DHHS (which manages CMS) to improve the Medicare program under Title XVIII of the Social Security Act (SSA), the Medicaid program under Title XIX of the SSA, and the efficiency and effectiveness of the health care system by encouraging the development of a health information system through the establishment of standards and requirements for the electronic transmission of certain health information

 c. Privacy Rule (August, 2002)

   i. HIPAA is first federal law that governs privacy of health information nationwide.

   ii. Prior to HIPAA privacy rule, there were no federal statutes or regulations of general application protecting the confidentiality of medical or personal information.

   iii. Ensures the protection of medical information shared with a covered entity, which are

    1. Health care providers

    2. Health plans

    3. Health care clearinghouses

   iv. Privacy rule restricts use and disclosure of personal health information and gives patients greater access to and protection of their medical records.

   v. Protects a patient's fundamental right to privacy and confidentiality; patients can expect

    1. Privacy regarding their privileged communication

    2. Security standards to ensure facilities, equipment, and patient information are safe from damage, loss, tampering, theft, or unauthorized access

   vi. Protected health information (PHI)

    1. Personal health information given to a covered entity

    2. Includes any information that is oral or is recorded on paper or electronically about a person's physical or mental health, services rendered, or payment for those services, and that includes personal information connecting the patient to the record

     3. Examples of PHI

       a. Patient's name or address

       b. Social Security or other identification numbers

       c. Physician's personal notes

       d. Billing information

     4. Authorization is required for the disclosure of PHI for purposes other than

       a. Treatment

         i. Covered entities may communicate freely with patients about treatment options and health-related information

       b. Payment

       c. Health care operations

     5. Authorization is required to use PHI for

       a. Use or disclosure of psychotherapy notes

       b. Research purposes, unless a documented waiver is obtained from the Institutional Review Board or privacy board

       c. Use and disclosure to third parties for marketing activities such as promoting services or selling lists of patients

vii. Release of information form must include

     1. A description of the information to be used or disclosed, written in clear language

     2. Whether or not it will result in financial gain for the covered entity

     3. Who will receive the information

     4. Expiration date

     5. Revocation

     6. Statement that information released pursuant to authorization may be subject to redisclosure by the recipient and no longer protected

     7. Signature of patient or legal representative

       a. If legal representative, then a description of his or her authority to act must be included on authorization form

viii. PHI can be used or disclosed without authorization but with patient agreement to

     1. Maintain a facility's patient directory

     2. Inform family members or other identified persons involved in the patient's care or notify them on patient location, condition, or death

     3. Inform appropriate agencies during disaster relief efforts

     4. Public health activities related to disease prevention or control

     5. Report victims of abuse, neglect, or domestic violence

     6. Health oversight activities such as audits, legal investigations, licensure, or for certain law enforcement purposes or government functions

     7. Coroners, medical examiners, funeral directors, or tissue/organ donations

     8. Avert a serious threat to health and safety

ix. Minimum necessary disclosure of PHI

     1. Covered entities must develop policies and practices to make sure the least amount of health information is shared.

     2. Employees must identify who regularly accesses PHI along with the types of PHI needed and the conditions for access.

     3. Does not apply to use or disclosure of medical records for treatment

    x. Notice of privacy practices

       1. Patients have the right to adequate notice concerning the use or disclosure of their PHI on the first date of service delivery or as soon as possible after an emergency. New notices must be issued when the facility's privacy practices change.

       2. Notice of privacy practices must

          a. Contain patient's rights and covered entities' legal duties

          b. Be made available to patients in print

          c. Be displayed at the site of service and posted on a web site whenever possible

       3. Once a patient has received notice of his or her rights, covered entities must make an effort to get written acknowledgment of receipt of notice of privacy practices from the patient, or document reasons why it was not obtained, and copies must be kept of all notices and acknowledgments.

    xi. Privacy rule grants patient rights over their PHI to include

       1. Receive notice of privacy practices at time of first delivery of service

       2. Request restricted use and disclosure, although the covered entity is not required to agree

       3. Have PHI communicated to them by alternate means and at alternate locations to protect confidentiality

       4. Inspect and amend PHI, and obtain copies, with some exceptions

       5. Request a history of disclosures for 6 years prior to the request

       6. Exceptions (disclosures for which an accounting is not required by covered entity) include disclosures

          a. Made for treatment, payment, health care operations, or with prior authorization

          b. To individuals of the PHI about themselves

          c. For use in the facility's directory or to persons involved in the individual's care or other notification purposes

          d. To meet national security or intelligence requirements

          e. To correctional institutions or law enforcement officials

          f. That occurred before the compliance date for the covered entity

       7. Contact designated persons regarding any privacy concern or breach of privacy within the facility or at DHHS

    xii. Rights of minors

       1. Parents have the right to access and control the PHI of their minor children, except when state law overrides parental control such as

          a. HIV testing of minors without parental permission

          b. Cases of abuse

          c. When parents have agreed to give up control over their minor child

   xiii. Responsibility of health care institution

       1. Allow patients to see and copy their PHI

       2. Designate a full- or part-time privacy official responsible for implementing the programs

       3. Designate a contact person or office responsible for receiving complaints

       4. Develop a Notice of Privacy Practices document

       5. Develop policies and safeguards to protect PHI and limit incidental use or disclosure

      6. Institute employee training programs so everyone knows about the privacy policies and procedures for safeguarding PHI

      7. Institute a complaint process, and file and resolve formal complaints

      8. Make sure contracts with business associates comply with the privacy rule

   xiv. HIPAA rules regarding psychotherapy notes

      1. Requires an authorization specifically allowing release of psychotherapy notes

      2. The rule defines psychotherapy notes as those taken by a mental health professional during a counseling session and kept separate from the rest of the medical record.

      3. Two key issues to determining which psychotherapy documentation is protected are

         a. Type of documentation

         b. Where the records are kept

      4. Not all documentation by a mental health professional requires special protection; only the notes from a therapy session.

      5. Other documentation is handled in a similar manner to the rest of the medical record and includes prescriptions, medication monitoring, session start and stop times, modality and frequency of treatments, clinical test results, and summary items.

      6. When psychotherapy notes are maintained in another or with another record (e.g., medical record), they lose their special confidentiality protection

   xv. Violation of privacy rule (civil and criminal penalties)

      1. Civil penalty of $100 up to a maximum of $25,000 per year for each standard violated

      2. Criminal penalty for knowingly disclosing PHI is up to $50,000 and 1 year in prison for obtaining or disclosing protected health information, up to $100,000 and up to 5 years in prison for obtaining or disclosing PHI under false pretenses, and up to $250,000 and up to 10 years in prison for obtaining or disclosing PHI with the intent to sell, transfer, or use it for commercial advantage, personal gain, or malicious harm

7. Health Record Documentation

  a. The record can serve and protect only when caregivers make a personal commitment to good medical record documentation.

  b. The record should be complete, accurate, and legible in order to:

     i. Keep the health care team informed about patient progress

     ii. Enable caregivers to coordinate their efforts properly

     iii. Supply clinicians data to evaluate and improve care

     iv. Help to ensure that timely decisions are made and communicated throughout the continuum of care

     v. Validate compliance to hundreds of requirements, including TJC accreditation standards and regulations established by federal, state, and local agencies

     vi. Furnish an objective basis for reimbursement by insurers

     vii. Provide a legal record of care rendered, thus defending against a malpractice claim

     viii. Furnish data to conduct research and clinical trials

  c. Patient record is used to:

     i. Establish duty

     ii. Determine if standards of care were met

          iii. Evaluate damages

          iv. Fix cause

   d. Departures from appropriate recordkeeping are used by the plaintiff's attorney to create the impression that care itself was negligent. These include:

          i. Alterations of entries without proper identification

          ii. Feuding among caregivers

          iii. Illegibility of written notes and orders

          iv. Late entries

          v. Missing data or test results

          vi. Omission of information

          vii. Time gaps

   e. Documentation Guidelines for Entries

          i. Entries should be complete, accurate, legible, timed, and signed by the author, using full name and credentials.

          ii. Entries should be made on or about the time of treatment.

          iii. Made on approved forms and filed by order of the chart

          iv. Made in the appropriate sequence in the record, avoiding gaps with previous entries and lapses in time

          v. Late entries should be clearly marked as such.

          vi. Entries by students, interns, and residents should be countersigned.

          vii. Only approved abbreviations and terminology should be used.

          viii. Corrections, addenda, and changes to entries should be done according to policy.

          ix. Adverse episodes and subsequent interventions should be written objectively.

8. Health Records in Court

   a. Definitions Relevant to Court Procedure

          i. Appeal: the process by which a decision of a lower court is brought for review to a court of higher jurisdiction, typically known as an appellate court

          ii. Court order: a written command or direction ordered by a court or judge

          iii. Cross examination: questioning of a witness by the opposing attorney

          iv. Defendant: the party against whom a complaint is brought

          v. Direct examination: initial questioning of a witness by the attorney who has requested the witness to testify

          vi. Jurisdiction: the power of authority which each court has to hear cases; a court's jurisdiction is determined by the subject matter of the case, the persons in the case, and by geographical area

          vii. Legal precedent: refers to a previous case decision that serves as an authority in identical or similar cases

          viii. Memorandum of law: a document prepared by an attorney, prior to trial, which outlines the case and notes past decisions that support the client's position; usually submitted to the court for reference

          ix. Motions: requests to the court made by plaintiff's or defendant's attorney

          x. Plaintiff: the party who brings a complaint against another

          xi. Pleadings: statements of complaint by plaintiff, answer from defendant, and possibly a counterclaim by defendant

          xii. Pretrial discovery: procedures whereby the attorneys for opposing sides in a case find out what information the opposing side possesses

xiii. Re-cross examination: second series of questions directed to a witness by the opposing attorney; takes place following redirect examination

xiv. Redirect examination: second series of questions directed to a witness by the attorney who had originally requested the witness to testify

xv. Res gestae: "things done," which means that hearsay statements made during an incident are admissible as evidence

xvi. Res ipsa loquitur: "The thing speaks for itself," which means that something is self-evident (e.g., erroneous surgical removal of healthy limb while leaving unhealthy limb)

xvii. Res judicata: "The thing is decided," which means the final judgment of a competent court is conclusive

xviii. Respondeat superior: "Let the master answer," which means that an employer is responsible for the legal consequences of an employee's actions

xix. Stare decisis: the doctrine that states that court decisions should be regarded as precedents for guidance in subsequent cases involving the same legal issues

xx. Summation: statement made by an attorney at the closing of a trial, summarizing the client's case

xxi. Summons: a court order notifying the defendant of a civil suit, and the date and place the defendant must appear to answer the complaint

xxii. Tort
  1. An injury or wrong committed against an individual or his or her property
  2. Any personal injury
  3. Types of torts (intentional and unintentional)
    a. Malpractice
    b. Negligence
    c. Intentional torts (assault and battery)
    d. False imprisonment
    e. Defamation

xxiii. Venue: the particular geographical area in which an action or prosecution may be brought to trial

xxiv. Voir dire: a preliminary examination to determine the competency of a witness or juror

b. Evidence
  i. Information that may be considered in the determination of a controversy taking place in a court of law
  ii. The means, sanctioned by law, of ascertaining the truth respecting a question of fact in a judicial proceeding
  iii. Best-evidence rule
    1. Original documents must be produced in a legal proceeding.
    2. Microfilm or other medium's reproductions are acceptable if the original record has been destroyed.
  iv. Types of evidence
    1. Direct: obtained from testimony of witnesses who possess actual knowledge of the facts of the case
    2. Indirect or circumstantial: facts that furnish reasonable ground for inferring the existence of some other connected facts
    3. Real or demonstrative: objects, documents, or anything that can be seen

4. Hearsay

    a. Evidence based on someone else's knowledge and observations, not on that of the witness

    b. Health records are hearsay evidence.

    c. Even though health records are hearsay, they may be entered into court as evidence in exception to hearsay rules because they are business records, which are admissible into court as evidence.

v. Admissibility

    1. Evidence that may be properly introduced in a legal proceeding

    2. The determination as to admissibility is based on legal rules of evidence and is made by the trial judge or a screening panel.

    3. For medical records to be admissible, they must meet the following

        a. Applicable to the business record rule

        b. The court must be confident that the information contained in the record is complete, accurate, and timely.

        c. The court must accept that the information was recorded as the result of treatment, not in anticipation of a legal proceeding.

    4. Discoverability

        a. Quality improvement, peer review, and incident reports are not discoverable in some states.

    5. Business record rule

        a. Records made and kept in the regular course of business may be entered into court as evidence.

        b. Medical records are business records.

vi. Legal proceedings

    1. Filing a civil suit

        a. Civil action is known by names of plaintiff and defendant, with plaintiff name listed first.

        b. Plaintiff's attorney pays fee and files a complaint or petition with clerk of the proper court to formally begin legal proceeding.

        c. Complaint states the facts on which the action is based, damages alleged, and the judgment or relief being sought.

    2. Civil pretrial procedure (see Table 3-6)

        a. Complaint

            i. Made by plaintiff

                1. Initial pleading in a lawsuit

                2. Plaintiff alleges a cause of action.

                3. Plaintiff request for wrong to be remedied by the court

        b. Answers to complaint by defendant

        c. Motions requesting court to make a variety of rulings

        d. Pretrial discovery

            i. Facilitates out of court settlements

            ii. Disclosure of facts and documents by one party at the request of the other

            iii. Obtained through depositions and interrogatories that are used to prepare the case for trial

                1. Deposition

                    a. Sworn statement of fact

                    b. Made outside of court

                    c. May be admitted as evidence in court

Table 3-6 Civil Pretrial Procedure

Complaint
Answers
Motions
Pre-trial discovery
Notice of trial
Memorandum of law

      2. Interrogatories
          a. Written questions presented to a party or witness
          b. Designed to gather information to assist parties prepare for trial
     e. Notice of trial: a trial date is set.
     f. Memorandum of law: a case description may be written by attorneys for both sides.
   3. Civil trial process
     a. Jury selection
     b. Opening statements by plaintiff's and defendant's attorneys
     c. Presentation of the plaintiff's case
     d. Presentation of defendant's case
     e. Plaintiff's rebuttal
     f. Answer to plaintiff's rebuttal
     g. Closing arguments
     h. Instructions to jury by judge
     i. Verdict read
     j. Judgment and execution for remedy or damages to be assessed
     k. Appeal by disappointed party if judge refuses to grant a post-trial motion for a new trial
 c. Health Information Practitioner's Proper Conduct as a Witness
    i. Review record and deposition prior to testimony
   ii. Make a copy of the record and paginate prior to taking to court
  iii. Take original record and copy to court
  iv. Request to submit copy of record in lieu of original into court as evidence
   v. Witness may refer to health record to refresh recollection.
  vi. Dress conservatively
 vii. Be polite, sincere, courteous
viii. Organize thoughts
  ix. Use simple and succinct terminology
   x. Pay attention to objections
  xi. Do not answer questions if not qualified to answer
 xii. Return original record to health care facility for proper storage

9. Negligence and Malpractice
  a. Principles of Liability
    i. Before an individual can bring a lawsuit to establish some form of liability (malpractice, negligence) against a health care provider, the individual must have established a relationship with that provider.
      1. Types of relationships
        a. Physician/patient
        b. Hospital/patient
        c. Hospital/physician
  b. Negligence
    i. Results when a person does not act the way a reasonably prudent person would act under the same circumstances
    ii. Results from a person committing an act, or failure to act as a reasonably prudent person would act in the given circumstance
    iii. When negligence results in patient injury, malpractice can be said to have occurred.
    iv. Careless conduct that is outside the generally accepted standard of care
      1. Standard of care
        a. What an individual is expected to do or not do in a given situation
        b. Established by professional associations, statute or regulation, or by practice
        c. Considered to represent expected behavior unless a court finds differently
    v. Negligence categorized
      1. Malfeasance: execution of an unlawful or improper act
      2. Misfeasance: improper performance of an act
      3. Malpractice
        a. Negligence or carelessness of a professional person such as a physician
        b. Patient injury or death due to negligence caused by a professional person such as a nurse, pharmacist, or physician
      4. Criminal negligence: reckless disregard for the safety or another; the willful indifference to an injury that could follow an act
    vi. Four components must be present for plaintiff to recover damages caused by negligence.
      1. Duty: a treatment or service owed to a patient (e.g., duty to give the right medication to the right patient)
      2. Breach: failure to perform to the applicable standard of care (e.g., nurse gave patient wrong medication)
      3. Cause: breach of duty, causing the resulting injury (e.g., patient suffered hallucinations, resulting in her getting out of bed without help and falling)
      4. Damage: patient injured (e.g., when she fell, she broke her hip)
        a. Three types
          i. Nominal: awarded for the vindication of a right in which minimal injury can be proved
          ii. Actual: compensatory damages are awarded to "make the plaintiff whole."
          iii. Punitive: exemplary damages are awarded above and beyond actual damages when there is proof of outrageous, malicious, or intentional conduct.

> Duty of Care + Breach of Duty of Care + Causation + Damages = *Negligence*

    vii. Statute of limitations: legislatively imposed time constraints that restrict the period of time after the occurrence of an injury during which a legal action must be commenced

    viii. Tort: an action brought when party believes that another party caused harm through wrongful conduct and seeks compensation for that harm

      1. Three categories of tort liability

        a. Negligent

          i. When a person does not act the way a reasonably prudent person would act under the same circumstance

          ii. Care rendered is outside the generally accepted standard of care.

        b. Intentional

          i. The person committed an act knowing that harm would likely occur.

          ii. Assault and battery

            1. The individual does not give permission or authority for an act.

            2. Assault occurs when an individual is placed in reasonable anticipation of being touched in a way that is insulting, provoking, or will cause the individual physical harm.

            3. Battery consists of physical contact involving injury or offense.

          iii. Defamation of character

            1. A communication about someone to another person that tends to injure the former person's reputation

            2. Slander: spoken character defamation

            3. Libel: written character defamation

          iv. False imprisonment: a health care provider's effort to prevent a patient from leaving a hospital when the patient insists on leaving (does not include mental illness or persons with contagious diseases)

          v. Fraud: a willful and intended misrepresentation that could cause harm or loss to a person or property

          vi. Invasion of privacy: negligent disregard for patient right of privacy

          vii. Willful infliction of mental distress: includes mental suffering resulting from such things as despair, shame, grief, and public humiliation

        c. Liability without fault: property liability, wherein a manufacturer, seller, or supplier of equipment or supplies is liable to one with whom there is no contractual relationship and who suffers harm from the equipment or supplies

    ix. Assumption of risk

      1. A method used to limit liability either completely or in part

      2. A plaintiff who voluntarily exposes himself to a known and appreciated danger may not recover damages caused by incurring that risk.

    x. Breach of contract: involves express contracts and the failure to perform these contracts

  xi. Defamation
   1. Wrongful injuring of another person's reputation
   2. May expose the person to ridicule, contempt, or hatred and tends to diminish the esteem, respect, goodwill, or confidence in which the person is held
  xii. Failure to warn: also referred to as failure to protect; a negligence theory that applies to a psychiatrist's failure to take steps to protect an innocent third party from a dangerous patient
  xiii. Good Samaritan statutes
   1. These statutes protect physicians and other rescuers from civil liability as a result of their acts or omissions in rendering emergency care.
   2. If, however, the rescuer acts in a willful, wanton, or reckless manner in providing emergency treatment, he or she cannot avail himself of the Good Samaritan statute as a defense.
  xiv. Invasion of privacy: the dissemination of information about another person's private, personal matters
  xv. Libel: defamation expressed in writing, pictures, or signs
  xvi. Medical abandonment: unilateral severing, by the physician, of the physician-patient relationship without giving the patient reasonable notice, at a time when there is a necessity for continuing care
  xvii. Repondeat superior
   1. "Let the superior respond" reflects the idea that the superior is responsible for the actions of the superior's employee or agent.
   2. Also referred to as vicarious liability
   3. Health care organization, such as hospital, is responsible for the negligent acts of its employees committed within the course and scope of their employment.
  xviii. Res ipsa loquitur: "the thing speaks for itself"
   1. Injury would not ordinarily occur without someone's negligence.
   2. The medical professional had exclusive control and management over the instrument or cause of the accident.
   3. The injury could not have occurred as a result of any action by the patient.
  xix. Slander: defamation expressed orally or with transitory gestures
  xx. Statute of limitation: a law that sets forth a fixed time period in which a lawsuit must be brought

10. Computer-Based Health Records
 a. Computer-Based Records as Evidence
  i. Courts have developed standards for establishing the trustworthiness of computerized records.
 b. Security
  i. Procedures must be in place to protect information from sabotage, hackers, and viruses.
  ii. Use passwords and other authorization devices that are changed at regular intervals
  iii. Access control that can limit who is able to view, enter, edit data, or print various sections of the record
  iv. Controls that prevent tampering with, changing, or editing of existing entries
  v. Audit trails that can locate sources of attempts at unauthorized access
  vi. Limitations on printouts of record
  vii. Automatic log-off protocols when terminal is unused for a period of time

      viii. Limited access to patient records by employees on a need-to-know basis

      ix. Encryption codes that prevent stored or transmitted data from being intercepted by unauthorized individuals

11. **Ethical Issues for Health Information Practitioners**

  a. Ethics

      i. A process of reasoned discourse among decision makers

      ii. Decision makers must carefully consider the shared and competing values and ethical principles that are important to the decision to be made.

  b. Ethical decision making requires everyone to consider the perspectives of others.

  c. Ethical decision making demonstrates respect for others and recognizes the importance of doing good, respecting others, not harming others, and treating people fairly.

  d. Core Ethical Responsibilities of Health Information Practitioner

      i. Maintain an accurate and timely patient database

      ii. Be honest and respectful toward patients, peers, and public

      iii. Protect the privacy of all patients

      iv. Demonstrate compassion to patients and peers

      v. Design forms to ensure that patients understand what they are signing

      vi. Coding for research and reimbursement, and coding accurately, to avoid fraud and abuse violations

      vii. Designing and implementing the health information system to ensure completeness, accuracy, and timeliness of documentation

      viii. Releasing patient information with special attention to, and protections assigned for, genetic, adoption, drug and alcohol treatment, sexual and behavioral issues

      ix. Complying with regulations and standards from many sources, including the government, accreditation and licensure organizations, and the health care facility

      x. Reporting quality review outcomes honestly and accurately

      xi. Ensuring that research and decisions supporting activities are accurate and reliable

      xii. Releasing accurate information for public health purposes for patients with communicable diseases

      xiii. Supporting managers, by providing accurate reliable information about patients, providers, and patterns of care

      xiv. Ensuring that the patient record (paper-based and electronic formats) meets the standards of privacy and security

      xv. Participating in activities to ensure that the needs of the health care facility are met and not jeopardized

      xvi. Serve as an advocate for the patient, health care team, and community

      xvii. Work in the emerging e-health system to ensure that high-quality information is provided to patients and that patient privacy is protected

      xviii. Comply with all laws, regulations, and policies that govern health information management

      xix. Ensure the privacy, confidentiality, and security of patient information and report violators to the proper authorities

      xx. Uphold the AHIMA codes of ethical standards

  e. Obligations to Employer

      i. Demonstrate loyalty to the employer

      ii. Protect committee deliberations

   iii. Comply with all laws, regulations, and policies that govern the health information system

   iv. Recognize both authority and the power associated with the job responsibility

 f. Obligations to Public

   i. Advocate change when patterns or system problems are not in the best interests of the patients

   ii. Refuse to participate in or conceal unethical practices

   iii. Report violations of practice standards to the proper authorities

---

Houston Honorary Hospital
Authorization for Release of Information

Name: _____   Medical Record #: _____

Address: _____   Phone: _____

Social Security #: _____   Date of Birth: _____

I authorize Houston Honorary Hospital to release my medical record information to the following person, facility, or agency:

Name: _____   Attention: _____   Phone: _____

Street: _____   City/Town: _____   State: ____   Zip: _____

The person filling out this form must provide details as to date(s) of requested information. Please note that a request for release of psychotherapy notes cannot be combined with any other type of request. Specify information to be released, e.g., Entire Record, Admission(s) Documentation, Discharge Summary(ies), Transfer Summary(ies), Evaluations, Assessments and Tests, Consultation(s) including names of consultant(s), Treatment Plan(s), ISP(s) & PSTP(s), Physical Exam & Lab Reports, Progress Note(s):

_____

_____

_____

_____

_____

_____

_____

Purpose for the authorization:

❑ The subject of the information or Personal Representative initiated the authorization (specific purpose not required)

or

❑ Continuity of care   ❑ Facilitate billing

❑ Referral   ❑ Obtain insurance, financial or other benefits

❑ Other purpose (please specify): _____

Figure 3-2 Sample Release of Information Form

Houston Honorary Hospital
Authorization for Release of Information *(continued)*

I understand that I have a right to revoke this authorization at any time. If I revoke this authorization, I must do so in writing and present it to the person at Houston Honorary Hospital. I understand that the revocation will not apply to information that has already been released pursuant to this authorization. This authorization will expire in 12 months unless otherwise specified (specify a date, time period or an event): _____
_____. I understand that once the above information is disclosed it may be redisclosed and no longer protected by federal or state privacy laws or regulations. I understand that authorizing the use or disclosure of the information identified above is voluntary. I need not sign this form to receive treatment or services from Houston Honorary Hospital. However, lack of ability to share or obtain information may prevent Houston Honorary Hospital, and/or other person, facility, or agency, from providing appropriate and necessary care.

_____   _____
Your signature or Personal Representative's signature   Date

_____
Print name of signer

THE FOLLOWING INFORMATION IS NEEDED IF SIGNED BY A PERSONAL REPRESENTATIVE

Type of authority (e.g., court appointed, custodial parent)

_____

Specially Authorized Releases of Information (please initial all that apply)

_____ To the extent that my medical record contains information concerning alcohol or drug treatment that is protected by Federal Regulation 42 CFR, Part 2, I specifically authorize release of such information.

_____ To the extent that my medical record contains information concerning HIV antibody and antigen testing that is protected by MGL c.111 §70F, or an HIV/AIDS diagnosis or treatment, I specifically authorize disclosure of such information.

_____   _____
Your signature or Personal Representative's signature   Date

INSTRUCTIONS:
1. This form must be completed in full to be considered valid.
2. Distribution of copies: original to appropriate medical record; copy to individual or Personal Representative.

Houston Honorary Hospital Form Authorization for Release of Information
Page 2 of 2
HIPAA-F-7 (4/22/08)

Figure 3-2 Sample Release of Information Form *(continued)*

§ THE STATE OF TEXAS	§ IN THE MATTER OF A
§ COUNTY OF COWBOYS	§ GRAND INVESTIGATION

TO THE SHERIFF OR ANY OTHER PEACE OFFICER

GREETINGS

WHEREAS the grand jury of Cowboys County is inquiring into certain offenses liable to indictment; and

WHEREAS Article 20.10 of the Texas Code of Criminal procedure provides that the attorney representing the state, in term time or in vacation may issue a summons or an attachment for any witness in the county, which summons or attachment may require the said witness to appear before the grand jury at a time fixed, or forthwith, without stating the matter under investigation; and

WHEREAS any Texas peace officer receiving this process shall execute the same forthwith by reading the same in the hearing of the said witness or by delivering a copy of this showing the time and manner of service, if served, and if not served, said officer shall show in his return the cause of his failure to serve it; and if the witness could not be found, he shall state the diligence he has used to find him, and what information he has as to the whereabouts of the witness;

NOW THEREFORE YOU ARE HEREBY COMMANDED to forthwith summon, the custodian of records, John Doe, Houston Honorary Hospital to appear before the 401st Judicial District Court Grand Jury for August Term, 2007 at 403 Tyson Street, 1st floor, Cowboy, Texas at 10 am on September 20, 2007.

FURTHER, you are directed that the said witness shall bring with him the following writing or other thing desired as evidence in accordance with Article 24.02 of the Texas Code of Criminal procedure, and more specifically described as follows:

PRODUCE TRUE AND CORRECT COPIES OF MEDICAL RECORD ON JOHN DOE; DATE OF BIRTH December 25, 200x.

Figure 3-3 Sample Subpoena Duces Tecum

§   IN THE DISTRICT COURT OF

§

§   COWBOYS COUNTY, TEXAS

§

§   1051st JUDICIAL DISTRICT

DIRECT QUESTIONS TO BE PROPOUNDED TO THE WITNESS, CUSTODIAN OF MEDICAL RECORDS FOR **Houston Honorary Hospital**

1. Please state your name and occupation.

2. Have you been served with a subpoena duces tecum for the production of medical records for John Doe?

3. Please state whether you have in your custody or subject to your control the records pertaining to John Doe.

4. Please hand the Notary Public propounding these questions a complete copy of all such records, reports, etc., described in the subpoena pertaining to Doe.

5. Are the records you have furnished the Notary Public in response to Question Number 4 a complete and accurate copy of the records described in the subpoena that you have on this individual?

6. Were records not produced that have been destroyed or purged?

7. Were these records kept in your regular course of business?

8. Is it in the regular course of your business, or of an employee in your office having personal knowledge of the acts recorded, to prepare the records or transmit the information included in the records of John Doe?

9. Were the records made at or near the time of the performance of the act recorded therein or reasonably soon thereafter?

10. Does the source of the information, and the method and circumstance of its preparation, establish the trustworthiness of the records, notes, and or reports?

_____

Signature of Custodian

BEFORE ME, THE UNDERSIGNED AUTHORITY on this day personally appeared _____, custodian of Medical Records for Houston Honorary Hospital known to me to be the person whose name is subscribed to the foregoing instrument in the capacity therein stated, and acknowledged to me that the answers to the foregoing questions are true as stated. I further certify that the records attached hereto are exact duplicates of the original records.

GIVEN UNDER MY HAND AND SEAL OF OFFICE, this the _____ day of _____ year of 200x.

_____

Notary Public in and for the State of Texas

My commission expires _____

Figure 3-4 Sample Deposition

STATE OF TEXAS   §   IN THE _____

Vs.   §   COURT IN AND FOR

_____   §   COWBOYS COUNTY, TEXAS

AFFIDAVIT

    Before me, the undersigned authority, personally appeared _____, who, being by me duly sworn, deposed as follows:

    My name is _____, I am of sound mind, capable of making this affidavit, and personally acquainted with the facts herein stated:

    I am the Custodian of the records of _____. Attached hereto are _____ pages of records from _____. These said _____ pages of records are kept by **Houston Honorary Hospital** in the regular course of business, at it was the regular course of business of **Houston Honorary Hospital**, for an employee or representative of **Houston Honorary Hospital**, with knowledge of the act, event, condition, opinion, or diagnosis, recorded to make the record or transmit information thereof to be included in such record; and the record was made at or near the time or reasonably soon thereafter. The records attached hereto are the original or exact duplicates of the original.

_____

Affiant

SWORN TO AND SUBSCRIBED before me the _____day of _____ of the _____ year.

_____

Notary Public
State of Texas

My commission expires _____

Figure 3-5 Sample Affidavit

This notice describes how medical information about you may be used and disclosed and how you can get access to this information. Please read it carefully.

Introduction to Privacy

We are required by law to maintain the privacy of your medical information. We are also required to give you this Notice about our privacy practices, our legal duties, and your rights concerning your medical information. We must follow the privacy practices that are described in this Notice while it is in effect. We reserve the right to change our privacy practices and the terms of this Notice at any time, provided such changes are permitted by law. We reserve the right to make the changes in our privacy practices and the new terms of our Notice effective for all medical information that we maintain, including medical information we created or received before we made the changes. If we make a significant change in our privacy practices, we will amend this Notice and make the new Notice available upon request.

You may request a copy of our Notice at any time. For more information about our privacy practices, or for additional copies of this Notice, please contact _____.

Joint Notice of Privacy

This Joint Notice applies to the privacy practices of Houston Honorary Hospital for the sole purpose of complying with the Health Insurance Portability and Accountability Act of 1996 (HIPAA), HIPAA Privacy Rules and with the Texas Medical Privacy Act, Texas Health & Safety Code § 181.

Uses and Disclosures of Medical Information

We use and disclose medical information about you for treatment, payment, and health care operations.

Treatment: We may use and disclose your medical information to a physician or other health care provider in order to provide treatment to you. This includes coordination of your care with other health care providers, and with health plans, consultation with other providers, and referral to other providers related to your care.

Payment: We may use and disclose your medical information to obtain payment for services we provide to you. Payment includes submitting claims to health plans and other insurers, justifying our charges for and demonstrating the medical necessity of the care we deliver to you, determining your eligibility for health plan benefits for the care we furnish to you, obtaining precertification or preauthorization for your treatment or referral to other health care providers, participating in utilization review of the services we provide to you and the like. We may disclose your medical information to another health care provider or entity subject to the federal Privacy Rules so they can obtain payment.

Health Care Operations: We may use and disclose your medical information in connection with our health care operations. Health care operations include:
- Quality assessment and improvement activities
- Reviewing the competence or qualifications of health care professionals, evaluating practitioner and provider accreditation, certification, licensing or credentialing activities
- Medical review
- Legal services and auditing, including fraud and abuse detection and compliance
- Business planning and development

(continues)

Figure 3-6 Sample Notice of Privacy Practices

- Business management and general administrative activities, including management activities relating to privacy, customer service, resolution of internal grievances, and creating de-identified medical information or a limited data set

We may disclose your medical information to another provider or health plan that is subject to the Privacy Rules, as long as that provider or plan has a relationship with you and the medical information is for their health care quality assessment and improvement activities, competence and qualification evaluation and review activities, or fraud and abuse detection and prevention.

On Your Authorization: You may give us written authorization to use your medical information or to disclose it to anyone for any purpose. If you give us an authorization, you may revoke it in writing at any time. Unless you give us a written authorization, we cannot use or disclose your medical information for any reason except those described in this Notice.

To Your Family and Friends: We may disclose your medical information to a family member, friend, or other person to the extent necessary to help with your health care or with payment for your health care. We may use or disclose your name, hospital location, and general condition or death to notify, or assist in the notification of (including identifying or locating) a person involved in your care. We may also disclose your medical information to whomever you give us permission. Before we disclose your medical information to a person involved in your health care or payment for your health care, we will provide you with an opportunity to object to such uses or disclosures. If you are not present, or in the event of your incapacity or an emergency, we will disclose your medical information based on our professional judgment of whether the disclosure would be in your best interest. We will also use our professional judgment and our experience with common practice to allow a person to pick up filled prescriptions, medical supplies, or other similar forms of medical information.

Facility Directory: We may use your name, your location, your general medical condition, and your religious affiliation in our facility directories. We will disclose this information to members of the clergy and, except for religious affiliation, to other persons who ask for you by name. We will provide you with an opportunity to restrict or prohibit some or all disclosures for facility directories unless emergency circumstances prevent your opportunity to object.

Disaster Relief: We may use or disclose your medical information to a public or private entity authorized by law or by its charter to assist in disaster relief efforts.

Health-Related Services: We may use your medical information to contact you with information about health-related benefits and services or about treatment alternatives that may be of interest to you. We may disclose your medical information to a business associate to assist us in these activities.

Business Associate: We may disclose your medical information to a company or individual performing functions or activities to or on our behalf.

Marketing: We will not use your medical information for marketing purposes without your authorization. Houston Honorary Hospital uses commercially purchased lists. We must obtain your authorization for all marketing purposes except for face-to-face conversations about services and treatment alternatives. You may also receive information through a membership program that you have joined. If you have opted in or have joined a membership program and you no longer wish to receive further

Figure 3-6 Sample Notice of Privacy Practices (continued)

information, please indicate this in writing by completing a marketing opt-out form, which you may get by calling 777-777-7777.

Fundraising: We may use your demographic information and the dates of your health care to contact you for our fundraising purposes. We may disclose this information to a business associate or foundation to assist us in our fundraising activities. If you would like more information on the Houston Honorary Hospital Foundation or a description of how you may opt out of receiving future fundraising communications, please indicate this in writing by calling 777-777-7777 and requesting an opt-out form.

Public Benefit: We may use or disclose your medical information as authorized by law for the following purposes deemed to be in the public interest or benefit:
- Public health activities including disease and vital statistics reporting, child abuse reporting, adult protective services, and FDA oversight
- Employers, regarding work-related illness or injury
- Cancer registry
- Trauma registry
- Birth registry
- Health oversight agencies
- In response to court and administrative orders and other lawful processes
- To law enforcement officials pursuant to subpoenas and other lawful processes, concerning crime victims, suspicious deaths, crimes on our premises, reporting crimes in emergencies, and for purposes of identifying or locating a suspect or other person
- To coroners, medical examiners, and funeral directors
- To organ procurement organizations
- To avert a serious threat to health or safety
- In connection with certain research activities
- To correctional institutions regarding inmates
- As authorized by state worker's compensation laws
- To the military, to federal officials for lawful intelligence, counterintelligence, and national security activities, and to correctional institutions and law enforcement regarding persons in lawful custody

Individual Rights

You have the right to review or receive a copy of your medical information, with limited exceptions. You may request that we provide copies in a format other than photocopies. We will use the format you request unless we cannot practicably do so. You must make a request in writing to obtain access to your medical information. You may obtain a form to request access or a copy of your medical information from the Release of Information department located at the facility where you obtain your medical care. There is a charge for a copy of your medical information.

Accounting of Disclosures

You have the right to receive an accounting of all uses and disclosures of your health information that was not authorized by you and that was not used by Houston Honorary Hospital for the sole purposes of treatment, payment, and health care operations. You must request this accounting in writing. This accounting is maintained for a period of 6 years beginning on April 14, 200x, the effective date of this Notice. You may obtain a form to request an accounting of disclosures from the Release of Information department located at the facility where you obtained your medical care. *(continues)*

Figure 3-6 Sample Notice of Privacy Practices *(continued)*

Restrictions: You have the right to request that we place additional restrictions on our use or disclosure of your medical information. We are not required to agree to these additional restrictions, but if we do, we will abide by our agreement (except in an emergency). You must make this request in writing.

Confidential Communications: You have the right to request that we communicate with you about your medical information by alternative means or to alternative locations. You must make your request in writing. We must accommodate your request if: it is reasonable; specifies the alternative means or location; and provides a satisfactory explanation of how payments will be handled under the alternative means or location you request.

Amendment: You have the right to request that we amend your medical information. Your request must be in writing, and it must explain why the information should be amended. We may deny your request if we did not create the information you want amended and the originator remains available or for certain other reasons. If we deny your request, we will provide you a written explanation. You may respond with a statement or disagreement to be appended to the information you want amended. If we accept your request to amend the information, we will make reasonable efforts to inform others (including people you name) of the amendment and to include the changes in any future disclosures of that information.

Electronic Notice: If you view this Notice on our Web site or by electronic mail (e-mail), you are entitled to receive a copy of this Notice in written form. Please contact us as directed below to obtain this Notice in written form.

Security of Your Information

Houston Honorary Hospital safeguards customer information using various tools such as firewalls, passwords, and data encryption. We continually strive to improve these tools to meet or exceed industry standards. We also limit access to your information to protect against its unauthorized use. The only Houston Honorary Hospital workforce members who have access to your information are those who need it as part of their job. These safeguards help us meet both federal and state requirements to protect your personal health information.

Questions or Concerns

If you would like more information about our privacy practices or have questions or concerns about this Notice, please contact the Privacy Office at the number listed below. If you believe your privacy rights have been violated, you may file a complaint, in writing, to the Houston Honorary Hospital Privacy Office located at
99999 Freeway, Suite 999 Houston, Texas 99999
or by calling 1-999-999-9999.

Or you may contact the U.S. Department of Health and Human Services (DHHS)
00000 Young Street, Suite 00000
Houston, TX 99999
Voice Phone 000-000-0000
FAX 000-000-0000
TDD 000-000-0000

To e-mail the DHHS Secretary or other Department Officials, send your message to hhsmail@os.dhhs.gov.

Figure 3-6 Sample Notice of Privacy Practices *(continued)*

PRACTICAL APPLICATION OF YOUR KNOWLEDGE

1. Answer the following questions on the organization of the legal system:

   a. What are the three levels of the government and the sources or documents that outline their power?

      1.

      2.

      3.

   b. What are the three branches of federal and state government and their duties?

      1.

      2.

      3.

   c. Distinguish between public and private law. Which usually deals with disputes between patients and health care providers?

   d. Discuss the rules of administrative agencies and give an example of an administrative agency that affects health care legislation.

2. Health Record Requirements and Retention Guidelines

    a. List the contents that should be included in an inpatient health record according to TJC.

    b. As manager of the health information department, you are constructing a retention schedule. Using AHIMA guidelines, state the length of time the following documents should be maintained:

Document	Retention Guideline
Adult patient health record	
Minor patient health record	
Diagnostic images (e.g., X-rays)	
Disease index	
Fetal heart monitor record	
Master patient index	
Operative index	
Physician index	
Register of births	
Register of deaths	
Register of surgical procedures	

3. Confidentiality, Consent, and Security of Health Records

    a. What is confidential information?

    b. Who is the owner of the health record?

    c. Who has the authority to release information from the health record?

    d. When is authorization not required to release PHI?

    e. What are the three elements of a privileged communication?

    f. State three types of consent.

    g. What is informed consent? What should be included in an informed consent?

    h. From what threats to the security of records must a health information practitioner protect those records?

4. Laws and Regulations Regarding Health Records

    a. Summarize the following federal legislation:

Legislation	Summary
Freedom of Information Act (1966)	
Drug Abuse and Treatment Act (1972)	
Privacy Act (1974)	
Natural Death Act (1989)	
Health Insurance Portability and Privacy Act (1996)	

5. Release of Information and Subpoenas

    a. To meet HIPAA requirements, a Release of Information form must collect what information?

    b. Subpoenas

        1. Match the term to its description or definition

            a. Subpoena duces tecum

            b. Subpoena ad testificandum

            c. Contempt of court

        1. _____ Results when a person fails to obey a subpoena and is punishable by fine or imprisonment

        2. _____ Court order that commands a person to come to court and produce whatever documents are named in the order

        3. _____ Court order that requires a person to appear in court to testify

    c. List eight common elements of a valid subpoena.

        1.

        2.

        3.

        4.

        5.

        6.

        7.

        8.

6. Health Insurance Portability and Accountability Act
  a. Discuss the administration simplification provisions.

  b. Discuss the privacy rule.

  c. What is PHI?

  d. Mark these statements concerning the HIPAA Privacy Rule as True or False.
   1. _____ The HIPAA Privacy Rule protects a patient's fundamental right to privacy and confidentiality.
   2. _____ A covered entity is a health care provider, health plan, or health care clearinghouse that transmits health information in electronic form.
   3. _____ PHI is anything that connects a patient to his or her health information.
   4. _____ After signing an authorization, the patient can decide to revoke it.
   5. _____ An authorization must contain an expiration date.
   6. _____ PHI includes all health information that is used or disclosed except PHI in oral form.
   7. _____ The health care facility must obtain patient agreement to use or disclose PHI for public health activities related to disease prevention.
   8. _____ In general, disclosure of PHI must be limited to the least amount needed to get the job done correctly.
   9. _____ The privacy rule gives patients the right to take action if their privacy is violated.
   10. _____ The privacy rule gives patients the right to request a history of routine disclosures.

7. Health Record Documentation

   a. List 10 guidelines for documentation in the health record.

   1.

   2.

   3.

   4.

   5.

   6.

   7.

   8.

   9.

   10.

   b. A physician charts the information of a patient in the wrong health record. Describe how the documentation can be corrected in each patient's record.

8. Health Records in Court
  a. Describe the following steps:

Step	Description
Complaint	
Answers	
Motions	
Pretrial discovery	
Notice of trial	
Memorandum of law	

  b. Describe the steps of the civil pretrial procedure.

  c. A patient sues your facility for malpractice. Describe the steps in a legal proceeding by which this case may be decided from its beginning to its conclusion.

9. Malpractice and Negligence

   a. Describe the four components that must be present for a plaintiff to recover damages caused by negligence.

      1.

      2.

      3.

      4.

10. Computer-Based Health Records

   a. List five methods to secure computer-based health records from unauthorized access.

      1.

      2.

      3.

      4.

      5.

11. Ethical Issues for Health Information Practitioners
    a. List 10 ethical obligations of the health information practitioner.
        1.

        2.

        3.

        4.

        5.

        6.

        7.

        8.

        9.

        10.

12. Define the Following Terms:

    a. Admissibility

    b. Advance directive

    c. Assault and battery

    d. Business record rule

    e. Evidence

    f. Defamation

    g. Defendant

    h. Deposition

    i. Hearsay

    j. Interrogatory

    k. Law

    l. Libel

m. Malpractice

n. Negligence

o. Plaintiff

p. Res gestae

q. Res ipsa loquitur

r. Res judicata

s. Respondeat superior

t. Stare decisis

u. Statute of limitations

v. Tort

w. Venue

TEST YOUR KNOWLEDGE

1. A nurse employed by your hospital gossiped about a discharged inpatient, which resulted in the patient's good reputation being questioned by his neighbor. This is known as what?
   a. Libel
   b. Slander
   c. Perjury
   d. Defamation

2. A third-party payer has requested copies of a patient's records. The patient has been diagnosed as having AIDS. The hospital's policy for release of information in this instance should ensure that the:
   a. record is sent by overnight express.
   b. physician gives consent for a copy of the record to be released.
   c. a subpoena duces tecum is received from the third-party payer.
   d. patient has signed a consent specifically authorizing release of this diagnosis.

3. A properly completed and signed authorization is required for release of all health information, except when a(n):
   a. patient has expired.
   b. patient presents to the hospital with a highly contagious disease that must be reported to the state health department.
   c. patient's spouse suspects the patient has AIDS and is afraid of contracting the disease.
   d. insurance company request copies of the patient's previous hospitalization record.

4. Which of the following is an example of respondeat superior?
   a. The hospital is held responsible for a pharmacist medication error.
   b. A physician with honorary staff status is sued by a current inpatient for malpractice.
   c. The director of nurses gives instructions to a staff nurse.
   d. The attending physician testifies against the surgeon in a malpractice case.

5. You are the supervisor of release of information and have been subpoenaed to bring records to court. With what document may you have been served?
   a. Subpoena duces tecum
   b. Subpoena ad testificandum
   c. Subpoena gestae
   d. Subpoena respondeat

6. Refusing to honor a subpoena may result in:
   a. the case being postponed.
   b. arrest of the attending physician.
   c. being held in contempt of court.
   d. receiving a court order.

7. According to the American Health Information Management Association, the suggested retention schedule for the master patient index is how long?
   a. 5 years
   b. 10 years
   c. 25 years
   d. Permanently

8. The statute of limitation sets:
   a. the maximum dollar amount that can be collected from a malpractice case.
   b. standards for the maintenance of pharmaceuticals.
   c. a minimum amount of time after an event occurs for a suit to be taken in court.
   d. a time period for the completion of medical records.

9. As supervisor of release of information you have been subpoenaed to court. You are qualified to testify in response to a subpoena duces tecum as to:
   a. the quality of care rendered by the medical staff to the patient.
   b. how the health records are maintained in the facility's regular course of business.
   c. the accuracy of a respiratory therapist's documentation.
   d. whether the confidentiality of the health information has been violated.

10. In a non-emergent situation, protected health information may be released to another hospital with the:
   a. written authorization of the patient.
   b. permission of the attending physician.
   c. death of the patient.
   d. receipt of a phone call from the patient's spouse.

11. Which of the following demonstrates the doctrine of res ipsa loquitur?
   a. A surgeon places a pacemaker in a patient.
   b. A surgeon erroneously leaves an instrument in a patient.
   c. A radiology technician takes an X-ray of the wrong leg of a patient.
   d. A nurse neglects to give a patient her prescribed medication.

12. A patient has a primary diagnosis of alcohol abuse and dependence. What information may be released without express authorization of the patient?
   a. Admission and discharge dates only
   b. The patient's physical health status
   c. The patient's attending physician's name
   d. No information at all

13. TJC requests to view a patient's health record, which contains a diagnosis of AIDS. The director of health information should:
   a. call the facility's attorney.
   b. deny access to TJC.
   c. obtain written authorization from the patient or legal representative.
   d. allow access to the record upon request of TJC.

14. Under the Freedom of Information Act (FOIA), a reporter requests a copy of a patient's record in a Veterans Administration hospital. How should the director of health information respond?
   a. Honor the request if it is in writing
   b. Refer the request to the media relations department
   c. Refuse to honor the request
   d. Tell the reporter the request will be honored with the receipt of a subpoena duces tecum

15. Which of the following is required to be present in an informed consent?
   a. Explanation of risks and benefits of treatment and or surgery
   b. List of referral physicians to obtain another expert opinion
   c. Alternative facilities that may treat the patient
   d. Cost of treatment and surgery

16. A school representative brings a minor to the facility with a broken arm, which requires surgery. Who may consent to the treatment of the patient?
   a. The school representative
   b. The minor patient
   c. The person with legal custody of the minor patient
   d. No consent is necessary in the emergent situation.

17. In a physician-owned clinic, the health record is the property of the:
   a. patient.
   b. admitting physician.
   c. physician-owned clinic.
   d. hospital to which the physician has admitting privileges.

18. A hospital fails to obtain informed consent prior to surgery on a patient. Which of the following may the hospital have performed?
   a. Slander and tort
   b. Defamation and liability
   c. Libel and tort
   d. Assault and battery

19. Tort claims have to do with what?
   a. Wrongful conduct that has caused harm in public law
   b. Unauthorized treatment
   c. Public and criminal wrongs
   d. Breach of contract

20. Health records may be admitted into court as evidence due to the:
   a. hearsay rule.
   b. business records rule.
   c. Privacy Act.
   d. HIPAA.

21. The powers of the three branches of the federal government are documented in the:
   a. United States Constitution.
   b. Act of Congress.
   c. administrative law.
   d. Articles of the Republic.

22. Bob brings a lawsuit against Houston Hospital for damages done to his knee during surgery. What term best describes Bob?
   a. Defendant
   b. Bailiff
   c. Plaintiff
   d. Attorney

23. Susan brings a lawsuit against Houston Hospital for wrongfully damaging her knee during surgery. What is this wrongful act called?
   a. Tort
   b. Slander
   c. Libel
   d. Assault

24. Austin Hospital is closed and sold to Houston Hospital. Which of the following entities owns the physical hospital health record?
   a. The patients
   b. Houston Hospital
   c. Austin Hospital
   d. The physicians who treated the patients

25. HIPAA privacy rules:
   a. take precedence over all other federal and state laws.
   b. are not relevant to children's hospitals.
   c. provide a federal foundation for privacy requirements of health information.
   d. are not subject to state laws.

26. PHI refers to _____ health information.
   a. private
   b. protected
   c. previous
   d. preliminary

27. A patient has submitted a request to view her psychotherapy notes. Under the HIPAA rules, the covered entity:
   a. must provide access without cost to patient.
   b. can demand that the patient pay to see her record.
   c. can deny access to the psychotherapy notes.
   d. can provide information to the patient's legal guardian.

28. Steve has submitted a written authorization to request a copy of his medical chart. However, Steve's psychiatrist has determined that access to his PHI might endanger his life or safety. What should the covered entity do concerning the request?
   a. Provide an appeals process to Steve for the denial
   b. Confirm the psychiatrist decision and deny the request
   c. Release requested information to Steve's legal guardian
   d. Release requested information to Steve

29. In regard to a patient's request for his PHI, which of the following statements is true?
    a. A cost-based fee may be charged to view the PHI.
    b. No fee may be charged for PHI.
    c. A cost-based fee may be charged for personnel expenses.
    d. A cost-based fee may be charged for making a copy of the PHI.

30. Steve submits a written request to Houston Hospital for a copy of his PHI on August 19. By what date must the covered entity comply?
    a. August 29
    b. September 3
    c. September 8
    d. September 18

31. Nurse Cecile makes an error in a patient's medical chart. What should she do?
    a. Remove the page with the error
    b. Obliterate the error
    c. Line through the error, then add her correction, stating "correction" or "error"
    d. Remove the page with error and add page with correction

32. Jennifer submits a written request to Houston Hospital for a copy of her PHI on August 19. The information is stored offsite. By what date must the covered entity comply?
    a. August 29
    b. September 19
    c. September 30
    d. October 18

33. Where can patients find a complete description of how PHI is used in a health care facility?
    a. Notice of privacy practice
    b. Medical staff rules and regulations
    c. Governing board bylaws
    d. HIM policies and procedures

34. The notice of privacy practice:
    a. provides patients with a fee scale of private rooms.
    b. must be provided to every individual at the first time of contact or service with the covered entity.
    c. gives the covered entity permission to release information to private insurance companies.
    d. explains to patients that the facility is a private institution and provides services on a fee-for-service basis.

35. The directory of patients maintained by a covered entity:
    a. requires patients to maintain their name and room number in the directory.
    b. allows patients to restrict information maintained on them in the directory.
    c. may not be released.
    d. must be maintained for 5 years.

36. Sworn testimony usually collected before a trial is a(n):
    a. subpoena.
    b. tort.
    c. deposition.
    d. complaint.

37. Bob brings a lawsuit against Houston Hospital for damages done to his knee during surgery. What term best describes Houston Hospital?
    a. Defendant
    b. Bailiff
    c. Plaintiff
    d. Complaintee

38. Elvis called in sick to work. His employer contacted his health care provider to verify his illness. Without the patient's authorization, employers are entitled to:
   a. no information except patient-authorized directory information of dates of admission and discharge.
   b. no information at all from their employee's records.
   c. any information, provided they will be paying for the health care treatment.
   d. no information except identifying information and the prognosis.

39. With proper written authorization from a patient, Houston Hospital obtains a copy of the patient's health record from Austin Hospital. Houston Hospital then releases the information from Austin Hospital to Dallas Hospital. What is this practice called?
   a. Redisclosure
   b. Release of information
   c. Voir dire
   d. Ad testificandum

40. With proper written authorization from a patient, Houston Hospital obtains a copy of the patient's health record from Austin Hospital. Houston Hospital then releases the information from Austin Hospital to Dallas Hospital. This practice is:
   a. never appropriate, because medical information should not be redisclosed.
   b. mandated by HIPAA to ensure continuity of patient care.
   c. regularly practiced due to the threat of medical lawsuits.
   d. noncompliant with HIPAA, but compliant with FIOA.

41. The health information manager is called to testify as a witness. She is asked questions concerning the medical competence of a psychiatrist. Her response should state:
   a. her honest opinion of the psychiatrist.
   b. she is not qualified to testify concerning his competence.
   c. give her honest opinion of the psychiatrist while supplying medical record copies of the psychiatrist to the bailiff.
   d. stall for time and ask the attorney to repeat the question.

42. As a witness for Houston Hospital, the health information manager should:
   a. refuse to turn over copies of medical records to the court that demonstrate negligence on the part of the hospital.
   b. never tell the court that medical records were not able to be retrieved or were lost.
   c. give copies of medical records to constable upon request.
   d. refuse to turn over copies of medical records to the court without a subpoena duces tecum or court order.

43. Public health laws mandate reporting of certain diseases, which do not require the patient's consent for release of this information. These include:
   a. deaths and herpes.
   b. births and viral meningitis.
   c. births and cancer cases.
   d. deaths and viral meningitis.

44. At Houston Hospital, the attending physician has:
   a. indirect ownership in the patients' records.
   b. no legal rights to the patients' records.
   c. the right to restrict the use of her records in quality assurance activities.
   d. the right to remove documents out of the medical records.

45. Manuel was in a severe car accident and unable to grant permission for treatment. Therefore, his wife:
- **a.** must obtain legal guardianship to speak for patient.
- **b.** has no right to consent to or deny treatment for Manuel.
- **c.** must obtain legal counsel to represent Manuel.
- **d.** may consent for his treatment.

46. Nipa was admitted to a Houston Community Hospital for gallbladder removal. Which of the following information about her is considered confidential?
- **a.** Previous history and treatment of a concussion
- **b.** Date of birth
- **c.** Address upon admission
- **d.** All information is considered confidential

47. Jim is 15 years old when treated for appendicitis with subsequent appendectomy. At what age will Jim be when his records may be destroyed, if the state's age of majority is 18 years of age?
- **a.** 18
- **b.** 25
- **c.** 28
- **d.** 30

48. LaToya, a 16-year-old student, is hospitalized for pneumonia. She was ambulatory and mentally competent upon admission. LaToya is a married mother of two. Her mother is contacted to be informed of her daughter's status. Who may authorize treatment for LaToya?
- **a.** LaToya
- **b.** LaToya's mom
- **c.** LaToya's husband
- **d.** No consent is required in an emergent situation.

49. Bob, a 93-year-old male, was admitted and treated for a myocardial infarction. Due to his history of Alzheimer's disease, his daughter is his legal guardian. Bob lives with his son. Upon discharge from the hospital, his primary physician requests copies of his medical record. Who is required to sign an authorization for release of the medical record information to the physician?
- **a.** Bob
- **b.** Bob's daughter
- **c.** Bob's son
- **d.** Due to continuity of care, an authorization is not mandatory.

50. Of the following, which requestor is NOT required to submit the patient's written authorization in order to obtain copies of the patient's medical record from the hospital?
- **a.** The patient
- **b.** The patient's attorney
- **c.** The patient's physician
- **d.** The hospital's attorney

Health Care Statistics, Research, and Epidemiology

1. Statistics
   a. Definition of Statistics
      i. The overall science of extracting information from a set of data and using the information to make inferences about that larger set of data
      ii. The study of variation
      iii. Descriptive statistics: statistical data concerning the attributes of a population
      iv. Inferential statistics: statistical data collected from a sample to make inferences about the population from which the sample is extracted
   b. Purposes of health care statistics; may be collected concurrently or retrospectively
      i. Strategic planning: determine changes to current structure of organization (e.g., equipment, staffing, facilities)
      ii. Compare past with current performance indicators
         1. Determine trends of medical staff
         2. Research and education
         3. Determine performance of ancillary units
         4. Quality improvement, credentialing, and utilization review
      iii. For accreditation compliance
         1. The Joint Commission (TJC, formerly the Joint Commission on Accreditation of Healthcare Organizations, JCAHO)
         2. Department of Health and Human Services (DHHS)
         3. Centers for Medicare and Medicaid Services (CMS)
         4. American College of Surgeons (ACS)
         5. American Osteopathic Association (AOA)
         6. Other organizations that have set standards and for which statistics can verify adherence to criteria
      iv. Health care agencies
         1. World Health Organization (WHO): the International Classification of Diseases (ICD) systems were developed under WHO.
         2. National Vital Statistics System (NVSS): responsible for the official vital statistics of the United States

3. National Center for Health Statistics (NCHS): federal government's principal vital and health statistics agency, which provides statistical information that will guide actions and policies to improve the health of the American public

4. Centers for Disease Control and Prevention (CDC): promotes health and quality of life by preventing and controlling disease, injury, and disability

5. State public health departments

c. Facilities That Maintain Health Care Statistics

   i. Acute-care
   ii. Long-term care
   iii. Home health care
   iv. Ambulatory care
   v. Veterinary care
   vi. Hospice
   vii. Psychiatric institutions
   viii. Insurance companies
   ix. Other facilities that provide health care

d. Standardized Data Sets for Health Care Statistics

   i. Uniform Hospital Discharge Data Set (UHDDS): minimum common core of data on Medicare and Medicaid hospital discharges
   ii. Uniform Ambulatory Care Data Set (UACDS): minimum common core of data on ambulatory visits
   iii. Minimum Data Set for Long-Term Care: federally mandated standard assessment form used to collect demographic and clinical data on nursing home residents, which are used to develop a resident assessment protocol (RAP) summary for each resident
   iv. National Committee on Vital and Health Statistics: revised the UHDDS and approved UACDS
   v. Data Elements for Emergency Department System (DEEDS): uniform collection of data in hospital based emergency departments
   vi. Health Plan Employer Data and Information Set (HEDIS): sponsored by the National Committee for Quality Assurance (NCQA); a set of standard performance measures designed to provide purchasers and consumers of health care with the information they need to compare the performance of managed health care plans

e. Health Information Practitioner's Role

   i. Decide if health information collected meets statistical needs of health care facility
   ii. Be aware of sources of data within the facility
   iii. Be prepared to merge other data with data from the health record
   iv. Collect quality health data
   v. Organize data into databases
   vi. Statistically analyze collected data
   vii. Develop, generate, and interpret health care statistical reports

2. Vital Statistics

   a. Crucial events in life such as births, deaths, adoptions, marriages, and divorces

   b. NCHS recommends standard forms, which most states adopt to develop birth, death, and fetal death certificates.

   c. States have responsibility for the preparation of birth, death, and fetal death certificates; local registrar maintains and forwards certificates to state registrar; and states share this information with the NCHS.

d. Certificates (birth, fetal death, death)

    i. Certificate of live birth is used for registration purposes and is composed of two parts. The first part contains information related to the child and parents, and the second part is used to collect data on the mother's pregnancy.

    ii. The fetal death certificate is completed when a pregnancy results in a stillbirth. It contains information about the parents (including occupational data), the history of the pregnancy, the cause and date of the fetal death, and significant conditions of the fetus or mother.

    iii. Data from death certificates are used to compile causes of death. Death certificates contain information on the decedent, place of death, medical certification, and disposition of the body.

3. **Analysis of Hospital Services**

  a. Basic Health Care Terms

    i. Hospital inpatient: a patient who is provided with room, board, and continuous general nursing services in an area of the hospital where patients generally stay at least overnight

    ii. Hospital newborn inpatient: a patient who is born in the hospital at the beginning of the current inpatient hospitalization. Newborns are usually counted separately in calculating some hospital performance indicators (e.g., average daily census, occupancy rate).

    iii. Inpatient hospitalization: a period in a person's life during which he or she is an inpatient in a single hospital without interruption, except by possible intervening leaves of absence

    iv. Inpatient discharge: the termination of a period of inpatient hospitalization through the formal release of the inpatient by the hospital; the term is used for patients who are discharged alive, against medical advice (AMA), or who died while hospitalized.

    v. Hospital outpatient: a hospital patient who receives services in one or more of the outpatient facilities when he or she is not currently an inpatient or home care patient

    vi. Census: number of patients present at any given time; see Table 4-1 as an example

    vii. Daily inpatient census: number of patients present at the official census-taking time (usually 12 midnight) each day, plus the number of patients admitted and discharged the same day

    viii. Inpatient service day: unit of measure denoting the services received by one inpatient in one 24-hour period

    ix. Total inpatient service days: sum of all inpatient service days for each of the days in the period under consideration; see Table 4-2

Table 4-1 Census
Patients in MICU on May 3, 200x at 11:30 AM
John Howard
Shirlyn Thomas
Carla Tyson
Census = 3

Table 4-2 Houston Hospital Total Inpatient Service Days	
Patient Name	**Inpatient Service Days for MICU**
John Howard	6
Shirlyn Thomas	9
Carla Tyson	13
Total	**28**

    x. Length of stay: the number of calendar days from admission to discharge; for example, discharged May 9, admitted May 3 = 6 days

        1. Patients admitted and discharged the same day are assigned one inpatient service day.

        2. Patients admitted on one day and discharged the very next day are assigned one inpatient service day.

    xi. Total length of stay: the sum of days' stay of any group of inpatients discharged during a specific period of time; see Table 4-3

    xii. Inpatient bed count: the number of available facility inpatient beds both occupied and vacant on a given day

    xiii. Inpatient bed count day: the unit of measure denoting the presence of one inpatient bed, either occupied or vacant, set up and staffed for use in one 24-hour period

    xiv. Hospital inpatient autopsy: the postmortem examination performed in a hospital facility (performed by a pathologist or other responsible physician) on the body of a patient who died during inpatient hospitalization

    xv. Hospital autopsy: post mortem examination of the body of an individual who at some time in the past was a previous patient but who was not an inpatient at the time of death; this is performed by a pathologist or an assigned physician on staff

    xvi. Nosocomial infection: infections acquired during hospitalization

  b. Inpatient Discharge Analysis

    i. Health record information is reviewed to determine types of services provided, length of stay, discharge status, and other data to assist in calculating hospital performance indicators.

  c. Gains and Losses (see Table 4-4)

Table 4-3 Total Length of Stay			
Patient Name	**Admitted**	**Discharged**	**Length of Stay (LOS)**
John Howard	January 3	January 9	6
Shirlyn Thomas	January 18	January 27	9
Carla Tyson	January 14	January 27	13
Total			**28**

Table 4-4 Gains and Losses	
Gains	**Losses**
Admissions to hospital (does not include DOAs)	Discharges (including deaths) from hospital
Transfers into hospital service or unit from another hospital service or unit	Transfers out of hospital service or unit to another hospital service or unit

d. Assigning a Patient to a Service or Unit
    i. Medical staff organized into services or units
    ii. Describes the professional activities of existing medical staff units or specialty clinical education programs

e. Common Services Rendered by a Hospital
    i. Internal medicine
    ii. Surgery
    iii. Obstetrics and gynecology
    iv. Neonatal medicine
    v. Anesthesiology
    vi. Pediatric medicine
    vii. Radiology
    viii. Diagnostic imaging
    ix. Neurology
    x. Psychiatry
    xi. Pathology

f. Reports from Discharge Data (may be calculated by service or unit or on a daily, weekly, monthly, or annual basis)
    i. Hospital performance indicators
        1. Number of admissions and discharges
        2. Average daily census
        3. Average length of stay
        4. Occupancy rate
        5. Mortality rates
        6. Autopsy rate
        7. Infection rates
        8. Consultation rate
        9. Other indicators of hospital performance
    ii. Information on patient demographics
    iii. Case mix (grouping of patients based on a set of characteristics)
    iv. Expected sources of payment
    v. Other relevant information

g. Hospital Performance Indicator Formulas for Commonly Computed Health Care Rates and Percentages

$$\text{Average Daily Census} = \frac{\text{Total service days for the unit for the period}}{\text{Total number of days in the period}}$$

$$\text{Average Length of Stay} = \frac{\text{Total length of stay (discharge days)}}{\text{Total discharges (includes deaths)}}$$

$$\text{Percentage of Occupancy} = \frac{\text{Total service days for a period}}{\text{Total bed count days in the period}} \times 100$$

$$\text{Hospital Death Rate (Gross)} = \frac{\text{Number of deaths of inpatients in period}}{\text{Number of discharges (including deaths)}} \times 100$$

$$\text{Hospital Death Rate (Net)} = \frac{\text{Number of deaths of inpatients in period} - \text{Inpatient deaths} < 48 \text{ hours}}{\text{Number of discharges (including deaths)} - \text{Inpatient deaths} < 48 \text{ hours}} \times 100$$

$$\text{Gross Autopsy Rate} = \frac{\text{Total inpatient autopsies for a given period}}{\text{Total inpatient deaths for the period}} \times 100$$

$$\text{Net Autopsy Rate} = \frac{\text{Total number of autopsies or inpatient deaths}}{\text{Total inpatient deaths minus unautopsied coroners' or medical examiners' cases}} \times 100$$

$$\text{Hospital Autopsy Rate (Adjusted)} = \frac{\text{Total hospital autopsies}}{\text{Number of deaths of hospital patients whose bodies are available for hospital autopsy}} \times 100$$

$$\text{Fetal Death Rate} = \frac{\text{Total number of intermediate and/or late fetal deaths for a period}}{\text{Total number of live births} + \text{intermediate and late fetal deaths for the period}} \times 100$$

$$\text{Neonatal Mortality Rate (Death Rate)} = \frac{\text{Total number of newborn deaths for a period}}{\text{Total number of newborn infant discharges (including deaths) for the period}} \times 100$$

$$\text{Maternal Mortality Rate (Death Rate)} = \frac{\text{Total number of obstetrical maternal deaths for a period}}{\text{Total number of obstetrical discharges (including deaths) for the period}} \times 100$$

$$\text{Caesarean Section Rate} = \frac{\text{Total number of caesarean sections performed in a period}}{\text{Total number of deliveries in the period (including caesarean sections)}} \times 100$$

4. Presentation of Data
   a. Data should be presented in a manner that catches the reader's attention, encourages interest, and makes data easy to interpret and use.
   b. Tables
      i. Columns of figures, each labeled to identify contents
      ii. Include title, date, and person who prepared table
      iii. Include narrative explanation of what table depicts (see Figure 4-1)

Houston Hospital January, 200X Statistics of code 250.00			
Gender	Age	LOS	Discharges
Male	25.6	8.3	85
Female	24.0	4.2	43

Figure 4-1 Example of a Table

c. Frequency Distribution
  i. Groups data into classes
    1. Rules for classes
      a. 5 to 15 classes.
      b. Smallest and largest figures represented.
      c. Each item fits into one class only.
      d. Classes should cover equal ranges of values.
      e. A histogram is an example.
d. Graphs
  i. Horizontal axis (independent variable)
  ii. Vertical axis (dependent variable)
  iii. Types of graphs
    1. Bar: used to report count values of categorical data (see Figure 4-2)
    2. Histogram: graphic representations of frequency distributions (see Figure 4-3)
    3. Line graph: used to provide a simple visual method of monitoring trends over time (see Figure 4-4)
    4. Pie chart: displays frequencies in each category (see Figure 4-5)
    5. Cause and effect diagrams: used to place factors that are expected to affect a problem, condition, or project in causal order; also called fishbone diagram (see Figure 4-6)

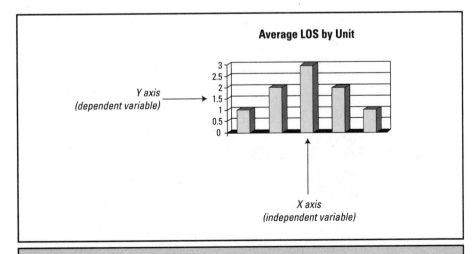

Figure 4-2   Example of a Bar Graph

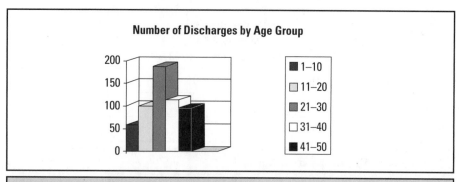

Figure 4-3   Example of a Histogram

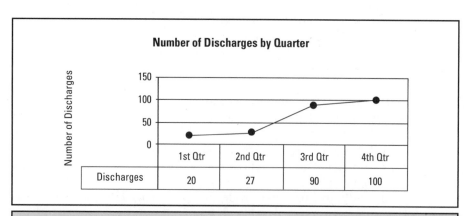

Figure 4-4   Example of a Line Graph

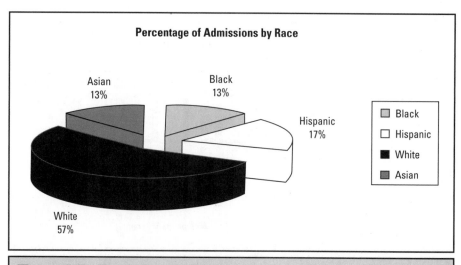

Figure 4-5   Example of a Pie Chart

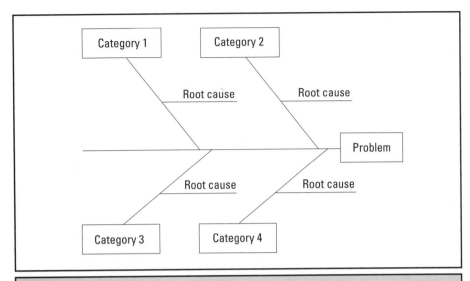

Figure 4-6   Example of a Cause and Effect Diagram

6. Pareto chart: similar to a bar chart or histogram; occurrences on chart are ordered from the most frequently occurring or most important category to the least frequent or least important (see Figure 4-7)
7. Scatter diagram: used to plot the points for two variables that may be related to each other (see Figure 4-8)
8. Frequency polygon graph: similar to a histogram; graph of a frequency distribution in line form rather than a bar graph (see Figure 4-9)

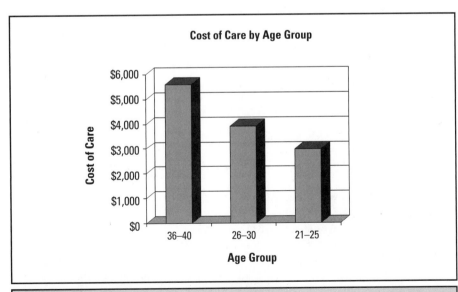

Figure 4-7   Example of a Pareto Chart

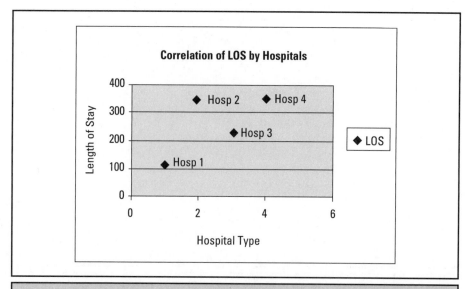

Figure 4-8   Example of a Scatter Diagram

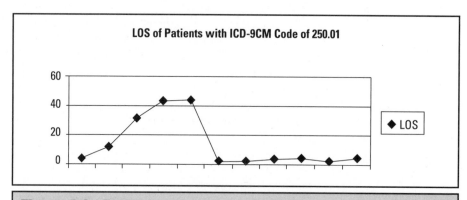

Figure 4-9   Example of a Frequency Polygon

5. Common Health Care Statistical Measures and Tests
    a. Terms and Definitions
        i. Population
            1. Any defined aggregate of objects, persons, or events (sum total) subject to statistical study
        ii. Parameter: statistic calculated on a population value
        iii. Sample
            1. Any sub-aggregate drawn from the population
            2. A small group drawn from the population in order to make inferences about that population
        iv. Estimate: any statistic calculated on a sample of observations
        v. Types of samples
            1. Random sample: sample in which every member of the population has an equal probability of being included (e.g., 15 names placed in a hat and 10 drawn out)

> **2.** Cluster sample: random selection of a number of subjects from naturally occurring groups or clusters; the unit chosen is not an individual but a group of individuals who are grouped together (e.g., persons living in a zip code)
> **3.** Stratified sample: samples of a population that consists of a number of subgroups or strata that may differ in characteristics being studied (e.g., ethnic groups)
> **4.** Systematic sample: a sample drawn by taking every n^{th} from a list of the population (e.g., from a list of 100 names, select every 10th name on list)
> **5.** Sampling error: the principle that the characteristics of a sample are not identical to the characteristics of the population from which the sample is drawn

b. Ratios, Proportions, and Rates

> **i.** These measures indicate the number of times something happened relative to the number of times it could have happened.
> **ii.** The general formula for calculating ratios, proportions, and rates is $x/y = z$, where x is a sample, y is the population, and z is the ratio, proportion, or rate.
> **iii.** Ratios: the quantities being compared may be expressed so that x and y are completely independent of each other, or x may be included in y
> **iv.** Proportions: a type of ratio in which x is a subset or sample of y and the numerator is always included in the denominator
> **v.** Rates: used to measure events over a period of time

c. Measures of Central Tendency

> **i.** Typical values tend to lie centrally within a set of data arranged according to magnitude
>> **1.** Mean: average calculated by adding the values of all observations and dividing the total by the number of observations
>> **2.** Median: middle-most value when values are ranked in numeric order
>> **3.** Mode: value that occurs most frequently
>>> **a.** When no value repeats more than once, there is no mode
>>> **b.** When several values repeat with the same frequency, each is the mode

d. Measures of Variability (also called measures of variation or measures of dispersion)

> **i.** The amount of variability of the measurement around the mean or median
> **ii.** The degree to which numerical data tend to be spread about an average value
>> **1.** Range: the difference between the highest and lowest values
>> **2.** Variance: how values are spread or dispersed around the mean; computed by squaring each deviation from the mean, summing them, and then dividing their sum by the degrees of freedom $(n - 1)$
>>> **a.** Degrees of freedom: any of the statistically independent values of a sample that are used to determine the property of the sample, as the mean or variance
>> **3.** Standard deviation
>>> **a.** How values are spread or dispersed around the mean
>>> **b.** The most common measure of variation
>>> **c.** The square root of the variance

131

     d. Small standard deviation implies data are close to mean and a large standard deviation implies data are more spread out from the mean.

     e. Example: December discharges for Houston Hospital had a mean of 6 days and a standard deviation of 2. Therefore, if a patient stayed in the hospital one standard deviation above the mean, he had a length of stay of 8 days (6 + 2 = 8). If a patient had a length of stay of 2 days, then he was in the hospital 2 standard deviations below the mean (6 − 2 − 2 = 4).

e. Normal Distribution

   i. Measures of central tendency and variation are interpreted as they relate to the normal distribution.

  ii. Theoretical family of distributions that may have any mean or any standard deviation

 iii. A bell-shaped curve (also referred to as normal curve) that is symmetrical about the mean

    1. 50% of observations fall above the mean and 50% fall below the mean.

    2. Each side of the mean extends to a tail.

     a. When the research hypothesis is directed to only one end of the curve, it is considered a one-tailed test. An alternative hypothesis (hypothesis that states there is an association between the independent and dependent variables) in which the researcher makes a prediction in one direction results in outcomes at one end of the curve.

     b. If the researcher makes no prediction about the direction of the results (more or less), the alternative hypothesis is two-tailed. Thus, the outcomes may fall at both ends of the curve.

    3. In Figure 4-10, the mean, median, and mode are all at 0.

    4. The standard deviation indicates how many observations fall within a certain range of the mean.

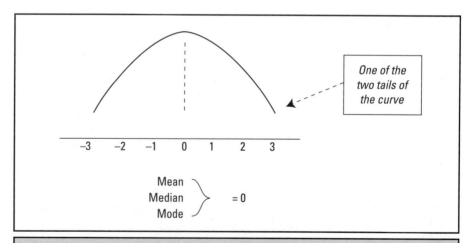

Figure 4-10　Example of a Bell-Shaped Curve

5. Values range from minus infinity to plus infinity, and

   a. 68.26% of all values fall within 1 standard deviation of the mean in each direction.

   b. 95.44% of all values fall within 2 standard deviations of the mean in each direction.

   c. 99.74% of all values fall within 3 standard deviations of the mean in each direction.

   d. Values that are more than 3 standard deviations from the mean in either direction are called outliers.

f. Test of Significance

   i. Purpose is to determine whether observed differences between groups, or relationships between variables in the sample being studied, are likely to be due to sampling error or are likely to reflect true differences or relationships in the population of interest.

   ii. The method utilized to test the null and alternative hypotheses

   1. Hypothesis

   a. Identifies the goal of the research and poses a tentative assumption to be tested

   b. Indicates the nature of the difference or relationship that is being tested

   2. Null hypothesis (symbolized as H_0) states there is no difference or relationship in the population under study.

   3. Alternative hypothesis states there is a difference or relationship in the population under study.

   iii. Commonly used methods to test the null hypothesis include T-test, Chi-square, Pearson correlation coefficient, regression analysis, and analysis of variance (ANOVA).

   1. T-test determines if there is a significant difference between two groups with respect to the independent and dependent variables. (See Figure 4-11.)

   a. Independent variable is the variable to be manipulated; also called the experimental or treatment variable.

   b. Dependent variable is the variable that is measured to determine the effects of the experimental treatment; also referred to as the control.

   2. Chi-square determines if there is a significant difference between observed and expected frequencies; used for nominal data.

   3. Pearson correlation coefficient (see Figure 4-12)

   a. Expressed as r

   b. Ranges from 0 to ± 1

   c. Used to assess the direction and degree of relationship between two variables

   d. As r approaches 0, there tends to be less correlation between the variables; as r approaches 1, there tends to be more correlation.

   e. Coefficient of determination

   i. r-squared (or r^2)

   ii. Tells how much of the variation in y is accounted for by the x variable

   iii. If $r = .80$, then $r^2 = .64$, and 64% of variation in y is accounted for by the x variable.

Houston Hospital Length of Stay of Patients on Unit A and Unit B

Unit A	Unit B
1	2
3	2
4	4
5	4
7	6
7	7
8	7
9	7

T-Test: Paired Two Sample for Mean

	Unit A	Unit B
Mean	5.5	4.875
Variance	7.428571429	4.696428571
Observations	8	8
Pearson correlation	0.955350077	
Hypothesized mean difference	0	
df	7	
t-stat	1.929612462	
P(T<=t) one-tail	0.047488246	
t Critical one-tail	1.894577508	
P(T<=t) two-tail	0.094976492	
t Critical two-tail	2.36462256	

If t-stat is > critical value, then reject H_0; if t-stat < critical value, accept H_0

Figure 4-11 Sample T-Test

Houston Hospital Length of Stay of Patients on Unit A, Unit B, and Unit C		
Unit A	**Unit B**	**Unit C**
1	2	5
3	2	6
4	4	6
5	4	7
7	6	8
7	7	9
8	7	10
9	7	10

	Unit A	**Unit B**	**Unit C**
Unit A	1		
Unit B	0.955350077	1	
Unit C	0.96780197	0.95	1

Unit B with C

Unit A with C

Figure 4-12 Sample Correlation Coefficient

4. Regression analysis determines the extent one or more explanatory variables can predict an outcome variable (see Figure 4-13).
   a. Coefficient of determination (r^2)
      i. Ranges from 0 to 1
      ii. Represents the squared correlation between the explanatory variable(s) and the outcome variable
      iii. The value of r^2 indicates the proportion of variability in the outcome that is explained by the predictor variable(s).
      iv. The closer r^2 is to one, the stronger the prediction.
      v. P-value associated with r^2 indicates the probability that the observed value of r^2 could occur through sampling error alone.
5. ANOVA determines if there is a significant difference between two or more groups (see Figure 4-14).
   iv. The computed result of the test of significance is called the test statistic or t-stat. The absolute value of the t-stat is compared to the critical value. If the t-stat is greater than the critical value, then the researcher will reject the null hypothesis.
      1. Measures the size of the difference or relationship observed in the sample

Houston Hospital Length of Stay of Patients on Unit A and Unit B

Unit A	Unit B
1	2
3	2
4	4
5	4
7	6
7	7
8	7
9	7

Summary Output

Regression statistics

Multiple r	0.955350077
r square	0.91269377
Adjusted r square	0.898142732
Standard error	0.869858605
Observations	8

r^2 means 91% of variation in unit B can be accounted to unit A

ANOVA

	df	SS	MS	F	Significance F
Regression	1	47.46007605	47.46007605	62.72361809	0.000215151
Residual	6	4.539923954	0.756653992		
Total	7	52			

	Coefficients	Standard Error	t-Stat	P-value	Lower 95%
Intercept	−0.357414449	0.800982857	−0.446219848	0.671090496	−2.317350327
Unit B	1.201520913	0.15171055	7.919824372	0.000215151	0.830298298

Figure 4-13 Sample Regression Analysis

2. The probability that the observed value of the test statistic could occur in the event that the null hypothesis is true is called the p-value, which ranges from 0 to 1.
   a. P-value answers the question: how likely is it that the observed difference or relationship is due to chance or due to sampling error?
   b. As the p-value approaches 0, the smaller the probability that the observed difference or relationship is due to chance or sampling error.

Houston Hospital Length of Stay of Patients on Unit A, Unit B, and Unit C

Unit A	Unit B	Unit C
1	2	5
3	2	5
4	4	6
5	4	7
7	6	7
7	7	8
8	7	9
9	7	10

ANOVA: Single Factor
Summary

Groups	Count	Sum	Average	Variance
Unit A	8	44	5.5	7.428571429
Unit B	8	39	4.875	4.696428571
Unit C	8	57	7.125	3.267857143

ANOVA

Source of variation	SS	df	MS	F	P-value	F crit
Between groups	21.58333333	2	10.79166667	2.10324826	0.147035257	3.466794851
Within groups	107.75	21	5.130952381			
Total	129.3333333	23				

If t-stat is > critical value, then reject H_0; if t-stat < critical value, accept H_0

Figure 4-14 Sample ANOVA

v. Level of significance (see Figure 4-15)
   1. Also referred to as alpha level and symbolized by the Greek letter α
   2. P-value is compared to level of significance to determine whether to accept or reject the null hypothesis; if the p-value is less than the alpha level, then the researcher will reject the null hypothesis.
   3. Common levels of significance are .05 and .01.
      a. At .05, the probability is smaller than 5 in 100 that the observed difference or relationship is due to sampling error or chance.
      b. At .01, the probability is smaller than 1 in 100 that the observed difference or relationship is due to sampling error or chance.
vi. Type I error: rejecting the null hypothesis when it is true
vii. Type II error: accepting the null hypothesis when it is false

Test of Significance

T-Test: Paired Two Sample for Mean .05 Level of Significance

	Unit A	Unit B
Mean	15.5	14.875
Variance	7.428571429	4.696428571
Observations	8	8
Pearson correlation	0.955350077	
Hypothesized mean difference	0	
df	7	
t-Stat	1.929612462	
P(T<=t) one-tail	0.047488246	
t Critical one-tail	1.894577508	
P(T<=t) two-tail	0.094976492	
t Critical two-tail	2.36462256	

p-value of a one- or two-tailed test at .05 level of significance; reject H_0

Figure 4-15 Sample Level of Significance Test

6. Research
   a. Scientific inquiry or question to increase the body of knowledge; may be applied or basic
      i. Applied research is directed toward improvement of actual practice.
      ii. Basic research is directed toward general explanations.
   b. Common Terms in Research
      i. Independent variable
         1. The variable to be manipulated
         2. Also called the experimental or treatment variable
      ii. Dependent variable
         1. The variable that is measured to determine the effects of the experimental treatment
         2. Also referred to as the control
      iii. Reliability: accuracy of the data in the sense of its reproducibility, i.e., the likelihood that the experiment will yield the same results on repeated trials
      iv. Validity
         1. Degree to which an instrument measures what it should measure
         2. Assesses relevance, completeness, accuracy (the result of an active effort to comprehend and verify; shows careful conformity to the fact or truth), and correctness (free from errors, mistakes, or faults)
   c. Scientific Method for Performing Research
      i. Define the problem (statement of the problem); determine population under study
      ii. Review the literature addressing previous or related investigations

iii. Formulate a hypothesis
    1. Define the null and alternative hypotheses
    2. State the independent and dependent variables
iv. Select a research method or design, including tools to be used
    1. Experimental
    2. Observational study
    3. Surveys and questionnaires
    4. Interviews
    5. Historical-prospective
    6. Participant observation
    7. Cross-sectional or prevalence study
    8. Cohort study
    9. Case control
v. Collect the data from sample abstracted from population
vi. Analyze the results
    1. Test of significance (T-test, chi-square, ANOVA, etc.)
    2. Compare computed result of p-value to alpha level or compare test statistic to critical value
    3. Accept or reject null hypothesis
vii. Draw conclusions

7. Epidemiology
  a. Definition
    i. The study of disease and the determinants of disease in populations
    ii. The study of clinical and health care trends or patterns and the ability to recognize trends or patterns within large amounts of data
    iii. The study of the distribution and determinants of diseases and injuries in human populations
  b. Common Epidemiological Terms
    i. Health: state of complete physical, mental, and social well-being, and not merely the absence of disease
    ii. Levels of prevention
      1. Primary: prevention by reducing exposure
      2. Secondary: early detection and treatment
      3. Tertiary: alleviation of disability resulting from disease
    iii. Rehabilitation: attempt to restore an affected individual to a useful, satisfying, and self-sufficient role in society
    iv. Risk factor: associated with an increased likelihood that the disease will develop at a later time
    v. Cohort: a group under study for a period of time
    vi. Epidemic: the occurrence in a community or region of a group of illnesses of similar nature, clearly in excess of normal expectancy
    vii. Endemic: the habitual presence of a disease or infectious agent within a geographical area or the usual prevalence of a given disease within such area
    viii. Prevalence rate (PR): the number of existing cases of a disease in a specified time period, divided by the population at that time; describes the magnitude of an epidemic

$$PR = \frac{\text{All new and preexisting cases of a specific disease during a given time period} \times 10^{10}}{\text{Total population during the same time period}}$$

1. Example:

$$\frac{\text{Number of children 12 years and under with bacterial meningitis in Houston, Texas} \times 10^{10}}{\text{Number of children 12 years and under in Houston, Texas}}$$

ix. Incident rate (IR): the number of newly reported cases of a disease in a specified time period, divided by the population at that time; used to compare the frequency of disease in populations

$$IR = \frac{\text{Total number of new cases of a specific disease during a given period of time} \times 10^{10}}{\text{Total population at risk during the same time period}}$$

1. Example:

$$\frac{\text{New Texas cases of children 12 years and under with bacterial meningitis in July 200x} \times 10^{10}}{\text{Number of Texas children 12 years and under in July, 200x}}$$

x. Relative risk (RR): used to determine which groups have a greater risk of developing the disease under study

$$RR = \frac{\text{Incidence rate exposed } (I_r e)}{\text{Incidence rate unexposed } (I_r o)}$$

xi. Epidemiological research
   1. Descriptive cross-sectional prevalence study
      a. Concurrently describes or examines the distribution of disease or characteristics and health outcomes at one specific point or period in time
      b. Used when little is known about the disease or characteristic under study
      c. Used to generate hypotheses, not to test them
   2. Case-control or retrospective
      a. Analytical study design in which a disease or health condition is examined to determine possible causes
      b. Researcher collects data on disease and controls by looking back in time.
   3. Prospective: determines whether the characteristics or suspected risk factors preceded the disease or health condition
   4. Cohort: prospective study in which subjects are separated into two groups based upon their exposures or health characteristics and then followed forward to determine whether they develop the disease
   5. Historical prospective: past records are used to collect information regarding the exposure characteristics or risk factors under study
   6. Experimental studies for clinical and community trials: modify the health characteristics that are found to cause the disease by using health care interventions that control progression of the disease or prevent the disease from occurring

PRACTICAL APPLICATION OF YOUR KNOWLEDGE

1. Health Care Statistics
   a. Define statistics.

   b. Explain the importance of maintaining health care statistics.

   c. What is the health information manager's role in health care statistics?

   d. Write the formulas for the following hospital performance indicators:
       i. Average daily census

       ii. Average length of stay

       iii. Occupancy rate

       iv. Death rate (gross vs. net)

       v. Gross autopsy rate

       vi. Net autopsy rate

       vii. Hospital-adjusted autopsy rate

   e. The Oncology Department Committee has established a quality monitor to report and review all cancer cases with the diagnosis of carcinoma of the lung, right upper lobe, and a frozen-section pathology report indicating normal lung tissue. What would be the correct formula to accurately calculate the percentage of cases that meet these criteria?

2. Vital Statistics
   a. Describe vital record information collected in health care institutions.

3. Statistical Measures
   a. Discuss the measures of central tendency.

   b. Describe the measures of dispersion.

   c. What does the standard deviation tell the researcher about the distribution?

   d. Explain the relationship of the confidence interval to the p-value.

   e. Explain the following terms:
      i. Test of significance

      ii. Level of significance

      iii. Test statistic

      iv. P-value

      v. Critical value

      vi. Confidence interval

      vii. T-test

     viii. ANOVA

     ix. Chi-square

     x. Pearson r correlation coefficient

     xi. Coefficient of determination

  f. Describe a normal distribution.

  g. Write the general formula for calculating ratios, proportions, and rates.

4. Research
  a. Define research.

  b. Describe various research methods.

  c. What test of significance would be used to determine the significant difference in frequencies between the two groups under study?

  d. List the steps in the scientific method of performing research.

  e. Define hypothesis, alternative hypothesis, and null hypothesis.

  f. Which hypothesis is tested utilizing the scientific method?

g. Considering a two-tailed test and given the data and T-test results in the table, decide if the researcher should accept or reject the following null hypothesis at the .05 level of significance:

H_0: There is no significant difference at the .05 level of significance in the monthly average length of stay of inpatients admitted in Texas and California acute-care hospitals for the past year.

Average Length of Stay in Texas and California Acute-Care Hospitals by Month

Month	Texas	California
Jan	5	11
Feb	7	12
Mar	6	12
Apr	10	13
May	7	9
Jun	7	9
Jul	7	7
Aug	8	13
Sep	9	19
Oct	12	19
Nov	4	5
Dec	5	7

T-test: Paired two sample for means

	Texas	California
Mean	7.25	11.33333333
Variance	5.113636364	19.33333333
Observations	12	12
Pearson correlation	0.804584565	
Hypothesized mean difference	0	
df	11	
t-stat	–4.866928756	
P(T<=t) one-tail	0.000248569	
t Critical one-tail	1.795883691	
P(T<=t) two-tail	0.000497139	
t Critical two-tail	2.200986273	

5. Epidemiology

    a. Discuss the importance of gathering epidemiology statistics in relation to an outbreak of a highly infectious disease.

    b. Prevalence rate

        i. Define.

        ii. Write the formula.

        iii. Give an example.

    c. Incidence rate

        i. Define.

        ii. Write the formula.

        iii. Give an example.

6. Computation of Hospital Performance Indicators

♪ The following calculations are reviewed with you in the statistical section of the audio entitled "Health Statistics, Research, and Epidemiology" tutorial. For questions a–c, utilize the following annual hospital report to calculate the requested hospital performance indicators.

Annual Statistics for General Hospital (non-leap year)

Admissions		Bed Count	
Adults and children	15,450	Adults and children	450
Newborns	680	Bassinets	60
Inpatient Service Days		Total Length of Stay	
Adults and children	125,031	Adults and children	89,231
Newborns	7090	Newborns	986
Discharges (including deaths)		Surgery Statistics	
Adults and children	15,684	Number of patients operated on	899
Newborns	623	Surgical procedures performed	926

Inpatient Deaths			Miscellaneous	
Total adults and children			Caesarean sections	95
Less than 48 hrs.	20		Deliveries	669
More than 48 hrs.	321		Obstetrical discharges	
Total newborns			(including deaths)	780
Less than 48 hrs.	10		Hospital infections	68
More than 48 hrs.	1		Post-op infections	18
Anesthesia deaths	2		Consultations	5800
Fetal deaths				
(Intermediate and late)	4			
Maternal deaths	1			
Post-op deaths	68			

Inpatient Autopsies			Other Autopsies	
Adults and children	18		Coroner's cases	2
Newborn	1		(Unavailable for autopsy)	
			Hospital outpatients	6

a. Calculate the average length of stay.

b. Calculate the death rate.

c. Calculate the gross autopsy rate.

d. If General Hospital had 1000 inpatient service days for March, what was the average daily census?

e. You are the newly employed statistician at Memorial Hospital. The management information system is currently being redesigned. In order to assure that the statistics are being calculated correctly, you manually calculate the statistics to assure accuracy. The following statistics are given for the month of July:

Memorial Hospital Occupancy Rate	
Category	**Number**
Admissions	929
Discharges	909
Discharge days	4988
Census days	5022
Beds	250
Patients remaining last day of month	184

What was the occupancy rate? Round off to one place behind the decimal.

TEST YOUR KNOWLEDGE

Use the following table for questions 1–4.

Month	Total Admissions	Total Discharges	Inpatient Service Days	Length of Stay	Bed Count
January	945	910	6750	6615	250
February	901	889	7130	6082	250
March	872	894	7470	5668	300

1. Calculate the average daily census for the month of January. Round off to a whole number.
   a. 213
   b. 216
   c. 218
   d. 237

2. Calculate the average daily census for the quarter. Round off to a whole number.
   a. 201
   b. 204
   c. 234
   d. 237

3. Calculate the average length of stay for the quarter. Round off to one place behind the decimal.
   a. 6.7
   b. 6.8
   c. 7.8
   d. 7.9

4. Calculate the occupancy rate for the quarter. Round off to one place behind the decimal.
   a. 75.4%
   b. 76.4%
   c. 88.8%
   d. 89.2%

5. The standard deviation (sd) describes the range of dispersion from the average or mean. The smaller the sd, the more the values in the distribution are:
   a. skewed around the mean.
   b. scattered out from the mean.
   c. varied from the mean of the population.
   d. closer to the mean.

6. A patient who is admitted into the hospital at 9:01 AM and expires at 11:58 PM the same day would be:
   a. counted as one inpatient service day.
   b. subtracted from the daily inpatient census count for the date of admission.
   c. reported based upon number of hours of care rendered instead of inpatient service days.
   d. subtracted from the daily inpatient census count for the next day following his/her death.

Use the following information for questions 7–11.

In the month of July, 7 adults, 1 child, and 1 newborn died at Houston Hospital. A total of 256 admissions and 237 discharges for adults and children were reported for the same month. Live births for July were 114 with 5 fetal deaths recorded (3 early, 1 intermediate, and 1 late). Autopsies were performed on 3 adults, the child, the newborn, and on 1 late fetal death case. One of the adult bodies was released to the coroner for examination. Additionally, 1 patient died in the emergency room and was autopsied. Three home care patients died and were brought to the hospital for autopsy.

7. What was the death rate (gross) for the month? Round off to two places behind the decimal.
   a. 2.95%
   b. 3.38%
   c. 3.52%
   d. 3.79%

8. What was the gross autopsy rate for the month? Round off to two places behind the decimal.
   a. 42.86%
   b. 55.56%
   c. 66.67%
   d. 77.78%

9. Calculate the net autopsy rate for the month. Round off to two places behind the decimal.
   a. 50.00%
   b. 55.56%
   c. 62.50%
   d. 66.67%

10. Calculate the fetal death rate for the month. Round off to two places behind the decimal.
   a. 1.72%
   b. 1.75%
   c. 4.20%
   d. 4.39%

11. What was the hospital adjusted autopsy rate for the month? Round off to two places behind the decimal.
   a. 41.67%
   b. 62.50%
   c. 69.23%
   d. 75.00%

12. Given that the researcher wants to set the p-value at .05, what would the alpha level be?
   a. .001
   b. .01
   c. .05
   d. .95

13. Calculate the mode for the following distribution: 2, 4, 5, 5, 6, 7, 10, 5
   a. 5.0
   b. 5.5
   c. 6.0
   d. 7.0

14. A researcher wants to test the following null hypothesis: There is no significant difference in the number of deaths at for-profit and not-for-profit hospitals. Which test of significance should the researcher use?
   a. T-test
   b. Pearson product moment correlation coefficient
   c. Regression analysis
   d. Chi-square

Comprehensive Review Guide for Health Information: RHIA and RHIT Exam Prep

15. Woman's Hospital had a total of 225 live births, 5 intermediate and late fetal deaths, and 4 early fetal deaths during the month of March. There were 235 newborn discharges for the month. Compute the fetal death rate for March.
- **a.** 1.77
- **b.** 1.78
- **c.** 2.17
- **d.** 4.00

16. In a normal distribution, a researcher calculated a mean of 15 and a standard deviation of 5. What is the value of 3 standard deviations below the mean?
- **a.** 0
- **b.** 8
- **c.** 10
- **d.** 12

17. The surgical department of Houston Hospital conducted a study on post-surgical deaths and age of patients. The researcher hypothesized, "there is a relationship between post-surgical deaths and the age of the patients." This statement is generally called what?
- **a.** Statement of the problem
- **b.** Hypothesis
- **c.** Independent variable
- **d.** Dependent variable

18. Mr. and Mrs. Howard are making plans to choose a community hospital that renders quality health care. They have narrowed the hospitals to four in the Houston area. They will make their final decision based on the local hospitals' post-op death rates. Based on the following data, which hospital will Mr. and Mrs. Howard decide to utilize?

Community Hospital

Community Hospital	Patients Operated Upon	Surgical Operations	Post-Op Deaths	Deaths
Get Well General	132	204	3	9
Stay Healthy Wellness Center	154	189	4	8
Houston Honorary	148	199	4	9
Tyson Memorial	163	213	3	7

- **a.** Get Well General
- **b.** Stay Healthy Wellness Center
- **c.** Houston Honorary
- **d.** Tyson Memorial

150

19. Based upon the following statistics during the month of December, what was the fetal death rate for Houston Hospital?

Fetal Deaths	
Fetal Deaths	**Number**
Early	240
Intermediate	40
Late	32
Births	980
Deliveries	994
Newborn discharges	1008

a. 6.84%
b. 7.31%
c. 7.43%
d. 31.85%

20. Calculate the gross autopsy rate for Houston Hospital given the following data.

Gross Autopsy Rate	
Category	**Value**
Discharges (including deaths)	1000
Death	
Total deaths	56
Inpatient deaths (including two coroner cases)	52
Outpatient deaths	2
Home care deaths	2
Autopsies	
Total autopsies	13
Inpatient autopsies	10
Outpatient autopsies	1
Home care autopsies	2

a. 17.86%
b. 19.23%
c. 23.21%
d. 25.00%

21. Houston Hospital has 520 beds and 70 bassinets, and discharged 1454 adult and child inpatients and 332 newborns during the month of September. A total of 9202 discharge days were recorded at the time of discharge for these adults and children and 1554 discharge days for newborns. Census days for adults was 9901, 331 for children and 905 for newborns. What was the average daily census for adults and children?
    a. 341
    b. 347
    c. 358
    d. 359

22. A normal distribution has a mean of 87 days and a standard deviation of 13. How many days are 3 standard deviations below the mean?
    a. 48
    b. 84
    c. 100
    d. 126

23. As Director of Health Information at Mercy Hospital, MiMi Goodstudy is responsible for assuring that the hospital statistics are recorded correctly. She reports that 14 patients were discharged from the medical service from June 1 through June 15. The length of stay for each patient was 17, 3, 4, 25, 8, 7, 13, 10, 5, 11, 9, 21, 3, and 1. What was the median stay for these patients?
    a. 8.0
    b. 8.5
    c. 9.0
    d. 9.5

24. As Director of Health Information at Mercy Hospital, Linda is responsible for assuring that the hospital statistics are recorded correctly. She reports that 14 patients were discharged from the medical service from June 1 to June 15. The length of stay for each patient was 17, 3, 4, 25, 8, 7, 13, 10, 5, 11, 9, 21, 3, and 1. What was the average length of stay for the first 15 days of June?
    a. 8.0
    b. 8.5
    c. 9.8
    d. 11.1

25. As Director of Health Information at Mercy Hospital, Tella is responsible for assuring that the hospital statistics are recorded correctly. She reports that 15 patients were discharged from MICU from October 1 to October 31. The length of stay for each patient was 20, 3, 17, 3, 4, 25, 8, 7, 13, 10, 5, 11, 9, 21, and 1. What was the average length of stay for these patients?
    a. 8.9
    b. 9.8
    c. 10.5
    d. 11.1

Use the following statistics of Houston Hospital for questions 26–27.

Houston Hospital January Statistics	
Category	**Value**
Beds	509
Admissions	1145
Census days	10,225
Discharges	1244
Deaths	20
Autopsies	13
Medical examiner cases	1

26. What was the net autopsy rate?
   a. 63.82%
   b. 65.01%
   c. 68.42%
   d. 100%

27. What was the death (gross) rate?
   a. 1.59%
   b. 1.61%
   c. 1.67%
   d. 1.71%

28. Calculate the average daily census for June.
   Admissions: 610
   Discharges: 673
   Patients remaining last day of month: 198
   Discharge days: 1055
   Beds: 301
   Inpatient service days: 1113
   a. 34
   b. 35
   c. 36
   d. 37

29. During March, 19 patients were discharged with a total of 209 discharge days. Which of the following may be calculated from the aforementioned data?
   a. Average daily census
   b. Average length of stay
   c. Average daily discharges
   d. Average monthly discharges

30. During the previous year, a large county in Texas reported 28 homicides to the Health Department. There were 35% from gunshot wounds, 25% from stabbings, 3% due to domestic violence, and 2% from road rage. Given the preceding data, what would be the best graphical presentation?
   a. One variable bar graph
   b. Line graph
   c. Table
   d. Pie chart

31. During the month of April, several patients had the exact same length of stay. The following reports number of patients with the same length of stay. What was the average length of stay?

Average Length of Stay	
Number of Patients	**Length of Stay**
1	105
209	3
311	2

a. 17.6
b. 12.3
c. 4.8
d. 2.6

32. The surgical department of Houston Hospital conducted a study on post-surgical deaths and age of patients. The researcher hypothesized, "there is no relationship between post-surgical deaths and the age of the patients." This statement is generally called the:
a. research hypothesis.
b. statement of the problem.
c. review of literature.
d. null hypothesis.

Use the following table for questions 33–39 about Houston Hospital.

Annual Patient Data for Houston Hospital		
Number	**January–May**	**June–December**
Beds	500	512
Bassinets	50	48
Admissions		
Adults	604	652
Children	201	198
Newborn live births	183	189
Discharges		
Adults	500	600
Children	150	205
Newborns	173	199
Deaths		
Adults	3	4
Children	0	2
Newborns	1	2
Inpatient Service Days		
Adults	4001	4500
Children	235	268
Newborn	498	606
Discharge Days		
Adults	4355	3998
Children	202	300
Newborn	500	599
Fetal Deaths		
Early	5	7
Intermediate	3	5
Late	1	3

33. Calculate the average daily census for newborns for the year.
   a. 2
   b. 3
   c. 4
   d. 5

34. Calculate the average length of stay for adults and children.
   a. 5.9
   b. 6.0
   c. 6.1
   d. 6.8

35. Calculate the average daily inpatient census (adults and children) for the year.
   a. 22
   b. 23
   c. 24
   d. 25

36. Calculate the newborn death rate.
   a. 0.81%
   b. 1.34%
   c. 4.03%
   d. 7.26%

37. Calculate the occupancy rate (adults and children) for the year.
   a. 2.44%
   b. 4.87%
   c. 5.46%
   d. 87%

38. Based upon the occupancy rate, how would you describe the financial solvency of the hospital?
   a. Excellent
   b. Very good
   c. Good
   d. Poor

39. Calculate the fetal death rate.
   a. 2.18%
   b. 3.17%
   c. 3.23%
   d. 6.45%

40. Based on the following statistics for the month of December, what was the fetal death rate for Houston Hospital?

Fetal Death Rate for Houston Hospital	
Category	**Value**
Live births	980
Deliveries	994
Newborn discharges	1008
Fetal deaths (early)	240
Fetal deaths (intermediate)	40
Fetal deaths (late)	32

   a. 6.84%
   b. 7.31%
   c. 7.43%
   d. 31.85%

Use the following information for questions 41–44.

Patient Jones was admitted to Houston Honorary Hospital on June 28 for tachycardia. The physician discharged Ms. Jones on July 8 with a discharge diagnosis of rule out stress.

41. How many discharge days were rendered to Ms. Jones upon discharge?
  a. 7
  b. 9
  c. 10
  d. 11

42. How many inpatient service days were rendered to Ms. Jones during June?
  a. 0
  b. 2
  c. 3
  d. 10

43. How may discharge days were rendered to Ms. Jones during June?
  a. 0
  b. 1
  c. 2
  d. 10

44. How many inpatient service days were rendered to Ms. Jones during July?
  a. 0
  b. 7
  c. 8
  d. 10

45. What was the average daily census in a 500-bed hospital that gave 14,942 inpatient service days and 15,001 discharge days during the month of October?
  a. 482
  b. 483
  c. 483
  d. 498

46. Last year, Houston Hospital averaged 98 births a month with a standard deviation of 6. January reported 107 births. How does the number of births in January compare to the average?
  a. It is 1 standard deviation above the mean.
  b. It is 1.5 standard deviations above the mean.
  c. It is 1 standard deviation below the mean.
  d. It is 1.5 standard deviations below the mean.

47. Given the Pearson r calculations in the following table, calculate the coefficient of determination of the patients' lengths of stays in July and August.

Patient Length of Stay (LOS) for July and August			
Patient	**July**	**August**	
Jones	15	16	
Tyson	12	15	
Thomas	11	12	
Howard	10	10	
Johnson	9	5	
Williams	2	2	
		July	**August**
Pearson r	July	1	
Pearson r	August	0.918506	1

a. .081
b. .843
c. 1.00
d. 1.91

48. A researcher tested to determine if there is a significant difference in the number of male and female HIM students at the .05 level of significance. In the study, the researcher observed a total of 16 students, 2 male and 14 female. Given the chi-square contingency table, how many male students should the researcher have postulated or expected?

Chi-Square Contingency Table		
	Male	**Female**
Expected	x	y
Observed	2	14

a. 0
b. 2
c. 8
d. 14

49. A physician's clinic sees 10 adolescent patients. Their weights were 79, 82, 78, 81, 87, 92, 99, 79, 80, and 84. What was the mean weight of the patients?
a. 79.0
b. 81.5
c. 83.0
d. 84.1

50. Given the following data and ANOVA results, decide if the researcher should accept or reject the following null hypothesis (H_0): There is no significant difference at the .05 level of significance in the number of inpatient autopsies performed at East, West, and North Hospitals for the past year.

Annual Autopsy Report for East, West, and North Hospitals

Month	East	West	North
January	4	2	12
February	4	1	12
March	4	1	34
April	5	1	5
May	7	1	43
June	1	2	23
July	0	2	20
August	0	4	19
September	6	1	16
October	7	5	23
November	4	3	17
December	5	2	12

Anova: Single factor

Summary

Groups	Count	Sum	Average	Variance
East	12	47	3.916666667	5.901515152
West	12	25	2.083333333	1.71969697
North	12	236	19.66666667	107.6969697

ANOVA

Source of Variation	SS	df	MS	F	P-value	F crit
Between groups	2242.388889	2	1121.194444	29.16784917	5.06887E-08	3.284924333
Within groups	1268.5	33	38.43939394			
Total	3510.888889	35				

a. Accept null hypothesis
b. Reject null hypothesis
c. Resulted in a Type I error
d. Not enough information to calculate

FORMULAS FOR COMMONLY COMPUTED HEALTH CARE RATES AND PERCENTAGES

$$\text{Average Daily Census} = \frac{\text{Total service days for the unit for the period}}{\text{Total number of days in the period}}$$

$$\text{Average Length of Stay} = \frac{\text{Total length of stay (discharge days)}}{\text{Total discharges (includes deaths)}}$$

$$\text{Percentage of Occupancy} = \frac{\text{Total service days for a period}}{\text{Total bed count days in the period}} \times 100$$

$$\text{Hospital Death Rate (Gross)} = \frac{\text{Number of deaths of inpatients in period}}{\text{Number of discharges (including deaths)}} \times 100$$

$$\text{Hospital Death Rate (Net)} = \frac{\text{Number of deaths of inpatients in period} - \text{Inpatient deaths} <48 \text{ hours}}{\text{Number of discharges (including deaths)} - \text{Inpatient deaths} <48 \text{ hours}} \times 100$$

$$\text{Gross Autopsy Rate} = \frac{\text{Total inpatient autopsies for a given period}}{\text{Total inpatient deaths for the period}} \times 100$$

$$\text{Net Autopsy Rate} = \frac{\text{Total inpatients for a given period}}{\text{Total inpatient deaths minus unautopsied coroners' or medical examiners' cases}} \times 100$$

$$\text{Hospital Autopsy Rate (Adjusted)} = \frac{\text{Total hospital autopsies}}{\text{Number of deaths of hospital patients whose bodies are available for hospital autopsy}} \times 100$$

$$\text{Postoperative Death Rate} = \frac{\text{Postoperative deaths}}{\text{Number of who die within 10 days of surgery}} \times 100$$

$$\text{Fetal Death Rate} = \frac{\text{Total number of intermediate and/or late fetal deaths for a period}}{\text{Total number of live births + intermediate and late fetal deaths for the period}} \times 100$$

$$\text{Neonatal Mortality Rate (Death Rate)} = \frac{\text{Total number of newborn deaths for a period}}{\text{Total number of newborn infant discharges (including deaths) for the period}} \times 100$$

$$\text{Maternal Mortality Rate (Death Rate)} = \frac{\text{Total number of obstetrical maternal deaths for a period}}{\text{Total number of obstetrical discharges (including deaths) for the period}} \times 100$$

$$\text{Caesarean Section Rate} = \frac{\text{Total number of caesarean sections performed in a period}}{\text{Total number of deliveries in the period (including caesarean sections)}} \times 100$$

$$\text{Infection Rate} = \frac{\text{Number of infection occurrences in a period}}{\text{Number of discharges in the period}} \times 100$$

$$\text{Postoperative Infection Rate} = \frac{\text{Number of infections in clean surgical cases in a period}}{\text{Number of surgical operations in the period}} \times 100$$

Quality Management and Performance Improvement

1. Clinical Quality Assessment
    a. Definitions of Terms
        i. Adverse event: the result of medical intervention in which the outcome was unforeseen and unexpected.
        ii. Benchmarking: performance comparison of one organization with that of a similar organization in that area
        iii. Compliance: process of meeting a prescribed set of standards or regulations to maintain active accreditation, licensure, or certification status
            1. Compulsory or voluntary
            2. Accreditation, licensure, certification
                a. Accreditation: the act of granting approval to a health care organization
                b. Licensure: the act of granting a health care organization or an individual health care practitioner permission to provide services of a defined scope in a limited geographical area
                c. Certification: approval for a health care organization to provide services to a specific group of beneficiaries
        iv. Error: an unintended act, either of omission or commission, or an act that does not achieve its intended outcome
        v. Indicator
            1. A quantifiable measurement or standard to distinguish acceptable from unacceptable performance.
            2. Performance measure that enables health care organizations to monitor a process to determine whether the organization is meeting process requirements
            3. May be established and implemented internally, externally, or generically
            4. May be written as ratio, such as number of admissions meeting criteria $\times$ 100 / number of admissions
        vi. Performance improvement: set of activities designed to increase the existing level of effectiveness or efficiency of existing performance
        vii. Quality: degree of excellence; superior in kind

       viii. Quality assurance: group of activities designed to measure the quality of a service, product, or process, with the intention to maintain a desired standard

       ix. Quality assessment: process of measuring and evaluating service activities to determine the current level of quality

       x. Quality control: a group of activities designed to detect and recognize positive and negative variances with the existing performance and to ensure predictable outcome

       xi. Quality improvements: methods or activities designated for the purpose of increasing the quality of a service or product

       xii. Quality management: the process of coordinating all quality activities as necessary towards the accomplishment of desirable performance outcome

       xiii. Sentinel event: an unexpected occurrence involving death or serious physical or psychological injury to a patient

       xiv. Root cause analysis: process for identifying the basic or causative factor that underlines variation in performance

       xv. Safety: all health care facilities are required to report all suspected and identified patient safety occurrences related to care or lack of care, that resulted, or could have resulted, to a patient.

       xvi. Total quality management: a mentality or philosophy based upon continuous quality improvement in the complete process of providing care

b. Historical Perspectives

       i. Through the law, regulations, standards, and required review processes, the federal, state, and local government and other stakeholders have influence in the quality management of health care facilities and their services.

           1. The 1700s

             a. In the mid-1700s, Pennsylvania Hospital becomes the model for the organization and development of hospitals.

             b. In 1760, New York State begins the practice of medical licensure.

             c. In 1771, New Jersey begins the practice of medical licensure.

           2. The 1800s

             a. In 1837, Massachusetts General Hospital sets limitations on clinical practice in the first granting of clinical privileges.

             b. In 1851, Massachusetts General Hospital establishes the first disease/procedure index by classifying patient disposition.

             c. In 1854, Florence Nightingale introduced new protocols for nurses during the Crimean War, that included Row nurses interacting with their patients and the ventilation and sanitation systems.

             d. In 1872, New England Hospital for Women and Children organizes a general training school for nurses.

             e. In 1874, American Medical Association encourages the creation of independent state licensing boards.

           3. The 1900s

             a. In 1910, Flexner Report indicates unacceptable variation in medical school curricula.

             b. In 1917, American College of Surgeons (ACS) establishes the Hospital Standardization Program (minimum standard of care).

c. In 1920, most medical colleges meet rigorous academic standards and are approved by the American Association of Medical Colleges.

d. In 1946, Hill-Burton Act establishes funding to build new hospitals.

e. In 1952, the Joint Commission on Accreditation of Hospitals (JCAH) was formed.

f. In 1953, JCAH published its first set of standards for hospitals.

g. In 1965, Congress passed the Social Security Amendment, which establishes Medicare and Medicaid coverage for citizens 65 years of age or older (PL 89-97).

h. In 1972, as a result of PL 92-603, professional standard review organizations (PSROs) are formed; they are now referred to as quality improvement organizations (QIOs).

i. In 1976, condition of participation was developed.

j. In 1980, the JCAH introduced accreditation standards.

k. In 1982, the Tax Equity and Fiscal Responsibility Act (TEFRA) changed the reimbursement structure from retrospective-determined cost-based payment to prospectively established fixed price determined by patients' final principal diagnosis, thus creating the prospective payment system (PPS).

l. In 1982, Peer Review Organizations (PRO) were created, now referred to as Quality Improvement Organizations (QIOs).

m. In 1982, state and regional peer review organizations contract with the Health Care Financing Administration (HCFA).

n. In 1983, prospective payment for Medicare was established (PL 98-21).

o. In 1983, HCPCS codes were developed and used to report health care services provided to Medicare and Medicaid (1986) patients treated in ambulatory care setting.

p. In 1985, JCAH revisited and revised its QA standards for monitoring and evaluating health care administrative and business operations.

q. In 1986, Health Care Quality Improvement Act (HCQIA; PL 99-660) established the National Practitioner Data Bank (NPDB), a clearinghouse to collect and release information to eligible parties for the purpose of identifying problematic or incompetent health care practitioners.

r. In 1985, JCAH developed a 10-step model for monitoring and evaluating effectiveness of QA efforts.

s. In 1986, condition of participation was expanded.

t. In 1986, JCAH developed the project called Agenda for Change.

u. In 1989, Agency for Health Care Policy and Research was created (PL 101-239).

v. In the 1990s, JCAH became the Joint Commission on Accreditation of Healthcare Organizations (JCAHO).

w. In the 1990s, JCAHO evaluation and monitoring standards expanded to include ambulatory care.

x. In 1991, the National Committee for Quality Assurance (NCQA) accredits managed care organizations (MCOs) using method similar to JCAHO.

y. In 1990, JCAHO monitoring and evaluation process expanded to include medical staff review activities.

z. In 1990, PRO is required to inform licensing boards of physician sanctions (PL 101-508).

aa. In 1992, accreditation manual transitioned from quality assurance to quality improvement.

bb. In 1994, JCAHO launched the Orion Project.

cc. In 1996, the Health Insurance Portability and Accountability Act (HIPAA) was passed (PL 104-191).

dd. In 1997, the ORYX initiative began to incorporate outcome measures and monitoring into health care accreditation processes.

ee. In 1990, Deming's total quality management philosophy begins to spread in U.S. health care.

ff. In 1990, JCAHO integrates quality improvement into the accreditation process.

gg. In 1993, Health Care Quality Improvement Program redirected PROs' focus toward improving quality.

4. The 2000s to present

   a. In 2001, ambulatory payment classification system is initiated.

   b. In 2002, HCFA becomes the Centers for Medicare and Medicaid Services (CMS).

   c. In 2002, peer review organizations (PROs) were renamed quality improvement organizations (QIOs).

   d. On April 14, 2001, the standard for privacy of individually identified health information (the privacy rule) took effect.

   e. By April 14, 2003, covered entity must comply.

   f. In January 2004, JCAHO begins unannounced tracer methodology for health care accreditation review process.

   g. On January 1, 2007, the JCAHO launched its new, shortened name—The Joint Commission (TJC)—and its new logo.

   h. During 2000s, TJC places emphasis on patient safety.

c. Pioneers of Quality Improvement (see Table 5-1)

   i. Avedis Donabedian

     1. Developed the three classes of quality assessment in health care

       a. Structure

         i. Indirectly assess care by looking at certain provider characteristics and the physical and organizational resources available to support delivery of care

         ii. Capability for providing care

         iii. Example: policies and procedures

       b. Process

         i. Interactions between patient and providers

         ii. Examines health care professional's decision-making processes as he or she directs a patient's course of treatment, or, at organizational level, investigates the procedures that guide operational decisions

         iii. Example: peer review of medical records

       c. Outcome

         i. Reviews end results or product of the patient's encounter with the system

         ii. Example: mortality rate

ii. Kaoru-Kaoru Ishikawa
  1. Early collaborator with Deming and Juran during their visits to Japan (1950s)
  2. Developed cause-and-effect diagram or fishbone
iii. Phillip Crosby
iv. W. Edwards Deming
v. Brian Joiner
vi. Joseph M. Juran

Table 5-1 Synopsis of Crosby, Deming, Joiner, and Juran's Philosophy of Quality Improvement

Crosby	Deming	Joiner	Juran
1. Quality means complete conformance to standards	1. Developed 14 principles and 7 deadly diseases	1. Developed the Joiner Triangle	1. Developed Trilogy process
2. Quality should mean zero defects	2. Emphasized quality processes	2. Believed quality must start at the top of the organization	2. Emphasized both quality process and quality outcomes
3. Advocated goal setting	3. Believed workers are naturally committed to excellent performance but managers desired directions	3. Believed in ensuring customer and staff loyalty and satisfaction	3. Believed in performance evaluation
4. Advocated merit pay	4. Disagreed with merit pay for performance	4. Advocated scientific approach to identifying cause of problem and developing solution plan	4. Advocated merit pay for performance
5. Advocated development of educational activities	5. Disagreed with continuous performance evaluation	5. Believed in teamwork, involvement, side-by-side management, and open door management	5. Advocated corrective action plan
6. Valued team decision making	6. Advocated continuous education for workers		6. Advocated team building and group process
	7. Advocated team building and group process		7. Believed in developing quality standards to monitor performance

    d. Quality Assessment Models

        i. Deming's 14 principles

            1. Create consistency towards purpose of the product or service

            2. Adopt new philosophy

            3. Focus on quality process flow of the product rather than mass inspection

            4. Price tag does not always indicate quality; end practice of rewarding based on price tag; embrace long-term relationship, trust, loyalty, and honesty

            5. Constantly assess and improve all processes

            6. Institute on-the-job training, job orientation, continued education, equipment training, etc.

            7. Institute leadership, remove workmanship barriers, be realistic, understand all staff cannot be above average

            8. Drive out fear (no one performs best under fear)

            9. Break down barriers within the organization by improving communication

            10. Eliminate numerical quotas; quota causes loss, chaos, dissatisfaction, burnout, boredom, turnover, etc.

            11. Eliminate quick-fix solution

            12. Eliminate inconsistent slogans and exhortation

            13. Create an open atmosphere of creativity; identify and uplift talented staff

            14. Involve everybody within the organization in working toward the transformation or improvement of the organization

        ii. Deming's seven deadly diseases in quality management

            1. Lack of vision, mission, plan, and purpose of the product or service

            2. Emphasizing short-time profits

            3. Inconsistent, unfair, and unmeasurable evaluation, and merit rating

            4. Employee job dissatisfaction

            5. Customer, vendor, and community dissatisfaction

            6. Excessive medical cost

            7. Excessive cost of liability

         iii. Juran's principles

            1. Product or service must meet customer's need

            2. Product or service must be free from deficiencies

    e. Quality Improvement

        i. Definition: characterized by the recipient of the service or product. Therefore, it is essential that quality is built into all services, processes, and products in health care delivery systems.

        ii. Methodologies and models for performing, assessing, and building quality into health care services

            1. Internal

                a. Vision

                b. Mission

                c. Goals

            2. External

                a. TJC

                    i. Joint Commission on Accreditation of Healthcare Organizations

                b. CARF

                    i. Commission on Accreditation of Rehabilitation Facilities

    c. QIOs (formerly PROs)

    d. Quality improvement organizations (formerly peer review organizations, or PROs)

        i. Peer review organizations

    e. CMS

        i. Centers for Medicaid and Medicare Services, previously known as Health Care Financing Administration (HCFA)

    f. HIPAA

        i. Health Insurance Portability and Accountability Act

  iii. Development and refinement of TJC standards relating to quality improvement (see Table 5-2)

  iv. In each of the cases in Table 5-3, the court ruled that the hospital and medical staff have the right and obligation to oversee quality of professional services rendered by the medical staff.

  v. Health care accrediting and licensing agencies (see Table 5-4)

f. Methods to Improve Quality

  i. Department of Health and Human Services (HHS)

    1. In November 2001, announced the quality initiative to assure quality health care for all Americans through accountability and public disclosure.

    2. Hospital Compare: a tool that provides information on 20 hospital quality measures that assess how well hospitals in a geographical area care for all their adult patients with particular medical conditions (see Table 5-5).

Table 5-2 Development and Refinement of TJC Standards Relating to Quality Improvement

Year	Responsibility
1952	Expanded standard of care
	Established structured set of standards
1972	Established a standard for medical audits
1975	Required hospitals to demonstrate consistency in care
1979	Required coordination and integration of all quality-of-care activities into hospital-wide program
1985	Ten-step model for quality evaluation introduced
	Hospital required to monitor the following: medical record, surgical cases, blood usage, drug usage, pharmacy, and therapeutics
1986	Launched *Agenda for Change*
1994	Accreditation manual for hospitals changes from departmental standards to functions critical to patient care
2004	Changed from scheduled and announced site visit to unscheduled and unannounced site visit with tracer methodology site review

Table 5-3 Relevant Court Cases

Year	Case	Decision
1965	Darling vs. Charleston Community Hospital	Court ruled that the hospital must assume certain responsibilities for care of the patient. The courts ruled that a hospital was negligent for permitting a general practitioner to perform orthopedic surgery. The court ruled that the hospital had a duty to apply reasonable standards to the practice of its physicians because it was responsible for the privileging of physicians on its staff.
1973	Gonzales vs. Nork and Mercy Hospital	The court found the hospital negligent if it knew, had reason to know, or should have known of the surgeon's incompetence.
1981	John vs. Misericordia Hospital	The court found that the hospital owes a duty to its patients in selecting medical staff members and granting privileges.

Table 5-4 Health Care Accrediting and Licensing Agencies

Abbreviation	Agency	Areas of Responsibility
AAAHC	Accreditation Association for Ambulatory Health Care	Specializes in assisting ambulatory health care organizations to improve quality of their services
ACS	American College of Surgeons	Initiated standard review in health care practices
CARF	Commission on Accreditation of Rehabilitation Facilities	Responsible for evaluating quality of care in organizations providing rehabilitative treatment
HEDIS	Health Plan Employer Data and Information Set	Responsible for collecting data on managed care plans
TJC (formerly JCAHO)	The Joint Commission (formerly Joint Commission on Accreditation of Healthcare Organizations)	Refined ACS standards and assumed responsibility for accreditation
NCQA	National Committee for Quality Assurance	Certifies qualified health care professional in quality assurance
NAHQ	National Association of Healthcare Quality	Certifies qualified health care professional in promoting continuous QI efforts

Table 5-5 Hospital Quality Measures

Condition	Measure
Acute myocardial infarction (AMI)/Heart attack	Aspirin at arrival
	Aspirin at discharge
	Beta-blocker at arrival
	Beta-blocker at discharge
	ACE inhibitor or angiotensin receptor blocker (ARB) for left ventricular systolic dysfunction
	Smoking cessation
	Thrombolytic agent received within 30 minutes of hospital arrival
	Percutaneous coronary intervention (PCI) received within 120 minutes of hospital arrival
Heart failure	Left ventricular function assessment
	ACE inhibitor or angiotensin receptor blocker (ARB) for left ventricular systolic dysfunction
	Comprehensive discharge instructions
	Smoking cessation
Pneumonia	Initial antibiotic received within 4 hours of hospital arrival
	Pneumococcal vaccination status
	Blood culture performed before first antibiotic received
	Smoking cessation
	Oxygenation assessment
	Appropriate initial antibiotic selection
Surgical infection prevention	Prophylactic antibiotic received within 1 hour prior to surgical incision
	Prophylactic antibiotics discontinued within 24 hours after surgery end time

Source: U.S. Department of Health and Human Services, Centers for Medicare and Medicaid Services. Available at: http://www.cms.hhs.gov/HospitalQualityInits/downloads/HospitalOverview200512.pdf.

    ii. Clinical practice guidelines
1. Systematically developed statements used to assist provider and patient decisions about appropriate health care for specific clinical circumstances
2. Developed with the goal of standardizing clinical decision making
3. Meant to be flexible and do not necessarily apply in every case
4. Example: American Diabetes Association recommends statins be considered for people with diabetes over the age of 40 who have a total cholesterol level ≥ 135 and that there be a blood pressure goal of < 130/80 mmHg for people with diabetes.

    iii. Clinical protocols
1. Treatment recommendations often based on guidelines
2. The step-by-step description of an accepted procedure recommended by an authoritative body
3. Example: If the blood sugar is > 150, give ____ units of a specific type of insulin. (It would also state how often the therapy could be given, and what tests or evaluations are to be performed and when, to determine the effectiveness of therapy, and when the physician must be contacted because something is not working.)
4. Protocols frequently take the form of branching grids, with yes and no answers, leading to directions based on the answers. (For example: Is blood sugar > 200? If yes, give [dose]; if no, is it < 100?)
5. Sources for clinical practice guidelines and protocols
   a. Agency for Healthcare Research and Quality (AHRQ)
   b. National Guideline Clearinghouse: a public resource for evidence-based clinical practice guidelines

    iv. Tools for implementing clinical guidelines and protocols
1. Critical paths: display goals for patients and provide the corresponding ideal sequence and timing of staff actions to achieve those goals with optimal efficiency
2. Clinical pathways: structured plans of care
3. Care maps: multidisciplinary standards that outline the processes of care and expected outcomes within predetermined time frames

    v. TJC recommends an evaluation and monitoring model to advance the transition from a quality assessment approach to a concept of improving quality. TJC developed a 10-step process to achieve the goals and objectives of a monitoring and evaluation program.
1. Assign responsibility
2. Delineate scope of care
3. Identify important aspects of care
4. Identify indicators
5. Establish thresholds
6. Collect and organize data
7. Initiate evaluation
8. Take actions to improve care and services
9. Assess the effectiveness of actions and maintain the gain
10. Communicate results to affected individuals and groups

     vi. Avedis Donabedian developed a sound model for assessing quality in the health care arena. Donabedian's model is based on the structure, process, and outcome models for assessing measurement approach to quality.

        1. Structure: measures the ability of the organization to coordinate all its resources such as physical, human resources, facility, technology, policies and procedures, financial, and other characteristics as needed to successfully support the delivery of health care services

        2. Process: measures the ability of the organization to foster and focus on positive interactions between the receiver of health care service and the provider of service throughout the course of the care

        3. Outcome: measures and focuses on the end result of the care provided and the overall satisfaction level of the patient with the care received

    vii. The plan, do, check, act (PDCA) system was developed by Walter Shewhart and W. Edwards Deming and became popular beginning in Japan. It has become one of the most commonly used models in quality improvement.

        1. Planning phase: data collection and analysis to propose a solution for an identified problem

        2. Do (or implementation) phase: tests the proposed solutions

        3. Checking phase: investigates the effectiveness of solutions over a period of time

        4. Act phase: formalizes the changes that have proved effective in the do and check stages

   viii. Brian Joiner, a supporter of W. Edwards Deming's philosophy, developed a seven-step method to assess quality.

        1. Define the project

        2. Study the current situation

        3. Analyze the potential causes

        4. Implement a solution

        5. Check the results

        6. Standardize the improvement

        7. Establish future plans

     ix. Re and Krousel Wood developed a six-step method.

        1. Record adverse or other outcomes of interest

        2. Use statistical techniques to determine variation

        3. Seek suggestions on a trial basis

        4. Monitor results

        5. If improvement occurs, implement suggestions and standardize

        6. Seek further suggestions for improvement

g. Project Management

     i. Rooted in engineering and oriented toward quantitative application methods

    ii. Initiation

        1. Occurs when participants observe there is a gap between organization performance and expected outcomes

        2. Project teams take on multiple tasks.
            a. Identify improvement opportunity
            b. Research and define performance expectations
            c. Implement process education
            d. Measure performance
            e. Document and communicate findings
            f. Analyze and compare internal and external data
     iii. Planning
        1. Identifies expected impact on organization
        2. Design
            a. Development of alternative solutions
            b. Gantt charts
                i. Project management tool used to schedule important activities
                ii. Charts divide a horizontal scale into days, weeks, or months and a vertical scale into project activities or tasks.
            c. PERT Charts
     iv. Execution
        1. Once plan is completed, execution begins
        2. Installation of equipment or construction begins
        3. Training
        4. Measure performance
     v. Closure
        1. Evaluation and control
  h. Role of HIM Staff in QI
     i. Participate in QI planning
     ii. Identify deviations from norm
     iii. Identify areas needing improvement
     iv. Provide chart/information
     v. Collect data
     vi. Analyze data
     vii. Benchmark collected data
     viii. Interpret data
     ix. Display data
     x. Present data
     xi. Implement required changes
     xii. Monitor and evaluate changes
     xiii. Communicate
     xiv. Update / revise / or create supportive policy
  i. Internal Customers of HIM: (quality improvement is fostered by identifying customers and their needs and tailoring services to meet customers' needs.)
     i. Other HIM staff within HIM department
     ii. Receptionists
     iii. Physicians
     iv. Laboratory technicians
     v. Nurses and other medical assistants
     vi. Business services
     vii. Radiology technician
     viii. Pharmacists and pharmacy staff
     ix. Janitorial staff
     x. Physical therapist, respiratory therapist
     xi. Social workers and social service staff

      xii. Patient advocates, volunteers

      xiii. Eligibility counselor

      xiv. Risk management staff

      xv. Utilization review staff

      xvi. Quality assurance staff

      xvii. Business associates

      xviii. Students and researchers

      xix. Office of patient financial service

      xx. Billing office

      xxi. Other departments

j. External Customer to HIM Department (Some external customers can also be internal customers at a given time, based on the role-reversal functions.)

      i. Patient

      ii. Vendor

      iii. Physician

      iv. Licensing agencies

      v. Accreditation agencies

      vi. Law enforcement agencies with needs to know

      vii. Medical examiners

      viii. Patient advocates

      ix. Patient's identified personal representatives

      x. Local, state, and federal agencies with needs to know

k. Data Collection

      i. The primary source of clinical data in the health care industry is the medical record, because it contains subjective and objective information related to the episode of care. Other data such as insurance, registry, reimbursement, and census data are considered to be secondary data sources, because data were taken from the medical record and entered into the subcategory of health-related records. Primary data are further classified into identifiable data or patient-specific data, and secondary data are further classified into aggregate or non-patient-specific data.

      ii. Methods for collecting data

         1. Questionnaire

         2. Survey

         3. Face-to-face interview

         4. Mail

         5. Phone

         6. Primary

         7. Secondary

l. Service and Products

      i. The HIM management must establish a service delivery and expectation standard for all services and products provided. It is important that the HIM staff knows the deadlines for the specific services or products the department has to offer.

      ii. See Table 5-6 for an example of service and product delivery.

m. Services and Products Offered by HIM Department

      i. Chart retrieval

      ii. Coding

      iii. Abstracting

      iv. Chart analysis

      v. Release of information

Table 5-6 Example of Service and Product Delivery

Service	Receivers of Service(s) (with a need to know)	Time Frame
Release of information	1. Business services within your facility 2. Risk management staff 3. Utilization review staff 4. Quality assurance staff 5. Business associates 6. Researchers 7. Office of patient financial service 8. Billing office 9. Patient 10. Health care providers 11. Licensing agencies 12. Accreditation agencies 13. Law enforcement agencies 14. Medical examiners 15. Patient advocates 16. Patient's identified personal representatives 17. Local, state, and federal agencies 18. Others	With the exception of stat request, all other requests are processed within 5 working days from the date received.

    vi. Disclosure tracking
    vii. Record processing
    viii. Filing
    ix. Chart maintenance
    x. Record imaging and indexing
    xi. Transcription
    xii. Hard copy and electronic storage
    xiii. Research processing
    xiv. Loose sheet processing
    xv. Chart tracking
n. Tools for Collecting and Displaying Data
    i. Data Analysis: determine what type of data are available, then determine how to display those data.
    ii. Types of Data
      1. Nominal: category of data that can be named. It is sometimes called categorical data. Gender and ethnicity are examples of nominal data. Nominal data are best displayed using bar graphs or pie charts.
      2. Ordinal: category of data that can be ranked or ordered. It is sometimes called ranked data. This type of data allows the

researcher to determine how respondents feel about a particular issue, for example by using a Likert scale (1 = strongly disagree, 2 = disagree, 3 = neutral, 4 = agree, and 5 = strongly agree). The data are best displayed using bar graphs and pie charts.

3. Discrete: category of data that represent a distinct and separate value. Number of children in the family, number of suspended claims, and number of coding errors are examples of discrete data.

4. Continuous: category of data that has infinite number as a possible value. Measurements that have decimal points or values such as vital signs are examples of continuous data. They are best displayed using histograms or run charts.

iii. Critical elements of data collection
   1. Understanding what to observe and collect
   2. Consistency of data collection
   3. Timeliness
   4. Design of data collection tools
   5. Design of users' guide or instruction sheet
   6. Orientation
   7. Criteria for data selection
   8. Data display and presentation

iv. Data analysis and presentation
   1. Bar graphs
      a. Simple: This can be used to measure different types of data that cannot be broken into subcategories, e.g., John has 5 misfiles; Susan has 20 coding errors; Paula processed 500 medical record disclosures in January.
      b. Clustered: gives a breakdown of simple bar graphs, e.g., John misfiled 2 OB charts and 3 ER charts. Susan has 5 codes that were missing fifth digits, 11 codes that were missing fourth digits, and 4 codes that were not appropriate for outpatient services. Paula processed 175 legal requests, 50 subpoena requests, 200 disability requests, and 75 insurance requests in the month of January.
      c. Stratified: allows display of total and subtotal at the same time
   2. Pareto chart: type of bar graph that displays categories of data in descending order of frequency or significance
   3. Pie chart: illustrates how an individual component of chart relates to the whole
   4. Radar chart: displays before and after data. It is used to identify the strengths and weaknesses of an activity. It also identifies opportunities for improvement.
   5. Run chart: a line graph that displays the progress and variations of data over time. It is also known as a time plot. It is used to identify existing processes needing improvement and to show whether the improvement was successful. Its trend and pattern can be identified easily by its movement away from the midpoint (average).
   6. Scatter diagram: indicates a relationship between two variables
   7. Storyboards: a graphic and/or text display tool used to communicate details of principal investigator's activities on a poster

v. Idea-generating techniques

    1. Brainstorming

        a. Used to generate ideas to encourage creativity and a free flow of ideas; example of a brainstorming topic can be customer-satisfaction form design

        b. Tips for conducting brainstorming session

            i. Allow each person to generate as many ideas as possible

            ii. Do not label any idea as good or bad

            iii. Provide a comfortable, free, and informal environment

            iv. Limit group to no less than 5 and no more than 13 people

            v. Limit discussion to one hour or less

    2. Nominal group technique

        a. Comparable to brainstorming

        b. The group members generate the ideas; however, after ideas are generated, they are objectively ranked or rated in the order of priority.

        c. It is a technique that allows group to narrow the focus of discussion or make decision without extended circular discussion.

vi. Data organization

    1. Cause and effect diagrams (also called fishbone diagram); utilized to separate root causes for an effect or problem

    2. Check sheet: indicates how often an event occurs (check sheets contribute to data for the creation of histograms, run charts, etc.)

    3. Decision matrix: grid design to rank ideas and proposals. It allows for scoring of each alternative and helps prioritize objectives.

    4. Flow chart

        a. Pictorial illustration of sequenced steps to complete a process

        b. Utilize multiple shapes (oval, rectangle, diamond), lines, and arrows to create a flowchart.

        c. Determine the starting point, the middle point, and the ending point of the process.

        d. All activities from end to finish must be arranged in a sequential order.

        e. The oval at the top indicates the starting point, and the oval at the bottom indicates the ending point.

        f. The rectangles in the middle indicate the activities that must be performed during the process.

        g. The diamond shapes indicate areas of the decision-making process.

        h. Benefits of flowchart usage (see Figure 5-1)

            i. Identifies unnecessary delay in process

            ii. Identify work redundancy, misunderstanding, and inefficiency

vii. Survey or questionnaire

    1. Gathers feedback from a large group of people

    2. Examples of auditing forms are in Table 5-7 and Table 5-8

o. Performance Improvement Plan

    i. Purpose of performance improvement

        1. All performance improvement plans must define the purpose of the plan. The plan also must be established in accordance with the organization's vision statement in mind. The plan will include the goals and objectives. For example, the purpose of a performance improvement plan for HIM release of information can be to

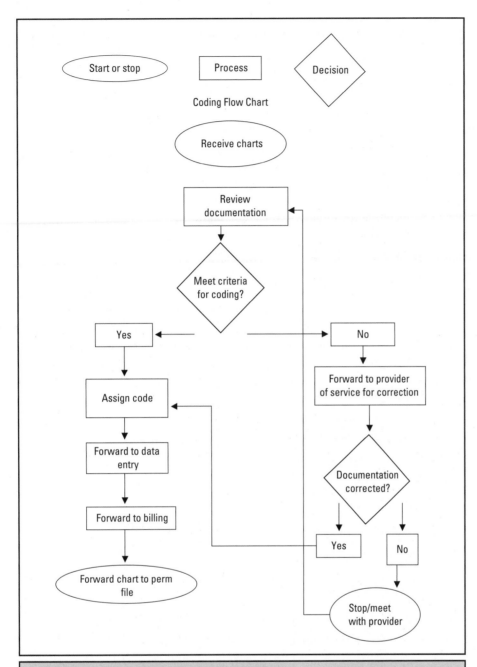

Figure 5-1 Example of a Flow Chart

Table 5-7 Example of an Auditing Form

	General Medical Records Auditing Form for Improving Medical Record Documentation		
#	**Criteria**	**Yes**	**No**
1	Does documentation in the medical record conform to the organization's policies?		
2	Are the documentations in the medical record legible?		
3	Are all entries dated?		
4	Is patient's identifying demographic information documented?		
5	Is there an evidence of consent for treatment?		
6	Does the medical record chart contain patient identification data?		
7	As appropriate, is there evidence of informed consent?		
8	Was the information documented in a timely manner?		
9	Was the documentation pattern uniform or consistent?		
10	Was there an evidence of provider authentication?		
11	Were the errors corrected appropriately?		
12	Was there evidence on known allergy documentation?		
13	Were all forms used in the chart approved by the organization?		
14	Did all forms in the chart belong to the same patient?		
15	Was there a documentation of history and physical?		
16	Was there evidence that a provider has reviewed consultation reports?		
17	Was documentation of reason for visit present?		
18	Was there documentation of present medical illness?		
19	Was there documentation of past medical histories?		
20	Was there documentation of clinical assessment?		
21	Were vital signs documented?		
22	Was there documentation of special studies ordered?		
23	Was there documentation of treatment plan?		
24	Was there documentation of medical findings or diagnosis?		
25	Was there documentation of referral?		

Table 5-8 Example of an Auditing Form

	Specific Medical Records Auditing Form for Assessment of Patient Care		
#	Criteria	Yes	No
1	Was patient assessed for pain?		
2	Is patient currently having pain?		
3	Was the location of the pain documented?		
4	Was the intensity of the pain documented?		
5	Was the duration of the pain documented?		
6	Was the quality of the pain documented?		
7	Was the associated contributing factor documented?		
8	Was current or previous intervention documented?		
9	Was the outcome of the intervention documented?		
10	Does patient assessment include physical assessment?		
11	Does patient assessment include social assessment?		
12	Does patient assessment include psychological assessment?		
13	Does patient assessment include spiritual assessment?		
14	Does patient assessment include cultural assessment?		
15	Was pain management or care plan documented?		
16	Was treatment or medication documented?		
17	Was the patient and/or patient's family educated regarding pain?		
18	Was the critical point regarding patient education documented?		
19	As appropriate, was the patient reassessed?		
20	Was patient care coordinated among other appropriate professionals?		

provide a framework to ensure all disclosures are disclosed efficiently in support of patient confidentiality and privacy.

    ii. Elements of performance improvement plan

        1. Statement of mission

        2. Statement of vision

        3. Objectives

        4. Organizational values and culture

        5. Leadership

        6. Organizational structure

        7. Performance measure objectives

        8. Methodology for improvement

        9. Annual review plan

        10. Communication models

    iii. Scope of activities

        1. Includes an overall assessment of the function to be performed, with special focus on continual process improvement for all related activities

        2. Example: The scope of HIM ROI performance improvement plan can include but is not limited to the following:

            a. Form design (authorization for uses and disclosures)

            b. Forms management and control

            c. Satisfaction of patients, providers, staff

            d. Validity of authorizations

            e. Disclosure logs

            f. Tracking of disclosure

p. Retention of Performance Improvement Data and Reports

    i. All performance improvement (PI) data and reports are kept according to the facilities policies and procedures relating to PI data retention. However, TJC recommends that PI data are kept for a minimum of 3 years, from one accreditation to another re-accreditation, and until any recommendations have been addressed fully.

    ii. Confidentiality statement

        1. All performance improvement information must be maintained in a locked file cabinet within the designated quality management service department or administrative offices as appropriate.

        2. The performance improvement data, reports, and minutes shall be accessible only to those participating in the program.

        3. Performance improvement information, records, proceedings, and communication submitted to performance improvement committees or their agents are protected from disclosure under state codes such as the Texas Health and Safety Code Ann. Section 161.031 and 161.032, Texas Medical Practice Act, Tex. Occ. Code Ann. Section 151.022(2), (8) and 160.007.

q. Continuous Quality Improvement (CQI)

    i. CQI is a never-ending cycle. It is a concept that came out of industry. Rather than creating a culture of blame if things do not go well, the focus is on a team approach to improvement that rewards the group when things get better.

    ii. Benefits of CQI

        1. A continuously learning organization

        2. Improvement projects that are strategically aligned to give knowledge to key customers, providers, and suppliers at every level of the hospital

    3. An integrated, customer-focused business plan for all organization functions

    4. Improved satisfaction among patients, physician, employees, and payers

    5. Reduced expenses as a result of removing waste, needless complexity, and rework

    6. Assistance with meeting accreditation standards

iii. FOCUS

    1. Find a process to improve

    2. Organize to improve a process

    3. Clarify what is known

    4. Understand variation

    5. Select a process improvement

iv. Process improvement plan model (see Figure 5-2)

    1. Plan

        a. Most complex part of the process; unrealistic planning will result in unachievable outcome

        b. Identify the specific service to improve

        c. Define the target population(s)

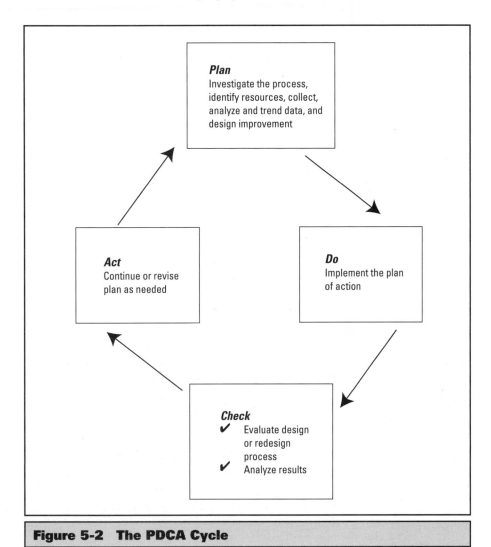

Figure 5-2   The PDCA Cycle

        d. Define the unique needs and characteristics of the target population(s)

        e. Define and acknowledge the deviation from standard

        f. Develop service to meet the needs of the target population(s)

        g. Determine data needed to monitor the improvement

        h. Create a timeline of resources, activities, training, and target dates

        i. Develop a data collection plan, the tools for measuring outcomes, and thresholds for determining when targets have been met

2. Do

        a. Directly correlated with the effectiveness of the plan phase

        b. Educate all staff as appropriate

        c. Develop continued or ongoing staff education plan

        d. Develop or revise policies and procedures

        e. Implement interventions

        f. Collect data to ensure validity and reliability of conformance to standard.

3. Check

        a. These are the assessments of the plan and do phases; used to validate effectiveness.

        b. Analyze collected data

        c. Study the results of data and evaluate reasons for variation

        d. Modify the plan as necessary

        e. Ask key questions

           i. What specifically is being assessed?

           ii. Does the tool capture the desired data?

           iii. What does the finding indicate about the process?

           iv. Were the desired outcomes achieved?

4. Act

        a. This is a determination phase.

        b. Act on what is learned and determine the next steps.

        c. A determination is made to continue with the plan as implemented or to revise the whole or certain steps of the plan due to findings.

        d. If the intervention is successful, work to make it part of standard operating procedure.

        e. If it is not successful, analyze sources of failure, design new solutions, and repeat the PDCA cycle.

r. Understanding TJC

    i. Accreditation process: to earn and maintain accreditation, a facility must undergo an on-site survey by a TJC survey team at least every 3 years. The objective of the survey is to evaluate the facility and provide educational guidance that will help the staff continue to improve the facility's performance.

    ii. Survey team: the survey team may spend several days at the facility observing activities, interviewing patients and staff, and reviewing documents. The team spends a significant amount of time observing staff provide care. The team may track a patient in person and or through medical records to find out how the systems and processes work in supporting patient care. The surveyors do not judge directly whether the care given to a specific patient is good or bad, right or wrong. Rather, they determine what activities are carried out, how well they are performed.

      iii. Evaluation: different members of the survey team may look at specific areas of the facility according to their expertise, but they work together closely at every step, integrating their findings to reach conclusions. At the end of the survey, the team scores the facility on how well it meets the standards.

      iv. Figure 5-3 provides a preparedness survey form; Figure 5-4 provides a mock survey form; Figure 5-5 provides a variance tracking record; and Figure 5-6 provides sample daily key notes.

2. Utilization Management

  a. Defined

      i. Utilization management or utilization review is a method of controlling health care costs and quality of care by reviewing the appropriateness and necessity of care provided to patients. Utilization management or utilization review is embedded in a hospital quality program. The goal of a utilization management department is to review the facility's efficiency in the provision of services and determine whether staff are using resources in the most cost-effective manner. Good utilization management prevents underutilization and overutilization of services, resources, and facilities are outcomes.

      ii. Public Law 92-603 of 1972 established professional standards review organizations (PSROs). These organizations comprise licensed physicians whose goal is to determine if services provided were medically necessary and cost effective.

      iii. TEFRA (1982) replaced PSROs with PROs. Fifty-three PROs, now known as quality improvement organizations (QIOs), are responsible for each state, territory, and the District of Columbia. These non-governmental agencies are empowered to evaluate performance relative to quality and appropriateness of service and can recommend punitive action to CMS.

      iv. CMS and TJC require UM (Utilization Management) programs by law.

      v. NCQA state managed care plans must monitor medical care delivered to detect possible over- or underutilization of services. Managed care plans must have a written UM (Utilization Management) plan and an appeals process.

  b. Some Medical Services Requiring Utilization Management

      i. Inpatient confinement

         1. Surgical and non-surgical confinements

         2. Skilled nursing facility

         3. Rehabilitation facility

         4. Inpatient hospice

         5. Maternity confinement

      ii. Reconstructive procedures and procedures that may be considered cosmetic

      iii. Selected durable medical equipment

      iv. Medical injectables

      v. Surgical procedures

      vi. Elective (nonemergent) transportation by ambulance or medical van and all transfers via air ambulance

      vii. All home health care services

      viii. Requests for in-network level of benefits for nonparticipating physicians and providers for nonemergent services

I.M. Standard	TJC Standard Example	Compliance Score				Responsible Person/ Target Date
		0	1	2	N/A	
I.M.	The hospital has a plan in place to continually meet the health information needs of the users.	☐	☐	☐	☐	
I.M.	The privacy and confidentiality of the health records are maintained.	☐	☐	☐	☐	
I.M.	Health information is maintained in a timely and accurate manner.	☐	☐	☐	☐	
I.M.	Health information is maintained in an efficient manner to effectively capture, retrieve, and disseminate the information.	☐	☐	☐	☐	

0=Insufficient compliance, 1=Partial compliance, 2=Satisfactory compliance, N/A=Not applicable
Based on: The Joint Commission. Comprehensive Accreditation Manual for Hospitals: The Official Handbook. Chicago, 2007.

Figure 5-3 Example of TJC Preparedness Survey Form

The following is a sample of a site visit survey to record the time, date, attendees, surveyed areas, survey methodology, findings, impressions, and recommended solutions.

Blank Form	Sample Completed Form
Date:	April 4, 20XX
Start: End:	Start: 10:30 AM End: 12:30 PM
Staff/Dept in Attendance:	Staff/Dept in Attendance:
	Jane: Nursing Department
	Debra: HIM Department
	Paul: Pharmacy Department
	Carol: Social Services Department
Area Surveyed:	Area Surveyed:
	Examination room
	Intake area
	Medical record
	Restroom
	Educational and instructional area
Method of Survey:	Method of Survey:
	Medical record review
	Environmental review
	Patient tracing
Findings:	Findings:
	1. Closed medical record review revealed 8 out of 25 charts reviewed have no documentation of H&P on surgical patients
Recommendation:	Recommendation:
	1. Conduct immediate focus audit
	2. Educate providers of service and support staff
	3. Educate HIM staff
	4. Conduct mock daily, weekly, or monthly reviews
Overall Impression:	Overall Impression:

Figure 5-4   Example of Blank and Completed JCAHO Survey Forms

Completed by: _____

Instructions:
- ➤ Record the area surveyed, e.g., lab
- ➤ Record the date the area was surveyed (some site visits may last for several days or weeks)
- ➤ Record the findings (activities rated below expected standards)
- ➤ Record the corrective action plan(s) needed to correct the deficiency
- ➤ Record the person responsible for the corrective action plan
- ➤ Record the status of the correction, with the date it was monitored or resolved
- ➤ Monitor and document until the problem is resolved within the established target date
- ➤ Communicate standard compliance status as appropriate

Area Surveyed	Date	Findings	Action	Contact Person	Progress/ Comment
					[ ] Resolved Date_____ [ ] Pending
					[ ] Resolved Date_____ [ ] Pending
					[ ] Resolved Date_____ [ ] Pending
					[ ] Resolved Date_____ [ ] Pending
					[ ] Resolved Date_____ [ ] Pending

Figure 5-5   Example of JCAHO Variance Tracking Record

1. Post site visit announcements
2. Always monitor and be aware of surroundings
3. Update, review, revise, and create policies and procedures as appropriate
4. Review all manuals and get clarification when needed
5. Assure that all posted signs are posted correctly
6. Organize your environment for positive impression
7. Correct any previously identified problems
8. Mentally and physically prepare yourself for the day
9. Be ready to discuss what you do
10. Be prepared to lead a tour of your facility
11. Think about how to educate the visitors about your service
12. Clear any obstructions in your area or hallway
13. Know the continuum process flow of your site
14. Have all keys available
15. Remember patient's rights, privacy, and confidentiality
16. Remember to wear comfortable, professional working clothes with name badge
17. Be ready to demonstrate that you are prepared in case of emergency
18. Know how to alert staff and patients during emergencies
19. Remember the types of safety in-services you have attended in the last year (fire, emergency preparedness, injury prevention, etc.)
20. Know the escape route
21. Know where, why, how, and when to use different types of fire extinguisher
22. You may have to explain your role during an internal or external disaster
23. Know emergency contact numbers (emergency, fire, etc.)
24. Check the environment for hazardous materials
25. Be familiar with abuse, neglect, exploitation, and advance directives
26. Check refrigerators, drawers, cabinets, and under the sink
27. Remember that it is not allowed in the premises if it is not listed on the MSDS list
28. Think about infection control at all times
29. Remember to always address the surveyor by name (Mr., Ms., Dr., etc.)
30. Know the mission, vision, and values statement
31. Always focus attention on patient
32. Be ready to explain or show how you trace patient through the continuum of care
33. Be ready to explain your role when critical lab value is identified
34. Think about your processes from the beginning of patient referral to the end
35. Remember it did not happen unless it was documented
36. Remember to document appropriately and completely
37. Log off on computers when you are done using them
38. Remember, do not place patient identifying information in the trash can—always shred
39. Remember HIPAA and patient confidentiality during disclosure of information
40. Be ready to discuss your organizational procedures during internal and external data abstractions for research and other legally mandated reporting

Figure 5-6   Example of JCAHO Daily Key Notes for Site Accreditation Visits

     ix. Dental implants and oral appliances

     x. Services that may be considered investigational or experimental

     xi. Special programs

         1. Mental health, substance abuse, or behavioral health services

         2. Maternity management programs, including genetic testing, antenatal testing, prenatal consultations and counseling

         3. Infertility programs

         4. Pharmacy precertification for certain pharmaceuticals

         5. Major organ transplant evaluations and transplants, including but not limited to kidney, liver, heart, lung, and pancreas, and bone marrow replacement or stem cell transfer after high-dose chemotherapy

         6. Outpatient imaging precertification for CTs (Computed Tomography Scan), MRI (Magnetic Resonance Imaging), nuclear cardiology, PET (Positron Emission Tomography) scans

c. Case Management

     i. Defined as coordination, development, and provision of patient care plans for the patients with complicated cases. The goal is to provide patient care plan in a cost-effective manner to patients with complicated cases.

     ii. Peer review

         1. Crucial component of Medicare reimbursement process

         2. Individual hospitals submit claims for payment of covered services to fiscal intermediary by way of a standardized billing form.

         3. For Medicare claims, fiscal intermediary transmits duplicate of all claims for a review period to PRO to determine:

            a. Whether services are reasonable and medically necessary

            b. Whether services could be furnished effectively on an outpatient basis as opposed to inpatient admission

            c. Medical necessity, reasonableness, and appropriate inpatient services

            d. Inappropriate medical or other practices resulting in inappropriate admission or fraudulent billing for reimbursement

            e. Validity of diagnostic and procedural information submitted to request reimbursement

            f. Completeness and adequacy of care provided

            g. Whether the quality of services meets professionally recognized standards of care

         4. The goal of the peer review is for the PRO physician reviewer to identify three primary issues.

            a. Utilization concerns

            b. Quality concerns

            c. Diagnosis Related Groups' concerns

d. Utilization Review Process

     i. Preadmission review (prospective review)

         1. Review prior to admission that determines if the procedure and reason for potential admission is appropriate and necessary

         2. Consists of comparing patient's medical condition with standard criteria that specify clinical indications for admission; criteria are intensity of service/severity of illness criteria (IS/SI)

     ii. Admission review: review at time of admission to determine medical necessity and appropriateness

      iii. Concurrent review: review of medical necessity for tests and procedures ordered during an inpatient hospitalization

      iv. Discharge review: review at time of discharge that determines if the patient meets specific discharge screen criteria. The discharge review may involve arranging appropriate home health care services for the discharged patient.

      v. Retrospective review: review conducted by the PRO for evaluation of quality issues, cost and outliers issues, and issues of utilization management and appropriateness of care

   e. Centers for Medicare/Medicaid Services (CMS)

      i. Scope of work

         1. Under the authority of the Health Care Financing Administration (now CMS), PSROs (now QIOs) began to phase out in 1982. Upon its closure, the peer review organization was enacted to ensure services provided for Medicare beneficiaries are

            a. Reasonable and medically necessary

            b. Of a quality that meets professionally recognized standards in health care

            c. Provided in the most effective and economic setting

         2. CMS current scope of work focused on

            a. Clinical quality outcomes

            b. Payment error prevention

3. Risk Management

   a. Definitions

      i. Risk management is the management of any event or situation that could potentially result in an injury to an individual or financial loss to the health care institution.

      ii. Consists of policies, procedures, and practices that reduce risk and liabilities for injuries that may occur

      iii. Objectives

         1. To create and maintain a safe, healthy, environment and enhance quality care

         2. To minimize risk of medical or accidental injuries and losses

         3. Provide cost-effective techniques to insure against financial loss

   b. Risk Management Program

      i. Elements

         1. Risk identification: identifying areas of existing or potential loss. The essential tool used to identify risk is the incident report.

         2. Risk control: prevention and control of risks and minimizing number of occurrences for which the facility may be held liable

         3. Risk financing: plan to financially cover losses; funds may include self insurance, insurance pools, and commercial insurance

      ii. Components

         1. Loss prevention and reduction

         2. Claims management

         3. Safety and security

         4. Employee programs

         5. Patient relations

      iii. Methodology

         1. Occurrence screening

             a. Adverse patient occurrences

             b. Potential compensable events

   2. Incident report
      a. Reportable incidents are written and investigated.
      b. Root cause analysis is done to determine underlying factors of a sentinel event.
   3. Patient advocacy
iv. Use of risk management information
   1. Improve system processes
   2. Increase patient and employee satisfaction
   3. Improve clinical outcomes
   4. Decrease risk factors
c. Reportable Events
   i. Adverse related events
      1. Unauthorized medication
      2. Omission
      3. IV infiltration
      4. Wrong dose
      5. Wrong patient
      6. Wrong medication
      7. Wrong site
      8. Wrong route
      9. Wrong dosage
      10. Wrong time
      11. Wrong technique
      12. Wrong drug preparation
      13. Wrong rate
      14. Drug interaction
      15. Drug allergy
      16. Food and drug interaction
      17. Deteriorated drug
   ii. Other types of reportable events
      1. Patient abuse
      2. Patient neglect
      3. Medically unstable at discharge
      4. Returning to intensive care unit within 24 hours of being transferred out
      5. Unplanned return to surgery for same condition
      6. Patient fall
      7. Missed diagnosis
      8. Delayed diagnosis
      9. Blood transfusion error
      10. Complication with anesthesia
      11. Unanticipated death
      12. Suicide/unsuccessful suicide attempt
      13. Prenatal death
      14. Inappropriate use of restraints
      15. Operative injury or complications
      16. Unexpected admission, readmission, or return to emergency center following inpatient or outpatient care for same condition
      17. Equipment failure
      18. Infant abduction
      19. Blood transfusion reaction
      20. Unauthorized inpatient departure
      21. Patient injury while in restraints

      iii. Sentinel events (unexpected occurrence involving death or serious physical or psychological injury)

          1. Surgery on wrong patient

          2. Infant discharged to wrong family

          3. Rape

          4. Blood transfusion related to blood group incompatibilities

          5. Surgery on wrong body part

          6. Unanticipated death

          7. Infant abduction

          8. Suicide

          9. Permanent loss of major function associated with medication or surgical error

4. Credentialing

  a. Defined

      i. The reviewing, verifying, validating, and evaluating of the key factors that determine an individual practitioner's ability to carry out certain patient care activities and granting of professional privileges

      ii. According to TJC, it is the "authorization granted by the governing board to a practitioner to provide specific patient care services in the hospital within defined limits, based on an individual practitioner's license, education, training, experience, competence, health status, and judgment."

      iii. Crucial role in maintaining high-quality professional care to the patients. Many legal and ethical landmarks have made it clear that the hospital has the obligation to select its staff carefully and to grant them privileges as appropriate in order to ensure the staff are highly educated, trained, experienced, qualified, and competent to deliver needed services.

  b. Purpose

      i. To ensure that medical staff members only perform procedures and services that they are qualified and competent to perform through training and experience

      ii. Key aspects

          1. Initial appointments to the medical staff

          2. Initial delineation and granting of clinical privileges

          3. Periodic reappointment to the medical staff

          4. Periodic renewal or revision of clinical privileges

  c. Medical Staff

      i. Functions of medical staff

          1. Adopt medical staff bylaws

          2. Provide patient care and carry out other professional responsibilities

          3. Actively participate in and exercise professional leadership in measuring, assessing, and improving the performance of the organizations within which they practice

          4. Continually improve the quality of health care services delivered

          5. Provide patient care within their professional competence

          6. Provide patient care as reflected in the scope of their clinical privileges

          7. Participate in ongoing measurement, assessment, and improvement of both clinical and non-clinical processes

      ii. Characteristics of medical staff

          1. Each medical staff member and all others with delineated clinical privileges are subject to medical staff and departmental bylaws, rules and regulations, and policies and are subject to review as part of the organization's performance improvement activities.

2. Each medical staff member is fully licensed.

3. Each medical staff member is permitted by law and by the hospital to provide patient care services independently in the hospital.

4. Each medical staff member has delineated clinical privileges that define the scope of patient care services he or she may provide independently in the hospital.

iii. Medical staff record maintenance

1. A separate record is maintained for each individual requesting medical staff membership or clinical privileges.

2. Complete applications are acted on within a reasonable period of time, as specified in the medical staff bylaws.

3. Each file is consistent with applicant's consents for inspection of records and documents pertinent to his or her licensure, specific training, experience, current competence, and ability to perform the privileges requested, and, if requested, applicant appears for an interview.

4. The bylaws, rules and regulations, and policies of the medical staff indicate that the applicant for reappointment or renewal of clinical privileges is required to submit any reasonable evidence of current ability to perform privileges that may be requested.

5. Each applicant pledges to provide for continuous care for his or her patients.

6. Signed acknowledgement for release and immunity from civil liability

iv. Required TJC medical staff bylaws

1. The method of selecting officers

2. The qualifications required for the medical staff position

3. The responsibilities and functions required for the position

4. The tenures of officers

5. The conditions and mechanisms for removing officers from their positions

6. Requirements for frequency of meetings and for attendance

7. Effective communication among the medical staff, hospital administration, and governing body

8. Mechanisms for corrective action, including indications and procedures for automatic and summary suspension of an individual's medical staff membership or clinical privileges

9. A description of the medical staff's organization, including categories of medical staff membership, when such exist

10. A description of appropriate officer positions, with the stipulation that each officer is a medical staff member

11. When necessary, the medical staff bylaws and rules and regulations are revised to reflect the hospital's current practices with respect to medical staff organization and functions.

12. The medical staff bylaws, rules and regulations, and policies and the governing body's bylaws do not conflict.

13. If significant changes are made in the medical staff bylaws, rules and regulations, or policies, medical staff members and other individuals who have delineated clinical privileges are provided with revised texts of the written materials.

14. Neither body may unilaterally amend the medical staff bylaws or rules and regulations.

15. Medical staff bylaws and rules and regulations create a framework within which medical staff members can act with a reasonable degree of freedom and confidence.

16. The medical staff implement a process to identify and manage matters of individual physician health that is separate from the medical staff disciplinary function.

17. There is an executive committee of the medical staff.

18. The executive committee's function, size, and composition and the method of selecting its members are defined in the medical staff bylaws.

19. The chief executive officer of the hospital or his or her designee attends each executive committee meeting on an ex-officio basis, with or without vote.

20. The participation of the medical staff in organization performance improvement activities

21. The mechanism by which medical staff membership may be terminated

22. There are mechanisms, including a fair hearing and appeal process, for addressing adverse decisions for existing medical staff members and other individuals holding clinical privileges for renewal, revocation, or revision of clinical privileges.

d. Types of Membership Privileges

   i. Appointment or reappointment of qualified applicants to an existing medical unit is designated by category, which describes the degree to which members use the facility, length of time of appointment, or some other factor specific to institution.

      1. Active

      2. Honorary

      3. Courtesy

      4. Faculty

      5. Associate or provisional

      6. Consulting

      7. Disaster

      8. House staff

      9. Temporary

e. Purpose of Clinical Privileges

   i. Delineates the types of procedures that can be performed by each provider of care

   ii. Delineates the types of care and treatment that can be carried out by each provider of care

   iii. Delineates the types of patients to whom the health care provider will be allowed to have access

f. Credentialing Application Process

   i. Practitioner applies for membership and requests clinical privileges.

      1. The medical staff bylaws and the medical staff rules and regulations delineate what needs to be collected and reviewed during the credentialing phase. They also delineate the processes and responsibilities for approval and denial of medical staff clinical privileges and membership.

      2. Categories of applicants

         a. Type one

            i. Physician

            ii. Dentist

            iii. Podiatrist

  b. Type two
    i. Physician assistant
    ii. Advanced nurse practitioner
    iii. Allied health providers
    iv. All other licensed and certified staff
  3. Applicant information
    a. Demographic and identifying information
    b. Education
    c. State licensure number
    d. State licensure expiration date
    e. Previous employers
    f. Prior malpractice claims
    g. Denial of medical privileges with other institutions
    h. Narcotics number
    i. Third-party payment program involvements
    j. Name of references/letter
    k. Acknowledgment of Medicare/Medicaid fraud regulations
    l. Revocation of medical privileges with other institution
    m. Suspension of medical privileges with other institution
    n. Voluntary relinquishment of licensure
    o. Involuntary relinquishment of licensure
ii. Credential verification
  1. Education
  2. Liability insurance coverage
  3. Current licensure
  4. Clinical competence
  5. Satisfactory health status
iii. Privilege delineation
  1. Process to determine specific procedures and services a practitioner is permitted to perform under jurisdiction of institution
  2. Applicant's documented experience
  3. The results of health care treatment and outcomes
  4. The conclusions drawn from performance-improvement activities as appropriate
  5. Benchmarking of staff activities is considered when delineating clinical privileges.
  6. Documentation of basis for granting privileges
  7. Classification or categorization of privileges is well defined, and the standards to be met by the applicant are stated clearly for each category.
  8. When medical staff clinical departments exist, all licensed independent practitioners are assigned to at least one clinical department and are granted clinical privileges that are relevant to the care provided in that department.
  9. There is a satisfactory method to coordinate appraisal for granting or renewal or revision of clinical privileges when an individual currently holding clinical privileges or applying for clinical privileges requests privileges that are relevant to the care provided in more than one department or clinical specialty area.
  10. The exercise of clinical privileges within any department is subject to the rules and regulations of that department and to the authority of the department head.

11. When there are no medical staff clinical departments, all individuals with clinical privileges have their privileges recommended and the quality of their care reviewed through designated medical staff mechanisms, described in the medical staff or governing body bylaws and rules and regulations.

12. Practitioners who diagnose or treat patients via telemedicine link are subject to the credentialing and privileging processes of the organization that receives the telemedicine service.

13. The medical staff recommends the clinical services to be provided by telemedicine.

14. Appraisal for reappointment to the medical staff or renewal or revision of clinical privileges is based on ongoing monitoring of information concerning the individual's professional performance, judgment, and clinical or technical skills.

15. The chief executive officer or his or her designee may grant temporary clinical privileges, when appropriate.

16. Disaster privileges may be granted when the emergency management plan has been activated and the organization is unable to handle the immediate patient needs.

17. Whatever mechanism for granting and renewal or revision of clinical privileges is used, evidence indicates that the clinical privileges are hospital-specific and based on the individual's demonstrated current competence.

18. Appointment or reappointment to the medical staff and the granting, renewal, or revision of clinical privileges is made for a period of no more than two years.

iv. Credentialing department chair
   1. Responsible for coordinating, reviewing, evaluating, and validating timeliness and appropriateness of submitted application
   2. Upon satisfactory, the Departmental Chair request for privilege verification
   3. Maintains documentation
   4. Forwards the application and the request for clinical privileges to Credentialing Committee for further review

v. Credentialing committee
   1. Functions in advisory capacity and is not empowered to make appointment
   2. Conducts peer review of applicant
   3. Makes recommendation for appointment and privileges to executive committee
   4. Aspects of role of credentialing committee
      a. Receive the reviewed application from departmental chair
      b. Review the application and the request for clinical privileges
      c. Forward its recommendation, membership application, and the request for clinical privileges to the executive credentialing review committee
      d. Can recommend approval with condition, approval with no restriction, or denial

vi. Executive committee
   1. Makes recommendation to governing board based upon
      a. The medical staff's structure
      b. The mechanism used to review credentials and to delineate individual clinical privileges

      c. Recommendations of individuals for medical staff membership

      d. Recommendations for delineated clinical privileges for each eligible individual

  2. Role of executive committee

      a. Gathers accurate, thorough, sufficient, and reliable information to ascertain that the professional staff applicants who were recommended for employment or contract are qualified and competent to be granted privileges for the appropriate task and services

      b. Forwards recommendations for appointment, reappointment, or denial of clinical privileges to the governing body

      c. Has governance responsibilities, delegated by the medical staff, within the organization

      d. Has the primary authority over activities related to the functions of the medical staff and over activities related to the quality of care, and functions of performance improvement of the professional services provided by individuals with clinical privileges

      e. Receives and acts on reports and recommendations from medical staff committees, clinical departments, and assigned activity groups

      f. The executive committee is empowered to act on behalf of the medical staffs in the related medical staff meetings.

vii. Governing board approves or denies membership and privileges.

  1. The governing body is ultimately responsible and accountable for the quality of services provided in its facility. Therefore, the final approval or denial of privileges remains the responsibility of the governing body. The credentialing and recredentialing are carried out according to the established and adopted bylaws, medical staff rules and regulations, and policies and procedures of the facility.

  2. The governing board depends on the reports and professional recommendation from its credentialing professional review committee. The governing board relies on its credentialing professional review committee to gather accurate, thorough, sufficient, reliable information to ascertain that the professional staff applicant who was recommended for employment or contract is qualified and competent to be granted privileges for the appropriate task and services.

  3. Role of governing board

      a. Approves medical staff bylaws

      b. Addresses and acknowledges its legal accountabilities and responsibilities to the patient population that it serves

      c. Establishes a quality-focused criteria-based process for selecting a qualified and competent medical staff

      d. Declares the final action for approval or denial of privileges

      e. Enhances collaboration and participation of assigned medical staff and other assigned leaders in developing, reviewing, and revising applicable policies and procedures to support credentialing process

      f. Depends on the reports and professional recommendation from its executive committee

    viii. Reappointment

        1. Practitioner profile

           a. Mechanism to integrate information compiled from quality management activities into credentialing process to determine reappointment

           b. Reappointment criteria may be different from initial appoint criteria

g. Continuing Education

    i. All individuals with clinical privileges participate in ongoing continuing education activities related to their granted privilege.

    ii. Continuing education must be documented, must be made available, and must become part of an indicator regarding qualifications for reappointment or renewal or revision of individual clinical privileges.

    iii. The educational activities must be related to the type of care performed by the particular medical staff and, in part, care offered by the hospital.

h. Credentialing Staff

    i. Functions

        1. Able to organize and prioritize work

        2. Able to follow instruction precisely

        3. Able to develop and/or implement policies and procedures

        4. Able to maintain confidentiality of information

        5. Able to coordinate heavy correspondence

        6. Able to secure hard-to-get but necessary information

        7. Has good handwriting and oral communication skills

        8. Knows credentialing and recredentialing requirements

        9. Knows proper terminology

i. Examples of credentialing process guidelines and credentialing data collection form (Figure 5-7, Figure 5-8, and Figure 5-9)

1. Credentialing, like an employment or contracting process, must be performed in a manner consistent with applicable local, state, and federal laws.
2. All staff participating in the credentialing process must be familiar with the local, state, and federal credentialing requirements.
3. The facility must ensure compliance with all applicable credentialing standards.
4. The applicant must sign an authorization for disclosure of information from requested third-party agents such as previous schools, employers, etc.
5. The facility must develop or adopt credentialing data collection tools.
6. The faculty must maintain adequate filing for general correspondence, confidential correspondence, and medical correspondence.
7. The faculty must maintain a tickler file for requested items.
8. Medical bylaws must include time frame for completing credentialing application process.
9. Applicant is responsible for providing all information the institution requests.
10. The applicant must conduct all requests for information at the direction, approval, and authority of the credentialing professional review committee.
11. Received information is treated as confidential and only shared as necessary within the credentialing review staff.
12. Sanctions and disciplinary action for redisclosure of information to other external agencies are addressed in the bylaws and the policies and procedures.
13. Credentialing information is requested promptly.
14. A checklist is used to identify what information is lacking in the application process.
15. The application for credentialing privilege is not complete until all required information has been received from all requested parties.
16. Decision to grant or deny privilege must be based on patterns of professional practice rather than a single occurrence, unless the single occurrence is considered to be a violation of the standard.
17. The governing board must communicate decision regarding the granting or denial of privileges to the applicant in writing.
18. Copies must be sent to the applicant's credentialing file, applicant, and performance improvement/risk management file.
19. The bylaws must provide appeal procedures for those who may wish to appeal adverse decisions.
20. With the exception of legal cases, all files regarding denials of privileges must be kept for a minimum of one year from the date decision was made.

Figure 5-7   Example of Credentialing Process Guidelines

Instructions: List all required items. Place a check mark in the box to indicate the item's completion.

	Items	Yes	No	Comment
1.	Application completed			
2.	Requested privileges specified			
3.	Attestation to correctness and completeness of information submitted			
4.	Authorization to request, disclose, and/or share information is signed			
5.	Special consent is signed as needed			
6.	Copy of state license is attached			
7.	Copy of board certificate or eligibility letter is attached			
8.	Proof of professional liability is attached			
9.	Names of three professional recommendations submitted			

Figure 5-8   Example of Data Collection Tool for Completion of Credentialing Application

Instructions: As applicable, write the date each item was sent out to the other third-party agent for verification, and the date each item was received, in the appropriate column.

	Items	Received Date	Pending	Sent Date	Contact Person
1.	Proof of professional liability verification				
2.	Three professional recommendations				
3.	Verification of past and/or pending professional disciplinary actions				
4.	Verification of voluntary and involuntary limitations, loss of clinical privileges, or reduction of privileges				
5.	Confirmation from national practitioner data bank (NPDB)				
6.	Confirmation from American Medical Association (AMA)				
7.	Confirmation from Drug Enforcement Agency (DEA)				
8.	Verification of educational background				
9.	Verification of training				
10.	Verification of employment history				
11.	Verification of prior membership termination				
12.	Verification and approval by credentialing committee				
13.	Recommendation for appointment forwarded to administrative staff				
14.	Appointment for recommendation by medical staff administration forwarded to governing board				
15.	Notification of approval, approval with conditions, or denial				
16.	Confirmation of physical and mental fitness to perform requested privilege				
17.	Conflict of interest statement signed				
18.	Signed statement of medical staff bylaws				
19.	Signed statement agreeing to report any malpractice and changes in related health status				

Figure 5-9   Example of Status Check Sheet for Credentialing Data Collection Process

PRACTICAL APPLICATION OF YOUR KNOWLEDGE

1. Quality Assessment and Performance Improvement
   a. Define the following terms:
      i. Quality

      ii. Quality improvement

      iii. Quality assessment

      iv. Total quality management

      v. Quality indicators

      vi. Benchmarking

      vii. Quality management

   b. Methods to Improve Quality
      i. List the TJC 10-step process to achieving the goals and objectives of a monitoring and evaluation program.

      ii. List and describe the Avedis Donabedian model for assessing quality in the health care arena.

      iii. What method was developed by Walter Shewhart and made popular by W. Edwards Deming? Define each of the four phases.

iv. What is the 7-step model that was developed by Brian Joiner to assess quality improvement?

v. List the 6-step model developed by Re and Krouse Wood.

vi. Describe the accomplishments of Crosby, Deming, Joiner, and Juran.

Crosby	Deming	Joiner	Juran

vii. Describe the philosophy of Crosby, Deming, Joiner, and Juran.

Crosby	Deming	Joiner	Juran

viii. List Deming's 14 principles.

ix. List Deming's 7 deadly diseases in quality management.

c. Court Cases
   i. Fill in the following blanks regarding the effects of court decisions on quality of health care services.

Court Cases		
Year	**Case**	**Decision**
	Darling vs. Charleston Community Hospital	Court ruled that the hospital must assume certain responsibilities for care of the patient. The courts ruled that a hospital was negligent for permitting a general practitioner to perform orthopedic surgery. The court ruled that the hospital had a duty to apply reasonable standards to the practice of its physicians because it was responsible for the privileging of physicians on its staff.
1973	*Gonzales vs. Nork and Mercy Hospital*	
1981		The court found that the hospital owed a duty to its patients in selecting medical staff members and granting privileges.

d. Spell out the following acronyms of external agencies influencing quality of health care.
   i. TJC (formerly JCAHO)

   ii. CARF

   iii. QIO (formerly PRO)

   iv. CMS

v. HCFA

vi. HIPAA

vii. TPR

e. Performance Improvement
   i. What is the purpose of performance improvement?

   ii. List the 10 core elements to be included in a performance improvement plan.
      1.

      2.

      3.

      4.

      5.

      6.

      7.

      8.

9.

10.

f. List some of the benefits of continuous quality improvement.
   i.

   ii.

   iii.

   iv.

   v.

g. List some of the internal customers of the HIM department.

h. List some of the external customers of the HIM department.

i. List ways to identify the needs of your customers.

j. List some of the services or products your department has to offer.

k. Draw the PDCA cycle and describe the activities of each step in the cycle.

l. Define CQI and its purpose.

m. Write out definitions for the acronym FOCUS.

F:_____

O:_____

C:_____

U:_____

S:_____

n. Describe data collection methods for performance improvement.

o. Is information collected during the CQI process confidential? Explain your answer.

2. Utilization Review

    a. List the three main goals of the QIO (formerly PRO) physician reviewers.

        i.

        ii.

        iii.

    b. Define the following segments of utilization review process:

        i. Preadmission review

        ii. Admission review

        iii. Concurrent review

        iv. Discharge review

        v. Retrospective review

3. Risk Management

    a. List three objectives of risk management.

        i.

        ii.

        iii.

    b. What are the 3 main elements of risk management?
        i.

        ii.

        iii.

4. Credentialing
    a. Define credentialing.

    b. What is the purpose of credentialing?

    c. List 10 elements of the information that is required for the applicant's credentialing file.
        i.

        ii.

        iii.

        iv.

        v.

        vi.

        vii.

viii.

ix.

x.

d. Identify the type of credentialing for which the professional practitioners in the following table can apply by placing a check mark under the appropriate category type.

Credentialing of Professional Health Practitioners		
	Category	
Practitioner	**Type One**	**Type Two**
Physician assistant		
Advanced nurse practitioner		
Physician		
Allied health provider		
Dentist		
Podiatrist		
Other licensed and certified providers		

e. List five types of membership privileges.
  i.

  ii.

  iii.

  iv.

  v.

    f. List five functions of the credentialing staff.

      i.

      ii.

      iii.

      iv.

      v.

5. Tools for Collecting and Displaying Data
    a. What is the primary source of health care data?

    b. What is the difference between primary and secondary sources of health care data?

    c. Give an example of both primary and secondary health care data.

    d. Define the following types of data and give examples of each.
      i. Nominal

      ii. Ordinal

    iii. Discrete

    iv. Continuous

e. List six critical elements of data collection.
    i.

    ii.

    iii.

    iv.

    v.

    vi.

f. Define the following data collection and data display tools:
    i. Bar graph

    ii. Pie chart

    iii. Radar chart

    iv. Run chart

    v. Scatter diagram

    vi. Storyboard

g. Use the following table to answer questions i–iv.

Requests for Medical Records vs. Number of Invalid Disclosures			
	Number of Requests	Invalid	Percent of Invalid Disclosures
January	592	7	1.18
February	560	10	1.78
March	452	48	10.61
Jan–Mar Quarter			
April	780	54	6.92
May	485	73	15.05
June	652	19	
Apr–May Quarter			
July	543	21	3.86
August	651	11	1.68
September	702	10	1.42
Jul–Sep Quarter			
October	486	41	8.43
November	385	45	12.93
December	620	9	1.45
Oct–Dec Quarter			
Total			

i. Calculate the percentage of invalid disclosures for the month of June.

ii. Calculate the totals for the quarter and the year.

iii. Which of the quarters has the greatest number of invalid disclosures?

iv. Which quarter demonstrates an improvement in proper medical record disclosure?

h. Matrix of performance improvement tools

    i. In the following table, place a check mark (✔) in the space next to the tool that will be most useful in collecting or displaying data during the following phases: *problem identification*, *data analysis*, *planning solution*, and *program evaluation*.

Problem-Solving Activities and Tools

Tools	Problem Identification	Data Analysis	Planning Solution	Evaluating
Brainstorming				
Cause and effect diagram				
Checklist				
Check sheet				
Control chart				
Flow chart				
Histogram				
Pareto chart				
Run chart				
Scatter diagram				

TEST YOUR KNOWLEDGE

1. Which of the following functions became mandatory under Title XVIII of the Social Security Act?
   a. Quality improvement
   b. Risk management
   c. Utilization review
   d. Quality assessment

2. The manager of the utilization review department wants to identify patients who are not suitable for inpatient admission and then redirect them to an appropriate health care setting to obtain health care services. When would the manager need to collect data?
   a. Prospectively
   b. Concurrently
   c. Retrospectively
   d. During long-term care review

3. Which of the following utilization review activities is being performed when a patient's record is reviewed at regular intervals to determine the appropriateness of care rendered and bed utilization?
   a. Preadmission
   b. Admission
   c. Continued stay
   d. Retrospective

4. At most, TJC accreditation is granted for ___ months.
   a. 12
   b. 18
   c. 36
   d. 48

5. Which of the following processes is not mandatory for health care facilities?
   a. Accreditation
   b. Certification
   c. Licensure
   d. AHA registration

6. In order to receive reimbursement for treating Medicare and Medicaid patients, health care organizations must:
   a. be contracted with PPS reimbursement.
   b. be contracted to HMO.
   c. meet the federal conditions of participation.
   d. accept major credit cards.

7. What action(s) would assist the manager of the health information management department in improving customer perception of the quality of services provided by the department?
   a. Establish a weekly turn-around time for all dictated reports
   b. Refuse to fax patient information to protect patient confidentiality
   c. Refuse to let other departments into medical records department
   d. Identify the specific customer needs in order to improve customer satisfaction with services

8. As related to quality patient care, physicians who are members of the ambulatory care clinics meet monthly to review documentation of treatment plan and patient outcomes. This type of review, in which a physician's health care documentation is reviewed by his/her professional colleagues, is known as what?
   a. Concurrent review
   b. Focused audit review
   c. Retrospective review
   d. Peer review

9. In a health care facility, who is responsible for the appropriateness and assurance of quality care?
   a. Chief executive officer
   b. Medical staff
   c. Governing board
   d. Hospital attorney

10. During a quality improvement audit, it was noted that a medical record coder was consistently up-coding certain diagnoses. The facility is conducting investigations to determine how much money to reimburse its third-party payers for overpayment. All of the following departments would receive data about the investigation *except* the _____ department.
    a. compliance
    b. billing
    c. health information management
    d. social services

11. The purposes of PROs include determining all of the following *except* whether:
    a. services provided were medically necessary.
    b. the quality of services provided met professionally recognized standards of health care.
    c. the care was provided in the most economical setting consistent with the patient's health care needs.
    d. the health care facility had met accreditation and licensing standards.

12. In addition to DRGs, TEFRA also introduced which of the following?
    a. Indicator measurement system (IMS)
    b. Peer review organizations (PRO)
    c. Quality improvement organizations (QIO)
    d. Centers for Medicare and Medicaid Services (CMS)

13. The purpose of _____ was to establish a continuous, data-driven accreditation process that uses performance measures and data focused on core measures.
    a. Agenda for change
    b. ORYX initiative
    c. ORION project
    d. Data aggregation

14. Which of the following is not the role of a HIM professional in a quality improvement process?
    a. Collect data
    b. Organize data
    c. Trend data
    d. Validate clinical data

15. The utilization manager reviews the record to determine which health care setting will be appropriate for the identified procedure. Which of the following functions is the manager performing?
    a. Retrospective
    b. Continued stay
    c. Preadmission
    d. Focused

16. Which of the following is *not* a TJC standard for medical staff quality improvement review?
    a. Blood usage
    b. Medical record
    c. Drug usage
    d. Form usage

17. Which of the following organizations was a forerunner for the evaluation of quality medical care in health care organizations?
    a. The Joint Commission (TJC, formerly JCAHO)
    b. Quality Improvement Organization (QIO, formerly PRO)
    c. Professional Standard Review Organization (PSRO)
    d. Centers for Medicare and Medicaid (CMS)

18. The members of which group are responsible for recommending clinical privileges to the governing body?
    a. Executive committee
    b. Medical staff
    c. Credentialing coordinator
    d. Credentialing staff

19. Which of the following organizations is responsible for evaluating the quality of health care services?
    a. Centers for Medicare and Medicaid Services
    b. Health Care Financing Administrations
    c. Peer review organizations
    d. Joint Commission Accreditation of Healthcare Organizations

20. During the credentialing process, the applicant was granted active membership. The applicant can utilize the clinical privilege for a maximum period of how long?
    a. More than 3 years
    b. Fewer than 5 years
    c. 2 years or fewer
    d. More than 10 years

21. Which of the following is not a type of idea-generation technique?
    a. Brainstorming
    b. Affinity diagrams
    c. Nominal group technique
    d. Benchmarking

22. Which of the following data organization methods is a tool that can be used to organize, categorize, and reduce information to a more usable form?
    a. Nominal group technique
    b. Matrix
    c. Bar graph
    d. Control chart

23. Which of the following is a sequential representation of steps in a decision-making process?
    a. Bar graph
    b. Run chart
    c. Flow chart
    d. Line graph

24. What type of data collection tool will be useful in collecting the number of charts reviewed for coding accuracy, the type of errors, and the number of errors made by each coder?
    a. Interview
    b. Check sheet
    c. Tally sheet
    d. Histogram

25. What will be the most effective data presentation tool to use in comparing staff productivity?
    a. Run chart
    b. Pareto chart
    c. Bar chart
    d. Cause and effect

26. Physician members of the psychiatry committee meet to review psychology cases that are referred for quality issues and that deviate from the Houston, Texas area standards of care. This type of review, in which a physician's record is reviewed by his or her professional colleagues, is known as what?
    a. Concurrent review
    b. Clinical pertinence review
    c. Peer review
    d. A physician reviewer

27. What does affinity grouping do?
    a. Organizes similar ideas into logical groupings
    b. Generates a large number of creative ideas from a group
    c. Plots the points for two variables to determine whether they are related to each other
    d. Displays frequencies of responses

28. In 1965, which of the following established legal liability for hospitals?
    a. P.L. 92-603
    b. CMS
    c. JCAHO
    d. *Darling vs. Charleston Community Memorial Hospital*

29. What does brainstorming do?
  a. Organizes similar ideas into logical groupings
  b. Generates a large number of creative ideas from a group
  c. Plots the points for two variables to determine whether they are related to each other
  d. Displays frequencies of responses

30. Quality improvement organizations were enacted by which group?
  a. TJC
  b. TEFRA
  c. HEDIS
  d. CMS

31. What is a scatter diagram used to do?
  a. Organize similar ideas into logical groupings
  b. Generate a large number of creative ideas from a group
  c. Plot the points for two variables to determine whether they are related to each other
  d. Display frequencies of responses

32. Which of the following terms refers to the process of planning for change?
  a. Change management
  b. TQM
  c. Change agent
  d. Benchmarking

33. Nurse Bob wants to display goals for patients and provide the corresponding ideal sequence and timing of staff actions to achieve those goals with optimal efficiency. Which should he use?
  a. Critical pathways
  b. Clinical protocols
  c. Critical guidelines
  d. Clinical pathways

34. In order to assure that patient care problems can be remedied immediately, Nurse Bob should perform which type of quality data collection?
  a. Preadmission screening
  b. Prospective
  c. Concurrent
  d. Retrospective

35. Nurse Bob wants to use the screening criteria for utilization review that most health care facilities utilize to determine the need for inpatient services and justification for continued stay. Which of the following should he use?
  a. Tracer methodology
  b. Clinical protocols
  c. Critical pathways
  d. Severity of illness

36. Bob, who is the manager of the utilization review department, wants to monitor and evaluate the prevention of inappropriate admissions. When should Bob collect data?
  a. Prospectively
  b. Concurrently
  c. Retrospectively
  d. Continued stay

37. Risk management is the:
  a. process of overseeing the medical, legal, and administrative aspects of health care management.
  b. group of processes used to measure how efficiently health care is managed.
  c. process of determining whether health care services meet predetermined criteria.
  d. mechanism to monitor and ensure customer satisfaction.

38. An attorney subpoenas the quality improvement committee meeting minutes of Houston Community Hospital. Should the minutes be released?
  a. Yes, or the hospital will risk being in contempt of court
  b. Yes, because all subpoenas must be honored
  c. No, the attorney needs a court order because a subpoena is not adequate
  d. No, because quality improvement committee meeting minutes are protected from subpoenas

39. Utilization management is the:
    a. process of overseeing the medical, legal, and administrative aspects of health care management.
    b. group of processes used to measure how efficiently health care is managed.
    c. process of determining whether health care services meet predetermined criteria.
    d. mechanism to monitor and ensure customer satisfaction.

40. The National Guideline Clearinghouse (NGC) provides:
    a. data concerning the competence of health care providers.
    b. clinical guidelines that may be used voluntarily.
    c. clinical guidelines that are mandated by the federal government.
    d. a mechanism to monitor and ensure customer satisfaction.

41. The clinician failed to obtain a signed consent form from Bob prior to surgery. His attorney may argue that Bob is a victim of:
    a. failed consent.
    b. improper consent.
    c. negligence.
    d. assault and battery.

42. "The hospital should have no more than 50% of the monthly discharged health information records delinquent" is an example of a:
    a. clinical standard.
    b. clinical guideline.
    c. clinical performance measure.
    d. clinical protocol.

43. TEFRA caused the reimbursement structure to change from a:
    a. manual to an electronic billing system.
    b. cost-based program to a retrospective payment.
    c. retrospective to a prospective payment system.
    d. retrospective to a concurrent utilization review system.

44. Which data bank is a result of HIPAA legislation?
    a. Fraud and Abuse Data Bank
    b. Healthcare Integrity and Protection Data Bank
    c. National Practitioner Data Bank
    d. Privacy Integrity Information Breach Data Bank

45. The goal of clinical practice guidelines is to:
    a. describe the outcomes of health care-related services.
    b. standardize clinical decision making.
    c. standardize the content of clinical pathways.
    d. regulate accreditation standards.

46. Which department will most likely be responsible for taking corrective action regarding the following quality indicator? "Ninety-five percent (95%) of physician appointments/reappointments will be completed within 90 days of receipt of all required application materials."
    a. Risk management
    b. Quality improvement
    c. Utilization management
    d. Credentialing

47. The standard for record completion is: "95% of discharged records must be coded within 30 days." Upon review of record coding statistics, 10 of the 100 discharged records were incomplete within the allotted time frame. Evaluate the department's standard.
    a. The standard was met.
    b. The standard was not achievable.
    c. The standard should be modified.
    d. The standard was not met.

48. You are assisting the nursing department in writing indicators to determine appropriate ratios and formulas and to determine data collection time frames. One important aspect of care is the documentation of patients' education. More specifically, the nursing department would like to assess its documentation of education on colostomy care for patients with new colostomies. Concerning the preceding scenario, what would be the most effective time frame for collecting the requested data?
   a. Prospectively
   b. Concurrently
   c. Retrospectively
   d. Ongoing

49. The utilization review coordinator reviews inpatient records at regular intervals to justify necessity and appropriateness of care to warrant further hospitalization. The utilization review activities being performed constitute a:
   a. preadmission review.
   b. continued stay review.
   c. retrospective review.
   d. discharge review.

50. Hospital Compare:
   a. was developed to publicly report valid information about the quality of care delivered in the nation's hospitals.
   b. established retrospective utilization management guidelines.
   c. grants accreditation to charitable health care organizations.
   d. provides statistical analysis of hospital quality indicators.

Information Technology and Systems

1. Time Line for the Evolution of Health Information Systems (Figure 6-1)
2. Information Technology
   a. Hardware
      i. Physical equipment of computers and computer systems
      ii. Consists of both electronic and mechanical equipment
   b. Software
      i. Set of instructions required to operate computers and their applications
      ii. Operating system software: sets of instructions that direct actual computer functions
      iii. Application software: set of instructions used to accomplish various types of processes

1960s–1970s	1980s	1990s	2000s
Financial Focus • Few clinical systems • In-house development • Shared systems • Turnkey systems • Transaction processing	**Continuing Financial Focus** • More clinical development • Standalone systems • Distributed systems • Management information systems (MIS)	**Focus on Clinical Systems** • Integration of systems • Executive information systems • Decision support systems • Enterprise-wide systems • Office automation • Virtual systems	**Standards** • E-health • Internet • Intranets • Extranets • Clinical repositories • Data warehouses • Data mining

Figure 6-1   The Evolution of Health Information Systems

    c. Categories of Computers
        i. Supercomputers
            1. Fastest and highest-capacity machines built today
            2. Can cost millions of dollars and are used in large-scale activities such as weather forecasting and mathematical research
        ii. Mainframe systems
            1. Only computers available until 1960s
            2. Can perform millions of instructions per second and hundreds of users can be connected at the same time
        iii. Midrange systems
            1. Minicomputers
                a. Introduced in 1960s
                b. Can support up to 4000 connected users at the same time via terminals consisting of a keyboard and a video screen
                c. Cheaper than mainframes
            2. Workstations
                a. Introduced in 1980s
                b. Very powerful desktop computers
                c. Comparable to midsize mainframe but sits on a desktop
                d. Used as servers to microcomputers connected through a network
        iv. Microcomputers
            1. Also called personal computers (PCs)
            2. Introduced in 1970s
            3. Variety of sizes, including desktop, laptop, palmtop, personal digital assistant, and pen-based
        v. Web appliances
            1. Used in conjunction with Internet to navigate the Web
            2. One device sits on top of a television and allows user to surf the Internet using a remote control device
            3. Do not have processing units or storage devices
    d. Computer Peripherals
        i. Peripherals are usually described in terms of input, processing and memory, output, storage, and communication
            1. Input devices: keyboard, microphone, scanner, pointing device such as a mouse, trackball, light pen, intelligent tablet, sensors for biometrics (e.g., fingerprints, handprints, and iris scans)
            2. Processing and memory: central processing unit (CPU) and capacity to hold the data being processed
            3. Output devices: printers, monitors, and speakers
            4. Storage devices: floppy disk drive, hard disk drive, magnetic tape, compact disk, zip disk, optical disk drive
            5. Communication devices: used to assist communications among computers, e.g., a modem
3. Information System
  a. Definition
        i. A collection of related components that interact to perform a task in order to accomplish a goal
        ii. The integration of several elements of a business process to affect a specific outcome
        iii. A process that refines raw facts into meaningful information
        iv. Provides opportunities to improve internal operations, create competitive advantage in the marketplace, improve patient care delivery, enhance research, and provide better service

b. System Characteristics
    i. A group of components that interact to accomplish a goal or an objective
    ii. Components interact with each other through defined relationships.
    iii. Self-adapt and respond to environmental changes
    iv. Composed of
        1. People
        2. Data
        3. Work processes
        4. Information technologies
    v. Elements
        1. Inputs
        2. Processing mechanisms
        3. Outputs

4. Design and Development of Health Information System (HIS)
  a. Six Components of an HIS
    i. Patient scheduling, admission, discharge, and transfer; system provides central notification about patients
    ii. Business and financial systems such as patient accounting and billing
    iii. Communication and networking applications transmit and manage messages among departments.
    iv. Departmental systems such as radiology and pharmacy
    v. Documentation systems used to collect, store, and retrieve patient data
    vi. Reminder and advice functions assist health care providers in planning patient care activities.
  b. System Software
    i. System
        1. Set of instructions that direct actual computer operation functions
        2. Acts as a conductor for all the hardware components and application software
    ii. Application: set of instructions used to accomplish various types of business processes
    iii. Three main system software
        1. Operating system: master program that manages the basic operations of the computer (OSX, Windows, Linux, UNIX)
        2. Utility programs: used to support, enhance, or expand existing programs (backup processes, virus protection, data recovery)
        3. Language translator: translates a program written by a programmer into machine language; includes graphical user interfaces (GUI) such as icons, forms
  c. Application Software
    i. Productivity: word processing, accounting, database management, graphic presentations, scheduling, e-mail, time management
    ii. Specialty software: programs specific for a particular industry (Encoders)
    iii. Education and reference: encyclopedias, anatomy atlases, library search engines
    iv. Entertainment: games, audio, video
  d. Programming Languages
    i. Machine language
        1. Binary representation
            a. 0,1
            b. 1 kilobyte = 1024 bytes

c. Typewritten page ≈ 2 kilobytes

d. Quantities of bytes

Name	Value in Bytes
Kilobyte (kb)	1024^1 or (1.024×10^3)
Megabyte (mb)	1024^2 or (1.049×10^6)
Gigabyte (gb)	1024^3 or (1.074×10^9)
Terabyte (tb)	1024^4 or (1.100×10^{12})

    ii. Assembly language

    iii. High-level languages

        1. BASIC

        2. COBOL

        3. FORTRAN

        4. PASCAL

        5. MUMPS

        6. JAVA

        7. HTML

        8. XML

    iv. Very high level languages: structured query language (SQL)

    v. Natural languages: artificial intelligence (technologies used in developing machines that imitate human qualities such as learning and reasoning)

e. Strategic Information System Planning

    i. Process of identifying and assigning priorities to the various upgrades and changes that might be made in an organization's information system

    ii. Ensures all changes contribute to the achievement of the organization's strategic goals and objectives

    iii. Establishes enterprise-wide priorities for information systems

    iv. Serves as a guide to make decisions of resource allocations

    v. Sets stage for system-development life cycle

    vi. Lead by the chief information officer

f. System Development Life Cycle (SDLC)

    i. Information engineering: a collection of processes used for the planning, analysis, design, and development of information systems on an enterprise-wide basis

    ii. After the chief information officer has led the development and establishment of a strategic plan for information systems, the organization will follow a structured process for selecting and implementing new computer-based systems.

    iii. There are many versions of the SDLC, but all include 4 major phases and 12 steps:

        1. System analysis

            a. Identify business issue or problem that needs to be solved

            b. Assess feasibility of the system and define the scope of project

            c. Assess information needs of users and define the functional requirements of system

            d. Provide a system that meets user and/or department needs and that also supports the strategic objectives of the organization

            e. Tools for system analysis

                i. Data dictionary

1. Detailed road map of the database
2. Defines each data field or column according to the following
   a. Name of computer
   b. Type of data field
   c. Length of data field
   d. Edits place on the data field
   e. Values allowed to be placed in the data field
   f. A clear definition of each value
3. Data modeling technique that is a repository for all primitive-level data structures and data elements within a system

Project:	Master Patient Index
Label:	Sex
Entry Type:	Data Element
Description:	Patient Gender
Alias:	None
Values:	M = Male F = Female

   a. Figure 6-2 provides graphic representation of the flow of data through a system. Can be a logical or physical data flow
   ii. Decomposition diagram: breaks down problems into smaller levels of detail; usually depicted in a hierarchy chart
   iii. Entity relationship diagram: data modeling technique that depicts the logical design of a database schema (see Figure 6-3)

Data Flow Name	Data Flow Symbol
External entity: receiving or sending data	
Process: changes inputs to outputs	
Data store: location of data storage	
Data flow	

Figure 6-2   Data Flow Diagram

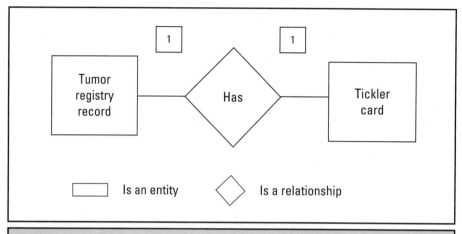

Figure 6-3 Entity Relationship Diagram (ERD)

      1. Entities are objects such as people, places, things, or events that make up the data of a database

      2. Relations are links or ties that exist between or among entities

      3. Attributes describe both entities and relationships

  2. System design

    a. Specify details of new system (logical and physical design)

    b. Decide how system will be designed or selected

      i. Built in-house

      ii. Turnkey (vendor selection, request for proposal)

    c. Data modeling

      i. Used as a plan for building complex organizational databases

      ii. Based on strategic plan for development of organizational information system

      iii. Provides graphical picture of the business data needs

      iv. Helpful in developing the general information systems master plan and identifying business data and how they relate to one another

      v. Steps in data modeling process

        1. Formation of data modeling team

        2. Selection of data modeling tools (e.g., computer-aided software engineering or CASE)

        3. Studying user requirements and defining these through the use of data modeling diagrams

          a. Identify scope of project

          b. Collect data about process to be automated

        4. Development of database design

      vi. Three levels of data models

        1. Conceptual

          a. Business data model

          b. One conceptual data model maintained for the enterprise that represents the information needs of the organization

      c. Defines the database requirements of the enterprise in a single description

      d. Used to develop external and internal models

      e. Input received from end users

      f. Contents consist of

         i. Diagrams (picture of data needs of enterprise)

         ii. Glossary (data dictionary)

         iii. Narratives (explain what diagram and glossary mean)

         iv. Access patterns (what data are accessed, how often, in what order to determine transaction times)

   2. External

      a. Also called logical data model

      b. View data by a specific group of users of a specific processing application

      c. Input received from end users

   3. Internal

      a. Also called physical data model

      b. Depicts how data are physically represented in the database

      c. Concerned with data structures, file organization, and mechanisms and techniques to most efficiently store data and make use of the database system

      d. IS develops without interaction of users

  vii. Computer-aided software engineering (CASE) tools

   1. Computerized development tools to improve the efficiency, accuracy, and completeness of the system development process

   2. Used in data modeling activity

   3. Create entity relationship diagrams (ERD)

   4. Assist in the electronic development of diagrams such as data models, data flow diagrams, and program structure charts, and data dictionaries

  viii. Rapid application development (RAD)

   1. Accelerated approach to information system analysis and design

   2. Assist with prototyping the system

   3. Initiated by conducting a joint application design session

  ix. Joint application design (JAD)

   1. Provides opportunity for substantial end-user input and speeds the development process

   2. Group of end users, analysts, and technical development professionals meet over a period of days to analyze the current system, identify goals and objectives for the new system, and identify the new system functions

3. System implementation

  a. Select project manager

  b. Make system operational

  c. Test system

  d. Train users

  e. Prepare site

  f. Install hardware and software

  g. Manage organization change and system impact

   h. Development of backup and recovery procedures

   i. Convert to new system

  4. System evaluation

   a. Evaluate system against established criteria

   b. Technical staff oversee

    i. System backups

    ii. Software upgrades

    iii. Equipment maintenance and replacement

    iv. Ongoing user training and assistance

    v. Disaster recovery

 iv. Twelve steps in system development life cycle

  1. Request for development

  2. Requirements and system analysis

  3. System design

  4. Specification of functions

  5. Coding of computer programs

  6. Testing of systems

  7. Development of system documentation

  8. User training

  9. User conversion

  10. Operating of the system

  11. System maintenance

  12. System changes and upgrades

 v. Nolan's six-stage theory

  1. An institution is at a certain maturity level in information technology at any given time

   a. Initiation: initiation of automation

   b. Expansion: growth of automation

   c. Control: management of information technology growth

   d. Integration: integrates systems through policies and procedures

   e. Data administration: databases developed and information is critical

   f. Maturity: growth of application is the focus on strategic importance of organization

5. Classification of Health Care Information Systems

 a. Various information system applications are currently utilized in the health care environment. Table 6-1 provides an overview of these applications.

6. Database Management System (DBMS)

 a. Database Management System (DBMS)

  i. An integrated set of programs that manages access to the database

  ii. Software that supports the operation of the database

  iii. Personal DBMS: used for small projects (e.g., personal address book)

  iv. Server-based DBMS: runs on a server computer and is separate application from a personal system (e.g., employee information—Oracle allows you to link multiple tables and also maintain consistency between them)

 b. Database

  i. A collection of stored data, typically organized into fields, records, and files

  ii. A structured computer file for data storage designed to enable editing the data, query and retrieval, and computer processing efficiency

Table 6-1 Classification of Health Care Information Systems

Functional Areas	Structure or Work Processes	Span Across the Health Care Enterprise	Purpose
Administrative 1. Admissions, Discharges, Transfers (ADT) 2. Human Resources 3. Materials management 4. Facilities management	**Access to Information** For example: Results reporting system	**Individual** For example: Word processing (Microsoft Word) Spreadsheets (Microsoft Excel) Presentation (Microsoft Powerpoint) Statistical (SPSS)	**Transaction Processing System (TPS)** Collects and stores data about transactions Manages the different kinds of transactions that occur in a health care facility For example: Patient admissions, employee time cards, supply purchases
Financial 1. Budgeting 2. Billing 3. Payments	**Access to Information Tools** For example: Results reporting system	**Workgroup** For example: E-mail	**Management Information System (MIS)** Supported by transaction processing systems Provides routine information to managers for decision making
			Enterprisewide System Automates information at the point of service, supports patient care, analyzes clinical practices *(continues)*

Table 6-1 Classification of Health Care Information Systems (continued)

Functional Areas	Structure or Work Processes	Span Across the Health Care Enterprise	Purpose
Clinical 1. EMR (Electronic Medical Record) 2. Results reporting 3. Patient care management 4. Order entry 5. Point of care documentation 6. Nursing services 7. Laboratory 8. Pharmacy 9. Clinical decision support 10. Research, QI, peer review	**Enforcement of Rules** For example: Automated system for application or practice guidelines and critical paths Automation of most or all work such as a computerized hospital information kiosk	**Organization** For example: Internet	**Decision Support System (DSS)** Using databases, it is an interactive system that helps managers solve problems and make decisions For example: Clinical DSS that alerts physician when lab results are outside normal range
Out-Patient 1. Appointment scheduling 2. Patient billing 3. Electronic insurance payment 4. Automatic payment posting 5. Patient collection and mail-merge 6. Medical record data capture and retrieval 7. Prescription writing 8. Report generation		**Outside the Organization**	**Executive Information System** Interactive system that allows top managers to answer "what if" queries and project trends Several databases are attached to type of system including external and internal operations and special management

Table 6-1 Classification of Health Care Information Systems (continued)

Functional Areas	Structure or Work Processes	Span Across the Health Care Enterprise	Purpose
Research 1. Data mart 　　Data subset 　　extracted 　　from larger 　　database 2. Data mining 　　Broadview 　　of data			**Expert System** Generates advice or suggests a decision A knowledge system built from a set of rules applied to specific problems
			Office Automation Day-to-day processing and communication tasks (word processing, spreadsheets, databases, e-mail)

c. Characteristics
    i. Building blocks of information
    ii. Organized integrated collection of data
    iii. Data is stored as a set of logical files that are accessed in a manner that is meaningful to its users.
    iv. Reduces redundant information
    v. Consistency of information
    vi. Standardization and flexibility of the information
d. Four Levels of Data Organization
    i. Item: data entity describes attribute of an object
    ii. Record
        1. Items that relate to an object or entity are combined into a record
        2. Each data item for a record occupies a field on the physical storage medium
        3. Size is measured by bytes or characters
    iii. File: collection of related records
    iv. Database: structured computer file for data storage

e. Five Major Database Models

    i. Relational: data stored in predefined tables that contain rows and columns similar to a spreadsheet

        1. Column or field is a basic fact (e.g., LAST_NAME, FIRST_NAME, DOB, RACE)

        2. Row or record is a set of columns or a collection of related data items. (e.g., Tyson, Carla, 9/20/1959, African-American)

        3. Key field uniquely identifies each row in a table; two types of keys:

            a. Primary key: ensures each row in a table is unique and does not change value; may be counter or randomly generated number

            b. Foreign key: column of one table that corresponds to a primary key in another table; together they allow two tables to be joined together

        4. All data are stored in tables with relationships between the tables.

        5. Relation is created by sharing a common data element.

        6. Stores currency, real numbers, integers

    ii. Hierarchical

        1. Supports treelike structure that consists of parent (root) and child segments; many-to-many relationships difficult to represent

        2. Each parent has a child or more; each child has only one parent

        3. User queries database; search seeks answer from parent to child

    iii. Network

        1. Similar to hierarchical, except that a child can have more than one parent

        2. Parent referred to as owner; child as member

        3. Supports many-to-many relationship

    iv. Object-oriented

        1. Stores objects of data

        2. Can model relational data or data types, such as graphics, movies, and audio

    v. Object-relational

        1. Combines best of relational and object-oriented

        2. Uses both traditional data types (currency, integers, and strings) and advanced data types (graphics, movies, and audio)

f. Types of Organizational Databases

    i. Transactional database

        1. Also called operational or production database

        2. Store and manage all the detailed data needed to support the operation of the entire health care facility

        3. Support all daily transactions of an organization (ADT, lab, accounting, inventory)

    ii. Analytical database

        1. Stores extracted pieces of data from selected transactional databases

        2. Designed to support high-level managers in making strategic and tactical decisions

        3. Used to analyze complex relationships, discover trends, perform "what-if" explorations

    iii. Distributed database

        1. Logically interrelated collection of stored data and a description of these data that are physically distributed over a computer network

    2. The database is split into a number of fragments, and each fragment is stored on one or more computers under the control of a separate DBMS.

    3. Database fragments serve specific local applications and are stored locally on a server but can also access other global databases and applications throughout the network.

  iv. External database

    1. Organizations obtain information from sources outside of the organization

    2. May access information from a commercial source via the Internet

  v. Data warehouse

    1. Provides organization the ability to access data from multiple databases and to combine the results into a single question and reporting interface

    2. Sets up large stores of data for strategic decision support analysis

    3. Selected data are extracted from multiple sources in the organization's information system.

    4. Subject oriented, integrated, time-variant, and nonvolatile collection of data in support of management's decision-making process

    5. Integrate organization-wide data into a single repository from which managers can pose ad hoc queries, run reports, and perform a variety of analyses

    6. Analytical databases designed to support strategic and tactical decision making

    7. Organization uses historical data and integrates them with a variety of analytical techniques to help solve problems.

    8. In order for the value of the data warehouse to be realized, techniques such as data mining must be applied.

  vi. Data mart

    1. Subset of a data warehouse that supports the requirements of a particular department or business function

    2. Focuses on the data needs for a specific department or business function, as opposed to a warehouse that stores data for the entire organization

    3. Tailored to meet needs of department

    4. Amount of historical data and level or granularity (detail) can be specific to needs of department.

  vii. Data mining

    1. Encourages a broad view of all data for a set of patients to explore relationships among the data that might not be readily apparent during the initial hypothesis

    2. The extraction of data from large databases to uncover previously unknown information to help managers make decisions

    3. Helps uncover previously unknown and hidden information trends

    4. Identifies patterns and relationships among variables using predictive modeling, database segmentation, link analysis, and deviation detection

    5. Must have a data warehouse to perform data mining

7. Information Security (see Table 6-2)

    a. Legislation Regarding Patient Privacy

        i. Privacy Act of 1974: safeguards privacy of health records in federal institutions

        ii. Health Insurance Portability and Accountability Act (HIPAA) of 1996: implemented security and privacy rules for health information

    b. Security Fundamentals for Health Information

        i. Protect privacy of patient-related data from intrusion

            1. Unauthorized use activity by authorized users

            2. Hackers

            3. Downloaded files

            4. Trojan horses

        ii. Ensure integrity of information

            1. Protect data and programs from accidental or unauthorized intentional change

            2. Ensure data entered into system are protected from unauthorized modification or deletion

        iii. Ensure availability of information to authorized users in a timely fashion

            1. Denial of user access may result from system intrusion such as a worm

            2. Unavailability may result from natural disaster or human error

    c. Security Program

        i. Establish a security organization (chief security officer, privacy officer)

        ii. Implement an employee awareness program

        iii. Conduct risk analysis and assessment

Table 6-2 Information Security (Definition of Terms)

Privacy	The right of an individual to limit access by others to some aspects of their person
Confidentiality	Based on a special doctor–patient relationship and refers to the expectation that the information collected will be used for the purpose for which it was gathered; limiting disclosure of private matters
Security	Means to control access and protect information from accidental or intentional disclosure to unauthorized persons and from alteration, destruction, or loss
Informational Privacy	The right of individuals to keep information about themselves from being disclosed to anyone

      iv. Establish access control (tracking system)

      v. Implement physical and management controls (passwords, lock doors, limit access)

      vi. Develop a disaster recovery and business community plan (disaster plan)

      vii. Implement network controls (viruses)

d. Prevention and Control

    i. Personnel

      1. Employees should only have access to information on a need-to-know basis

      2. Should sign confidentiality agreements and be made aware of privacy and security policies and procedures

      3. Terminate or revise information access upon employee leaving or moving within the organization

    ii. Physical: equipment and information should be secure from threats and unauthorized access

    iii. Hardware

      1. Should be secured from extreme temperatures, power outages, and other environmental threats

      2. Should be installed according to manufacturer instructions

    iv. Software

      1. System in place for system development life cycle (SDLC)

      2. Access to specific applications should be limited

        a. Integrity controls (file record counts, hash totals, block counts, check sums)

        b. System should automatically log all transactions

        c. Audit trails

    v. External

      1. Firewalls

        a. System to prevent access to a private network from the outside or limit access to the outside from within

        b. Types

          i. Proxy server

          ii. Packet filter

          iii. Application gateway

      2. Encryption: changes readable text into a set of different characters and numbers based on a mathematical algorithm

      3. Internet security: secure socket layer (SSL) protocol; Web servers that support an SSL session have an address that begins with *https* instead of *http*

    vi. Communication

      1. Authentication

        a. System knows user is authorized

          i. Passwords: use should include password aging and should allow only one log-in per user identification at a time

          ii. Tokens or cards: card generates a unique sequence of numbers, and, through an algorithm, assigns the user access privileges for an application

          iii. Biometric devices: unique trait of a human that can be used for automatic recognition, such as fingerprints, retinal eye patterns, or speech

          iv. Access controls: granted by role of user and the permitted roles for specific information access

8. Emerging Technologies
- **a.** Videoconferencing
  - **i.** Provides video, audio, computer, and imaging system connectivity
  - **ii.** Allows several physicians to collaborate
  - **iii.** Information from computerized patient record (CPR) can be viewed on the same screen with a physician's image and diagnostic imagery.
- **b.** Groupware: combines different document types with the corresponding work process into a tightly integrated work flow
- **c.** Information Kiosk: computer station to which patients and others have access for information on a variety of subjects
- **d.** Speech recognition: technology that permits interaction with system using voice
- **e.** Telephone Interface Systems
  - **i.** Private branch exchanges (PBX)
  - **ii.** Circuit-switching technology
  - **iii.** Packet-switching technology
  - **iv.** Computer-telephone integration
- **f.** Computer telephone applications and caller assistance: call control, caller identification, collection of call event data, and caller interaction
- **g.** Internet protocol (IP) telephony: allows real-time calls to be initiated through the Internet instead of public telephone system
- **h.** Web centers: telephone support for the facility's Web site
- **i.** Fax on demand: user selects from a list of available fax sources by keying in the corresponding number of a fax title or from multiple fax messages via the telephone.
- **j.** Telemedicine
  - **i.** Exchange of medical information between sites via electronic communications for the health and education of the patient or health care provider and for improving patient care
  - **ii.** Uses bandwidth to transmit various forms of information (bandwidth is a measure of how much information can be transmitted simultaneously through a communication channel and is measured in bits per second, or bps)
  - **iii.** Types include facsimile (fax), audio, still images, and full-motion video
- **k.** Three-dimensional imaging: contains all three spatial dimensions and is easier to understand when viewed
- **l.** Personal digital assistants (PDAs): allow for portable computing and rapid access to information sources
- **m.** Wireless networking: provides network connectivity without ethernet or other wires
- **n.** Smart Cards
  - **i.** Credit-card size cards that contain integrated circuit technology
  - **ii.** Integrated circuit contains a processor and memory subsystem.
  - **iii.** A portable and secure way to carry information
- **o.** Virtual private network: creates the illusion of a fast, secure network, but shares a public network such as the Internet or other IP network

9. Internet Technologies
- **a.** Network Architecture
  - **i.** The way a computer network is set up; its basic design or architecture

    ii. Two main types of network architectures
        1. Local area network (LAN)
            a. Connects computers in a relatively small area (room, building)
            b. Client-server network
            c. Peer-to-peer network
            d. Hybrid network (mixture of client-server and peer-to-peer)
        2. Wide area network (WAN)
            a. Connects devices across a large geographical area (state or world), such as the Internet
            b. Consists of two or more connected LANs

b. Internet
    i. Consists of thousands of loosely connected networks (LANs, WANs) and no single group is responsible for it; each network on the Internet is independent, but each network communicates with the Internet using the same networking language.
    ii. Protocols
        1. Relies on software called browsers
        2. TCP/IP protocol for transmission of data
        3. IP refers to unique network address that is assigned to each computer on the Internet.
        4. The specific algorithm assigned to the transfer of data through Web browsers is the hypertext transfer protocol (HTTP).
        5. HTTP determines how information is formatted and transmitted and what action browsers take in response to commands (HTTPS is secure mode).
    iii. Tools for preparing documents to be viewed through browser
        1. HTML: hypertext markup language
        2. SGML: standard generalized markup language
        3. XML: extensible markup language
    iv. JAVA
        1. Programming language
        2. Allows construction of stand-alone applications that can be transferred across the Web and run independently on a client computer
        3. Applets
            a. Small programs (applications) at the top of HTML page that run on client side
            b. Available through the user's Web browser
            c. Temporarily downloaded to the user's machine and performs calculations in real time
        4. Servlet: functions like an applet but resides on server side, not client side
    v. Security tools
        1. Provide encryption for Internet connections
        2. Organizations should use secure socket layer (SSL)
        3. CMS requires all Internet transmissions containing patient data to be sent using SSL to protect patient confidentiality
        4. Allows browser and server of the Web transmission to authenticate identities and encrypt the data transfer

c. Intranet
    i. Special form of a LAN
    ii. Networking capability within one organization that uses Internet technologies, software that uses HTML, and Web-browser software

to accomplish computer communications within the organization

    iii. Servers are located inside a firewall or security barrier and can be accessible only to authenticated users on a specific network

  d. Extranets

    i. Similar to intranet

    ii. Provides network connectivity between suppliers to allow direct connection between networks

  e. E-commerce: the marketing, buying, selling, and support of products and services over the Internet, intranets, and extranets

    i. Allows consumers to learn about medicines they are taking, buy medicines, learn about diseases and disease prevention, and other activities

    ii. Involves electronic data interchange (EDI) and electronic funds transfer (EFT) payment systems

    iii. Multiple uses

      1. Physician referral services

      2. Lists of health care classes and seminars

      3. Information on clinical trials

      4. Uses Internet to create bulletin boards, electronic surveys, newsletters, and e-mail information on diagnoses and treatment of diseases

      5. External links to federal agencies and other organizations that provide health care

      6. Builds strategic alliance with customers, suppliers, consultants, and competitors

  f. E-health: provision of health information and services through Internet technologies

    i. Storing personal health data

    ii. Reference information on a variety of health issues

    iii. Manage health care superstores

10. Electronic Health Records

  a. Definitions

    i. Health care information: all information, oral or recorded in any form, related to any care, service, or procedure to diagnose, treat, or maintain the physical or mental condition of an individual identified patient. It is obtained in the course of a patient's health care from a health care provider, from the patient, from a member of the patient's family or an individual with whom the patient has a close personal relationship, or from the patient's legal representative.

    ii. Patient medical record: primary repository for information concerning a patient's health care, uniquely representing patients and serving as a dynamic resource for the health care industry

    iii. Health informatics: science that deals with health information, its structure, acquisition, and uses

    iv. Computer-based patient record: an electronic patient record that resides in a system specially designed to support users by providing accessibility to complete and accurate data, alerts, reminders, clinical decision-support systems, links to medical knowledge, and other aids

    v. Electronic health record (EHR)

      1. Any information relating to the past, present, or future physical or mental health or condition of an individual; resides in electronic systems used to capture, transmit, receive, store, retrieve, link, and manipulate multimedia data for the primary purpose of providing health care and health-related services

2. Form of computer-based health record in which information is stored by whole files instead of by individual data elements

3. EHR should do the following
   a. Have a positive impact on workflow operations
   b. Improve administrative process
   c. Include uniform core data elements and standardized coding
   d. Use common data dictionary
   e. Perform searches
   f. Provide 24-hour access with rapid retrieval
   g. Link to other information systems
   h. Provide real-time alerts and possible remedies

4. EHR building blocks
   a. Data: raw material of information system
   b. Information: collection of data that contains meaning when processed
   c. Knowledge: formalization of the relationships among elements of information and data
   d. Infrastructure: technology architecture required to maintain EHR
   e. Registration: admission, discharge, transfer
   f. Data interface standards
      i. Health Level 7 and vocabulary dictionaries and interface engines are used to transfer data, sometimes translating or reformatting as required.
      ii. May be transferred to repositories for future use
      iii. Designed to deliver the individual patient's information to the care team via the clinical workstation, where the content and presentation capability take over

5. EHR vocabularies
   a. Used to represent and communicate concepts, including symptoms, diagnoses, procedures, and health status
   b. Text processing: computer processing of natural language
   c. Natural language processing: all terms and expressions used by a discipline in its models
   d. Script-based system: combines keywords and scripts; may be a predesigned expression that represents information about consequences of care processes

b. Health Evaluation through Logical Processing (HELP)
   i. Comprehensive hospital information system that combines clinically based modules with a financial database
   ii. Integrates information from admitting, radiology, pharmacy, pathology, nursing, respiratory therapy, and clinical laboratories
   iii. Creates an EHR
   iv. Designed to
      1. Accommodate research subsystems to facilitate clinical research, including cost and quality components
      2. Combine communications and clinical alert features through time-drive and data-drive rules

c. Health Level Seven (HL7)
   i. Electronic interchange of clinical, financial, and administrative information among disparate health information systems

   ii. Allows for the transmission of data from one computer to another

   iii. Used for intrainstitution transmission of orders; clinical observations and clinical data, including test results; admission, transfer, and discharge records; and charge and billing information

  d. Institute of Medicine established to do the following

   i. Examine current state of medical record systems

   ii. Identify impediments to development and use of improved record systems

   iii. Identify ways to overcome impediments

   iv. Develop a research agenda to advance medical record systems

   v. Develop a plan for improved medical record systems, including means for updating systems

   vi. Recommend policies and other strategy to achieve improvements

11. **Information Resources Management (IRM)**

 a. Encompasses all the management concepts concerned with the creation, usage, storage, and disposal of information in a business setting

 b. Provides the plan to integrate all information processes, computer and manual, and all information technologies associated with computers, telecommunications, office automation, distributed processing, and selection and implementation of computer systems

 c. Assumes that information is a valuable resource that must be managed, no matter what form it takes or in what medium it is stored

 d. Chief information officer (CIO) is the senior-level executive manager of IRM and is responsible for leading the strategic information system planning process, helping the leadership team use information systems in support of strategic planning and management, and overseeing the organization's IRM functions

12. Role of Health Information Manager in Information Systems

 a. Information broker: intermediary between a client and an information product or group of services

 b. Advocate for effective system development or selection by assuming prominent role in the system development life cycle

 c. Custodian of patient health information, regardless of media on which it is maintained

 d. Establishes policies, procedures, systems, and safeguards to ensure patient health information is documented, maintained, and disclosed in accordance with all health information laws, regulations, and standards

 e. Ensures the functionality of electronic health record systems with respect to the practice of health information management and its support of other business functions of the organization

 f. Under the Information Engineering Domain

  i. Strategic planning: identification of goals and the critical success factors of the enterprise

  ii. Data modeling: development of a detailed logical database design

  iii. Process modeling: analyzing the processes of an organization, usually on a departmental basis

  iv. Data administration: administrative rather than technical functions associated with data and database management

  v. Interface design: content or layout of screens and reports; may use CASE tools such as screen painters, report generators, or prototyping software

 g. Information Retrieval and Analysis, and Policy Development

PRACTICAL APPLICATION OF YOUR KNOWLEDGE

1. Discuss the evolution of information systems in health care.

2. List and describe the various categories of computer systems.

3. List five programming languages.

4. Define an information system and give an example.

5. Distinguish between system and application software.

6. Describe the following five types of information systems.
   a. Transaction processing system (TPS)

   b. Management information system (MIS)

   c. Executive information system (EIS)

   d. Expert system (ES)

   e. Decision support system (DSS)

7. Match the type of information system with the scenario in which it would be best used (TPS, MIS, EIS, ES, DSS).

a. _____ The CEO of Houston Ambulatory Care Clinic is performing strategic planning. She needs to ask "what-if" questions to assist with the process.

b. _____ The admissions, discharge, and transfer system.

c. _____ Dr. Johnson queries the system with a patient's symptoms to obtain possible diagnoses.

d. _____ Dr. Thomas obtains an alert stating that his patient's lab values are higher than the norm.

e. _____ Odell Tyson, R.N., is charge nurse for the medicine unit. She queries the system to obtain the census.

8. Considering the four levels of data organization, use the relational database table to label the item, record, and file.

Relational Database Table

ID	Last Name	First Name	Address	Date of Birth	Dx Code	Pr Code	Amount Owed
1.	Tyson	Carla	1458 Spruce	9/20/1959	250.00		$50
2.	Thomas	Shirlyn	889 Oh	2/6/1972	141.03	74.1	$10
3.	Johnson	Casandra	394 Pleasant	3/27/1970	852.02	01.24	$30
4.	Rodriquez	Marilyn	789 Gerind	5/9/1980	864.15	50.61	$65
5.	Stariha	Carolyn	225 Needville	4/16/1972	403.91	39.95	$87
6.	Rodriguez	Irma	745 Valley	12/5/1984	414.00	36.06	$34

a. If a researcher wanted to obtain all patients from a database with the last name of "Rodriquez," what method would he/she use to extract the data?

b. With the method you identified in the previous question, list at least three types of reports that can be obtained from the above file.

c. Select the phrase that best describes each term.

1. _____ record
2. _____ field
3. _____ database
4. _____ query
5. _____ data dictionary
6. _____ table
7. _____ entity

a. smallest storage unit for data
b. list of information describing the field
c. question asked by user, answer to which is in database
d. columns (fields) and rows of related information in a database
e. collection of related data items treated as a unit
f. persons, locations, things, or concepts that can be collected or stored as data
g. a collection of stored data, typically organized into fields, records, and files

9. Compute the following:

    a. A discharge summary is one typewritten page. Approximately how many kilobytes is the discharge summary?

    b. An operative report is 3072 bytes in length. How many kilobytes is the report?

    c. A transcription company types approximately 5000 reports a month. The average report is 4.5 kilobytes in length. How many megabytes are needed to store the transcribed documents?

10. The ambulatory care clinic is planning to implement an electronic health record system. The health information director needs to make a graphical representation of the proposed flow of the information in the electronic medical record. What tool for system analysis will assist with this graphic representation?

11. Discuss the administrative, financial, clinical, outpatient, and research information systems and give an example of each.

12. Define the functions of a database management system.

13. Discuss the five major database models.

14. Describe the relational database and how data is arranged and manipulated.

15. Distinguish among data warehouse, data mart, and data mining.

16. List and explain the four major phases of the system development life cycle.

17. Discuss methods to assure the security and protection of health information.

18. Explain authentication tools used by information systems.

19. Discuss how intranets and extranets utilize Internet technologies.

20. Identify network protocols used with the Internet.

21. Explain functional requirements and expectations for the electronic health record.

22. Discuss the role of the health information professional with regard to information systems.

23. Why is a firewall needed in an information system?

24. You have just been hired for the position of Chief Information Officer at Houston Memorial Hospital. Discuss what your duties include.

25. What are e-commerce and e-health?

TEST YOUR KNOWLEDGE

1. Which of the following is an example of a clinical information system?
   a. Executive information system
   b. Results reporting
   c. ADT
   d. Master patient index

2. Which job title is most appropriate to manage the information resource management in a health care institution?
   a. Chief Information Officer
   b. Health Information Manager
   c. System Analyst
   d. Data Administrator

3. The physicians of the pediatric clinic need a system to assist with diagnosing patients. Which of the following systems will be most advantageous?
   a. Executive information system
   b. Extranet
   c. Management information system
   d. Decision support system

4. In order to make the electronic medical record documentation more efficient for the surgery nursing service, which of the following systems should be employed?
   a. Point of care
   b. Decision support system
   c. Admission, discharge, and transfer system
   d. Data mart

5. The CEO needs a system to assist with strategic planning and making "what-if" decisions. What is the information system that will best meet her needs?
   a. Executive information system
   b. Expert system
   c. Decision support system
   d. Data warehouse

6. The pharmacy department requests a focused information system that will allow it to research its historical data in great detail. Which system should the pharmacy use?
   a. Data warehouse
   b. Data mining
   c. Data mart
   d. Expert system

7. In an electronic health record system, how are sonograms processed?
   a. Video
   b. HTML
   c. Images
   d. Audio

8. The Houston Hospital information system requires a mechanism for recording access and transactions of its users. What authentication tool can be implemented?
   a. Ethernet
   b. Token ring
   c. Turnaround document
   d. Token card

9. In the system analysis phase of the system development life cycle, which tool is used to break down problems into smaller levels of details?
   a. Entity relationship diagram
   b. Hierarchy chart
   c. Data dictionary
   d. Flow chart

10. The health information department is going to store 2500 discharge summaries on optical disk. Each discharge summary is approximately 3072 bytes in length. How many kilobytes of space are needed to store the data?
    a. 3k
    b. 30.72k
    c. 7500k
    d. 7,680,000k

11. Health Level Seven (HL7) allows for the:

a. communication and clinical alerts through time drive and data drive.

b. electronic interchange of clinical, financial, and administrative information among disparate health information systems.

c. creation of an electronic health record to accommodate research subsystems that facilitate clinical research.

d. integration of information from admitting, radiology, pharmacy, pathology, nursing, respiratory therapy, and clinical laboratories.

12. GUI is an acronym for _____, which provides an environment using icons, tool bars of pull-down menus, and click, point, and drag with the mouse.

a. assembly level language

b. graphical user interface

c. binary system

d. COBOL

13. Houston Hospital has been collecting data on physician credentialing for 4 years. The credentials specialist wants to retrieve all the physicians in the database who are pediatricians. Which tool should be used to run the report?

a. XML

b. HTML

c. HTTP

d. SQL

14. You want to depict the movement of patient information from the time of admittance to the point of discharge. Which of the following tools is most appropriate?

a. Data modeling

b. Decomposition diagram

c. Hierarchy chart

d. Data flow diagram

15. You are developing a Web page for the health information department. Which software would you most probably use?

a. COBOL

b. PASCAL

c. HTML

d. JAVA

e. Both c and d

16. As HIM director, you are involved in a project to assist the systems analyst in creating a central repository of all data elements utilized in the master patient index database. An example of this documentation includes: Length: 1 character, Type: alphanumeric, Value: M=Male and F=Female. This resource is known as what?

a. Data flow diagram

b. Decision table

c. Entity relationship diagram

d. Data dictionary

17. Bob has been hired to implement an information system for the radiology department. Which of the following will provide him with the ability to determine the best staffing pattern for efficient patient care?

a. Executive information system

b. Decision support system

c. Knowledge management system

d. Expert system

18. Bob, as director of nursing, suggests a point-of-care system, which should include a(n):

a. clinical decision support system.

b. executive decision support system.

c. knowledge management system.

d. robotics component for assessing vitals.

19. Which of the following is supported by a tactical database?

a. Executive information system

b. Results reporting

c. ADT

d. Staff scheduling

20. Houston Hospital requires a transaction-oriented information system. Which of the following might they purchase?
   a. R-ADT system
   b. Medical decision support
   c. Executive information system
   d. Electronic mail

21. Bob is programming the management information system for the entry of discharge summaries. Which data type should he use to code the discharge summary?
   a. Image
   b. Numeric
   c. Text
   d. Audio

22. Barbette plans to query the database in order to determine the number of female discharges, age 20–25, with an ICD-9-CM diagnostic code of 250.01, during December of last year. Which of the following might she use?
   a. Rich text language
   b. Integrated text language
   c. Knowledge-based language
   d. Structured query language

23. The CEO of Houston Hospital wants an information system that combines data with analysis tools to facilitate "what-if" questions for posing future optional scenarios. Which should she purchase?
   a. Expert system
   b. Executive information system
   c. Decision support system
   d. Both executive information system and decision support system

24. ICD-9-CM codes are which type of data?
   a. Text
   b. Numeric
   c. Alphanumeric
   d. Alpha

25. During system analysis, Bob uses a tool that shows relations between data. What is he using?
   a. Data dictionary
   b. Entity relationship diagram
   c. Data flow chart
   d. Relational flex chart

26. JAVA compilers are usually found in:
   a. Web browsers.
   b. spreadsheets.
   c. databases.
   d. word processors.

27. Which of the following is an attribute for an MPI entry?
   a. Admission date
   b. Physician order entry
   c. Medical record
   d. Financial record

28. The CIO of Houston Hospital suggests a system designed to provide diagnostic and other expert advice to clinicians from various resources. Which should she purchase?
   a. Clinical information system
   b. Picture archiving and communication system
   c. Clinical decision support system
   d. Executive information system

29. An order entry system is a component of a:
   a. clinical decision support system.
   b. clinical information system.
   c. executive information system.
   d. database management system.

30. Benefits of an electronic medical record over a paper-based system include no lost charts and:
   a. improved hands-on patient care.
   b. better clinician bedside manners.
   c. decreased allergic drug reactions.
   d. better data collection.

31. An application of a clinical information system would be in _____ management.
    a. quality improvement
    b. financial
    c. human resource
    d. materials

32. Which of the following health information applications lends itself well to automation?
    a. Patient communication
    b. Follow-up with clinicians
    c. Indexing
    d. Employee counseling

33. Master programs that manage the basic operations of the computer are called:
    a. utility programs.
    b. language translators.
    c. operating systems.
    d. user interfaces.

34. The process of sorting through the organization's data to identify unusual patterns is called:
    a. data mining.
    b. language translation.
    c. operating systems.
    d. user interfaces.

35. A type of database where data are stored in predefined tables that contain rows and columns similar to a spreadsheet is called a(n) _____ database.
    a. executive
    b. objective
    c. subjective
    d. relational

Use the following table to answer questions 36–37. Choose the best answer.

Sample Relational Database

Name	Gender	Age	City
Washington	Female	24	Houston
Applegate	Male	44	Houston
Matthews	Female	12	Sugar Land

36. The preceding is a relational database table. What is an alternative name for each row?
    a. File
    b. Record
    c. Field
    d. Relation

37. The preceding is a relational database table. What is an alternative name for each column?
    a. File
    b. Record
    c. Field
    d. Relation

38. Barbette is reading her email and the following window pops up.

> Medical Record Committee meeting today, 3 PM

This is an example of a(n):
a. reminder.
b. alert.
c. JAVA.
d. GUI.

39. Dr. Bob ordered Zithromax for his newborn patient. A window pop-up read the following:

> Patient 2 days old. Do you want to continue with this medication order?

This is an example of a(n):
a. reminder.
b. alert.
c. JAVA.
d. GUI.

40. The pharmacy department wants to set up a database to research and study adverse reactions to Coumadin. Which of the following should be established?
a. External data model
b. Conceptual data model
c. Internal data model
d. Data mart

41. Dr. Bob queries the EHR to determine the best medication for his 2-day-old newborn. Which system would be most beneficial?
a. Executive decision support
b. Clinical decision support
c. Tactical decision support
d. Operational decision support

42. Houston Hospital utilizes wireless laptops for documenting in the EHR. Which security protocol system provides the strongest security?
a. WEP
b. WiFi
c. WPA
d. TCP/IP

43. An interface engine:
a. serves as bridge between applications.
b. allows for point to point connection.
c. is a type of hardware.
d. is a type of software.

44. Within an e-mail there is an embedded object that enables direct access to another related Web page. What type of link is the embedded object?
a. Hyperspace
b. Hypertext
c. GUI
d. JAVA

45. Based upon the following table, calculate the payback period in years for the purchase of a scanner.

Cost Chart	Year 1	Year 2	Year 3	Year 4
Current system cost	$3000	$3000	$3000	$3000
New system cost	$5300	$1100	$1100	$1100
Yearly difference in cost	$2300	$1900	$1900	$1900
Cumulative difference in cost	($2300)	($400)	$1500	$3400

a. 1
b. 2
c. 3
d. 4

46. Barbette, director of HIM, writes a proposal for an electronic chart tracking system. She states that the purchase of the $30,000 system will save approximately $9000 per year in personnel time. She has conducted a:
   a. cost-benefit analysis.
   b. break-even analysis.
   c. cost-effectiveness analysis.
   d. payback period.

47. In order to improve patient safety, Dr. Bob encourages administration to purchase an EHR with medication alerts. Which of the following has he conducted?
   a. Cost-benefit analysis
   b. Break-even analysis
   c. Cost-effectiveness analysis
   d. Payback period

48. The manager of record retrieval requires a system to assist with making day-to-day decisions. Which system would be most effective?
   a. Tactical decision support system
   b. Executive decision support
   c. Clinical decision support
   d. Operational decision support

49. The HIM department has set up and installed the new scanner, trained users, and performed testing. They are in the _____ phase of system implementation.
   a. system conversion
   b. system development
   c. system performance
   d. system start-up

50. Which individual is mostly likely to use a tactical decision support system?
   a. CEO
   b. Director of HIM
   c. Coding supervisor
   d. Physician

Biomedical Sciences

The following is a common list of drugs, the conditions they treat, and the tests used to determine the diagnosis.

Common Drug References

Drug	Conditions Treated	Diagnostic Tests
acetaminophen (Tylenol)	Fever and pain Simple headaches and muscle aches The minor aches and pains of the common cold and flu Backache Toothache Minor pain of arthritis Menstrual cramps Pain due to teething, immunizations, tonsillectomy, and childhood illnesses	Physical examination Temperature monitoring
albuterol (Proventil)	Bronchial spasms (including asthma and bronchial spasm due to exercise)	Allergy testing Bronchoscopy Chest radiography Chest ultrasonograph Chest X-ray Pulmonary function test Pulmonary ventilation scan
alprazolam (Xanax) [Tranquilizer]	Symptoms of anxiety Anxiety disorders	Psychological examination Physical examination

(continues)

Common Drug References *(Continued)*

Drug	Conditions Treated	Diagnostic Tests
amitriptyline (Elavil) [Member of the group of drugs called tricyclic antidepressants]	Mental depression May be prescribed for bulimia (an eating disorder), chronic pain, the prevention of migraine headaches, and the pathological weeping and laughing syndrome associated with multiple sclerosis	Psychological examination Physical examination
amlodipine (Norvasc)	High blood pressure (hypertension) Angina pectoris	Stress test EKG Blood pressure monitoring CAT scan
amoxicillin (Amoxil) [Antibiotic for bacterial infections]	Gonorrhea Middle ear infections Skin infections Upper and lower respiratory tract infections Infections of the genital and urinary tract	Physical examination Culture Urine test Blood test if needed
amoxicillin clavulante (Augmentin)	Lower respiratory, middle ear, sinus, skin, and urinary tract infections caused by specific bacteria that produce a chemical enzyme called beta lactamase that makes some infections particularly difficult to treat	Physical examination Culture Urine test Blood test if needed
atovastatin calcium (Lipitor) [Cholesterol-lowering drug]	Elevated cholesterol levels	HDL and LDL blood tests
azithromycin (Zithromax) [Antibiotic related to erythromycin]	Mild to moderate skin infections Upper and lower respiratory tract infections, including pharyngitis (strep throat), tonsillitis, sinus infections, worsening of chronic obstructive pulmonary disease, and pneumonia Sexually transmitted infections of the cervix or urinary tract Genital ulcer disease in men In children: Middle ear infection Pneumonia Tonsillitis Strep throat	UGI Physical examination Culture Urine test Blood test if needed
cephalexin (Keflex, Keftab) [Cephalosporin antibiotics]	Bacterial infections of the respiratory tract, middle ear, bones, skin, and reproductive and urinary systems	Physical examination Culture Urine test Blood test if needed

Common Drug References *(Continued)*

Drug	Conditions Treated	Diagnostic Tests
cimetidine (Tagamet) [Histamine blocker]	Heartburn Acid indigestion Sour stomach	UGI
cisplatin (Platinol)	Various types of cancers, including sarcomas, some carcinomas (e.g. small cell lung cancer and ovarian cancer), lymphomas, and germ cell tumors	Biopsy
codeine	Pain	Physical examination
cyclobenzaprine HCL (Flexeril) [Muscle relaxant that, when combined with rest and physical therapy, provides relief of muscular stiffness and pain]	Muscle spasms resulting from injuries such as sprains, strains, or pulls	Physical examination
cyclosporine (Sandimmune Neoral)	Organ transplant surgery to help prevent rejection of organs (kidney, heart, or liver) by suppressing the body's immune system and to avoid long-term rejection in people previously treated with other immunosuppressant drugs	Bleeding time Platelet aggregation test Clot retraction test Blood count (WBC, RBC)
dexamethasone (Decadron)	Inflammation and symptoms from a variety of disorders, including rheumatoid arthritis and severe cases of asthma Primary or secondary adrenal cortex insufficiency (lack of sufficient adrenal hormone) Severe allergic conditions, such as drug-induced allergies Blood disorders, such as various anemias Certain cancers (along with other drugs) Skin diseases, such as severe psoriasis Collagen (connective tissue) diseases, such as systemic lupus erythematosus Digestive tract disease such as ulcerative colitis High serum levels of calcium associated with cancer Fluid retention due to nephrotic syndrome (a condition in which damage to the kidneys causes the body to lose protein in the urine) Eye diseases such as allergic conjunctivitis With other drugs, lung diseases such as tuberculosis	Blood count (WBC, RBC)

(continues)

Common Drug References *(Continued)*

Drug	Conditions Treated	Diagnostic Tests
diazepam (Valium) [Benzodiazepine]	Anxiety disorders, including short-term relief of the symptoms of anxiety Symptoms of acute alcohol withdrawal Relax muscles Relieve the uncontrolled muscle movements caused by cerebral palsy and paralysis of the lower body and limbs Involuntary movement of the hands (athetosis) Tight, aching muscles With other medications, convulsive disorders such as epilepsy	Psychological examination Physical examination
digoxin (Lanoxin) [Improves the strength and efficiency of the heart, which leads to better circulation of blood and reduction of the uncomfortable swelling that is common in people with congestive heart failure]	Congestive heart failure Certain types of irregular heartbeat Other heart problems	Stress test EKG Blood pressure monitoring CAT scan
diltiazem HCL (Cardizem)	Angina pectoris (chest pain usually caused by lack of oxygen to the heart due to clogged arteries)	Stress test EKG Blood pressure monitoring CAT scan
ferrous sulfate (Feosol) [Form of the mineral iron, which is important for many functions in the body, especially for the transport of oxygen in the blood]	Dietary supplement Iron deficiencies and iron deficiency anemia	Blood count (RBC) Blood screen
fluoxetine (Prozac) [Selective Serotonin Reuptake Inhibitors (SSRI)]	Depression Obsessive-compulsive disorder (OCD) Panic disorders	Psychological examination Physical examination

Common Drug References *(Continued)*

Drug	Conditions Treated	Diagnostic Tests
haloperidel (Haldol)	Mental disorders such as schizophrenia Tics (uncontrolled muscle contractions of face, arms, or shoulders) and the unintended utterances that mark Tourette's syndrome Short-term treatment of children with severe behavior problems, including hyperactivity and combativeness Severe nausea and vomiting caused by cancer drugs Drug problems, such as LSD flashback and PCP intoxication Symptoms of hemiballismus (a condition that causes involuntary writhing of one side of the body)	Psychological examination Drug screen Complete blood count
heparin [Anticoagulant, a blood thinner]	Prevents the formation of blood clots	Bleeding time Platelet aggregation test Clot retraction test
herazasin HCL (Hytrin)	High blood pressure (hypertension) Symptoms of benign prostatic hyperplasia (BPH)	Stress test EKG Blood pressure monitoring CAT scan
hydrocodone bitatrate (Vicodin) [Narcotic analgesic (painkiller) and cough reliever with a non-narcotic analgesic]	Moderate to moderately severe pain Cough	Physical examination
levothyroxine sodium (Levoxyl synthroid) [Synthetic thyroid hormone]	Thyroid gland not making enough hormone Enlarged thyroid (a goiter) or at risk for developing a goiter Cancers of the thyroid Thyroid production low due to surgery, radiation, certain drugs, or disease of the pituitary gland or hypothalamus in the brain	T3 T4 TSH

(continues)

Common Drug References *(Continued)*

Drug	Conditions Treated	Diagnostic Tests
lisinopril (Prinivil)	High blood pressure (hypertension)	Stress test EKG Blood pressure monitoring CAT scan
loratadine (Claritin) [Antihistamine]	Sneezing, runny nose, stuffiness, itching, and tearing eyes caused by hay fever or other upper respiratory allergies Swollen, red, itchy patches of skin caused by hives	Bronchoscopy Chest radiography Chest ultrasonograph Chest X-ray Pulmonary ventilation scan
lorazepan (Ativan) [Benzodiazepines drug class]	Anxiety disorders Relief of the symptoms of anxiety	Psychological examination Physical examination
meperidine (Demerol) [Narcotic analgesic]	Moderate to severe pain	Physical examination
metaformin HCL (Glucophage) [Oral antidiabetic medication]	Type 2 (non-insulin-dependent) diabetes	FBS, PPBS, GTT, c-peptide, glucagon Blood urea nitrogen (BUN) and plasma creatinine test to detect kidney function
methyldopa (Aldomet)	High blood pressure (hypertension)	Stress test EKG Blood pressure monitoring CAT scan
metoclopramide HCL (Reglan) [Increases the contractions of the stomach and small intestine to help the passage of food]	Symptoms of diabetic gastroparesis	UGI LGI
metoprolol tartrate (Lopressor) [Beta blocker]	High blood pressure (hypertension) Angina pectoris (chest pain usually caused by lack of oxygen to the heart due to clogged arteries) Myocardial infarction (heart attack)	Stress test EKG Blood pressure monitoring CAT scan

Common Drug References *(Continued)*

Drug	Conditions Treated	Diagnostic Tests
nabumetone (Relafen) [Nonsteroidal anti-inflammatory drug]	Inflammation, swelling, stiffness, and joint pain associated with rheumatoid arthritis and osteoarthritis	Physical examination
nadolol (Corgard)	Angina pectoris (chest pain, usually caused by lack of oxygen to the heart due to clogged arteries) High blood pressure (hypertension)	Stress test EKG Blood pressure monitoring CAT scan
naproxen (Anaprox, Aleve) [Nonsteroidal anti-inflammatory drugs]	Mild to moderate pain and menstrual cramps Inflammation, swelling, stiffness, and joint pain associated with rheumatoid arthritis and osteoarthritis (the most common form of arthritis), and for ankylosing spondylitis (spinal arthritis), tendinitis, bursitis, acute gout, and other conditions May be prescribed for juvenile arthritis	Physical examination
nifedipine (Procardia XL) [Calcium channel blocker]	High blood pressure (hypertension)	Stress test EKG Blood pressure monitoring CAT scan
nitroglycerin (Nitro-dur, NitroQuick, Nitrogard)	Angina pectoris	Stress test EKG Blood pressure monitoring CAT scan
oxybutynin HCL (Ditropan) [Relaxes bladder muscles]	Incontinence	Physical examination
oxytocin (Pitocin)	Induce labor Increase the strength or duration of labor contractions	Fetal monitor Labor and delivery assessment

(continues)

Common Drug References *(Continued)*

Drug	Conditions Treated	Diagnostic Tests
paroxetine HCL (Paxil) [Selective Serotonin Reuptake Inibitor (SSRI)]	Serious, continuing depression that interferes with patient's ability to function Obsessive-compulsive disorder (OCD) Panic disorder Generalized anxiety disorder Social anxiety disorder Post-traumatic stress disorder Major depression	Psychological examination Physical examination
phenobarbital sodium (Bellatal, Luminal) [Barbiturate that depresses the activity of the brain and nervous system]	Induce sleep Insomnia (for up to 2 weeks) Prevent and treat seizures	CAT scan Complete blood work-up EKG EEG
potassium (K-Dur)	Low potassium levels in people who may face potassium loss caused by digitalis, non-potassium-sparing diuretics, and certain diseases	Potassium (K+)
prednisone (Deltasone) [Steroid drug]	Inflammation Symptoms in rheumatoid arthritis and severe cases of asthma Abnormal adrenal gland development Allergic conditions (severe) Blood disorders Certain cancers (along with other drugs) Diseases of the connective tissue including systemic lupus erythematosus Eye diseases of various kinds Flare-ups of multiple sclerosis Fluid retention due to nephrotic syndrome Lung diseases, including tuberculosis Meningitis (inflamed membranes around the brain) Prevention of organ rejection Rheumatoid arthritis and related disorders Severe flare-ups of ulcerative colitis or enteritis (inflammation of the intestines) Skin diseases Thyroid gland inflammation Trichinosis (with complications)	Bronchoscopy Chest radiography Chest ultrasonograph Chest X-ray Pulmonary ventilation scan

Common Drug References *(Continued)*

Drug	Conditions Treated	Diagnostic Tests
promethazine HCL (Phenergan) [Antihistamine]	Nasal stuffiness and inflammation and red, inflamed eyes caused by hay fever and other allergies Itching, swelling, and redness from hives and other rashes Allergic reactions to blood transfusions With other medications, anaphylactic shock (severe allergic reaction) Sedative and sleep aid for both children and adults Prevent and control nausea and vomiting before and after surgery Prevent and treat motion sickness With other medications, for pain after surgery	Physical examination Culture Urine test Blood test if needed
propoxyphene (Darvon, Darvocet-N, Propoxy)	Pain	Physical examination
propranolol HCL (Inderal) [Beta blocker]	High blood pressure (hypertension) Angina pectoris (chest pain usually caused by lack of oxygen to the heart due to clogged arteries) Changes in heart rhythm Prevention of migraine headache Hereditary tremors Hypertrophic subaortic stenosis (a condition related to exertional angina) Tumors of the adrenal gland Reduce the risk of death from recurring heart attack	Stress test EKG Blood pressure monitoring CAT scan
quinopril (Accupril) [ACE inhibitor class]	High blood pressure (hypertension) Congestive heart failure	Stress test EKG Blood pressure monitoring CAT scan
randitidine HCL (Zantac)	Decrease the production of stomach acid Irritation to the stomach lining Ulcers and other gastrointestinal conditions	UGI
simvastatin (Zocor) [Cholesterol-lowering drug for people at high risk of heart disease]	LDL levels ≥130 Bypass surgery or angioplasty to clear clogged arteries	HDL and LDL blood tests

(continues)

Common Drug References *(Continued)*

Drug	Conditions Treated	Diagnostic Tests
streptokinase (Streptase) [Clot-dissolving medication]	Myocardial infarction (heart attack) Pulmonary embolism	Stress test EKG Blood pressure monitoring CAT scan
tetracycline (Sumycin Panmycin) [Broad-spectrum antibiotic often used as an alternative for people who are allergic to penicillin]	Bacterial infections such as Rocky Mountain spotted fever, typhus fever, and tick fevers Upper respiratory infections Pneumonia Gonorrhea Amoebic infections Urinary tract infections Severe acne Trachoma (a chronic eye infection) and conjunctivitis (pinkeye)	Physical examination Culture Urine test Blood test if needed
theophylline (Theo-dur) [Oral bronchodilator medication]	Symptoms of asthma, chronic bronchitis, and emphysema	Bronchoscopy Chest radiography Chest ultrasonograph Chest X-ray Pulminary ventilation scan
tobramycin ointment (Tobradex) [Topical antibiotic]	Bacterial infections of the eye	Physical examination Culture Urine test Blood test if needed
tramadol HCL (Ultram)	Moderate to moderately severe pain	Physical examination
trimethoprim and Sulfamenthoxazole (Bactrim) [Antibacterial combination drug]	Certain urinary tract infections Severe middle ear infections in children Long-lasting or frequently recurring bronchitis in adults that increases in seriousness Inflammation of the intestine due to a severe bacterial infection Traveler's diarrhea in adults Pneumocystis carinii pneumonia (also for prevention of this pneumonia in people with weakened immune systems)	Physical examination Culture Urine test Blood test if needed

Common Drug References *(Continued)*

Drug	Conditions Treated	Diagnostic Tests
warafin sulfate (Coumadin) [Anticoagulant, a blood thinner]	Prevent and/or treat a blood clot that has formed within a blood vessel or in the lungs Prevent and/or treat blood clots associated with certain heart conditions or replacement of a heart valve Aid in the prevention of blood clots that may form in blood vessels anywhere in the body after a heart attack Reduce the risk of death, another heart attack, or stroke after a heart attack	Bleeding time Platelet aggregation test Clot retraction test
zolpidem tartrate (Ambien) [Relatively new drug chemically different from other common sleep medications like Halcion and Dalmane]	Insomnia (difficulty falling asleep or staying asleep, or early awakening)	Psychological examination Physical examination

Common Pharmacology Abbreviations

aa	of each
ac	before meals
ad	right ear
as	left ear
A.U.	both ears
B.I.D	two times a day
BP	blood pressure
cc	cubic centimeter
gm	gram
h.s.	at bedtime
I.M.	intramuscular
IV	intravenous
mg	milligram
ml	milliliter
mm	millimeter
npo	nothing by mouth
O.D.	right eye
O.S.	left eye
O.U.	both eyes
p.c.	after meals
P.O.	orally
p.r.n.	as needed
qam	every morning
Q.D.	once a day
Q.H.	every hour
Q.I.D.	four times a day
Q.O.D	every other day
S.L.	sublingually
Stat	immediately
T.I.D	three times a day
ud	as directed
ung	ointment

TEST YOUR KNOWLEDGE

1. A patient is admitted with a diagnosis of pneumoconiosis. Which of the following may be used as a definitive diagnostic test?
   a. Pulmonary device test
   b. Pulmonary function test
   c. Bronchodilators
   d. Bronchoinhalers

2. A patient is admitted with chest pain. The physician wants to rule out angina pectoris. He performs an ECG. What would the ECG show?
   a. Low HDL
   b. High HDL
   c. Ischemia
   d. Increased blood flow

3. A patient is admitted with angina pectoris. Which of the following drugs may the patient be prescribed?
   a. Fosomax
   b. Procardia
   c. Premarin
   d. Codeine

4. A patient is admitted with angina pectoris. From which of the following drug groups may the patient receive his/her prescription?
   a. Calcium channel blockers
   b. Cox 2 Inhibitors
   c. Antiemetics
   d. Antidyskinetics

5. A patient is diagnosed with arthritis. Which of the following drugs might be prescribed?
   a. Robaxin
   b. Flonase
   c. Celebrex
   d. Albuterol

6. A patient is experiencing nausea from a Caribbean cruise. Which drug group might the patient receive a prescription from?
   a. GABA agents
   b. Antiadrenergics
   c. Ophthalmic prostaglandins
   d. Antiemetics

7. A pulmonary function test may be used to rule out which of the following diagnoses?
   a. Goiter
   b. Urologic pathologies
   c. Ophthalmic neurosis
   d. Bronchiectasis

8. Abnormal results in the thrombin time may be indicative of:
   a. multiple myeloma.
   b. bronchiectasis.
   c. decreased oxygen.
   d. pneumoconiosis.

9. ACE inhibitors are used to treat which condition?
   a. Asthma
   b. Diabetes
   c. Psychosis
   d. Hypertension

10. Increased plasma bilirubin levels are associated with:
    a. hemolytic anemias.
    b. neuropathy.
    c. diabetes.
    d. renal disease.

11. Because the lung tissue is spongy, the chest X-ray is:
    a. not a good radiography study to rule out pneumonia.
    b. a good radiography study to rule out pneumonia.
    c. inconsistent with diagnosing lung diseases.
    d. incapable of diagnosing lung diseases.

12. A patient with cretinism on thyroid scan would show a(n) _____ in _____ uptake.
   a. decrease; iodine
   b. increase; iodine
   c. decrease; sodium
   d. increase; sodium

13. A physician may prescribe _____ to treat patients with diabetes insipidus.
   a. SSRIs
   b. statins
   c. sulfonylureas
   d. vasopressin injections

14. An increase in the fibrinogen assay test results may indicate which condition?
   a. Hepatitis
   b. Diabetes insipidus
   c. Anemia
   d. Hypertension

15. Thiazolidinediones may be used to treat:
   a. depression.
   b. high cholesterol.
   c. diabetes mellitus.
   d. asthma.

16. Which of the following is used to treat cretinism?
   a. Potassium iodide
   b. Alpha-adrenergic blockers
   c. Biguanides
   d. Thyroid hormone replacement

17. Beta-adrenergic blocking drugs are used to treat which condition?
   a. Anxiety
   b. Premature labor
   c. Hypertension
   d. Alcoholism

18. A physician may use _____ to treat a patient with a diagnosis of urethritis.
   a. potassium
   b. antibiotics
   c. diuretics
   d. anticoagulants

19. Increased BUN levels are usually caused by inadequate excretion due to what condition?
   a. Alcoholism
   b. Cardiac arrhythmias
   c. Renal disease
   d. Liver disease

20. An abnormal intravenous pyelography (IVP) result may be obtained if the patient has a condition associated with the:
   a. heart.
   b. veins.
   c. kidneys.
   d. lungs.

21. Which of these tests is a primary screen for diabetes mellitus?
   a. Liver enzymes
   b. Fasting blood sugar test
   c. BUN
   d. ELISA

22. For which diagnosis might ampicillin, cephalosporins, and sulfonamides be prescribed?
   a. Electrolyte imbalance
   b. Crohn's Disease
   c. CVA
   d. UTI

23. ACE inhibitors may be prescribed to treat which condition?
   a. Hypertension
   b. Congestive heart failure
   c. Angina pectoris
   d. High cholesterol

24. Nitroglycerin may be prescribed to treat which condition?
   a. Hypertension
   b. Congestive heart failure
   c. Angina pectoris
   d. High cholesterol

25. Beta blockers may be prescribed to treat which condition?
   a. Electrolyte imbalance
   b. Myocardial infarction
   c. Diabetes mellitus
   d. High cholesterol

26. An ECG is used to diagnose:
   a. heart conditions.
   b. renal conditions.
   c. cerebrovascular accidents.
   d. bronchospasms.

27. Epinephrine is used to treat:
   a. heart conditions.
   b. renal conditions.
   c. cerebrovascular accidents.
   d. bronchospasms.

28. A KUB is used to diagnose:
   a. heart conditions.
   b. renal conditions.
   c. cerebrovascular accidents.
   d. bronchospasms.

29. A cerebral angiography is used to diagnose:
   a. heart conditions.
   b. renal conditions.
   c. cerebrovascular accidents.
   d. bronchospasms.

30. Elevated triglyceride levels are associated with:
   a. an increased risk for atherosclerosis.
   b. a diet high in vegetable fats.
   c. non-insulin-dependent diabetes mellitus.
   d. decreased HDLs in postmenopausal women.

31. An increase in blood potassium levels may be indicative of what condition?
   a. Diabetes
   b. Bronchospasms
   c. CVA
   d. Renal failure

32. _____ is not an antipsychotic drug.
   a. Thorazine
   b. Haldol
   c. Zyprexa
   d. Theophyline

33. Variations from normal in the spirometry may indicate which diagnosis?
   a. Cancer of the sigmoid colon
   b. Bronchitis
   c. Alcohol dependence
   d. Cystic fibrosis

34. Pharmacokinetics refers to a patient's _____ of medication.
   a. refusal
   b. acceptance
   c. metabolism
   d. route

35. Demerol may be prescribed for:
   a. emesis.
   b. severe pain.
   c. blocking drug absorption.
   d. inflammation.

36. Alpha-adrenergic blocking drugs stimulate:
   a. vasoconstriction.
   b. vasodilation.
   c. hunger.
   d. dreams.

37. An increase in the activated partial thromboplastin time (APTT) indicates a:
   a. bleeding disorder.
   b. renal condition.
   c. liver condition.
   d. psychotic episode.

38. Decreased plasma BUN levels are associated with which condition?
   a. Glomerulonephritis
   b. Acute tubular necrosis
   c. Liver failure
   d. Chronic gout

39. An abnormal bronchoscopy test may indicate the presence of a:
   a. goiter.
   b. heart condition.
   c. ulcer.
   d. respiratory condition.

40. Hyponatremia is usually indicative of which condition?
  a. Cystic fibrosis
  b. Diabetes mellitus
  c. Diabetes incipidus
  d. Excess body water

41. NSAIDs are used to treat:
  a. asthma.
  b. hypertension.
  c. dementia.
  d. arthritis.

42. A patient diagnosed with leukocytopenia would show a(n) _____ in _____.
  a. increase; WBC
  b. increase; RBC
  c. decrease; WBC
  d. decrease; RBC

43. A patient diagnosed with leukocytosis would demonstrate a(n) _____ in _____.
  a. increase; WBC
  b. increase; RBC
  c. decrease; WBC
  d. decrease; RBC

44. SSRIs may be used to treat:
  a. hypertension.
  b. arthritis.
  c. depression.
  d. UTI.

45. Ditropan is categorized with:
  a. statins.
  b. urinary antispasmodics.
  c. sulfonylureas.
  d. ACE inhibitors.

46. Digoxin may be used to treat:
  a. an ulcer.
  b. CHF.
  c. excessive fluid retention.
  d. high cholesterol.

47. Nitroglycerin may be used to treat:
  a. an ulcer.
  b. angina.
  c. excessive fluid retention.
  d. high cholesterol.

48. Intravenous vasodilators may be used to:
  a. treat an ulcer.
  b. treat a hemorrhage.
  c. induce labor.
  d. treat malignant hypertension.

49. Which of the following may be prescribed for lowering cholesterol?
  a. Zocar
  b. Zithromax
  c. Zantac
  d. Xanax

50. Increased plasma creatinine levels are associated with:
  a. liver failure due to cirrhosis.
  b. early stages of muscular dystrophy.
  c. excessive loss of kidney function.
  d. ingestion of creosote.

Clinical Classification Systems

1. **Documentation and Coding Quality**
   a. Accurate coding is contingent upon complete, accurate, legible, and timely documentation.
   b. ICD-9-CM and CPT coding drives reimbursement and is a mechanism used to determine utilization of services and the quality of care rendered to patients.

2. **Nomenclature and Classification System**
   a. Nomenclature is a list of proper names for diseases and operations; each listing may include a code number.
      i. Standard Nomenclature of Disease and Operations (SNDO)
      ii. Standard Nomenclature of Medicine (SNOMED)
      iii. Standard Nomenclature of Medicine Clinical Terminology (SNOMEDCT)
   b. Classification is a system of assigning code numbers to diseases and operations; related diseases may be grouped together.
      i. ICD-9-CM
      ii. ICD-10 (planned replacement of ICD-9-CM volumes 1 and 2)
      iii. ICD-10-PCS (planned replacement of ICD-9-CM volume 3)
      iv. ICD-O
      v. DSM-IV (Diagnostic and Statistical Manual of Mental Disorders)

3. **Why We Code**
   a. Research
   b. Reimbursement
   c. Predict Health Care Trends
   d. Plan for Future Health Care Needs
   e. Evaluate Use of Health Care Facilities
   f. Study Health Care Costs

4. **ICD-9-CM**
   a. International Classification of Disease, 9th revision, Clinical Modification
   b. Uses
      i. Translate descriptive information into numerical codes for disease, injuries, conditions, and procedures
      ii. Classify morbidity (sickness) and mortality (death)
      iii. First published by World Health Organization (WHO) in 1979

      iv. Volumes of ICD-9-CM
- **1.** Volume 1: tabular list
- **2.** Volume 2: index
- **3.** Volume 3: procedure index and tabular list

c. ICD-9-CM Guidelines of Coding
- **i.** Uniform Hospital Discharge Data Set Terms (UHDDS)
  - **1.** Admitting diagnosis
    - **a.** Working diagnosis
  - **2.** Principle diagnosis
    - **a.** The condition established after study to be chiefly responsible for occasioning the admission of the patient to the hospital for care
  - **3.** Other diagnoses
    - **a.** Additional conditions that affect patient care
  - **4.** First-listed diagnoses
    - **a.** Term used in lieu of a principle diagnosis in an outpatient setting
  - **5.** Principal procedure
    - **a.** Performed for definitive treatment, or one that is necessary, to care for a complication
    - **b.** If more than one procedure, relates to principal diagnosis
  - **6.** Other procedures
    - **a.** Sequenced after principal procedure

d. Official Guidelines Developed by 4 Groups:
- **i.** American Hospital Association (AHA)
  - **1.** Maintains central office on ICD-9-CM
  - **2.** Approves official coding guidelines
  - **3.** Publishes coding clinic
- **ii.** American Health Information Management Association (AHIMA)
  - **1.** Certifies coders
  - **2.** Provides coding education
  - **3.** Sponsors Council on Coding and Classification and the Society for Clinical Coding
  - **4.** Approves official coding guidelines
- **iii.** Centers for Medicaid and Medicare Services (CMS)
  - **1.** Maintains the procedure classification
  - **2.** Approves official coding guidelines
- **iv.** National Center for Health Statistics (NCHS)
  - **1.** Maintains the disease classification
  - **2.** Approves official coding guidelines
  - **3.** Official ICD-9-CM coding guidelines can be found at http://www.cdc.gov/nchs/datawh/ftpserv/ftpicd9/ftpicd9.htm#guidelines.

5. Format of ICD-9-CM Coding Book
- **a.** Volume 1 (tabular list of diseases and injuries)
  - **i.** Chapter
    - **1.** Divided by conditions that affect a specific body system and conditions according to etiology
  - **ii.** Section
    - **1.** Groups of 3-digit categories
  - **iii.** Category
    - **1.** Three-digit code numbers
  - **iv.** Subcategory
    - **1.** Four-digit code numbers

          v. Subclassification

              1. Five-digit code numbers and the most specific code

   b. Volume 2 (alphabetic index of diseases and injuries)

        i. Main terms

              1. Usually identify disease conditions

        ii. Subterms

              1. Indicate site, type, or etiology for a condition or injury

        iii. Carryover lines

              1. Used when complete entry cannot fit on a single line

        iv. Code number and modifier

              1. ICD-9-CM code with modifying term (if any)

        v. Connecting word

              1. Expresses the relationship between main term or subterm, indicating an associated condition or etiology

                  a. With, in, due to

   c. Volume 3 (alphabetic index and tabular list of procedures)

        i. Index procedure

              1. Alphabetic listing of procedures

        ii. Tabular procedure

              1. Numeric listing of procedures

   d. Tables

        i. Hypertension

        ii. Neoplasms

        iii. Drugs and chemicals

6. Conventions

   a. Abbreviations NEC (not elsewhere classified), NOS (not otherwise specified)

   b. Punctuation

        i. Brackets [ ]—enclose synonyms, alternative wording, and explanatory phrases

        ii. Parentheses ( )—supplementary words that may or may not be present

        iii. Braces { }—enclose a series of terms each modified by statement appearing at right of brace

        iv. Colon :—used in tabular list after incomplete term needing modifier

   c. Symbols (section mark, lozenge)

   d. Bold and Italicized Typefaces

   e. Includes and Excludes Notes

   f. Use Additional Code, If Desired

   g. Code also Underlying Disease

   h. Code Also

   i. Omit Code

   j. Eponyms

   k. Main Terms

   l. Joined Main Terms

   m. Non-Essential Modifiers

   n. Not Elsewhere Classifiable (NEC)

   o. Cross Reference Notes

   p. Hypertension Table

   q. Neoplasm

   r. Etiology and Manifestation of Diseases

7. Guidelines for Inpatient Coding

   a. Basic ICD-9-CM Coding Guidelines

        i. Use both alphabetic indexes and tabular list.

        ii. Assign codes to the highest level of detail.

      iii. Assign residual codes (NEC and NOS) as appropriate.

      iv. Assign combination codes when available.

      v. The appropriate code(s) from 001.0 through V84.8 must be used to identify diagnoses, symptoms, conditions, problems, complaints, or other reason(s) for the encounter or visit.

      vi. Selection of codes 001.0 through 999.9 frequently will be used to describe the reason for the admission or encounter. Theses codes are from the section of ICD-9-CM for the classification of diseases and injuries.

      vii. Codes that describe signs and symptoms, as opposed to diagnoses, are acceptable for reporting purposes when a related definitive diagnosis has not been established by the provider.

      viii. Signs and symptoms that are integral to the disease process should not be assigned as additional codes unless otherwise instructed by the classification.

      ix. Additional signs and symptoms that may not be associated routinely with a disease process should be coded when present.

      x. Assign multiple codes as required.

      xi. Assign the combination code only when that code fully identifies the diagnostic conditions involved or as the alphabetic index directs.

      xii. Code unconfirmed diagnoses as if established.

      xiii. If the same condition is described as both acute (sub-acute) and chronic, and separate subentries exist in the alphabetic index at the same indentation level, code both and sequence the acute (sub-acute) code first.

      xiv. Coding of late effects generally requires two codes sequenced in the following order:

          1. The condition or nature of the late effect is sequenced first.

          2. The late effect code is sequenced second.

      xv. Code any condition described at the time of discharge as "impending" or "threatened" as follows:

          1. If it did occur, code as confirmed diagnosis.

          2. If it did not occur, reference the alphabetic index to determine if the condition has a subentry term for "impending" or "threatened" and also reference main term entries for "impending" and for "threatened."

          3. If subterms are listed, assign the given code.

          4. If the subterms are not listed, code the existing underlying condition(s) and not the condition described as "impending" or "threatened."

  b. Refer to ICD-9-CM Official Guidelines for Coding and Reporting set forth by CMS and NCHS, both part of DHHS

8. ICD-9-CM Coding by Chapters

  a. Infectious and Parasitic Diseases

      i. Bacteremia is bacteria in the blood, as confirmed by culture, but may be transient. It denotes a laboratory finding, not an acute illness, but can progress to septicemia when there is a more severe infectious process or an impaired immune system.

      ii. Septicemia or sepsis is a severe infection that is characterized by release of toxins into the bloodstream and the presence of bacteria in the blood. Negative or inconclusive blood cultures do not preclude a diagnosis of septicemia in patients with clinical evidence of the condition.

       iii. Urosepsis NOS is coded to urinary tract infection. Some physicians use this term to mean sepsis due to a urinary tract infection. When documentation is not clear, query the physician.

b. Neoplasms

       i. Codes can be located in the neoplasm table.

       ii. Categories include malignant, benign, carcinoma in situ.

       iii. Invasive means extension of tumor to other sites (metastatic).

       iv. Benign means the tumor is not invasive and will not spread to other sites; usually cured by total excision of tumor.

       v. Carcinoma in situ is undergoing malignant changes, but still confined to point of origin.

       vi. If the primary malignant tumor has been excised, but patient is still undergoing treatment, e.g., chemotherapy or radiation therapy, the primary malignancy code is used.

       vii. Secondary site (metastatic site) is sequenced as principal when reason for admission is based entirely on the secondary malignancy.

       viii. If the secondary site is specified without mention of the primary site, or if the primary site is unknown, code 199.1 (malignant neoplasm, NOS) for the primary site.

       ix. Contiguous sites are identified by a fourth-digit 8 (i.e., other specified sites) when the neoplasm overlaps the boundaries of two or more contiguous sites. Do not use a fourth-digit 8 to replace fourth-digit 9 (unspecified) to avoid using an unspecified code.

c. Endocrine, Nutritional, and Metabolic Diseases

       i. Insulin-dependent diabetes mellitus (IDDM), type 1

       ii. Non-insulin-dependent diabetes mellitus (NIDDM), type 2

       iii. The abbreviation IDDM is not enough to code insulin-dependent diabetes mellitus; the physician must document type 1.

       iv. Fifth digit is needed to specify controlled versus uncontrolled. When poorly controlled is documented, query the physician to see if he/she means uncontrolled.

       v. If a patient is admitted for dehydration due to acute renal failure, sequence the acute renal failure as principal even though treating the dehydration with IV fluids resolves the renal failure.

d. Diseases of the Blood and Blood-Forming Organs

       i. For sickle cell anemia, use addition code to specify type of crisis, e.g., acute chest pain syndrome; code sickle cell anemia with crisis as principal, followed by acute chest pain syndrome as secondary diagnosis.

       ii. If patient is admitted for treatment of anemia due to chronic disease, (e.g., end stage renal disease, neoplastic disease, or other chronic disease), code first the anemia followed by the chronic disease.

       iii. Anemia, thrombocytopenia, and neutropenia documented on same admission should be coded to pancytopenia (284.8), which is a type of aplastic anemia that represents deficiency of all three elements of the blood.

e. Diseases of the Respiratory System

       i. Respiratory failure should be coded as principal diagnosis when a patient is admitted in respiratory failure caused by a respiratory condition such as pneumonia, asthma, emphysema, or chronic obstructive pulmonary disease (COPD) or a chronic non-respiratory condition like myasthenia gravis.

  ii. Respiratory failure should be coded as a secondary diagnosis when a patient is admitted in respiratory failure due to a non-respiratory condition, such as congestive heart failure (CHF), myocardial infarction (MI), poisoning/overdose, or cerebral vascular accident (CVA).

f. Diseases of the Digestive System

  i. For gastrointestinal (GI) bleeding resulting from an identified GI lesion, such as angiodysplasia, ulcers, gastritis, diverticulitis, etc., the combination code should be used. Only exception is when physician clearly states the bleeding is unrelated to the GI lesion identified; then both the GI lesion and the GI bleeding are coded.

  ii. Arteriovenous malformation (AVM) is a term used interchangeably with angiodysplasia. Although the alphabetic index leads to congenital anomaly, do not use this code until physician has indicated it is congenital.

g. Complications of Pregnancy, Childbirth, and the Puerperium

  i. Normal delivery (650) can be coded if infant is single, full-term, born alive, delivered without instruments or surgery, occiput (vertex) or head-first presentation, and no complications before or after labor; 650 can be used if physician performed an episiotomy.

  ii. Fifth-digit 0 should not be used, as the hospital record should have enough data present to use fifth digits 1 to 4.

   1. 1: delivered this admission with/without antepartum condition

   2. 2: delivered this admission, but developed complications after delivery

   3. 3: antepartum; discharged undelivered

   4. 4: delivered on previous admission, but admitted with postpartum complication

  iii. Conditions of pregnancy can be indexed under the condition, pregnancy, or delivery.

  iv. Always assign outcome of delivery as secondary diagnosis.

  v. When instrumentation or surgery is used to delivery the baby, always use the condition that required the instrumentation or surgery as the principal diagnosis.

  vi. Because ICD-9-CM assumes conditions are complicating the pregnancy unless the physician specifically states otherwise, codes from 630-676 should be used as the principal diagnosis. Often an additional code outside of Chapter 11 will be needed to fully code a condition affecting the pregnancy. If the physician states the condition is not complicating the pregnancy, code the condition first and V22.2 (incidental pregnancy) as a secondary diagnosis.

h. Diseases of the Circulatory System

  i. ICD-9-CM assumes a cause-and-effect relationship with hypertension and renal disease; when both are mentioned, use combination code. Exception to the rule is acute renal failure (584.9 and 401.9).

  ii. Hypertensive or "due to" indicates a cause-and-effect relationship and combination coding should be used.

   1. Examples

    a. Hypertensive cardiovascular disease (HCVD) is coded 402.90.

    b. Hypertension and renal failure is coded 403.91.

  iii. Hypertension with congestive heart failure should not be coded using the combination codes 401.9 and 428.0.

  iv. Use hypertension table in index.

     v. Non-Q-wave myocardial infarction is coded under 410.7, subendocardial, with fifth digit specifying episode of care.

     vi. Impending MI that does not progress to a MI should be coded to intermediate coronary syndrome.

     vii. CHF has been expanded to specify the CHF as systolic, diastolic, or both, with an additional code for the CHF.

     viii. CVA should be coded at the highest level of specificity. In some facilities, use of the radiologist's findings can be used to provide specificity needed to code "infarction."

     ix. CVA most likely due to cardioembolism should be coded to cerebral embolism with/without infarction. The condition is common in patients with atrial fibrillation.

     x. Residuals (e.g., hemiplegia, dysphagia, aphasia, etc.) that resolve before discharge are not coded.

i. Burns

    i. Burns should be coded to the highest degree at each given site.

      1. Second- and third-degree burns of the forearm should only be coded to the third degree.

    ii. When multiple degrees of burns are present, use the highest degree burn as the principal diagnosis.

      1. For a first-degree burn of the finger, second-degree burn of the toe, and third-degree burn of the chest, the third-degree burn of the chest should be the principal diagnosis.

    iii. Code percentage of body surface as an additional code, if specified.

    iv. Non-healing burns are coded to acute burns.

j. Poisoning and Adverse Effects of Drugs

    i. Terms for poisoning include wrong medication taken or given, overdose, taking prescribed dose and drinking alcohol, and taking too much of prescribed dose.

    ii. Taking less than prescribed dose does not constitute a poisoning.

    iii. An adverse effect of a drug includes taking prescribed dose and having a reaction from the drug.

    iv. Always code an E code for the drug causing the adverse effect.

k. V Codes

    i. Key terms include admission for, examination, history, observation, aftercare, problem, and status.

    ii. V codes also show birth status of newborns and are used as a principal diagnosis.

    iii. V codes show outcome of delivery and are used as secondary diagnoses.

    vi. V codes show history of and are appropriate to code if affecting a patient's care.

l. E Codes

    i. External causes of injury and poisoning.

    ii. Adverse effects of medicinal drugs and biological substances.

    iii. Late effects of external causes.

    iv. Misadventures and complications of care.

    v. Terrorism.

9. ICD-9-CM Procedural Coding

  a. Conventions for Volume 3 are essentially the same as those used in the disease classification.

  b. The alphabetic index is organized by main terms, which are printed in bold typeface. Main terms usually identify the type of procedure performed rather than the anatomic site involved.

    c. A main term may be followed by a series of terms in parentheses that are nonessential modifiers.

    d. A main term also may be followed by a list of subterms or modifiers that do have an effect upon the selection of the appropriate code for a given procedure.

    e. NEC is used for two purposes, which can only be determined by referring to the tabular list.

        i. With ill-defined terms, as a warning that specified forms of the procedure are classified differently.

        ii. With terms for which a more specific category is not provided in the tabular list, and no amount of additional information will alter the selection of the code.

    f. Omit Code

        i. Terms that identify incisions are listed as main terms in the alphabetic index.

        ii. If the incision was made only for the purpose of performing further surgery, the instruction omit code is given.

    g. Synchronous procedures are coded for some operative procedures if it is necessary to record the individual components of the procedure.

    h. Notes are used to list fourth-digit subclassifications for those categories that used the same fourth-digit subdivisions.

        i. In these cases, only the three-digit code is given for the individual entry.

        ii. The user must refer to the note following the main term to obtain appropriate fourth-digit subclassification.

    i. Eponyms are operations named after a person.

        i. They are listed as main terms in their appropriate alphabetic sequence and under the main term "operation."

        ii. A description of the procedure or anatomic site affected usually follows the eponym.

10. CPT-4 and HCPCS

    a. The Common Procedural Terminology 4th Edition (CPT-4) was developed in 1960 by American Medical Association. Its main purpose is to standardize the classification and reporting of health care services to facilitate reimbursement. It describes medical, surgical, and diagnostic services and is revised and updated annually.

    b. CMS adopted CPT as level I of the Healthcare Common Procedure Coding System (HCPCS).

    c. Content of CPT

        i. Nine chapters (sections)

            1. Introduction

            2. Evaluation and management (E/M)

            3. Anesthesia

            4. Surgery

            5. Radiology

            6. Pathology and laboratory

            7. Medicine

            8. Appendices

            9. Index

        ii. Section format includes section, subsection, heading, and subheading.

            1. Section: surgery

            2. Subsection: respiratory

      3. Heading: trachea and bronchi

      4. Subheading: incision

  iii. Punctuation, typeface, and symbols

      1. Semicolon and indention

      2. Boldface type

      3. Symbols

         a. Triangle △

            i. Code whose description changed

         b. Bullet •

            i. New code

         c. Sideways Double Triangle ▷◁

            i. New or revised text

         d. Plus +

            i. Add on codes

         e. Bull's eye ⊙

            i. Administration of conscious sedation

         f. Circle with slash ⊘

            i. Not permitted to be appended with modifier 51 multiple procedures

         g. Circle with arrow ➤

            i. Directs coder to an AMA-published reference

 iv. Modifiers

      1. Used to indicate that a performed service or procedure has been altered by some specific circumstance but not changed in its definition

         a. To report only the professional component of a procedure or service

         b. To report a service mandated by a third-party payer

         c. To indicate that a procedure was performed bilaterally

         d. To report multiple procedures performed at the same session by the same provider

         e. To report that a portion of a service or procedure is reduced or eliminated at the physician's discretion

         f. To report assistant surgeon services

  v. Unlisted procedures: due to advances in medicine, physicians or other health care professionals may perform services or procedures that have not yet been designated with a specific CPT code. Each section of the CPT book identifies an unlisted procedure code for these procedures. Use of an unlisted procedure code requires a special report or documentation to describe the service.

  vi. Add-on codes: codes that describe procedures or services that must never be reported as stand-alone codes. These procedures and services are always performed in addition to the primary procedure or service and are identified by the "+" symbol.

 vii. Unbundling: reporting a procedure or service using separate codes for each part of the procedure when one comprehensive code covers all the parts.

viii. Separate procedure: identified by the inclusion of the term (separate procedure) in the code descriptor. A code designated as a separate procedure may not be reported when it is an integral component of another procedure or service.

          ix. How to use the index
             1. Main terms
             2. Subterms
             3. Code ranges
             4. Crossreferences

d. General Rules for CPT Coding

    i. Identify the procedures and services to be coded by carefully reviewing the health record documentation.

    ii. Consult the index under the main term for the procedure performed and consult any subterms under the main term.

    iii. If the term is not located under the procedure performed, check the organ or site, condition, or eponym, synonym, or abbreviation.

    iv. Note the code number(s) found opposite the selected main term or subterm.

    v. Check the code(s) or code range in the body of the CPT codebook.

        1. When a single code number is provided, locate the code in the body of the CPT codebook.

        2. When two or more codes separated by a comma are shown, locate each code in the body of the CPT codebook.

        3. When a range of codes is shown, locate the range in the body of the CPT codebook.

    vi. Read and be guided by any coding notes under the code, at the subheading, heading, subsection, or section level.

    vii. Never code directly from the index.

    viii. Assign the appropriate modifier(s) when necessary to complete the code description.

    ix. Assign the appropriate code.

    x. Continue coding all components of the procedure or service using the above steps.

e. CMS administers HCPCS, which includes two (formerly three) levels of codes.

    i. Level 1: current procedural terminology

    ii. Level 2: alphanumeric procedure and modifier codes, codes representing items, supplies, and non-physician services not covered by the CPT codes

    iii. Level 3: local procedure and modifier codes used prior to 2003. Additional Level 2 codes are used now to compensate for the loss of the Level 3 codes.

11. ICD-10

  a. Copyrighted by WHO

  b. Used to code and classify mortality data from death certificates

  c. Replaced ICD-9 for this purpose as of January 1, 1999

12. ICD-10-CM

  a. The codes in ICD-10-CM are not currently valid for any purpose or use.

  b. Proposed to replace ICD-9-CM Volumes 1 and 2 with implementation based on the process for adoption of standard under the Health Insurance Portability and Accountability Act of 1996

13. ICD-10-PCS

  a. Proposed new procedure coding system being developed as a replacement for ICD-9-CM, Volume 3

PRACTICAL APPLICATION OF YOUR KNOWLEDGE

1. History of Coding
   a. Explain the purpose of coding.

   b. Define DRGs and explain their impact on hospital reimbursement.

   c. List cooperating parties responsible for maintaining and updating ICD-9-CM.

   d. Explain APC's impact on outpatient coding.

2. Important Definitions
   a. Define principal diagnosis.

   b. Explain how complications may affect a patient's length of stay.

   c. Explain the difference between diagnostic and therapeutic procedures and its significance in determining the principal procedure.

3. Principles of CPT

    a. List the two levels of HCPCS.

    b. Explain the purpose of modifiers.

    c. Where are guidelines for CPT found?

4. CPT Coding Terms

    Match each of the following terms with its definition:

        a. Global surgical package   **d.** Separate procedures

        b. Add-on codes   **e.** Comprehensive code

        c. Unbundling   **f.** Starred surgical procedures

    1. ____ When this note is in parentheses in the code description, it represents services that are commonly an integral part of a more extensive procedure.

    2. ____ This term refers to the use of multiple procedure codes for a group of services or procedures that actually can be identified by one comprehensive code.

    3. ____ These are items that are included in the CPT code for the defined surgical service.

    4. ____ This is used to describe a procedure or service at the highest level of complexity.

    5. ____ These are codes in the CPT manual that are submitted in addition to other codes.

    6. ____ These are considered minor surgical procedures to which the global surgical package does not apply.

♪ **5.** Code the following scenarios. These coding scenarios are reviewed with you in the Clinical Classification Systems portion of the audio review. Use ICD-9-CM for questions a–j and CPT for questions k–o.

   a. A patient with CRF due to HTN was admitted for dialysis. Hemodialysis was given.

   b. Patient was diagnosed with adenocarcinoma of the lower outer quadrant of the left breast. A mastectomy was performed 2 weeks ago. No metastasis was found. The patient is now admitted for chemotherapy.

   c. A patient was admitted with GSW to the abdomen. Exploratory laparotomy was performed and a hepatic laceration was noted and sutured without any complications.

   d. A patient with a history of a previous CVA 8 years ago with residual right hemiparesis is admitted with an acute embolic cerebral infarction. The patient has a history of CHF and receives Lasix during this admission. The patient is later transferred to rehabilitation.

   e. A female who was 39 weeks pregnant delivered a breech female infant by classical Caesarean section for a low fetal heart rate (bradycardia). The Caesarean section wound became an infection and the patient stayed in the hospital an additional 3 days for antibiotics.

   f. A 55-year-old male was admitted due to a traumatic brain injury resulting in subarachnoid hematoma. The patient experienced a loss of consciousness of 5 minutes. A craniotomy with evacuation of the hematoma was performed. The patient recovered without any immediate complications.

   g. A 40-year-old male with type 2 diabetes is admitted with uncontrolled glucose levels that result in ketoacidosis. (The patient also has diabetic proliferative retinopathy that will be treated as an outpatient day surgery.)

h. A preterm delivery of a single live born female by low cervical Caesarean section due to mild pre-eclampsia. There was no history of hypertension prior to pregnancy. There were no postpartum complications.

i. A patient was admitted with unstable angina due to coronary artery disease (CAD). Percutaneous transluminal coronary angioplasty (PTCA) was performed with stent insertion. (Drug eluting)

j. A 34-week, preterm, 1565-gram male infant was delivered by Caesarean section. The infant was ABO incompatible. The infant Coombs were positive, which confirmed the diagnosis. The infant is jaundiced due to the ABO incompatibility. Phototherapy was started.

k. Repair of a reducible right inguinal hernia with hydrocelectomy of the spermatic cord. Patient is 5 months old and male.

l. Hand laceration (3 cm), forehead (12 cm), and neck (5 cm). The lacerations were repaired with sutures in layered closure.

m. Pars plana victrectomy with membrane peeling and panretinal photocoagulation on the left eye.

n. Orchioplexy for undescended testes by inguinal approach. (Bilateral)

o. Laparoscopic cholecystectomy with intraoperative cholangiogram.

TEST YOUR KNOWLEDGE

1. Nonessential modifiers are enclosed in:
   a. braces.
   b. slanted brackets.
   c. parentheses.
   d. square brackets.

2. A late effect is a(n):
   a. disease that lasts more than a year after diagnosis.
   b. external cause of accident or injury.
   c. readmission for the same problem within 7 days of the previous admission.
   d. residual effect of an acute illness or injury.

3. The interaction of two prescribed drugs taken as directed is considered a(n):
   a. accident.
   b. poisoning.
   c. late effect.
   d. adverse effect.

4. How would a coder report a definitive procedure performed in conjunction with an exploratory laparotomy?
   a. Code both procedures, but list the definitive procedure first
   b. Code only the exploratory laparotomy
   c. Code the definitive procedure only
   d. Ask the surgeon before assigning any procedures

5. Which diagnosis is sequenced first in the following burn case: second-degree burn of the leg; third-degree burn of the wrist; and first-degree burn of the foot.
   a. Second-degree burn of the leg
   b. First-degree burn of the foot
   c. Third-degree burn of the wrist
   d. The diagnosis listed first by the attending physician

6. A system that provides a method of arranging related disease entities in groups for the reporting of statistical data is a:
   a. CPR.
   b. nomenclature system.
   c. register.
   d. classification system.

7. DRGs are part of a case-mix classification system that assigns inpatient discharges to only one DRG per episode of care. On which data elements is the assignment made?
   a. Diagnoses, procedures, patient's age, and patient's disposition at discharge
   b. Principal diagnosis and principal procedure
   c. Surgical procedure, patient's age, and patient's financial class
   d. Principal diagnosis, severity of illness, and patient's disposition at discharge

8. A coder reads a procedure note, but fails to find an appropriate CPT code that matches the procedure performed. When the bill goes out to the fiscal intermediary, a special report is prepared and sent with a(n):
   a. starred procedure.
   b. unlisted procedure.
   c. unbundled procedure.
   d. separate procedure.

9. How are brackets used in ICD-9-CM?
   a. To enclose words or numbers within Volume 2
   b. To designate synonyms, alternate wordings, abbreviations, or explanatory phrases
   c. To enclose supplementary words that may or may not be present in the diagnostic statement
   d. To indicate additional codes that must be used

10. Which of the following is not a section of CPT?
 a. Surgery
 b. Psychiatry
 c. Radiology
 d. Anesthesiology

11. Probable, possible, and suspected condition(s) of patients are coded as if they exist if the condition(s) are:
 a. treated while the patient is in the hospital.
 b. not treated while the patient is in the hospital.
 c. ruled out while the patient is in the hospital.
 d. diagnosed prior to admission.

12. Key terms for using V codes are:
 a. delivery of, possible cause, or due to.
 b. threatened to, impending case, or late effect of.
 c. admission for, history of, observation, or status.
 d. prior to, late effect of, possible, or probable.

13. If a baby is born at Hospital A and transferred to Hospital B the first day of life, the V30 code should be used by which hospital(s)?
 a. A and B
 b. A only
 c. B only
 d. Inappropriate for use by either facility

14. What is code 650 used for?
 a. Multiple live births, delivered head first
 b. Multiple live births, caesarean section, forceps delivery
 c. Single newborn, stillborn
 d. Single live newborn, delivered head first and full term

15. A complication is a condition that:
 a. was diagnosed prior to admission to the hospital.
 b. was caused by a nosocomial infection.
 c. arises while the patient is in the hospital.
 d. is a sentinel event that is reported to JCAHO

16. E codes are:
 a. sometimes used as principal diagnoses.
 b. mandatory for pregnancy determination.
 c. used voluntarily by the health care organization.
 d. never used as principal diagnoses.

17. When locating a term for coding a neoplasm diagnosis, one should access:
 a. the alphabetic index.
 b. the tabular index.
 c. both the alphabetic and tabular indexes.
 d. the table of neoplasms.

18. The word "and" should be interpreted to mean "and" as well as "_____."
 a. or
 b. with
 c. see
 d. see also

19. A patient has right side hemiplegia from a CVA last year. This year the patient is admitted and discharged for an appendicitis. How should the hemiplegia be coded?
 a. Acute hemiplegia
 b. Late-effect hemiplegia
 c. Due to CVA
 d. Not treated, therefore not coded

20. ICD-9-CM 192 code is used for malignant neoplasm of other and unspecified parts of the nervous system. Code 192.1 reads "cerebral meninges, Dura (mater), Falx (cerebelli) (cerebri)." The terms listed in parentheses are:
   a. to be coded as complications or cormorbidities.
   b. synonyms or alternative phrasing for the preceding word.
   c. supplementary words or nonessential modifiers.
   d. eponyms for the preceding word.

21. What are V codes used to classify?
   a. Factors influencing health status and contact with health services
   b. External causes of injury and poisoning
   c. Late effects of external causes
   d. Misadventures and complications of care guidelines

22. A patient is admitted because of threatened abortion and subsequently aborted. Threatened abortion should:
   a. not be coded; code underlying condition.
   b. be coded as a late effect of the underlying condition.
   c. be coded as confirmed diagnosis.
   d. not be coded; code as complete abortion.

23. What are E codes used to classify?
   a. Factors influencing health status and contact with health services
   b. External causes of injury and poisoning
   c. Injuries and poisonings
   d. Symptoms, signs, and ill-defined conditions

24. CMS uses which of the following as the HCPCS level 1 codes?
   a. CPT codes
   b. All ICD-9-CM codes
   c. DRGs
   d. E codes of ICD-9-CM

25. What does the filled-in dot (·) appearing to the left of a CPT code designate?
   a. Add-on code
   b. New and revised test in coding notes
   c. Code's terminology has been revised
   d. New code in the current edition

[Use of ICD-9-CM and CPT coding books are required for the remaining portion. (*Note:* Because the exams are computerized, you will not need your coding books while sitting for the national RHIA and RHIT examinations.)]

26. Immediately after delivery, a critically ill neonate receives care under the direction and supervision of a pediatrician. What is the CPT-4 code?
   a. 99295
   b. 99285
   c. 99245
   d. 99205

27. During surgery, Ms. Johnson demonstrates distress and the physician must discontinue the procedure. What modifier may be used to report that the physician discontinued the procedure?
   a. -22
   b. -52
   c. -53
   d. -57

28. Bob was treated because he had right-leg paralysis due to poliomyelitis from childhood.
   a. 344.30, 138
   b. 344.31, 138
   c. 342.01, 138
   d. 138, 344.31

29. Bob was admitted with seizures and has a history of malignant neoplasm of the liver. Further diagnostic testing revealed metastasis of the liver cancer to the kidney.
   a. 198.0, 780.39, 155.0
   b. V10.07, 780.39, 198.0
   c. 155.0, V10.07, 198.0, 780.39
   d. 198.0, 780.39, V10.07

30. A 78-year-old woman is treated for severe malnutrition, percutaneous endoscopic gastrostomy.
   a. 262, 43.11
   b. 261, 43.11
   c. 263.2, 43.11
   d. 263.9, 43.11

31. A 13-year-old girl is admitted with sickle cell anemia with crisis.
   a. 282.61
   b. 282.62
   c. 282.62, V13.09
   d. 282.64

32. Patient is stated to have anxiety with depression.
   a. 300.4
   b. 300.00
   c. 300.10
   d. 300.00, 311

33. Bob is 65 years old and has aspiration pneumonia with pneumonia due to Staphylococcus aureus. He also has emphysema.
   a. 507.0, 482.41, 492.8
   b. 482.41, 507.0, 492.8
   c. 482.41, 492.8
   d. 507.0, 483.31, 492.8

34. Patient has acute and chronic cholecystitis with cholelithiasis. Laproscopic cholecystectomy attempted and converted to open.
   a. 574.10, 574.00, 51.22, 51.23
   b. 574.01, 574.10, 51.22
   c. 574.20, 51.22, 51.23
   d. 574.00, 574.10, 51.22, 51.23

35. The patient has an acute urinary tract infection due to *E. coli.*
   a. 599.84, 041.4
   b. 041.4, 599.0
   c. 599.0, 041.4
   d. 599.0

36. Single newborn delivered at 42 weeks gestation; manually assisted delivery.
   a. 645.11, V27.0, 73.59
   b. 645.21, V27.0, 73.59
   c. 645.21, V27.0, 73.51
   d. 650, V27.0, 73.51

37. Bob had a recurrent internal derangement of the right knee. Physician performed a diagnostic arthroscopy of the knee.
   a. 718.66, 80.26
   b. 718.36, 80.26
   c. 718.36, 80.16
   d. 718.66, 80.16

MOCK MEDICAL RECORDS

Instructions for questions 38–50:

Following are inpatient, day surgery, and outpatient observation medical records. Code the following medical records using ICD-9-CM and CPT-4 (for outpatient and day surgery records) codes.

38.

HOUSTON HEALTH CARE CENTER

History and Physical

Patient name: *Case 1*

Present complaint: Gallstones and hyperbilirubinemia

Past history:

    Pertinent surgeries: None

    Pertinent medical illness: Hypertension

    Current medications: Zestril

    Allergies: None

    Smoking: None

    Alcohol: None

Vital signs:

    Pulse: 21   **Respiratory Rate:** 12   **Blood pressure:** 140/93

General: Alert, oriented. No acute distress

Pertinent lab: Hyperbilirubinemia

HEENT: No mass or deformity

Torso/Breast: No mass or deformity

Heart: Normal rhythm, no murmur or gallop

Lungs: Clear to auscultation

Abdomen: Epigastric and RLQ pain

Pelvic/Rectal: No mass or tenderness

Extremities: No edema or tenderness

Neurological: Intact

Impressions: Choledocholithiasis

Treatment and plan: Endoscopic retrograde cholangiopancreatography (ERCP)

Signature: _____ MD

H&P

HOUSTON HEALTH CARE CENTER
Procedure Note

Preoperative diagnosis: Gallstones and hyperbilirubin

Procedure: Endoscopic retrograde sphincterotomy with stone extraction

Surgeon: Dr. Xxxxx

Anesthesia: Versed, meperidine (Demerol), and benzocaine (Cetacaine)

Postoperative diagnosis: Choledocholithiasis

Drains, complications: None

Estimated blood loss: None

Findings: Choledocholithiasis

Signature: _____ MD

Procedure Note

HOUSTON HEALTH CARE CENTER
Operative Report

Preoperative diagnoses: 1. Status post-endoscopic retrograde cholangiopancreaticogram with choledocholithiasis and choledochotomy
2. Cholecystitis
3. Cholelithiasis

Postoperative diagnoses: 1. Status post-endoscopic retrograde cholangiopancreaticogram with choledocholithiasis and choledochotomy
2. Cholecystitis
3. Cholelithiasis

Procedure performed: Laparoscopic cholecystectomy

Anesthesia: General endotracheal anesthesia

Estimated blood loss: Minimal

Complications: None

Findings: 1. Inflamed gallbladder with mucinous, clear material
2. Multiple stones

Procedure in detail: The patient was prepped and draped in the supine position.

A small supraumbilical incision was made and carried down through the subcutaneous tissue using electrocautery. The linea alba was identified and divided. The finger was bluntly inserted through the preperitoneal space into the peritoneum. Stay sutures of #2-0 Vicryl were placed to the right and left of midline.

A Hasson trocar was passed into the abdomen, and the abdomen was insufflated with air. There were no hemodynamic changes.

Examination revealed a distended, mildly inflamed gallbladder. There were some adhesions between the liver capsule and the anterior abdominal wall.

A 10-mm trocar was placed in the upper midline and two 5-mm trocars in the right upper quadrant. The gallbladder was aspirated using a long needle. Clear material was returned. After the gallbladder was aspirated flat, it was grasped and elevated up over the liver. Some mild adhesions of the gallbladder to the duodenum were taken down, and the dissection was begun at the level of the infundibulum/cystic duct junction.

The cystic duct was easily identified, clipped twice proximally and once distally, and divided. The cystic artery was easily identified, clipped twice proximally and once distally, and divided. The gallbladder was dissected free from the underlying liver bed without entering the liver parenchyma. The gallbladder was drawn out through the umbilicus and opened on the back table. There was clear, milky, mucoid fluid with multiple stones but no evidence of any tumor. The bed was then examined, and there was no bleeding.

(continues)

Op Report

HOUSTON HEALTH CARE CENTER
Operative Report *(Continued)*

This was thoroughly irrigated and aspirated, including Morrison pouch in the lateral aspect of the right lobe. The trocars were removed sequentially with no evidence of any bleeding. The 10-mm trocar sites were closed with #2-0 Vicryl at the fascia. All four trocar sites were closed at the skin with a running, subcuticular suture of #4-0 Vicryl after being thoroughly irrigated, and dry dressings were applied.

The patient tolerated the procedure well and had no hemodynamic oxygenation problems.

Dictated and reviewed by: _____ MD

Op Report

HOUSTON HEALTH CARE CENTER
Surgical Pathology Report

Clinical information

    Preoperative diagnosis: Acute cholecystitis

    Postoperative diagnosis: Same as above

Tissue

    Source description: Gallbladder

Gross description:

The specimen is received in formalin in a container labeled with the patient's name, Ella Dawson and medical record number and designated "gallbladder." It consists of an opened gallbladder measuring 10 cm in length and 5 cm in circumference. The serosa is tan-pink. The wall measures 0.2 cm in thickness.

The mucosa is unremarkable. Also present in the container are two irregular lobulated tan-yellow stones. Representative sections are submitted in cassettes A1-A3.

    3 blocks, 3 H&E

    Azk:Mbv

Diagnosis:

    Gallbladder, cholecystectomy: Acute and chronic cholecystitis. Cholelithiasis.

Path Report

HOUSTON HEALTH CARE CENTER
Operative Note

Preoperative diagnosis: Choledocholithiasis s/p ERCP

Procedure: Laparoscopic cholecystectomy

Surgeon: Dr. Xxxxx

Anesthesia: General

Postoperative diagnosis: Cholecystitis and cholelithiasis

Drains, complications: None

Estimated blood loss: Minimal

Findings: Inflamed gallbladder; mucinous, clear material; multiple gallstones.

Signature: _____ MD

Op Note

Answer Sheet for Case 1

Code this inpatient medical record using ICD-9-CM diagnoses and procedure codes.

Principal diagnosis:

Secondary diagnoses (if any):

Principal procedure:

Other procedures (if any):

39.

HOUSTON HEALTH CARE CENTER
History and Physical

Patient name: *Case 2*

Present complaint: 28-year-old, gravida 2, para 1 with chief complaint of incompetent cervix here for cerclage insertion.

Past history:

　Pertinent surgeries: None

　Pertinent medical illness: None

　Current medications: None

　Allergies: No known allergies

　Smoking: None

　Alcohol: None

Vital signs:

　Pulse: 101　　**Respiratory rate:** 20　　**Blood pressure:** 131/80

General: Alert, oriented, no acute distress

Pertinent lab:

HEENT: No mass or deformity

Torso/Breast: No mass or deformity

Heart: Normal rhythm, no murmur or gallop

Lungs: Clear to auscultation

Abdomen: Gravid

Pelvic/Rectal: No mass or tenderness

Extremities: No edema or tenderness

Neurological: Intact

Impressions: Incompetent cervix at 12 weeks

Treatment and plan: McDonald's cerclage insertion

Signature: _____ MD

H&P

HOUSTON HEALTH CARE CENTER
Operative Report

Procedure: McDonald's cerclage placement

Diagnosis: Intrauterine pregnancy at 12 weeks with cervical incompetence

Anesthesia: Epidural

Findings and technique: Preoperatively, her internal os was approximately 1 cm dilated. The posterior cervix was approximately 2 cm long, and the interior cervix was approximately 1 cm long. At the end of the procedure, the knot could be felt at the 12 o'clock position and the internal os was closed to digital examination.

The patient was in the dorsal lithotomy position. She had an internal and an external perineal prep and was draped for the procedure. A Mersilene band on two needles was used with one needle placed in at the 6 o'clock position and brought out at 3 o'clock, and replaced at the same position and brought out at 12 o'clock. The other needle was taken in at 3 o'clock and brought out at 9 o'clock, and then replaced and brought out at 12 o'clock position. The Mersilene band then was tied at the 12 o'clock position until the internal os was closed. It was palpable at the end of the procedure, and the two ends were cut long. The patient received perioperative antibiotics, and her heart tones were Dopplerable before the procedure. The procedure was without complications, and the patient was taken to the recovery room in stable condition.

Op Report

HOUSTON HEALTH CARE CENTER
Operative Note

Preoperative diagnosis: Incompetent cervix at 12 weeks

Procedure: Cerclage insertion

Surgeon: Dr. Xxxxx

Anesthesia: General

Postoperative diagnosis: Incompetent cervix at 12 weeks

Drains, complications: None

Estimated blood loss: None

Signature: _____ MD

Op Note

HOUSTON HEALTH CARE CENTER
Discharge Note/Discharge Order

Hospital course: Uncomplicated

Discharge instructions:

Medication: None

Activity: As tolerated

Diet: As per instructions

Follow-up: 2 weeks in office

Discharge status: Stable

Final diagnosis: Incompetent cervix at 12 weeks

Signature: _____

Discharge

Answer Sheet for Case 2

Code this inpatient medical record using ICD-9-CM diagnoses and procedure codes.

Principal diagnosis:

Secondary diagnoses (if any):

Principal procedure:

Other procedures (if any):

40.

HOUSTON HEALTH CARE CENTER

History and Physical

Patient name: *Case 3*

Present complaint: Numbness in left hand

Past history:

    Pertinent surgeries: Right carpal tunnel release

    Pertinent medical illness: None

    Current medications: Avapro

    Allergies: None

    Smoking: Yes

    Alcohol: Yes

Vital signs:

    Pulse: 112   **Respiratory rate:** 20   **Blood pressure:** 122/80

General: Alert, oriented, no acute distress

Pertinent lab:

HEENT: No mass or deformity

Torso/Breast: No mass or deformity

Heart: Normal rhythm, no murmur or gallop

Lungs: Clear to auscultation

Abdomen: No mass or tenderness

Pelvic/Rectal: Deformed

Extremities: Left hand with numbness and decreased sensation

Neurological: Median neuropathy

Impressions: Carpal tunnel syndrome, left hand

Treatment and plan: Carpal tunnel release

Signature: _____ MD

H&P

HOUSTON HEALTH CARE CENTER
Operative Report

Preoperative diagnosis: Carpal tunnel syndrome left wrist

Postoperative diagnosis: Carpal tunnel syndrome left wrist

Operation: Decompression of medial nerve, left wrist

Surgeon: Dr. Xxxxx

Anesthesia: Bier block

Estimated blood loss: Less than 500 cc

Procedure: Under Bier block anesthesia, preparation was done with Betadine scrub, Betadine solution, and sterile draping. Curvilinear incision was made based on the lunar side of the longitudinal wrist crease and carried up to the proximal flexor wrist crease. This was carried through subcutaneous tissue. Range retractors were inserted. The median nerve was visualized using the microscope at the proximal edge of the transverse carpal ligament. The nerve was protected and, using curved dissecting scissors, the transverse carpal ligament was sectioned under direct vision. The nerve was quite compressed. After the ligament had been sectioned, the wound was closed with interrupted 5-0 nylon sutures and sterile dressings were applied. The patient tolerated the procedure well and circulation to the extremity was intact at the completion of the procedure.

Op Report

HOUSTON HEALTH CARE CENTER
Operative Note

Preoperative diagnosis: Carpal tunnel syndrome

Procedure: Carpal tunnel release, left hand

Surgeon: Dr. Xxxxx

Anesthesia: General

Postoperative diagnosis: Carpal tunnel syndrome

Drains, complications: None

Estimated blood loss: None

Signature: _____ MD

Op Note

HOUSTON HEALTH CARE CENTER
Discharge Note

Hospital course: Stable

Discharge instructions:

    Medication: As per instructions

    Activity: As tolerated

    Diet: As per instructions

    Follow-up: Month

Discharge status: Discharged when criteria for discharge were met

Final diagnosis: Carpal tunnel syndrome

Signature: _____

Discharge

Answer Sheet for Case 3

Code this day surgery medical record using ICD-9-CM diagnostic and CPT-4 procedural codes.

Principal diagnosis:

Secondary diagnoses (if any):

CPT code(s):

41.

HOUSTON HEALTH CARE CENTER
History and Physical

Patient name: _Case 4_

Present complaint: R knee pain

Past history:

    Pertinent surgeries: None

    Pertinent medical illness: None

    Current medications: None

    Allergies: None

    Smoking: No

    Alcohol: No

Vital signs: Stable

General:

Pertinent lab: Normal

HEENT: No mass or deformity

Torso/Breast: No mass or deformity

Heart: Normal rhythm, no murmur or gallop

Lungs: Clear to auscultation

Abdomen: No mass or tenderness

Pelvic/Rectal: No mass or tenderness

Extremities: R knee tender medial joint

Neurological: Intact

Impressions: Torn medial meniscus

Treatment and plan: Arthroscopy

Signature: _____ MD

H&P

HOUSTON HEALTH CARE CENTER
Operative Report

Procedure: Arthroscopic partial medial meniscectomy

Diagnosis: Torn medial meniscus

Anesthesia: General

Technique: After induction with general anesthesia, a standard three-portal approach of the knee was evaluated. Mild synovitic changes were noted in all three compartments. The anterior cruciate ligament was intact, as was the lateral meniscus, and there were only slight synovitic changes in the anterior compartment. The anterior portion of the medial meniscus had a flap tear, which was debrided with an aggressive resector.

After all instruments were withdrawn, 4-0 nylon horizontal mattress stitches were used to close the wound and pressure dressings were applied. The patient was awakened and removed to the recovery room in good condition.

Op Report

HOUSTON HEALTH CARE CENTER
Operative Note

Preoperative diagnosis: Torn medial meniscus

Procedure: Arthroscopic meniscectomy

Surgeon: Dr. Xxxxx

Anesthesia: General

Postoperative diagnosis: Torn medial meniscus

Drains, complications: None

Estimated blood loss: None

Findings: Torn medial meniscus

Signature: _____ MD

Op Note

HOUSTON HEALTH CARE CENTER
Discharge Note

Hospital course: Good

Discharge instructions:

Medication: As per instructions

Activity: As tolerated

Diet: As per instructions

Follow-up: 3 days

Discharge status: Stable

Final diagnosis: Torn medial meniscus, right knee

Signature: _____

Discharge

Answer Sheet for Case 4

Code this day surgery medical record using ICD-9-CM diagnostic and CPT-4 procedure codes.

Principal diagnosis:

Secondary diagnoses (if any):

CPT code(s):

42.

HOUSTON HEALTH CARE CENTER
History and Physical

Patient name: *Case 5*

Present complaint: 38-year-old, gravida 2, para 2, LMP two weeks ago, no form of birth control, currently desires permanent sterilization.

Past history:

    Pertinent surgeries: Laparoscopy 10 years ago for ovarian cyst

    Pertinent medical illness: None

    Current medications: Multivitamin

    Allergies: No known allergies

    Smoking: None

    Alcohol: None

Vital signs:

    Pulse: 70   **Respiratory Rate:** 18   **Blood pressure:** 152/95

General: Alert, oriented, no acute distress

HEENT: WNL

Torso/Breast: No mass or deformity

Heart: Normal rhythm, no murmur or gallop

Lungs: Clear to auscultation bilaterally

Abdomen: Soft, not tender

Pelvic/Rectal: Deferred to OR

Extremities: No edema or tenderness

Neurological: Grossly intact

Impressions: Multiparity desires permanent sterilization

Treatment and plan: To OR for scope bilateral tubal ligation

Signature: _____ MD

H&P

HOUSTON HEALTH CARE CENTER
Operative Report

Procedure: Scope bilateral tubal ligation using Falope rings

Diagnosis: Multiparity desiring permanent sterilization

Anesthesia: General endotracheal

Fluids: 400 cc in

Estimated blood loss: Minimal

Procedure in detail: The patient was taken to the operating room where general anesthesia was induced without difficulty. She was placed in the dorsal lithotomy position and prepped and draped in the usual sterile fashion.

An infraumbilical incision was made with a scalpel and a 10-mm trocar was inserted through this incision until peritoneal placement was attained. This was confirmed using the low pressure of CO_2 gas. The camera was inserted and attention was then turned to the suprapubic incision site. A 5-mm trocar was inserted here without difficulty. The Falope ring applicator was then passed through this. Both tubes were identified and followed to the fimbriated ends. Approximately 3 cm from the cornua, the tube was grasped and the Falope ring was applied on both sides without difficulty. Both had good knuckle of the tube with good blanching noted. Pictures were taken. The rest of the pelvic anatomy appeared normal. The gas was evacuated from the abdomen. Both trocars were removed. The incision was closed with subcuticular 3-0 Vicryl. She tolerated the procedure well and went to the recovery room in stable condition.

Complications: None

Counts: All counts were correct.

Dictated by: _____ (Resident)

Reviewed by: _____ (Surgeon)

Op Report

HOUSTON HEALTH CARE CENTER
Operative Note

Preoperative diagnosis: Multiparity, desires permanent sterilization

Procedure: Bilateral tubal ligation with Falope rings

Surgeon: Dr. Xxxxx

Anesthesia: General

Postoperative diagnosis: Multiparity, desires permanent sterilization

Drains, complications: None

Estimated blood loss: Minimal

Signature: _____ MD

Op Note

HOUSTON HEALTH CARE CENTER
Discharge Note/Discharge Order

Hospital course: Uncomplicated

Discharge instructions:

Medication: Vicodin 1-2 tablets every 4 hours as needed

Activity: Do not attempt to make any important decision for a period of 24 hours. Do not drive for 24 hours.

Diet: Advance as tolerated when awake, alert, and oriented.

Follow-up: 2 weeks in office

Discharge status: Stable

Final diagnosis: Multiparity, desires permanent sterilization s/p bilateral tubal ligation

Signature: _____

Discharge

Answer Sheet for Case 5

Code this day surgery medical record using ICD-9-CM diagnostic and CPT-4 procedural codes.

Principal diagnosis:

Secondary diagnoses (if any):

CPT code(s):

43.

HOUSTON HEALTH CARE CENTER

History and Physical

Patient name: *Case 6*

Present complaint: 25-year-old female patient with pilonidal cyst with continuous drainage, swelling, and pain

Past history:

Pertinent surgeries: None

Pertinent medical illness: hypothyroidism and depression

Current medications: Synthroid, Paxil, Zyprexan, and multivitamins

Allergies: No known allergies

Smoking: None

Alcohol: None

Vital signs:

Pulse: 86   **Respiratory Rate:** 10   **Blood pressure:** 128/80

General: Alert, oriented, no acute distress

HEENT: WNL

Torso/Breast: No mass or deformity

Heart: Normal rhythm, no murmur or gallop

Lungs: Clear to auscultation bilaterally

Abdomen: Soft, not tender

Pelvic/Rectal: WNL

Extremities: No edema or tenderness

Neurological: Grossly intact

Impressions: Patient with obvious pilonidal cyst.

Treatment and plan: Pilonidal cystectomy

Signature: _____ MD

H&P

HOUSTON HEALTH CARE CENTER
Operative Report

Procedure: Pilonidal cystectomy

Diagnosis: Pilonidal cyst

Anesthesia: General endotracheal and 30 cc of 0.25% Marcaine with epinephrine as a local block

Operative findings: Small superficial subcutaneous sinus and pilonidal cyst, at midline within the buttocks.

Complications: None

Counts: All counts were correct.

Procedure in detail: The patient was taken to the operating room and placed supine on the stretcher, then subsequently induced with general anesthesia. Once the patient was orally endotracheally intubated, she was flipped into a prone position onto two rolls, with care taken not to put any undue pressure on her breasts. Once the patient was positioned in a prone position, the buttocks were spread and held with tape. The area between the buttocks was fully prepped and draped in the usual surgical sterile fashion. A lacrymal probe was used to go through a sinus that tracked into the midline and opened up at midline with a slight extension superiorly. Once the cavity was delineated, local anesthesia was injected into circumferential tissues and deep through the cyst, using 0.25% Marcaine with epinephrine, approximately 30 cc. After local anesthesia was injected, Bovie electrocautery was used to open up the sinus tracts and the edges were cauterized, in order to allow better drainage of the cavity. The cavity was subsequently scraped and cleaned. Once the entire cavity was fully debrided and skin edges were excised, hemostasis was achieved using Bovie electrocautery. The cavity was packed using a moist 4 × 4 and another 4 × 4 was placed on top and held in place using tape. The patient was subsequently rolled back into a supine position on the stretcher and then awoke from general anesthesia, extubated, and taken to the post-anesthesia care unit, in an alert and hemodynamically stable condition.

Dictated by: _____ (Resident)

Reviewed by: _____ (Surgeon)

HOUSTON HEALTH CARE CENTER
Operative Note

Preoperative Diagnosis: Pilonidal cyst

Procedure: Pilonidal cystectomy

Surgeon: Dr. Xxxxx

Anesthesia: General endotracheal and 30 cc of 0.25% Marcaine with epinephrine as a local block.

Postoperative diagnosis: Pilonidal cyst

Drains, Complications: None

Estimated blood loss: Minimal

Signature: _____ MD

Op Note

HOUSTON HEALTH CARE CENTER
Discharge Order

Hospital course: Uncomplicated

Discharge instructions:

Dressing: Sitz baths 3 times a day and after each bowel movement. Change gauze to wound 3 times a day.

Medication: Darvocet n-100, one or two tablets by mouth, if needed for pain

Activity: Do not attempt to make any important decision for a period of 24 hours. Do not drive for 24 hours.

Diet: Resume

Follow-up: 2 weeks in office

Discharge status: Stable

Final diagnosis: Pilonidal cyst

Signature: _____

Answer Sheet for Case 6

Code this day surgery medical record using ICD-9-CM diagnostic and CPT-4 procedure codes.

Principal diagnosis:

Secondary diagnoses (if any):

CPT code(s):

44.

HOUSTON HEALTH CARE CENTER
History and Physical

Patient name: _Case 7_

Present complaint: This is a 53-year-old man with flank pain.

History of present illness: The patient started having left flank pain in October of last year. At that time, he was seen at a local emergency room, and a CT scan demonstrated a 7-mm proximal stone in the left ureter that he was told would pass. Because the patient did not have any more pain, he did not follow up, but in December of last year he had another episode of recurrent pain, and this time a repeat CT scan demonstrated the stone had dropped to the lower part of the ureter, causing obstruction at the level of the sacroiliac joint. The patient came to me and was asymptomatic and had a negative urinalysis, but a KUB and review of his X-rays demonstrated the stone to be visible in the pelvis of the left ureter and the patient was advised to have extracorporeal shock wave lithotripsy. He has been on Flomax to prevent potential postprocedure urinary retention.

Past history:

  Pertinent surgeries: None

  Pertinent medical illness: Hypertension

  Current medications: Atenolol (Flomax) 25 mg daily

  Family history: The patient's father died at the age of 72 of unknown cause, per patient. The mother died at the age of 86 from liver cancer.

  Allergies: No known allergies

  Smoking: None

  Alcohol: None

Vital signs:

  Pulse: 70   **Respiratory Rate:** 18   **Blood pressure:** 152/95

General: The patient is well developed and well nourished in no acute distress.

HEENT: WNL

Torso/Breast: No mass or deformity

Heart: Normal sinus rhythm, no murmur or gallop

Lungs: Clear to auscultation bilaterally

Abdomen: Soft, there is no organomegaly or tenderness

(continues)

H&P

HOUSTON HEALTH CARE CENTER

History and Physical *(Continued)*

Genitourinary: There is no costovertebral angle (CVA) tenderness. The patient has a normal circumcised penis, bilateral descended normal testes, and a 15 g, benign-feeling prostate.

Extremities: No edema or tenderness

Impressions: This is a patient with an obstructing left lower third ureteral calculus admitted for extracorporeal shock wave lithotripsy (ESWL)

Signature: _____ MD

H&P

HOUSTON HEALTH CARE CENTER
Operative Report

Procedure: Left extracorporeal shock wave lithotripsy

Diagnosis: Ureteral calculus

Anesthesia: Local

Shocks: 4000 to left ureter

Flouro: 7.5

Patient's position: Prone

Procedure in detail: The primary operative procedure consisted of extracorporeal shock wave lithotripsy using the Litotron lithotripter. The patient was positioned on the treatment table. Biaxial fluoroscopy was utilized to localize the stone(s). When added, additional radiographic snapshots were utilized to assist localization. Multiple firing of the electromagnetic shock wave source as noted above was made to effect pulverization of the stone(s). Upon completion of the procedure, the patient was transferred back to the recovery room for observation.

Complications: None

Dictated and reviewed by: _____ MD

Op Report

HOUSTON HEALTH CARE CENTER
Operative Note

Preoperative diagnosis: Ureteral calculus

Procedure: Left extracorporeal shock wave lithotripsy

Surgeon: Dr. Xxxxx

Anesthesia: Local

Postoperative diagnosis: Ureteral calculus

Signature: _____ MD

Op Note

HOUSTON HEALTH CARE CENTER
Discharge Note/Discharge Order

Hospital course: Uneventful

Discharge instructions:

Medication: None

Activity: As tolerated

Diet: Advance as tolerated

Follow-up: 3 days

Discharge status: Stable

Final diagnosis: Ureteral calculus

Signature: _____

Discharge

Answer Sheet for Case 7

Code this day surgery medical record using ICD-9-CM diagnostic and CPT-4 procedure codes.

Principal diagnosis:

Secondary diagnoses (if any):

CPT code(s):

45.

HOUSTON HEALTH CARE CENTER
Face Sheet

Patient name: *Case 8*

Final diagnosis: Obscured vision after cataract extraction.

Procedures: YAG laser posterior capsulotomy, right eye

Face Sheet

HOUSTON HEALTH CARE CENTER
Laser Operative Summary Report

Patient name: *Case 8*

History: Progressive loss of vision in right eye over past 4–6 months. Macular hole surgery 4 years ago and cataract surgery 3 years ago.

Medications: Levoxyl, Premarin, Lantac

Allergies: Penicillin and codeine

Physical find: Cloudy capsule right eye

Visual activity: OD 20/50 Ocular tension OD 15

Slit lamp: OD cloudy posterior capsule

Fundus: OD macular scarring

Vital signs: BP: 135/81   Pulse: 69   Mental status: Alert

Diagnosis: OD cloudy capsule

Procedure: YAG laser capsulotomy

Anesthesia: Topical

Contact lens: Yes, Abraham

Area/Pattern: OD

Parameters: 1. # Pulses: 13

           2. Spot size: N/A

           3. Power: 3.1 mW

           4. Duration:

Complications: None

Patch: No

Return visit: 1 hour

Diet: Regular

Activity: As tolerated

Signature: _____ MD

Op Report

Answer Sheet for Case 8

Code this day surgery medical record using ICD-9-CM diagnostic and CPT-4 procedural codes.

Principal diagnosis:

Secondary diagnoses (if any):

CPT:

46.

HOUSTON HEALTH CARE CENTER
History and Physical

Patient name: _Case 9_

History: This child has had recurrent ear infections over the last 4 months. He has received several courses of appropriate antibiotic therapy, to which he initially responds well but relapses soon after discontinuation of the drug. He had his first episode at the age of 5 months. The child also suffers from cough variant asthma for which he is on inhaler frequently. He has no known risk factors for otitis media, other than an older sibling having had tubes placed at the age of 2 years old.

Physical examination: Clinical examination today showed evidence of a left acute otitis media. The right ear also had an otitis media with effusion. Nose and throat were normal.

Recommendations: This child is a candidate for placement of pressure-equalizing (PE) tubes. I have discussed the procedure, its complications, and outcome with his mother, who has consented for this. I have also recommended a course of high-dose amoxicillin to cover the child in view of the presence of acute otitis media.

Signature: _____ MD

H&P

HOUSTON HEALTH CARE CENTER
Operative Report

Diagnosis: Chronic otitis media with effusion

Procedure: Myringotomy left and right with insertion of pressure-equalizing tubes left and right

Anesthesia: General mask

Estimated blood loss: Less than 1 cc

Complications: None

Condition: Satisfactory

Indication for surgery: This is a 10-month-old male with a history of recurrent otitis media not responding satisfactorily to antibiotic therapy. Clinical examination showed inflamed tympanic membranes. There was evidence of effusion behind both tympanic membranes. In addition, there was also evidence of a recent acute episode of otitis media. In view of the recurrent nature of his problem, it was decided to proceed with insertion of PE tubes.

Procedure: The patient was brought to the operating room and general anesthetic was administered via a face mask. Right ear was first examined under the microscope. The external auditory canal was cleared of cerumen. An anterior inferior myringotomy was performed. A mucoid effusion was suctioned out of the middle ear and a blue Pope tympanostomy tube was inserted. The opposite ear was examined under the microscope. The external auditory canal was cleared of cerumen. An anterior inferior myringotomy was performed. Mucoid effusion was suctioned out of the middle ear and a blue Pope tympanostomy tube was inserted. No complications were encountered. Antibiotic ear drops were instilled in both ears. The patient was then handed back to the anesthesiologist in satisfactory condition and taken to the recovery room.

Dictated and reviewed by: _____ (Surgeon)

Op Report

HOUSTON HEALTH CARE CENTER
Operative Note

Preoperative diagnosis: Chronic otitis media with effusion

Postoperative diagnosis: Chronic otitis media with effusion

Procedure: Myringotomy left and right with insertion of pressure-equalizing tubes left and right

Surgeon: Dr. Xxxxx

Anesthesia: General endotracheal

Complications: None

Signature: _____ MD

Op Note

HOUSTON HEALTH CARE CENTER
Discharge Note/Discharge Order

Hospital course: Uncomplicated

Discharge instructions:

Medication: Tylenol, prn
Cortisporin 3 drops, 3 times a day for 3 days

Activity: Encourage child to rest at home the first day after surgery

Diet: Regular

Follow-up: 2 weeks in office

Discharge status: Stable

Final diagnosis: Chronic otitis media with effusion

Signature: _____

Discharge

Answer Sheet for Case 9

Code this day surgery medical record using ICD-9-CM diagnostic and CPT-4 procedural codes.

Principal diagnosis:

Secondary diagnoses (if any):

CPT code(s):

47.

HOUSTON HEALTH CARE CENTER
Face Sheet

Patient name: *Case 10*

Final diagnosis: New onset angina, coronary artery disease
History of coronary stent insertion
History of myocardial infarction
Diabetes mellitus, history of smoking, hypertension, hypercholesterolemia

Procedures: Left heart catheterization
Selective angiogram (Judkins technique)
Left ventriculogram

Reason for admission: Left heart catheterization and selective coronary angiography.

Indications for procedure: 1. Known coronary artery disease, status post coronary angioplasty with stent insertion of the right coronary artery.
2. New onset angina

History of present illness: This 50-year-old man with a history of a non-Q wave myocardial infarction 6 weeks ago, status post angioplasty at that time, presented back to the clinic with further worsening of his angina, and was referred for cardiac catheterization. The risks and benefits of cardiac catheterization have been discussed with the patient.

He has done relatively well since the angioplasty until recently, when he was admitted for additional problem, which was a diverticular perforation. There was a small area of ischemia on the inferior wall following the evaluation for preoperative clearance for drainage of the diverticular abscess.

He has no PND, orthopnea or peripheral edema. However, on his last consultation he did complain of new onset chest pain on exertion. In conjunction, the finding of coronary ischemia remains of concern in that he may have developed restenosis of his previous coronary stent. I have discussed this with the patient and he wishes to go ahead with cardiac catheterization.

Coronary artery disease risk factors: Risk factors include hypertension and hypercholesterolemia. He has a history of diabetes. No history of asthma. He has a family history of heart disease. He is an ex-smoker.

Past medical/surgical history: As described above, myocardial infarction 6 weeks ago with stenting of the right coronary artery.

Allergies: Allergic to penicillin. He denies any allergies to iodine or seafood.

(continues)

Face Sheet

HOUSTON HEALTH CARE CENTER
Face Sheet *(Continued)*

Review of systems: Unremarkable, he has no bowel disturbance or urinary tract disturbance. He has no neurological symptoms.

Current medications:

1. Lisinopril 0.5 mg qd
2. Metoprolol 50 mg bid
3. Plavix 75 mg qd
4. Aspirin 325 mg qd
5. Lipitor 10 mg qd
6. Niaspan 500 mg bid. He was noted to have an extremely low HDL in the hospital and therefore was started on Niaspan to try and raise his HDL. He appears to be tolerating all of his medications relatively well at this point in time.

Physical examination:

Vital signs:

Blood pressure was 140/70, pulse 72 and regular

Neck: JVD flat. No carotid bruits

Heart: S1 and S2 normal

Chest: Clear

Abdomen: Soft and nontender

Extremities: No peripheral edema

Assessment and plan: The patient is clinically stable with no fever and is planning elective surgery for his diverticular perforation. Given the inferolateral ischemia and new onset angina, I recommend a cardiac catheterization.

Signature: _____ MD

Face Sheet

HOUSTON HEALTH CARE CENTER

Procedure Note

Left heart cath, selective coronary (Judkins technique), and left ventriculogram

Findings: LM: normal

LAD: mild disease

Ramus: 60-65% stenosis

CX: mild disease

RCA: patent stent

Assessment and plan: Continue medical treatment and discharge after bed rest

Proc Note

Answer Sheet for Case 10

Code this outpatient observation medical record using ICD-9-CM diagnostic and CPT-4 procedural codes.

Principal diagnosis:

Secondary diagnoses (if any):

Principal procedure:

Other procedures (if any):

CPT code(s):

48.

HOUSTON HEALTH CARE CENTER
History and Physical

Patient name: *Case 11*

Present complaint: Tonsillitis

Present illness: 12-year-old male with recurrent episodes of acute tonsillitis

Review of systems: Negative

Past history: Negative

Allergies: NKA

Current medication: None

Physical examination:

Vital signs:

   Pulse: 84   **Respiratory Rate:** 16   **Temperature:** 98° F

   Age: 12   **Sex:** M

General: No acute distress

HEENT: PERRL, TM's nl, tonsils +3 enlarged with deep crypts

Chest and lungs: Clear

Heart: R R + R

Abdomen: Soft

Pelvic/Genitalia: defer

Neurological: WNL

Extremities: No edema

Impressions: Chronic tonsillitis

Treatment and plan: Tonsillectomy, possible adenoidectomy

Signature: _____ MD

H&P

HOUSTON HEALTH CARE CENTER
Operative Report

Preoperative diagnosis: 1. Chronic nasal obstruction

2. Chronic tonsillitis

3. Adenoid hypertrophy

Postoperative diagnosis: 1. Chronic nasal obstruction

2. Chronic tonsillitis

3. Adenoid hypertrophy

Procedures performed: Tonsillectomy and adenoidectomy

Anesthesia: General

Complications: None

Estimated blood loss: 5 cc

Indications and findings: This 12-year-old has had recurrent episodes of pharyngitis as well as chronic nasal obstruction. He is totally unable to breathe through his nose.

Findings at the time of surgery included very small tonsils, but a very large adenoid pad in the nasopharynx that obstructed the air flow through his nose. There was also pus in the nasal cavities. The adenoidectomy was accomplished by using a suction cautery.

Description of procedure: The patient was taken to the operating room and was placed on the table in the supine position. He was put to sleep under general anesthetic and intubated. The table was then turned for the procedure.

Using a Crowe-Davis mouth gag in place, the nasopharynx was first inspected. This was accomplished by passing a red rubber catheter through the nose and retracting the soft palate. Upon inspection, it was clear that the adenoid tissue was very enlarged. Using a suction cautery, this was substantially reduced. Also, the nose was irrigated copiously with cold saline to flush out all of the pus. Any bleeding in the nasopharynx was stopped with the electrocautery.

Attention was then turned to the tonsils which were both rather small. The right tonsil was removed. The left tonsil was cauterized. The airway was good. There was no bleeding. The patient was then awakened in the operating room, extubated, and taken to the recovery room.

Dictated and reviewed by: _____ (Surgeon)

Op Report

HOUSTON HEALTH CARE CENTER
Operative Note

Preoperative diagnosis: Chronic tonsillitis

Postoperative diagnosis: 1. Chronic nasal obstruction
                                          2. Chronic tonsillitis
                                          3. Adenoid hypertrophy

Procedure: Tonsillectomy and adenoidectomy

Surgeon: Dr. Xxxxx

Anesthesia: General

Drains, complications: None

Estimated blood loss: 5 cc

Findings: Chronic nasal obstruction; chronic tonsillitis; adenoid hypertrophy

Signature: _____ MD

Op Note

HOUSTON HEALTH CARE CENTER
Discharge Note/Discharge Order

Diagnosis: 1. Chronic nasal obstruction
2. Chronic tonsillitis
3. Adenoid hypertrophy

Procedure: Tonsillectomy and adenoidectomy

Diet: Clear liquid; advance as tolerated

Activity: At liberty

Discomfort: Tylenol with codeine elixir 3 tsp/po q 4 prn. Amoxil 250 mg po bid

Follow-up: In 2 weeks

Condition at discharge: Stable

Signature: _____

Discharge

Answer Sheet for Case 11

Code this day surgery medical record using ICD-9-CM diagnostic and CPT-4 procedural codes.

Principal diagnosis:

Secondary diagnoses (if any):

CPT code(s):

49.

HOUSTON HEALTH CARE CENTER
History and Physical

Patient name: *Case 12*

Present complaint: Undescended testicles

Present illness: 13-year-old male with undescended testicles and urinary incontinence

Review of systems: Negative

Past history: Reactive airway disease

Past surgical history: Newborn circumcision

Allergies: NKA

Current medication: Rhinocort

Physical examination:

Vital signs:

   Pulse: 84   Respiratory Rate: 16   Temperature: 98° F

   Age: 13   Sex: M

General: No acute distress

HEENT: Normal

Chest and lungs: Clear to auscultation bilaterally

Abdomen: Soft, non-tender

Pelvic/Genitalia: Circumcised, bilateral testes with external ring in scrotum

Neurological: Non focal

Extremities: Normal

Impressions: Bilateral undescended testes

Treatment and plan: Bilateral orchiopexy

Signature: _____ MD

H&P

HOUSTON HEALTH CARE CENTER
Operative Report

Preoperative diagnosis: Undescended testicles

Postoperative diagnosis: Undescended testicles

Procedures performed: Bilateral orchiopexy

Anesthesia: General

Complications: None

Procedure in detail: After anesthesia was administered, the patient was prepped and draped in sterile fashion and placed in the supine position. We made small inguinal incisions on both sides and dissected down external oblique fascia and opened at the external ring. The testes were low in the canal. They were mobilized and brought up into the wound. The gubernacular and lateral attachments were then divided. The testes were then mobilized back into the ring. A closed processus vaginalis was present on each side and this was dissected from the cord structure and transected to further lengthen the cord vessels.

The tunica was then opened over the testes. The appendix testis and appendix epidymidis was present on the left side. No appendages were on the right. Both testes were very small. The left testis measured about 9 mm and the right 8 mm, but the volume of the testes was also reduced. The epididymal attachments were normal.

A Dartos pouch was created in the usual way. The testes were brought down to the pouch and secured there with Vicryl suture. Both incisions were closed with absorbable suture. Steri-Strips were placed across the incisions. The patient tolerated the procedure well.

Dictated and reviewed by: _____ (Surgeon)

Op Report

HOUSTON HEALTH CARE CENTER
Operative Note

Preoperative diagnosis: Undescended testicles

Postoperative diagnosis: Undescended testicles

Procedure: Bilateral orchiopexy

Surgeon: Dr. Xxxxx

Anesthesia: General

Drains, complications: None

Findings: Undescended testicles

Signature: _____ MD

Op Note

HOUSTON HEALTH CARE CENTER
Discharge Note/Discharge Order

Diagnosis: Undescended testicles

Procedure: Bilateral orchiopexy

Diet: Regular

Activity: No straddle toys or bicycle riding

Discomfort: Tylenol with codeine 5-10 ml po q 4 as needed for pain.

Follow-up: In 3 weeks

Condition at discharge: Stable

Signature: _____

Discharge

Answer Sheet for Case 12

Code this day surgery medical record using ICD-9-CM diagnostic and CPT-4 procedural codes.

Principal diagnosis:

Secondary diagnoses (if any):

CPT code(s):

50.

HOUSTON HEALTH CARE CENTER
Face Sheet

Patient name: *Case 13*

Final diagnosis: Screening for colon cancer
Family history of colon cancer

Procedures: Colonoscopy

Face Sheet

HOUSTON HEALTH CARE CENTER

History and Physical

Present complaint: Family history of colon cancer

Past history: None

Current medications: None

Allergies: NKA

Smoking or drinking: No

Physical examination:

    General: Alert

    HEENT: No mass or deformity

    Torso/Breast: No mass or deformity

    Heart: Normal rhythm

    Lung: Clear to auscultation

    Abdomen: No mass or tenderness

    Extremities: No edema or tenderness

Neurological: Intact

Impression: Family history of colon cancer

Treatment and plan: Colonoscopy

Signature: _____ MD

H&P

HOUSTON HEALTH CARE CENTER
Procedure Note

Preoperative diagnosis: Family history of colon cancer

Postoperative diagnosis: Colon polyps

Procedure: Colonoscopy with polypectomy

Medications: Demerol 50 mg; Versed 2.0

Findings: 4-mm polyp at sigmoid

Pathology results: Tubular adenoma with villious component
    Follow up biopsy results in 1–2 weeks
    Repeat colonoscopy in 2–3 years

Signature: _____ MD

Op Note

HOUSTON HEALTH CARE CENTER
Discharge Note/Discharge Order

Hospital course: Stable

Discharge instructions:

Medication: None

Activity: As tolerated

Diet: As per instructions

Follow-up: 1–2 weeks

Discharge status: Discharged when criteria met

Final diagnosis: Colon polyp

Signature: _____

Discharge

Answer Sheet for Case 13

Code this day surgery medical record using ICD-9-CM diagnostic and CPT-4 procedural codes.

Principal diagnosis:

Secondary diagnoses (if any):

CPT code(s):

Organization, Management, and Supervision

1. Management
   a. Defined
      i. People who get things done through other people; contrasted with people who actually do the work
      ii. Process of coordinating individual and group actions toward the accomplishment of organizational goals in a manner that is acceptable to the larger social cultural system
      iii. Process of planning, organizing, and leading the activities of an organization
   b. What Managers Do
      i. Get things done through other people
      ii. Have and use authority to get things done
      iii. Communicate
      iv. Solve problems
      v. Provide direction
   c. Mintzberg's Managerial Roles (Table 9-1)
   d. Levels of Management
      i. Supervisory
         1. Oversee the organization's efforts at the staff level and monitor the effectiveness of everyday operations and individual performance against established standards
         2. Ensure that the organization's human assets are used effectively and that its policies and procedures are carried out consistently
      ii. Middle
         1. Primarily concerned with facilitating the work performed by supervisory and staff-level personnel as well as by executive leaders
         2. Develop, implement, and revise the organization's policies and procedures, under the direction of executive managers
         3. Execute the organizational plans developed at the board and executive levels
         4. Provide the operational information that executives need to develop meaningful plans for the organization's future

Table 9-1 Mintzberg's Managerial Roles	
Managerial Activities	**Related Roles**
Interpersonal	Figurehead
	Liaison
	Leader
Informational	Monitor
	Disseminator
	Spokesperson
Decisional	Entrepreneur
	Disturbance handler
	Resource allocator
	Negotiator

    iii. Executive management
        1. Hired by the board, or by the chief executive officer with board approval
        2. Responsible for working with the board to set the organization's future direction and establish its strategic plan
        3. Ensures that the organization uses its assets wisely, fulfills its current mission, and works toward achieving a meaningful vision for the future
        4. Oversees broad functions, departments, or groups of departments
        5. Establishes the policies of health care organizations and leads their quality improvement and compliance initiatives
        6. Works with community leaders to make sure that the health care organization contributes to the well-being of the community it serves
        7. Titles include
            a. Chief executive officer
            b. President
            c. Executive vice president
            d. Senior vice president
            e. Vice president
            f. Director
   iv. Board of governors or board of directors
        1. Ultimately responsible for the operation of the health care organization
        2. Final authority in setting the organization's strategic direction, mission, and vision and general philosophy and ethical base
        3. Represents the interests of the organization's owners
            a. Types of owners
                i. Federal government
                ii. State government
                iii. Local government

        iv. Investment group

        v. Educational institution

        vi. Religious organization

        vii. Public group

            1. Stockholders elect board members.

            2. In for-profit entities, investors purchase stock on stock exchanges and receive a share of the profits.

        viii. Private group

            1. Board members are appointed.

            2. May operate as not-for-profit charitable organizations

    4. Consist of chairperson and 10 to 20 board members

e. Landmarks in Management as a Discipline

    i. Scientific

        1. Earliest attempt to study management in a scientific manner, emphasizing worker efficiency achieved through the "one right way" to perform a task, as determined by the expert who possesses a scientific understanding of the work achieved by methodic study

        2. Max Weber (1864–1920): proposed organizations become bureaucracies

        3. Frederick Taylor (1856–1915): attempted to study management scientifically by conducting time and motion studies

        4. Henry Gantt (1861–1919): developed charting method (Gantt chart) that is still used for project management

    ii. Administrative

        1. To compensate for scientific management's exclusion of senior management, administrative management argued that management was a profession and could be learned.

        2. Henri Fayol (1841–1925): identified five management functions and 14 principles (see Table 9-2)

            a. Planning

            b. Organizing

            c. Leading (directing)

            d. Controlling

    iii. Humanistic

        1. Focused on how to treat employees

        2. Initiated the human relations movement

        3. Hawthorne effect

            a. Experiment conduct by Mayo and Roethlisberger from 1924–1932 to test the effect of lighting level in the workplace on productivity

            b. Concluded positive attention and human relations improved performance

    iv. Human resource management

        1. Abraham Maslow (1908–1970): suggested hierarchy of needs to help explain behavior and provide guidance for managers on how to better motivate workers

            a. Physiological needs

            b. Safety

            c. Social belonging

            d. Self-esteem

            e. Self-actualization or creativity needs

Table 9-2 Fayol's Management Principles

Principle	Description
Specialization of labor	Work allocation and specialization allow concentrated activities, deeper understanding, and better efficiency.
Authority	The person to whom responsibilities are given has the right to give direction and expect obedience.
Discipline	The smooth operation of a business requires standards, rules, and values for consistency of action.
Unity of command	Every employee receives direction and instructions from only one boss.
Unity of direction	All workers are aligned in their efforts toward a single outcome.
Subordination of individual interest	Accomplishing shared values and organizational goals takes priority over individual agendas.
Remuneration	Employees should receive fair pay for work.
Centralization	Decisions are made at the top.
Scalar chair	Everyone is clearly included in the chain of command and line of authority from top to bottom of the organization.
Order	People should clearly understand where they fit in the organization, and all people and material have a place.
Equity	People are treated fairly, and a sense of justice should pervade the organization.
Tenure	Turnover is undesirable, and loyalty to the organization is sought.
Initiative	Personal initiative should be encouraged.
Espirit de corps	Harmony, cohesion, teamwork, and good interpersonal relationships should be encouraged.

2. Douglas McGregor (1906–1964): recognized the shift in conceptual models from assumptions that workers were incapable of independent action to beliefs in their potential and high performance
   a. Theory X
      i. Presumes workers inherently dislike work and avoid it.
      ii. Employees have little ambition and mostly want security.
      iii. Managerial direction and control are necessary.

    b. Theory Y

        i. Assumes work is as natural as play

        ii. Motivation could be both internally and externally driven.

        iii. Under the right conditions, people will seek responsibility and be creative.

v. Operations management: developed out of need to better understand how products and services could be manufactured and delivered

    1. Forecasting: previous conditions are projected into the future.

    2. Linear programming: used to identify an optimal decision, given a set of planned constraints or limited resources.

    3. Break-even analysis: helps planners determine the level of sales at which total revenues equal the total costs. Revenues beyond that are profit.

    4. Queuing theory: mathematical theory for determining the flow of customers or for designing optimal wait times for services.

    5. Simulation and inventory modeling: based on computerization and systems concepts. Key components and processes of a system are represented in a computer model so that planner can experiment with different operating strategies and designs to get the best results before committing to their actual implementation.

    6. PERT

        a. Allows large, long-term, and complex projects to be shown graphically in order to clarify critical task sequences, potential bottlenecks, and the time required for them.

        b. For complex situations, computer decision support can help explore and optimize decisions.

vi. Contemporary management

    1. Peter Drucker (1909–2005)

        a. Formulated practice of strategy by integrating formulation, tactical planning, and budgeting into a single system of management

        b. Elaborated on the technique of management by objectives (MBO), in which clear target objectives could be stated and measured and could direct behavior

            i. Four elements

                1. Top management plans and sets goals

                2. Managers with subordinates set individual objectives related to organizational goals

                3. Autonomy in the means of achieving objectives

                4. Regular review of performance in obtaining objectives

    2. W. Edwards Deming (1900–1993)

        a. Focused on quality improvement instead of quotas, because workers spent too much time trying to look good or protect themselves by seeking short-term objectives and ignoring long-term and critical outcomes

        b. Total quality management (TQM)

            i. Purported to overcome the limitations of MBO

            ii. Offered a way to build in high performance by maximizing employee potential and continuous improvement of process

f. Basic Components of Management

    i. Effectiveness

        1. Ensures that the utilization of resources accomplishes the objectives (products or services)

        2. Effectiveness is a product of productivity, performance, and efficiency.

    ii. Functions
        1. Planning
        2. Organizing
        3. Directing (leading)
        4. Controlling
    iii. Resources
        1. External
            a. Human resources
            b. Money
            c. Materials
            d. Machinery
        2. Internal
            a. Creativity
            b. Coordination
            c. Cooperation
            d. Communication
            e. Common sense
    iv. Objectives
        1. Something toward which effort is directed
        2. Purposes to be achieved
        3. Direct an organization in the face of change
g. Functions of Management (planning, organizing, directing, controlling)
    i. Planning
        1. Choose a destination, evaluate alternatives, and decide the specific course
        2. Determine what work must be done
        3. Define roles and mission
        4. Most important of management functions
        5. To plan effectively managers must
            a. Understand the mission and vision of the organization
            b. Work-group goals should be measurable, reflect organizational and personal priorities, and be challenging yet attainable.
            c. Goals should be flexible and capable of responding to changing conditions.
        6. In planning, managers perform the following:
            a. Define objectives
            b. Set courses of action
            c. Arrange matters in advance
            d. Determine what work must be done
            e. Define role and mission
        7. Planning involves
            a. Choosing a destination
            b. Evaluating alternative routes
            c. Deciding on the specific course to reach the chosen destination
        8. Stages of planning
            a. Setting the stage: a period to gather data to understand the environment facing the organization and its individual parts
            b. Setting goals
               i. Goal is a long-range aim, a destination to which the organization commits itself. Goals tend to be general, unqualified statements that describe the outcome or attribute the organization seeks to achieve.

      ii. Goals should
        1. Be specific
        2. Reflect organizational priorities and personal priorities
        3. Be measurable
        4. Be challenging yet attainable
        5. Relate to critical success factors
  c. Plan development
      i. Mission statement: organization's overall purpose and philosophy
      ii. Strategic planning: philosophical analysis of what the organization is (its mission), what it hopes to be (its vision), and innovative ways of achieving the type of future that will ensure the organization's survival and effectiveness
      iii. Long-range plans: shorter term than strategic plans (typically 1–5 years)
      iv. Tactical planning: operational and budgetary planning designed to accomplish immediate and short-term plans
        1. Operational plans: 1 year or less, day to day, time, talent, tasks
        2. Intermediate: programmatic plans of 1 year or less
        3. Short-range: includes financial and budgetary planning
  d. Implementation
      i. Planning flexibility: a good plan can be altered easily and adjusted in light of change.
      ii. Contingency plan: plans that take into account conditions different from those assumed to provide the foundation for the primary plan.
      iii. Paradox of planning: the areas in which plans are most likely to be inaccurate are the areas in which they are most needed, and the areas in which plans are most accurate are those in which they are less essential.
  e. Feedback or review
      i. Control necessary to ensure that plans meet the goals established early in the process; emphasis is on the result and whether or not activities are proceeding according to plan.
      ii. MBO is a systematic and organized approach that allows management to focus on achievable goals and to attain the best possible results from available resources; it involves participative goal setting and evaluation based on results.
9. Approaches to planning
  a. Gap analysis answers the questions
      i. Where are we today?
      ii. Where do we want to go?
      iii. How are we going to get there?
  b. SWOT is an organization's review of its
      i. Strengths
      ii. Weaknesses
      iii. Opportunities
      iv. Threats
10. Tools related to the planning function
  a. Policies: general broad guidelines to action that relate to goal attainment and translate overall objectives into comprehensible

and practical terms; should be consistent; require judgment but not complex interpretation

b. Procedures: plans for action; a series of related steps designed to accomplish a specific task; developed to define the task clearly, achieve uniformity of practice, and facilitate training

c. Rules: plans that depict a required prohibited course of action accurately; require no decision making or interpretation but rather require or limit specific action authoritatively and officially

d. Objectives: more specific statements that define the expectations or outcomes given by the goal statement

  i. Routine objectives: ongoing, continue from year to year
  ii. Innovative objectives: involve solving a special problem, a new project, or similar non-recurrent assignment
  iii. Improvement objectives: require continuous performance improvement

e. Standards: measures established to serve as criteria or levels of reference for determining the accomplishment of objectives

ii. Organizing

1. Defined as distributing or allocating resources toward the accomplishment of the objectives of the defined plan

2. Classifying and dividing the work into manageable units

3. Has a formal and an informal structure

4. Staffing

a. Determining the requirements for ensuring the availability of personnel to perform the work

b. Selecting personnel and appointing people to organizational positions

c. Developing personnel to provide opportunities for people to increase their capabilities in line with organizational needs

d. Determining personnel needs; analyzing the work for personnel capabilities required

5. Components of organization

a. Organizational chart: a schematic representation of the manner in which work is arranged and related so it can be performed

b. Responsibility: the obligation of an individual to carry out assigned tasks to the best of his or her abilities; two major types of relationship responsibility

  i. Line: positions that have direct responsibility for accomplishing the objectives of an organization
  ii. Staff: positions that assist and advise the manager in accomplishing objectives

c. Authority: the right given to each position holder to command the behavior for which the position is responsible

d. Unity of command: states that an employee should have one and only one immediate boss

e. Span of control: the number of immediate subordinates a manager can manage effectively

f. Scalar principle: chain of command; the authority flows down the chain of command from the top to the lowest level

g. Accountability: the obligation to account for the results expected

h. Delegation: act of passing one's rights or authority to another in order to prohibit or require actions on the part of another; the conveyance of responsibility and authority from superior to subordinate

iii. Directing (Leading)

1. Leading: stimulating members to meet objectives; getting all members of a work group to contribute effectively and efficiently to the achievement of the organization's objectives
2. Bringing about the human activity required to accomplish objectives
3. Assigning: charging individual employees with job responsibilities or specific tasks to be performed
4. Motivating: influencing people to perform in a desired manner
5. Communicating: achieving effective flow of ideas and information in all desired directions
6. Coordinating: achieving harmony of group effort toward the accomplishment of individual and group objectives
7. Centralization: only limited amount of authority is delegated; provides closer control of operations, uniformity of policies, procedures, practices
8. Decentralization: significant amount of authority delegated to lower levels of organization; enables faster decision making without resorting to higher-level consulting; excellent training experience for promotion to higher level management; may result in decisions better adapted to local conditions
9. Flow charting: used to collect information on the steps of work process and to analyze and improve the process; identifies problems; helps eliminate duplication, workstation travel time, delays

iv. Controlling

1. Tools or methods that help a supervisor measure the progress of work against performance standards with sufficient time to take corrective action if there are deviations; tools must be measurable, economical, and timely.
2. Ensuring the effective accomplishment of objectives; clear objectives include:
   a. An action verb that describes an observable performance
   b. Conditions under which the action is to occur
   c. Statement of the standard or quality of performance (or competency) that is acceptable
   d. Time limits for completion of the action
3. Establishing standards: devising a gauge of successful performance in achieving objectives
4. Measuring performance
   a. Assessing actual versus planned performance
   b. Feedback mechanism for planning
   c. Determines whether planning has been effective and takes steps to ensure goals
   d. Assess employee performance
5. Corrective action
   a. Bringing about performance improvement toward objectives

    b. Detecting and correcting significant variations in the results obtained from planned activities by means of variance analysis

      i. Determines cause of deviation (deviation is the gap between actual performance and the established standard for that performance)

      ii. Review of deviation from standards found from monitoring

      iii. Financial planning

6. Requirements for controlling

    a. An understanding of what is necessary to meet standards defined in objectives and goals

    b. Monitoring to determine actual performance and compare it to the expected performance

    c. Mechanism to ensure that adequate resources exist to meet standards and take corrective action

7. Four basic steps to controlling

    a. Establish standards of performance: standards are criteria for determining the characteristics of acceptable performance and progress, utilizing scientific methods, simulation, past performance record, benchmarking

    b. Use controls to compare actual performance with standards

    c. Determine causes of deviation from standards

    d. Correct deviations from plans, standards, and expectations

8. Productivity: measures of the number of items created or the number of services accomplished per staff hour that meet established levels of quality; e.g., an employee coded 10 records in one hour, and 9 records were coded with 100% accuracy; therefore, the coder had a productivity of 9 or 90%.

9. Quality and quantity monitors (see Table 9-3)

Table 9-3 Quality and Quantity Monitors

Quality	Quantity
Direct inspection	Employee-reported volume log
Checklist	Stopwatch or time and motion studies
Questionnaire	Work sampling
Benchmarking	
Work simplification	

h. Role of Supervisor in Management

    i. Oversees the organization's efforts at the staff level, monitors the effectiveness of everyday operations, and measures individuals' performances against established standards

    ii. Supervisor

        1. Works in small groups

        2. Hands-on functions

        3. Staff training, recruitment, and retention

        4. Directs, schedules, and monitors daily work

        5. Revises procedures

        6. Conducts performance reviews

        7. Has advanced technical skills

i. Change Management

    i. The management of change within the organization

    ii. Organizational development: process of an organization reflecting on its own processes and consequently revising them for improved performance

    iii. Change agent

        1. Specialist in organizational development who facilitates the change brought about by the innovation

        2. Stages of change agents' work

            a. Scouting

            b. Entry and contracting

            c. Diagnosis or data gathering and feedback

            d. Planning

            e. Implementation

            f. Evaluation

            g. Termination

    iv. Stages of change

        1. Kurt Lewin's model (3 stages)

            a. Unfreezing

                i. Presenting the discrepancies between the status quo and the desired goals

                ii. Creates a state of cognitive dissonance, which is an uncomfortable awareness of two incompatible perceptions or beliefs

                iii. Motivates the person to resolve dissonance, usually by changing the situation to make the perceptions congruent

            b. Moving to the new desired state for the organization

            c. Refreezing: New barriers are reinforced to become as stable and institutionalized as the previous status quo was.

        2. Elizabeth Kübler-Ross's stages of grief

            a. Shock and denial

            b. Anger and resentment

            c. Bargaining and negotiation

            d. Depression and despair

            e. Acceptance and reorientation

2. Leadership

    a. Multiple Aspects

        i. The interpersonal influence directed toward attainment of a specific goal or goals

        ii. Ability to inspire and influence others; process of influencing the behavior of group members

   iii. The process by which one individual influences others to accomplish goals

   iv. Takes the part of a manager who influences subordinates to accomplish desired goals within a business organization

   v. Art of mobilizing others to want to struggle for shared aspirations

  b. Characteristics of Effective Leadership

   i. A strong drive for responsibility and devotion to completing tasks

   ii. Persistent in the pursuit of established goals

   iii. Innovation and originality in problem solving and decision making

   iv. Self-confident; strong personal identity

   v. Exercise initiative and make things happen

   vi. Willing to accept the consequences of actions

   vii. Deals effectively with stress and willing to tolerate frustration

   viii. Ability to influence the actions of others

  c. Leadership Practices

   i. Empower and motivate others

   ii. Recognize valuable ideas

   iii. Serve as a symbol of the work group's identity

   iv. Create a vision

   v. Renew the tangible (including people) and intangible resources

   vi. Network externally to promote data/information dissemination to customers

   vii. Demonstrate credibility to maintain trust

   viii. Listen and keep in touch internally and externally with regard to the organization

   ix. Maintain a standard of excellence

  d. Leadership Styles

   i. Bureaucratic: derives authority from the organization's set of rules and regulations; leads through reliance on rules and regulations and on formal grant of authority derived from higher levels of management

   ii. Laissez-faire: free reign or hands-off management; most successful in highly professional setting with knowledge-based workers who have a high sense of professional commitment

   iii. Democratic: utilizes a decision-making process that allows others to participate and takes others' opinions into consideration

   iv. Autocratic

    1. Rules with unlimited authority and undisputed power; monarch

    2. Efficiency results from arranging work so that human elements have little effect

    3. Are usually formal leaders who use their positions as the way to influence the behavior of others

   v. Transactional: strives to create an efficient workplace by balancing task accomplishment with interpersonal satisfaction

   vi. Transformational: promotes innovation and organizational change; charismatic or has ability to inspire and motivate people beyond what is expected with exceptionally high levels of commitment

  e. Types of Power

   i. Reward: ability to withhold or provide rewards for performance

   ii. Expert: leader has knowledge or expertise that is of value

   iii. Referent: personal characteristics that are appealing to the constituency, and the constituency follow out of admiration, charismatic impact, or the desire to be like the leader

   iv. Legitimate: comes from the authority of one's rank and position in the chain of command

   v. Coercive: utilizes punishment to maintain control

   vi. Information: persuasive content of the message, apart from personal characteristics of messenger

   vii. Representative: followers democratically delegate power to the leader for the purpose of representing their interests and making decisions on their behalf.

3. Communication

 a. Transference of understanding between two parties (individual or organizations); may be verbal, nonverbal, or written

 b. Understanding the Communication Process

   i. Who is speaking

   ii. Message content

   iii. Medium of transmission

   iv. Context of letter, written inquiry, or spoken message

   v. Consequences of interaction

 c. Nonverbal Communication

   i. Movements and gestures

   ii. Expressions

   iii. Dress

   iv. Silence (people may not speak yet ideas are exchanged)

   v. Gestures vary from one culture to another and may affect communication

 d. Communication Model

   i. Sender: originator of a stimulus (message)

   ii. Encoding: act that begins the communication process

   iii. Decoding: process of understanding the message

   iv. Filtering: altering of a message as it passes through the personalities of either the sender or receiver

   v. Receiver: one who receives the message

   vi. Noise: anything that changes or interferes with the message but is not part of either the receiver or sender

   vii. Feedback loop: connects the receiver and the sender; by evaluating feedback, the sender can gain valuable insight into the way the message is being received.

 e. Communication Process Model

   i. Downward (e.g., to subordinates)

   ii. Laterally (e.g., to colleagues)

   iii. Diagonally (e.g., from superior to subordinate outside of department)

   iv. Upward (e.g., to superior)

 f. Barriers to Communication

   i. Message overload

   ii. Message complexity

   iii. Personal distortion mechanisms

    1. Inattention

    2. Premature evaluation

    3. Lack of a common vocabulary

   iv. Psychological distortion mechanisms

    1. Rationalization

    2. Denial

 g. Rules for Effective Interpersonal Communication

   i. Be clear and concise

   ii. Use vocabulary that is common to the individual or group

               iii. Check to make sure the message was received clearly and accurately

               iv. Try not to communicate in great haste

               v. Listen to others

               vi. Keep a written record of communication

   h. Listening Skills

      i. Avoid distractions

      ii. Evaluate the sender, and make adjustments for a different frame of reference

      iii. Seek to sort out the major theme and key points of the message to reduce the amount of information that must be retained

      iv. Consider factors surrounding the message to learn its full meaning

      v. Seek further clarification if needed

      vi. Respond to the message thoughtfully

4. Conflict

   a. Disagreement within the organizational setting between two or more parties, or between two or more positions, regarding how to best attain the organization's goals

   b. Sources of Conflict

      i. Differences in goals

      ii. Resource competition

      iii. Communication failure and misinterpretation of information

      iv. Disagreement over performance standards

      v. Organizational structure incongruities

   c. Strategies for Managing Group Conflict

      i. Avoidance

      ii. Smoothing

      iii. Dominance or power intervention

      iv. Compromise

      v. Confrontation

   d. Strategies for Resolution

      i. Know background of conflict

      ii. Evaluate background of those in the conflict

      iii. Analyze the relationship between conflicting parties

      iv. Realize the benefits to be derived from resolving conflict

5. Solving Problems

   a. Making a choice between two or more alternatives

   b. Styles of Decision Making

      i. Problem avoider: ignores signals of possible problem eruption

      ii. Problem solver: solves problems

      iii. Problem seeker: actively looks for opportunities to plan, anticipate, and solve possible problems before they occur

   c. Decision making is a systematic way of solving problems.

   d. Decision-Making Process

      i. Define the real problem, after awareness of the symptoms

      ii. Set criteria for making the decision while analyzing available information

      iii. Generate relevant alternative solutions to the problem

      iv. Analyze and evaluate these alternatives

      v. Select the best alternatives for a solution

      vi. Implement the chosen alternatives

      vii. Monitor and evaluate the decision's effectiveness

   e. Problem-Solving Techniques

      i. Multi-dimensional approach

    1. Define problem by determining the magnitude of problem and writing a problem statement

    2. Assess the context by determining your authority to act and identifying whom to involve

    3. Weigh the alternatives

        a. Gather information about causes and solutions

        b. Identify criteria for evaluating alternatives

        c. Generate and rate alternatives and select best solution

    4. Create an implementation plan

        a. Evaluate and assign resources

        b. Identify implementation activities and completion dates

        c. Identify whom to inform

  ii. Brainstorming: maximizes ideas and generates alternatives

  iii. Nominal group technique

    1. Generate possible solutions in writing

    2. Present ideas to group

    3. Rank ideas anonymously

  iv. Delphi technique

    1. Elicit group input while controlling for bias and distortion

    2. Group members never meet, and their responses to questionnaire are anonymous.

    3. Identify future trends

f. Work-Group Dynamics

  i. Formal

    1. Those designated by and sanctioned by the organization

    2. Groups adhere to the scalar principle of organizational power.

    3. Receive legitimacy from the organization itself

    4. Communication flows according to organizational design.

  ii. Informal

    1. Created by the employees themselves

    2. Not sanctioned by the organization

  iii. Basic group forms

    1. Functional

    2. Task

    3. Interest

    4. Peer

    5. Committees

        a. Formal groups created by organization

        b. Have a specific purpose

        c. Structure

        d. Committee chairperson and members

6. Human Resource Management (HRM)

a. Human resource planning is proactive and improves utilization of resources by providing a planned method of matching personnel with organizational or departmental goals and objectives; it ensures long-term health of the organization's human assets.

b. Effective human resource planning can prevent termination or layoffs and provide directives for recruitment and training.

c. Human resource planning assures that manager can overcome both external and internal challenges.

d. Human resource activities should be performed with the organization's unique mission, culture, size, and structure in mind and take into consideration the greater social, political, legal, economic, technological, and cultural environments in which it operates.

    e. Contributes to success of organization by enhancing its productivity, quality, and service

    f. Ensures compliance with legal and regulatory requirements

        i. The Joint Commission (TJC): voluntary accreditation

        ii. Occupational Safety and Health Act (OSHA): ensures safe and healthy work environment

        iii. National Labor Relations Act (NLRA, also called Wagner Act): gives employees right to collective bargaining and outlaws unfair labor practices

        iv. Health care amendments to the NLRA: extend the coverage and protection of the Act to employees of nonprofit hospitals and other health care organizations

        v. Labor Management Relations Act (Taft-Hartley Act): outlaws unfair labor practices by unions

        vi. Labor Management Reporting and Disclosure Act: forces unions to represent their members' interests properly

        vii. Civil Rights Act (Title VII): prohibits discrimination based on race, color, religion, sex, or national origin, and ensures equal employment opportunity

        viii. Vietnam Era Veterans' Readjustment Assistance Act: affirmative efforts to provide employment for qualified disabled veterans and veterans of the Vietnam era

        ix. Age Discrimination in Employment Act: protects employees between the ages of 40 and 70

        x. Americans with Disabilities Act: outlaws discrimination against people with disabilities and requires reasonable accommodations for them in the workplace

        xi. Family and Medical Leave Act (FMLA): grants unpaid leave and provides job security to employees who must take time off for medical reasons for themselves or family members

        xii. Pregnancy Discrimination Act: extends Title VII (of the Civil Rights Act of 1964) prohibitions against discrimination based on gender by broadening the definition to include pregnancy status, childbirth, and related medical conditions

        xiii. Employee assistance program (EAP)

        xiv. Termination including retirement and layoffs

        xv. Counseling and discipline

        xvi. Grievance procedures

        xvii. Employee and labor relations, including policy development and employees' rights and privacy protection

        xviii. Employee health, security, and safety

        xix. Compensation and benefits

            1. Wage and salary administration

            2. Payroll systems

            3. Performance incentive program

            4. Employee benefit program

        xx. Employee development

            1. Orientation

            2. Training

            3. Career development

4. Performance evaluation
5. Retention of valuable employees
6. Alternative staffing structures (flextime, job sharing, home-based work, outsourcing)

xxi. Staffing and selection
1. Recruitment: process of finding, soliciting, and attracting new employees
2. Screening and staff selection
3. Job analysis, design, and process engineering
   a. Job evaluation provides a formal procedure to determine relative worth of each position in the organization.
   b. Tools used to evaluate jobs include job ranking, job grading, factor comparison, and point system.
4. Job description elements
   a. Date
   b. Author
   c. Organization
   d. Job grade or classification
   e. Supervisory relationships
   f. Job status
   g. Job summary
   h. Essential functions, duties, and activities
   i. Job specifications
   j. Working conditions

g. Role of Health Information Professionals in Human Resources
  i. Staffing structures and work scheduling
  ii. Write job or position descriptions
  iii. Establish performance standards
    1. Set for both quantity and quality
    2. Should be objective and measurable
  iv. Develop policies and procedures
    1. Policy: statement about what an organization or department does
    2. Procedure: describes how work is done, how it is related to a department's policies, and how policies are carried out
  v. Recruit, select, and hire staff
  vi. Orientation of new employees: introduce new staff to the mores, behaviors, and expectations of the organization
  vii. Training and development
    1. Teach staff specific skills, concepts, or attitudes
    2. Ongoing in-service education to teach staff about skills, facts, attitudes, and behaviors, largely through internal programs
    3. Continuing education facilitates the efforts of staff members to remain current in the knowledge base of their trade or profession through external programs and meeting external standards.
    4. Career development continuously expands the capabilities of staff beyond a narrow range of skills toward a more holistically prepared person.
  viii. Empowerment of staff
  ix. Performance reviews
  x. Counsel and discipline staff
  xi. Conflict and grievance resolution
  xii. Maintain employee records

7. **Strategic Management**
  a. Strategy is a course of action designed to produce a desired outcome.
  b. Skills of Strategic Managers
    i. Monitor trends
    ii. Reflect on how trends may affect the future
    iii. Consider how changes in one area may affect changes in other areas
    iv. Set a course for change and help others visualize it
    v. Coach others to be partners in advancing a change agenda
    vi. Implement plans effectively
    vii. Question the status quo
  c. Elements of Strategic Management
    i. Vision
    ii. Issues
    iii. Goals
    iv. Strategies
    v. Tactics
    vi. Measure the results

8. **Project Management**
  a. Application of knowledge, skills, tools, and techniques to project activities in order to meet project requirements
  b. Concerned with completing a project within the expected cost and timeline with high-quality results
  c. A project team is responsible for task execution on project activities, resulting in an end product.
  d. Project team manager functions
    i. Set the project expectations
    ii. Create the project plan and recruit the project team
    iii. Manage and control project
    iv. Recommend plan revisions
    v. Execute change control
    vi. Prepare, document, and communicate project information
  e. Project Management Process
    i. Project definition
      1. Determine project scope and define project deliverables
      2. Estimate the project schedule and cost
      3. Prepare the project proposal
    ii. Project planning
      1. Identify project activities
      2. Construct the project network
        a. Determine dependencies among tasks
        b. Utilize a project schedule to determine when particular tasks can begin and when they are scheduled to end
      3. Estimate activity duration and work effort
      4. Conduct risk analysis and put contingencies in place for all risks
    iii. Project implementation
      1. Hold a kickoff meeting
      2. Perform project tasks and produce deliverables
      3. Track progress and analyze variance
      4. Establish change control
      5. Communicate project information
      6. Prepare the final report
      7. Celebrate success
  f. Project Management Life Cycle (see Table 9-4)

Table 9-4 Project Management Life Cycle	
Cycle	**Description**
Project definition	This process will determine the project objectives, activities, assumptions, high-level cost estimates, and anticipated schedule.
Planning and organization	A detailed project plan delineates the tasks to be performed, the resources necessary for each task, and the estimated task duration, start, and finish. The project team is established.
Tracking and analysis	By tracking project progress and analyzing it against the original plan, the project manager is able to determine when the project is not moving forward as planned.
Project revisions	When the analysis reveals project deviations, the plan may need to be modified in order to meet the project objectives.
Change control	This is the process of managing change request to the original project definition.
Communication	This process occurs throughout the project life cycle. Project information is collected from and disseminated to all stakeholders.

9. Work Design and Performance Improvement
   a. Associated with designing, redesigning, and implementing effective and efficient work processes within an organization
   b. Components of work processes and the development and use of performance standards and various methodologies in performance improvement
   c. Methods of Work Division
      i. Staffing involves determining the type and number of employees needed and what kind of work schedule is needed.
      ii. Work division
         1. Serial work division: consecutive handling of tasks or products by individuals who perform a specific function in sequence
         2. Parallel work division: concurrent handling of tasks
         3. Unit work division: simultaneous assembly, in which everyone performs a different specialized task at the same time
      iii. Work distribution analysis is used to determine whether a department's current work assignments and job content are appropriate.

    iv. Work scheduling ensures

        1. A core of employees on duty at all times when services must be provided

        2. A pattern of hours to be worked and days off that employees can be reasonably sure will not be changed except in extreme emergencies

        3. Fair and just treatment of all employees with regard to hours assigned

    v. Management of work procedures

        1. Job procedure: a structured, action-oriented list of sequential steps involved in carrying out a specific job or solving a problem

        2. Procedure manual: compilation of all procedures used in a specific unit, department, or organization

    vi. Work environment

        1. Addresses space, equipment, aesthetics, and ergonomics

        2. Work flow

            a. The established path along which tasks are sequentially completed by any number of staff to accomplish a function

            b. Well-designed work flow is critical to achieving optimum efficiency and productivity.

        3. Space and equipment

            a. Workspace design can influence morale, productivity, and job satisfaction.

            b. Should address

                i. Physical environment

                ii. Office space utilization

                iii. Furniture and equipment

                iv. Space-planning techniques, guidelines, and standards

            c. Four types of office space needed

                i. Private office space

                ii. General office space

                iii. Service area

                iv. Storage area

        4. Aesthetics

            a. Aesthetics of physical environment have great physiological and psychological effects on employees.

            b. Elements

                i. Lighting: sufficient brightness, exposure to natural light.

                ii. Color of walls and furniture: influences how employees feel.

                iii. Auditory impacts: music and sound incorporated into work environment may improve working conditions and relieve both mental and visual fatigue.

                iv. Temperature, moisture content, circulation: at least 2000 cubic feet per person per hour should be circulated to maintain a healthy respiratory atmosphere, and a range of 68 to 72 degrees Fahrenheit is generally acceptable.

        5. Ergonomic management

            a. Assesses employee workspace for comfort and safety

            b. Educates staff on how to care for themselves to reduce injuries and discomfort

d. Performance and Work Measurement Standards

  i. Work is the task to performed; performance is the execution of the task.

  ii. Managers must determine what work is to be done, what performance standards are achievable and appropriate, and how to measure performance, and then monitor work for variance from the standard.

  iii. A standard is a performance criterion established by custom or authority with the purpose of assessing factors such as quality, productivity, and performance.

  1. Communicated to staff via rules, polices, regulations, job descriptions, verbal confirmation

  2. Criteria for setting effective standards

   a. Understandable

   b. Attainable

   c. Equitable

   d. Significant

   e. Legitimate

   f. Economical

  3. Qualitative and quantitative standards

   a. Qualitative standards specify quality levels such as accuracy and error rate; also referred to as service.

   b. Quantitative standards specify level of measurable work expected for a specific function; also referred to as productivity.

  4. Key indicator: live (versus retroactive) measurement thresholds that alert a department to its level of competent customer service

   a. Complaints

   b. Surveys to access accreditation, legal, or regulatory standards the organization has failed to meet in one or more areas

  5. Developing standards

   a. Benchmarking

    i. Based on research into the performance of similar organizations and programs or on standards established by national or local sources

    ii. Steps in benchmarking

     1. Identify peer organization that has outstanding performance

     2. Study the best practices within that organization

     3. Act to implement those best practices

   b. Work measurement

    i. Process of studying the amount of work accomplished and the amount of time it takes to accomplish it

    ii. Supports manager to

     1. Set production standards

     2. Determine staff requirements

     3. Establish incentive pay

     4. Determine direct costs by function

     5. Compare performance standards

     6. Identify activities for process/method improvement

    iii. Accomplished through

     1. Analysis of historical data

     2. Employee self-logging (time ladder, volume logs)

        3. Measurement (stopwatch to record time to complete task)

        4. Work sampling (random sample of observations of work)

6. Performance measurement

  a. The process of comparing the outcomes of an organization, work unit, or employee to established performance plans and standards

  b. The results of performance measurement process are expressed as percentages, rates, ratios, averages, and other quantitative assessments.

  c. Performance controls

    i. Specific monitors (controls) are established by the manager and outcome data are collected.

    ii. Outcome data are then analyzed to determine the extent to which actual performance corresponds to the performance expectations established during the planning process.

    iii. Effective monitoring criteria include flexibility, simplicity, economy, timeliness, focus on exceptions.

  d. Variance analysis: Analysis of the performance factors involved in the work (people, supplies, equipment, and money) helps determine needed changes.

  e. Assessment of employee performance

    i. Monitor and measure outcomes and performance

    ii. Compare performance to established goals and standards

    iii. Evaluate variance and develop action plan

    iv. Take appropriate action

  f. Principles of performance improvement: determine why actual output varies from expected output and then take actions to increase the effectiveness, efficiency, and adaptability

  g. Performance improvement methodologies

    i. System analysis and design

      1. Determine need for the system and the system requirements

      2. Analyze system requirements

      3. Propose system design or redesign

      4. Evaluate the proposed system

      5. Implement the system

      6. Conduct ongoing evaluation and maintenance

      7. Use basic tools of system analysis (work distribution chart, movement diagram, flow process chart)

    ii. Continuous quality improvement (CQI)

      1. Constancy of variation

      2. Importance of data

      3. Vision and support of executive leadership

      4. Focus on customers

      5. Investment in people

      6. Importance of team

      7. Improvement model utilizing FOCUS-PDCA

        a. Find a process to improve

        b. Organize a team

        c. Clarify the knowledge

   d. Understand causes of variation

   e. Select process of improvement

   f. Plan, Do, Check, Act

  8. CQI techniques and tools

   a. Brainstorming: generates a large number of creative ideas

   b. Affinity grouping: allows team to organize and group similar ideas together

   c. Nominal group technique (NGT): brings agreement about an issue or an idea that the team considers most important by ranking ideas according to importance

   d. Multi-voting technique: variation of NGT in which team members rate the issue using a distribution of points or colorful dots

   e. Root cause analysis: fishbone diagram

   f. Pareto chart: ranking of multi-voting and nominal group process displayed visually from highest to lowest

   g. Force field analysis: visual display of data generated through brainstorming

   h. Check sheet: data collection tool that permits recording and compiling observations or occurrences

   i. Scatter diagram: data analysis tool used to plot points of two variables suspected of being related to each other in some way

   j. Histogram: data analysis tool used to display frequencies of response

   k. Run chart: displays data points over a period of time

   l. Statistical process control chart: plots points over time to demonstrate how a process is performing

 iii. Reengineering

  1. Focuses on the potential revamping of the entire process to achieve improvement

  2. Expectations of reengineering

   a. Increased productivity

   b. Decreased costs

   c. Improved quality

   d. Maximized revenue

   e. More satisfied customers

10. **Financial Management**

 a. Definitions

  i. Financial data: individual elements of organizational financial transactions

  ii. Financial transaction: the exchange of goods or services for payment or the promise of payment

  iii. Asset: items or resources that belong to the organization and have a future value

  iv. Liabilities: amounts owed to various creditors and vendors

  v. Revenue: the monies received for services provided

  vi. Expenses: the cost to provide a service

  vii. Equity: the difference between revenues and expenses

  viii. Profit: money received from the payer less the actual cost to complete the service, assuming the cost is less than the cash received

        ix. Accounting

             1. Process of recording, summarizing, and reporting the business history of a firm

             2. Involves the collection, recording, and reporting of financial data

                 a. The benefits of the financial data should exceed the cost of obtaining them.

                 b. The data must be understandable.

                 c. The data must be useful for making decisions.

             3. Six concepts of accounting activity

                 a. Entity

                 b. Going concern

                 c. Stable monetary unit

                 d. Time period

                 e. Conservatism

                 f. Materiality

             4. Principles of accounting

                 a. Reliability

                 b. Cost

                 c. Revenue

                 d. Matching

                 e. Consistency

                 f. Disclosure

    b. Financial Accounting

        i. Authorities

             1. Financial Accounting Standards Boards

             2. Securities and Exchange Commission

             3. Centers for Medicare and Medicaid Services

             4. Internal Revenue Service

        ii. Financial statements

             1. Balance sheet: snapshot of the accounting equation at a point in time

$$\text{Assets} - \text{Liabilities} = \text{Owner's Equity}$$

             2. Income statement

                 a. Shows the difference between revenues and expenses

                 b. Shows the results of operations and other activities affecting the profits of the firm

$$\text{Profit (Operating Income)} = \text{Revenue} - \text{Expenses}$$

             3. Cash flow statement

                 a. Shows changes in the cash and cash equivalent balances of a company for a specific fiscal period

                 b. Begins with the net income of the company and then makes a series of adjustments to convert to a cash basis

                 c. Cash flow results from three activities.

                     i. Operating

                     ii. Investing

                     iii. Financing

             4. Analyzing financial statements

                 a. Liquidity ratios

                     i. To evaluate current debt-paying and operating ability

    ii. Cash and nearness to cash

$$\text{Working Capital} = \text{Current Assets} - \text{Current Liabilities}$$

$$\text{Current Ratio} = \frac{\text{Current Assets}}{\text{Current Liabilities}}$$

$$\text{Quick Ratio} = \frac{\text{Quick Assets}}{\text{Current Liabilities}}$$

  b. Efficiency ratios
    i. Show how efficiently a company uses its assets
    ii. How quickly accounts receivable are collected
    iii. How quickly inventories are converted to cash
    iv. Accounts receivable turnover determines the average collection period for accounts.
    v. Debt to equity ratio indicates what proportion of equity and debt the company is using to finance its assets.

$$\text{Accounts Receivable Turnover} = \frac{\text{Net Credit Sales}}{\text{Average Accounts Receivable}}$$

$$\text{Debt to Equity Ratio} = \frac{\text{Long Term Debt}}{\text{Stockholdler's Equity}}$$

  c. Profitability ratios
    i. Useful in evaluating the company's operating performance
    ii. Profit margin shows how much of the sales dollars end up as profit for the company.

$$\text{Profit Margin} = \frac{\text{Net Income}}{\text{Net Sales}}$$

5. Inventory and depreciation
  a. Inventory
    i. Valuing products in inventory that are acquired at different prices or costs
    ii. First in, first out (FIFO)
    iii. Last in, first out (LIFO)
  b. Depreciation determines how to account for a long-term asset being used up over its useful life.
6. Investment decisions
  a. Compounding: value of investment is determined by length of time the investment is in place.
  b. Discounting: opposite of compounding; determines how much one must invest today at a compound interest rate of x to receive a given amount at the end of n years
  c. Rate of return
    i. Annual net inflows or outflows are averaged over the project's life for each project.
    ii. The asset value of investment value is averaged over the life of the project as well.
    iii. The asset value is depreciated on a straight-line basis for the life of the program.
  d. Payback period: how long it will take to get initial investment back for a project

      e. Net present value: difference between the present value of the investment cash outflow required for a project and the present value of future net free cash inflow from a project

c. Budgets

    i. Numeric documents that translate the goals, objectives, and action steps into forecasts of volume and monetary resources needed

   ii. Budgets are planned and prepared consistent with the strategic plan.

$$\text{Actual Dollars Spent} - \text{Dollars Budgeted} = \text{Variance}$$

$$\frac{\text{Actual Dollars Spent} - \text{Dollars Budgeted}}{\text{Dollars Budgeted}} \times 100 = \text{Variance Percentage}$$

  iii. Types of budgets

    1. Statistics budget

      a. Historical data are used to predict the future and plan the budget.

      b. Historical data include discharges by services, payer type, DRG, length of stay by DRG, diagnosis, procedures, ambulatory visits, type and number of home health visits, number of emergency room visits.

    2. Operating budget: managers predict cost of labor, supplies, and other expenses to support work volume of a particular department.

    3. Master budget: consolidation of all operating budgets

    4. Rolling budget: a budget established at the beginning of an accounting period is continually amended to reflect variances that arise due to changing circumstance.

    5. Flexible budget: Predicated on volume; supplies, labor, and other variable expenses are budgeted in proportion to the anticipated volume.

    6. Zero-based budget: requires management to justify all activities performed by a department before allocating any funding

    7. Capital budget

      a. Planning for capital equipment acquisitions and renovations

      b. Incorporates long- and short-term operating needs as they relate to equipment

      c. Capital equipment usually has a cost in excess of a stated amount (e.g., $500), a useful life of more than one year, and is tagged for tracking with an identifying number.

d. Reimbursement Methodologies

    i. Facility must be able to evaluate the underlying cost of providing services and to compare its actual reimbursements to the potential reimbursements based on charges.

   ii. All individual patient charges are captured in the patients' accounts.

  iii. Charges and underlying costs of the services provided are maintained in a database called a Chargemaster.

    1. Chargemaster is a database that collects information on all of the goods and services the facility provides to patients.

    2. Used to facilitate charge capture by centralizing and standardizing charge data within the facility

e. Payment for Health Care Services (Table 9-5)

    i. Historical aspects of health care in the United States have led to the third-party payer concept.

      1. A third party (insurance company) pays for services provided by the health care organizations or practitioners to the insured.

Table 9-5 Types of Payment for Health Care Services in the United States

Time Period	Method of Payment
Prior to 1930s	Direct out-of-pocket remuneration
After 1930s	Establishment of insuring agents that served a forerunner for Blue Cross and other insurance companies Growth in number of hospitals as consumers demanded more services for premiums paid
Mid-1960s	Government-subsidized Medicare Further encouraged hospitals to provide services without regard to cost due to Medicare reimbursement for services
1982	Tax Equity and Fiscal Responsibility Act mandated a prospective payment system (PPS), resulting in the implementation of DRGs
Present	Various reimbursement methods currently in use, including prenegotiated amounts, reimbursement based on a discount on billed charges, per diem payments, reimbursement based on audited costs, DRGs, ambulatory care groups, resource utilization groups, and payment for services at billed or full charges

2. The payer often receives premium payments from the insured's employer.
3. Federal and state governments also cover or insure non-employees in Medicare and Medicaid programs.
4. Reimbursement has extended beyond hospital providers to home health agencies, skilled nursing facilities, outpatient departments, ambulatory surgery centers, and rehabilitation facilities.
f. Cost Allocation Methods
   i. Step-down method
      1. Supported by Medicare in its cost-reporting requirements.
      2. Indirect departments that receive the least amount of service from other indirect departments and provide the most service to other departments have their costs allocated first.
      3. Allocation is based on the ratio of services provided to each department or some other basis such as square footage, employees, or worked hours.
   ii. Double-distribution method
      1. Similar to step-down
      2. Assumes that the allocation of cost cannot be linear and that some indirect departments need to be allocated or distributed to less commonly dispersed or distributed departments before the costs of these departments are fully allocated

        iii. Simultaneous-equations methods

           1. Also known as algebraic or multiple apportionment method

           2. Permits multiple allocations to occur through sophisticated mathematical software and the use of simultaneous mathematical equations

g. Role of the Health Information Professional in the Budgeting Process

    i. Responsible for identifying and recording the appropriate clinical codes to describe the patient's interaction with the organization

    ii. Assure timely and accurate coding

    iii. Aggregate and maintain documentation that supports reimbursement

    iv. Communicate budgetary requirements

    v. Develop and maintain the department budget and understand what caused variation or variance from the budget

PRACTICAL APPLICATION OF YOUR KNOWLEDGE

1. Management
   a. Describe the basic components of management.
      i. Effectiveness

      ii. Functions

      iii. Resources

      iv. Objectives

   b. Define and give examples of each management function.
      i. Planning

      ii. Organizing

    iii. Directing (Leading)

    iv. Controlling

c. Match each statement with the correct management function.
(Planning = P, Organizing = O, Directing = D, Controlling = C)

    i. _____ Manager meets with his staff weekly to give orders and encourage suggestions.

    ii. _____ Supervisor of release of information (ROI) gives assignments to staff.

    iii. _____ Manager sets the short range goals for the department.

    iv. _____ The director of health information delegates a project to a subordinate.

    v. _____ Manager makes a "to-do" list for the day.

    vi. _____ Manager praises employee for doing a good job with a project.

    vii. _____ Main file supervisor trains filing clerk on terminal digit order.

    viii. _____ Subsequent to performing benchmarking, a supervisor sets productivity standards.

    ix. _____ Supervisor motivates staff to work weekends.

    x. _____ Director sets goals and timeline for completion.

    xi. _____ Coding supervisor hires three analysts.

    xii. _____ The management teams restructure the staff and their duties.

    xiii. _____ The supervisor establishes a sequence of actions to follow in reaching the objectives of the barcoding project.

    xiv. _____ The CEO of the facility defines the mission of the organization.

    xv. _____ The supervisor of record processing disciplines an employee for tardiness.

d. Using the following table, develop and write supervisor job duties that correspond to the appropriate management function.

Supervisor Job Duties	
Planning	Organizing
Directing (Leading)	Controlling

e. Define the following terms and identify to which management function (planning, organizing, directing, or controlling) they correspond.

    i. Strategic plan

    ii. Operational plan

    iii. Policy

    iv. Procedure

     v. Goal

     vi. Rule

     vii. Objectives

     viii. Mission statement

     ix. Authority

     x. Lines of authority

     xi. Delegation

xii. Unity of command

xiii. Span of control

xiv. Scalar principle

xv. Staff

xvi. Line

f. Evaluate centralization and decentralization issues.
   i. Centralization

   ii. Decentralization

g. Define productivity and describe the various types of quality and quantity monitors.

h. Discuss motivation and the basic theories of motivation.

i. Discuss the role of supervisors.

j. Compare and contrast the definitions of management and leadership.
   i. Management

   ii. Leadership

2. Leadership
  a. Differentiate among the approaches to leadership theories.
    i. Classical approaches

    ii. Behavioral approaches

b. Define and contrast the following:
  i. Theory X

  ii. Theory Y

  iii. Theory Z

c. Match the following statements with the correct McGregor management theory. (Theory X = X, Theory Y = Y)

  i. _____ People are naturally lazy, and they prefer to do nothing.

  ii. _____ People work mostly for money and status rewards.

  iii. _____ The main force keeping people productive in their work is the fear of being demoted or fired.

  iv. _____ People are naturally active, and they set goals and enjoy striving.

  v. _____ People are naturally dependent upon leaders.

  vi. _____ People seek many satisfactions in work.

  vii. _____ People understand and care about what they are doing and can devise and improve their own methods of doing work.

  viii. _____ People need a sense that they are seen as capable of assuming responsibility and self-correction.

  ix. _____ People seek to give meaning to their lives by identifying with nations, communities, causes, and unions.

  x. _____ People have little concern beyond their immediate and material interest.

  xi. _____ People need to be encouraged and assisted.

  xii. _____ People need to be told, shown, and trained in proper methods of work.

  xiii. _____ People appreciate being treated with courtesy.

  xiv. _____ People crave genuine respect from their fellow humans.

  xv. _____ People constantly grow, and it is never too late to learn.

d. Discuss the various leadership styles.
    i. Bureaucratic

    ii. Laissez-faire

    iii. Democratic

    iv. Autocratic

e. Match the following with the correct leadership styles. (Bureaucratic = B, Laissez-faire = L, Democratic = D, Autocratic = A)

    i. _____ The president of the institution allows all five of his vice presidents free reign in managing their respective departments.

    ii. _____ The supervisor allows the employees to participate in deciding the filing system to utilize.

    iii. _____ An employee wears sandals to work. The supervisor sends the employee home because the rule states, "Employees must wear hard-toed shoes."

    iv. _____ When an employee offers suggestions for a more efficient department, the director states he will only incorporate ideas that he thinks are best.

    v. _____ During the holiday season, the supervisor arranged the main file room job duties so that the work would continue to be performed regardless of the employees utilizing their vacation.

    vi. _____ The director of health information exerts minimum effort in the supervision of her assistants.

    vii. _____ The manager disciplined his staff for not precisely following the policy and procedure about release of information.

    viii. _____ The CEO has an organization-wide meeting to obtain the ideas of the entire staff concerning optimizing financial resources.

f. Discuss the following types of power.
   i. Reward

   ii. Expert

   iii. Referent

   iv. Legitimate

   v. Coercive

   vi. Information

   vii. Representative

3. Communication

    a. Utilizing the communication model, identify the encoding, filtering, noise, decoding, and feedback in the following scenario. Also, how could the listening process be improved?

        i. The manager of ROI is training a new employee on telephone etiquette and taking telephone requests for release of information. The employee asks the manager follow-up questions for clarification of the procedure. The ROI office has a waiting area where authorized users make record requests. Within the ROI office, there are two photocopy machines, four telephone lines, and five physically active employees.

4. Problem Solving

    a. Using the decision-making process and the multi-dimensional approach to problem solving, determine a solution to the following.

        i. As supervisor, you are responsible for assuring that productivity is not jeopardized during the holiday season. Three out of five of your employees have requested to utilize one week of vacation time during the holiday season. All three employees must utilize their vacation time within this year or they will lose these hours.

Decision-Making Process	Multi-Dimensional Approach

5. Human Resource Management

 a. You own a release of information company with 10 employees. Due to the expansion of your business, you need to hire an additional employee. One candidate for the position is six months pregnant. You decide not to hire her based upon the demands of the job and her pregnancy condition. She reports you to the EEOC. How do you defend your decision?

 b. List and describe 10 legal and/or regulatory requirements that have affected human resource management.

 c. What should be the result of job analysis?

 d. Explain the elements of a job description.

 e. List major activities in the recruitment process.

 f. Discuss employee counseling and discipline.

 g. What is the health information practitioner's role in training and development?

6. Strategic Management
   a. Discuss necessary skills of a strategic manager.

   b. Describe the elements of strategic management.

7. Project Management
   a. What is project management?

   b. Discuss the steps in the project management life cycle.

8. Work Design and Performance Improvement
   a. The number of sick-leave days taken for the main file area has increased by 50% from the previous year. The major complaints by the employees have been back strain. What steps might the manager implement to decrease the number of sick days taken by employees?

   b. Define benchmarking and describe why it is used.

c. Differentiate between brainstorming and the nominal group process.

d. Discuss the importance of the work environment on employee production.

e. Given the following scenario, design a workflow diagram for optimum productivity.

    i. The health information department of a 150-bed hospital has 8 employees. The average length of stay is 3 days, with an average of 1201 discharges per month. The hospital uses a serial-unit record and TDO filing system. The department has one manager, one coder, one analysis clerk for the physician completion area, one assembly clerk, one statistician, one release of information clerk, and two main file clerks.

9. Financial Management

    a. Why do health information managers need to know about budgetary terms, processes, and types of budgets?

    b. How does the health information practitioner contribute to the master budget?

    c. List the major functional areas in financial accounting.

d. How do health care institutions get paid for services provided to patients and/or clients?

e. Explain the role of the health information professional in the budgeting process.

f. Describe various cost allocations methods.

10. Computation of Management and Personnel Problems

♪ The following calculations are reviewed with you on the audio entitled "Organization, Management, and Supervision."

a. It takes approximately 20 minutes to assemble and analyze a chart for deficiencies. If there are 16,020 discharges for the month, how many personnel hours are needed for this volume of work?

b. A coding supervisor at Count General Hospital needs to determine the number of full time equivalents (FTEs) necessary to code 750 discharges per week. It takes an average of 15 minutes to code each record and each coder will work 40 hours per week. How many FTEs are required?

c. All employees are to get a 3.5% increase in pay at the beginning of the new fiscal year, which is July 1. Employees will also get an 8% merit increase on their anniversary. The director of the health information department currently makes $45,000 per year. What will her salary be as of August 25 next year, which is her anniversary date?

d. The director of health information is contemplating purchasing or leasing a new dictation system. The director calculates the payback period and rate of return on investment. The facility's required payback period is 4 years with a required rate of return of 30%. If the equipment costs $40,000 and generates $10,000 per year in savings, what would the payback period for this equipment be?

e. In a health information department, the coding staff earns and works the following hours. What is the routine (40 hours/week) cost of staffing the coding area of this health information department?

Employee	# Hours Worked per Week	Hourly Wage
Coder A	45	$25
Coder B	40	$30
Coder C	49	$35
Coder D	36	$37

TEST YOUR KNOWLEDGE

Use the following table for questions 1–2.

Employee	June 200x	August 200x
Irma	95%	98.5%
Casandra	94%	89%
Bunmi	98.2%	100%
Shirlyn	92.4%	98.3%

Productivity of four employees was calculated as follows:

1. Which employee has shown the most improvement?
   a. Irma
   b. Casandra
   c. Bunmi
   d. Shirlyn

2. Which employee needs to be counseled concerning her productivity?
   a. Irma
   b. Casandra
   c. Bunmi
   d. Shirlyn

3. As the supervisor of the birth certificate process, you conduct a monthly review of the birth certificates processed versus the certificates returned from the Bureau of Vital Statistics. Based on your review, a total of 468 birth certificates were filed and 12 were returned. What is the accuracy of processing birth certificates?
   a. 85.9%
   b. 94.4%
   c. 97.4%
   d. 100%

4. You have owned and managed a transcription company for just over 4 years with great efficiency. You have six employees, including two sales associates and four transcribers. Occasionally an employee tries to suggest changes, but you have success with the present system and you tell them to just follow the established procedures. What is your style of management?
   a. Democratic
   b. Laissez-faire
   c. Participatory
   d. Autocratic

5. Each procedure should indicate how it is related to a department's:
   a. rules.
   b. objectives.
   c. policies.
   d. standards.

6. The production of a coder has been consistently lower than the others. You suspect he is not efficient with his time. Which tool would most accurately measure his production?
   a. Work sampling
   b. Production time study
   c. Time log
   d. Standard time data

7. _____ power is based on a follower's perception that an influencer has the capacity to administer some favorable incentive.
   a. Coercive
   b. Reward
   c. Legitimate
   d. Expert

8. Which management function involves scheduling, budgeting, and selecting and setting objectives?
   a. Planning
   b. Organizing
   c. Directing
   d. Controlling

9. James is the director of HIM and Linda is his manager of the main file room. James sees one of Linda's subordinates give a medical record to a physician without following the proper procedure. James immediately goes to Linda to have her correct the clerk and the situation. To which organizational principle is James adhering?
   a. Organizational function
   b. Scalar principle
   c. Span of control
   d. Unity of command

10. The workflow in a department is complicated and congested. In order to study and correct the situation, which technique is the manager most likely to use?
    a. Flow process chart
    b. Movement diagram
    c. Work distribution chart
    d. Procedure flow chart

11. You own a transcription company with 13 employees. Due to the decrease of your business, you need to dismiss 2 employees. In order to assure that you abide by federal regulations, you determine the 2 employees to be dismissed based upon their:
    a. age.
    b. productivity.
    c. war time service.
    d. salary.

12. A supervisor of quality improvement exerts _____ authority when she directs an employee in her section.
    a. functional
    b. line
    c. coercive
    d. staff

13. A process of allocating the cost of non-patient-revenue-generating departments to patient-generating departments can be accomplished through which method?
    a. Step-down
    b. Single distribution
    c. Double indemnity
    d. Math equations

14. The major advantage of written communication is the:
    a. fact that the message can be reinforced by other communication.
    b. opportunity to not receive feedback.
    c. ability to get the message across clearly and without interpretation.
    d. opportunity to develop the message carefully prior to dissemination.

15. Procedures provide for _____ in performing the task.
    a. flexibility
    b. guidelines
    c. standardization
    d. examples

16. A Gantt chart is useful in which of the following management activities?
    a. Scheduling
    b. Recruitment
    c. Purchasing
    d. Workflow

399

17. A hospital has been in operation for 4 years. It has an average of 18,000 admissions a year. The facility has expanded and expects 24,000 admissions next year. There are 6000 linear feet of filing space available, and half has been used. The facility experienced a 38% readmission rate and expects a 40% future readmission rate. If this is a unit record system, how many new file folders will be needed for next year?
    a. 9600
    b. 14,400
    c. 14,880
    d. 33,600

18. The director of the HIM department is preparing a training manual for specific functional areas in the department. What should be the determining factor for providing training?
    a. Length of employment
    b. Cost of training
    c. Educational levels
    d. Functional area objectives

19. A billing clerk is working one hour each day before clocking in at her scheduled start time. She explains that the workload is massive and in order to keep current, she must start work early. Because she has not been compensated for her hours worked, what federal regulation is being violated?
    a. National Labor Relations Act
    b. Labor Management Reporting and Disclosure Act
    c. Civil Rights Act
    d. Fair Labor Standards Act

20. A hospital averages 72 discharges per day. Coders must average 27 records per day. How many full time coders does the department need?
    a. 2
    b. 3
    c. 4
    d. 5

21. What statement best defines management?
    a. Management is getting things done by using the function of management.
    b. Management is the art of getting things done through people.
    c. Management is getting things done through systems.
    d. Management is working through and with systems.

22. Positions of authority that advise and recommend a course of action are called:
    a. line authority.
    b. authority.
    c. advisory authority.
    d. staff authority.

23. Positions that have authority to direct the tasks of subordinates are called:
    a. line authority.
    b. authority.
    c. staff authority.
    d. direct line authority.

24. According to Henry Mintzberg, all are considered managerial roles *except*:
    a. interpersonal activity.
    b. editing activity.
    c. decisional activity.
    d. informational activity.

25. In orientating a new employee, you inform her that her immediate supervisor is Kimberly Smith, the record completion supervisor. This is what principle of management?
    a. Scalar chain
    b. Unity of direction
    c. Order
    d. Unity of command

26. Introducing a new employee to the organizational structure and illustrating how the person contributes to the objectives of the department is what principle of management?
    a. Scalar chain
    b. Unity of direction
    c. Order
    d. Unity of command

27. There is a staff of 20 people in record completion. The manager organizes them in groups of 4 and assigns each team to a group of physicians to assist them in completing patient records. This is an example of organizing work by:
   a. customer.
   b. project.
   c. territory.
   d. product.

28. An organization chart identifies all of the following *except*:
   a. line of authority.
   b. responsibilities.
   c. wages and benefits.
   d. span of control.

29. The organizing function involves:
   a. defining roles.
   b. budgeting.
   c. motivating.
   d. structuring.

30. A tool used to analyze manual operations and steps in a work process is called a (an) _____ chart.
   a. organization
   b. flow process
   c. work process
   d. work distribution

31. Delegating authority:
   a. is not recommended by good leaders.
   b. frees the team leader to focus on more important and complex assignments.
   c. decreases the leader's productivity.
   d. delays decision making.

32. To classify work into manageable units is to:
   a. plan.
   b. control.
   c. direct.
   d. organize.

33. Development of goals for the future year and the development of a plan for professional development are elements of:
   a. employee's job description.
   b. employee's handbook.
   c. employee's performance review.
   d. employee's discipline record.

34. Space costs, rent, and salaries of management team are considered:
   a. fixed costs.
   b. controls.
   c. variable costs.
   d. revenue.

35. Determining whether plans or goals are being achieved can be defined as:
   a. planning.
   b. organizing.
   c. controlling.
   d. directing.

36. Directing includes all of the following *except*:
   a. leading.
   b. actuating.
   c. taking corrective action.
   d. communicating.

37. Choose the best order for the steps in problem solving.
   a. Define problem; generate alternatives; implement alternatives; analyze problem
   b. Define problem; analyze the root of the problem; generate alternatives; implement alternatives; evaluate
   c. Analyze root of problem; generate alternatives; select best alternative; implement alternatives; evaluate
   d. Define problem; analyze the root of the problem; generate alternatives; select best alternative; implement alternatives; evaluate

38. _____ power occurs when the follower perceives that the leader has valuable knowledge.
   a. Coercive
   b. Reward
   c. Referent
   d. Expert

401

39. Power based on a follower's desire to identify with a charismatic leader is _____ power.
  a. coercive
  b. reward
  c. referent
  d. expert

40. A statement of the organization's overall purpose and philosophy is called the:
  a. mission statement.
  b. value statement.
  c. strategic plan.
  d. statement of objectives.

41. A tool used to determine the amount of time workers are spending on a task is called a:
  a. flow process chart.
  b. movement diagram.
  c. work distribution chart.
  d. Pert chart.

42. The ideal office temperature is about _____ degrees Fahrenheit.
  a. 70
  b. 60
  c. 65
  d. 50

43. A tool used to identify alternative courses of action for problem solving is called a:
  a. flow process chart.
  b. movement diagram.
  c. work distribution chart.
  d. decision tree.

44. A method to establish standards that involves comparison of one organization's performance with another organization is called:
  a. stop watch studies.
  b. work sampling.
  c. benchmarking.
  d. monitoring.

45. A grievance policy should do all of the following *except*:
  a. state the goals and purpose of the process.
  b. communicate critical time limits.
  c. exclude employees on probation.
  d. describe each stage of the process.

46. A human resource tool that depicts visually who is able to fill projected vacant positions is known as a:
  a. replacement chart.
  b. staffing table.
  c. human resource audit.
  d. job analysis.

47. Interpersonal influence directed toward attainment of a specific goal or goals can be defined as:
  a. planning.
  b. leadership.
  c. management.
  d. delegation.

48. The feedback mechanism is considered to be:
  a. planning.
  b. controlling.
  c. organizing.
  d. directing.

49. The 85/15 rule of total quality management proposes:
  a. 85% of work problems are the result of faulty systems rather than unproductive people.
  b. 85% of work problems are the result of unproductive people rather than faulty systems.
  c. 85% of work problems are the result of bad management rather than faulty systems.
  d. 85% of work problems are the result of faulty systems and bad management.

50. Which theory suggests that in the right conditions people will seek responsibility and be creative?
  a. Theory X
  b. Theory Y
  c. Theory of motivation
  d. Maslow's need theory

Mock Exam

There are 200 questions in this exam. You have 4.5 hours to complete it. You will need your coding books and a calculator. Questions are grouped by subject area, thus allowing you the ease of determining the subject areas that require further study and your personal attention. You may use the enclosed CD to scramble the questions; the actual national exams will have the subject areas scrambled.

Choose the best answer.

1. The primary purpose of the health record is to:
   a. teach health care students.
   b. study patient outcomes.
   c. foster continuity of care.
   d. monitor public health.

2. Quantitative analysis ensures:
   a. the discharge summary is present when required and is authenticated.
   b. that the patient record reflects the progression of care.
   c. identification of inconsistent documentation.
   d. identification of inaccurate documentation.

3. The evaluation of patient documentation that compares the patient's pharmacy drug profile with the medication administration record for consistency is an example of what?
   a. Quantitative analysis
   b. Qualitative analysis
   c. Statistical analysis
   d. Legal analysis

4. Thomas General Hospital health information department currently uses 2000 linear filing inches to store medical records and plans to purchase new open-shelf units. Each of the shelves in a new 6-shelf unit measures 36 linear filing inches. It is estimated that an additional 500 filing inches should be planned to allow for 6 years of expansion. How many new file shelving units should be purchased?
   a. 14
   b. 12
   c. 24
   d. 22

5. The Charity Hospital health information department located 2588 out of 2694 records that were requested. What is the record retrieval rate?
   a. 96%
   b. 96.06%
   c. 98%
   d. 105%

6. Electroconvulsive therapy or any therapy that uses painful stimuli:
   a. is no longer used in psychiatric institutions.
   b. cannot be withdrawn by the patient.
   c. requires special care and meticulous documentation.
   d. cannot be reimbursed by third-party payers.

7. The total amount of inpatient discharges at Howard General for the month of December was 1873. However, only 673 of the discharged records were complete at the time of discharge. Calculate December's incomplete health record rate.
   a. 34%
   b. 34.3%
   c. 60%
   d. 64.1%

8. A new health information department has purchased 600 units of 6 shelf files and plans to implement a terminal digit filing system. How many shelves should be allocated to each primary number?
   a. 6
   b. 32
   c. 36
   d. 100

9. _____ help(s) to prevent misfiles and aids in rapid storage and retrieval.
   a. File folders
   b. Color coding
   c. Terminal digit filing
   d. Unit numbering system

10. According to federal regulations, the Veteran's Affairs hospitals are expected to keep their patient records for how many years?
   a. 10 years from the last date of activity
   b. 30 years from the last date of activity
   c. 65 years from the last date of activity
   d. 75 years from the last date of activity

11. The basic tools of a manual record-tracking system are:
   a. out guides and requisitions.
   b. color-coded charts and requisitions.
   c. out guides and color-coded charts.
   d. out guides and a transfer notice.

12. AHMIA recommends that records are destroyed in a manner that prevents their reconstruction. The destruction documentation should include all of the following *except*:
   a. date of destruction.
   d. method of destruction.
   c. time of destruction.
   d. a statement that the records were destroyed in the normal course of business.

13. Secondary purposes of the health record are related to the environment in which patient care is provided. What is an example of a secondary purpose of the health record?
   a. Patient care delivery
   b. The assessment of compliance with standards of care
   c. Patient care management
   d. Patient care support processes

14. In 2003, the Institute of Medicine added this to the list of secondary purposes of the health record.
   a. Policy making and support
   b. Public health and homeland security
   c. Conduct research and development
   d. Study patient outcomes

15. Upon arriving at the emergency room, a patient reports, "My stomach has been tied in knots for two days." The patient's chief complaint is documented in the:
   a. consent for special procedures.
   b. medical history and physical examination.
   c. anesthesia report.
   d. operative report.

16. You are asked to prepare a research paper on sexually transmitted diseases. Your population of study will be males, ages 14–18. Which index could best assist you in this project?
   a. Physician index
   b. Procedure/operations index
   c. Disease index
   d. Numbers index

17. Dr. Mills wants to evaluate the number of patients she saw in the month of January. Which secondary data source would best assist her?
   a. Physician index
   b. Master patient index
   c. Numbers index
   d. Disease and procedure index

18. John Doe dies en route to the health care facility. There is a question about the cause of his death. The family members request an examination to determine and/or confirm the cause of death. What is the report of this examination called?
   a. Autopsy report
   b. Pathology report
   c. Operative report
   d. Consent to treatment

19. A person whom has been injured in a car accident, shot, stabbed, or has experienced a violent fall would be included in which database?
   a. Diabetes registry
   b. Cancer registry
   c. Trauma registry
   d. Birth defects registry

20. A key to locating patient records is the:
 a. admission and discharge register.
 b. master patient index.
 c. number index.
 d. register of births and deaths.

21. All are beginning steps in the forms design process, *except*:
 a. identify purpose of the form.
 b. identify uses of the form.
 c. identify potential users of the form.
 d. make sure forms are not duplicated.

22. An example of an administrative form is:
 a. the birth and death certificate.
 b. consultation report.
 c. interval summary.
 d. progress notes.

23. The Patient Self-Determination Act, effective December 1991, allows patients to give instructions about their wishes in special medical situations. These instructions are called:
 a. consent to special procedures.
 b. advance directives.
 c. acknowledgment of patient rights.
 d. consent to treatments.

24. TJC requires the history and physical to be completed within:
 a. 24 hours.
 b. 24 hours, or sooner if surgery is to be performed.
 c. 48 hours.
 d. 72 hours after admission.

25. What are the four major sections of a problem-oriented medical record?
 a. Database, problem list, initial plans, progress notes
 b. Problem list, SOAP notes, nursing notes, graphic sheets
 c. History and physical, problem list, SOAP notes
 d. Initial plans, problem list, SOAP notes, nursing notes

26. The integrated patient record format is defined as:
 a. arrangement according to the source of the information.
 b. association of treatment and therapies with patient problem.
 c. arrangement according to documentation of a logical, organized plan of clinical thought by practitioners.
 d. organization of reports in strict chronological order without any division by source.

27. Doug Douglas was an inpatient at Thomas Memorial for pancreatitis in July. His medical record number is 10-16-88. He came back to Thomas Memorial in August for gastritis. Thomas Memorial files according to the serial numbering and filing system. Of the following, what possible new number would Mr. Douglas receive?
 a. 10-16-88
 b. 88-16-77
 c. 40-62-40 and then combined into 10-16-88
 d. There is no need for a new number or new record folder.

28. Mrs. Bobette has an oophorectomy done at Houston Medical Center. She returns four months later to have a salpingectomy. Houston Medical Center uses the unit numbering and filing system. How would her record be filed?
 a. She would receive a new medical record number and new folder.
 b. Old records would be brought forward and combined with a new record with a new medical record number.
 c. The Medical Center would use the same medical record from the prior admission and add new medical information.
 d. She would receive a new medical number and a new record would be added to the previous record.

29. You are a file clerk at Manuel Memorial Hospital, which uses the serial-unit numbering and filing system. In this type of system:
  a. the patient is given a new medical record number for each admission.
  b. a new number is given to the patient for each admission, and the old record is brought forward and combined with the new, thus producing a unit record.
  c. the patient uses the same medical record number for each admission.
  d. records are filed in alphabetical order.

30. A numbering system that consists of placing extra pairs of digits illustrating order or position of individuals in the household is:
  a. serial.
  b. serial-unit.
  c. family numbering.
  d. social security numbering.

31. You are working at a 200-bed facility, as a Health Information Specialist II. In the file room, you see the following series of charts on the file shelf: 76-44-07, 77-44-07, 78-44-07, 79-44-07. This is an example of _____ filing.
  a. straight numeric
  b. terminal digit
  c. middle digit
  d. terminal-middle digit

32. When may a final progress note be substituted for a discharge summary?
  a. When patients are admitted for less than 48 hours with minor problems
  b. When the patient stay did not require surgery
  c. In cases of breach childbirth
  d. When no consultation was requested

33. A health record that uses both manual and electronic processes is described as a _____ health record.
  a. electronic
  b. computerized
  c. traditional
  d. hybrid

34. In paper forms design and production, the body and close of the form:
  a. contain the title and subtitle.
  b. explain the purpose of the form.
  c. contain the main content of the form.
  d. explain production considerations.

35. The "A" in the SOAP format of documenting progress notes is:
  a. what the practitioner identifies through the history, physical exam, and other diagnostic tests.
  b. the approach that will be used to resolve problems.
  c. the combination of the subjective and objectives statements that result in a conclusion.
  d. what patient states as a problem.

36. If a patient is admitted to a health care facility on three different occasions and receives three different health record numbers, what numbering system is in use?
  a. Serial
  b. Unit
  c. Alphabetic
  d. Terminal-digit

37. The Centers for Disease Control and Prevention is concerned with:
  a. distribution of major grant funding to the state government and private sector.
  b. producing and disseminating scientific and policy-relevant information.
  c. communicable diseases, environmental health, and foreign quarantine activities.
  d. major medical research.

38. The Centers for Medicare and Medicaid Services (formerly HCFA) is involved in:
  a. health care for the elderly, disabled, and poor.
  b. health care grant funding.
  c. research on communicable diseases.
  d. quality of health care for the aged.

39. All are considered hospital patients *except*:
    a. observation patients.
    b. ambulatory care patients.
    c. inpatients.
    d. long-term care patients.

40. Diagnostic methodologies and stage at the time of diagnosis are data components that are found in what type of registry?
    a. Trauma
    b. Cancer
    c. Birth defects
    d. Diabetes

41. The surgical department of Houston Hospital conducted a study on post-surgical deaths and age of patients. The researcher hypothesized, "There is no relationship between post-surgical deaths and the age of the patients." This statement is generally called the:
    a. statement of problem.
    b. research hypothesis.
    c. alternative hypothesis.
    d. null hypothesis.

42. A researcher wanted to test the following null hypothesis at the .05 level of significance: "There is no significant difference in the length of stays of patients at Hospital X and Hospital Z." The ANOVA results indicated a p-value of .0003. What should the researcher conclude based upon a two-tailed test?
    a. Reject the null hypothesis
    b. Accept the null hypothesis
    c. Expand the review of literature
    d. Rephrase the statement of the problem

43. What does the standard deviation of a sample or population express?
    a. The coefficient of nondetermination
    b. The coefficient of determination
    c. The average of the values in a set
    d. The dispersion of values from the mean

44. The most difficult step in the research process, and probably the most important, is:
    a. conducting review of literature.
    b. isolating the specific research problem.
    c. calculating the statistics.
    d. analyzing the data.

45. A Type I error is when the researcher:
    a. accepts the null hypothesis when it is false.
    b. underestimates the population parameters.
    c. rejects the null hypothesis when it is true.
    d. draws conclusions with insufficient sample size.

46. The researcher calculated a Pearson r of .76. What was the coefficient of determination?
    a. .24
    b. .42
    c. .58
    d. 1.52

47. The Pearson's product-moment correlation coefficient determines:
    a. variability of data scores from the mean.
    b. the significant difference between three or more sample means.
    c. the strength of the relationship between two or more variables.
    d. the significant difference between two sample means.

48. The variable that causes a change in the other variable is called a(n) _____ variable.
    a. dependent
    b. independent
    c. confounding
    d. extenuating

49. A researcher tested the following null hypothesis at the .05 level of significance: "There is no significant difference in the length of stays of patients at Hospital X and Hospital Z." The ANOVA resulted in a p-value of .09. How should the researcher evaluate the null hypothesis based upon a two-tailed test?

  a. Reject the null hypothesis

  b. Accept the null hypothesis

  c. Lower the level of significance

  d. Re-test due to Type 2 error

50. The September average length of stay for Houston Rehabilitation Hospital was 67 days with a standard deviation of 3. What was the length of stay for a patient who stayed in the hospital two standard deviations below the mean?

  a. 58

  b. 61

  c. 64

  d. 65

51. Mr. and Mrs. Howard are making plans to choose a community hospital that renders quality health care. They have narrowed the hospitals to four in the Houston area. They will make their final decision based on the local hospitals' anesthesia death rates. Based upon the data in Table 10-1, which hospital will Mr. and Mrs. Howard decide to utilize?

Table 10-1 Community Hospitals				
Community Hospitals	**Patients Operated Upon**	**Anesthetics Administered**	**Anesthetic Deaths**	**Deaths**
Get Well General	122	194	3	11
Stay Healthy Wellness Center	144	179	4	9
Houston Honorary	138	189	4	10
Tyson Memorial	153	203	3	8

  a. Get Well General

  b. Stay Healthy Wellness Center

  c. Houston Honorary

  d. Tyson Memorial

52. Calculate the hospital net autopsy rate for Houston Hospital given the data in Table 10-2.

Table 10-2	
Discharges (including deaths)	1089
Death	
Total deaths	56
Inpatient deaths (including two coroner cases)	52
Outpatient deaths	2
Home care deaths	2
Autopsies	
Total autopsies	13
Inpatient autopsies	10
Outpatient autopsies	1
Home care autopsies	2
Coroner cases	2

  a. 17.86%
  b. 20.00%
  c. 25.00%
  d. 26.79%

53. Houston Hospital has 520 beds and 70 bassinets and discharged 1454 adult and child inpatients and 332 newborns during the month of September. A total of 9202 discharge days were recorded at the time of discharge for these adults and children and 1554 discharge days for newborns. Census days were 9901 for adults, 331 for children, and 905 for newborns. What was the average daily census for adults and children?
  a. 341
  b. 347
  c. 358
  d. 359

54. Patient Jones was admitted to Houston Honorary Hospital on March 24 for tachycardia. The physician discharged Ms. Jones on April 9 with a discharge diagnosis of rule out stress. How many discharge days were rendered to Ms. Jones upon discharge?
  a. 7
  b. 9
  c. 16
  d. 17

55. As Director of Health Information at Houston Hospital, Tella Johnson is responsible for assuring that the hospital statistics are recorded correctly. She reports that 15 patients were discharged from MICU during October. The length of stay for each patient was 20, 3, 17, 3, 4, 25, 8, 7, 13, 10, 5, 11, 9, 21, and 1. What was the average length of stay for these patients?
  a. 8.9
  b. 9.8
  c. 10.5
  d. 11.1

Use the following table to answer questions 56–57.

Table 10-3	
Discharges	13,642
Deaths	225
Hospital autopsies	75
Coroner cases	10
Live births	1525
Newborn discharges	1502
Newborn deaths	0
Intermediate and late fetal deaths	63
Intermediate and late fetal autopsies	11

56. Houston Hospital had these statistics for a non-leap year. What was the death rate?
   a. .092%
   b. .91%
   c. 1.49%
   d. 1.65%

57. Houston Hospital had these statistics for a non-leap year. What was the adjusted hospital autopsy rate?
   a. 34.88%
   b. 35.01%
   c. 40.23%
   d. 41.01%

58. Houston Woman's Hospital had a total of 225 live births, 5 intermediate and late fetal deaths, and 7 early fetal deaths during the month of March. There were 235 newborn discharges for March. Compute the fetal death rate for the month.
   a. .51%
   b. 1.77%
   c. 1.78%
   d. 2.17%

59. Honors Hospital has 410 beds and 60 bassinets and discharged 1274 adults and children and 322 newborns during the month of April. There were a total of 8482 discharge days for adults and children and 1154 discharge days for newborns. The census days for adults and children were 9173 and census days for newborns were 1265. What was the percentage of occupancy for adults and children?
   a. 66.7%
   b. 68.8%
   c. 72.2%
   d. 74.6%

60. Honorary Hospital operated on 58 inpatients during the month of June. Of these, 3 patients expired 5 days post-surgery. Two expired on the 15th day after receiving their operations. All 58 patients received an epidural anesthesia. Four of the deaths were determined to be caused by the anesthesia. What was the postoperative death rate?
    a. 5.17%
    b. 5.56%
    c. 8.62%
    d. 13.79%

61. Responsibilities for planning and implementing clinical quality assessment programs consist of all of the following *except*:
    a. identify potential clinical quality problems.
    b. determine method for studying potential problems.
    c. participate in regular departmental meetings across the organization.
    d. inform administration of all potential problems.

62. Physician members of the psychiatry committee meet to review psychology cases that are referred for quality issues and that deviate from the Houston, Texas area standards of care. This type of review, in which a physician's record is reviewed by his or her professional colleagues, is known as a _____ review.
    a. concurrent
    b. clinical pertinence
    c. peer
    d. physician

63. The coding section of the health information department has noticed an increase in the number of errors. They gathered together to generate a large number of creative ideas from a group. Which of the following techniques did they use?
    a. Brainstorming
    b. Affinity grouping
    c. Pert networking
    d. Root cause analysis

64. _____ display goals for patients and provide the corresponding ideal sequence and timing of staff actions to achieve those goals with optimal efficiency.
    a. Critical pathways
    b. Clinical protocols
    c. Critical guidelines
    d. Clinical pathways

65. Concurrent quality data collection provides what benefit?
    a. Multiple chart reviews save time.
    b. Patient care problems can be remedied immediately.
    c. Bias is eliminated with anonymous chart review.
    d. Fewer staff are required to perform the review.

66. What does TJC label a serious patient incident that should have a root cause analysis prepared?
    a. Risk assessment
    b. Safety indicator
    c. Intensity review
    d. Sentinel event

67. Concerning clinic records, the health information department states that 100% of records requested will be retrieved prior to patients' appointments. This is an example of a:
    a. performance evidence.
    b. practice indicator.
    c. performance measure.
    d. practice guideline.

68. Activities intended to ensure that facilities' resources are used appropriately on the basis of the patients' needs are termed:
    a. performance improvement.
    b. utilization management.
    c. accounts payable.
    d. resource management.

69. Dr. Houston has applied for reappointment to the medical staff. Which activity must the credentialing staff perform?
 a. Query the National Practitioner Data Bank
 b. Request a history of previous medical staff appointments
 c. Assemble a portfolio of patients treated
 d. Acquire references from patients treated

70. Dr. Houston erroneously removed a patient's healthy kidney. The administrative and legal procedures to be initiated are known as:
 a. potentially compensable event.
 b. safety assessment.
 c. risk management.
 d. claims management.

71. Leaders who have developed methods for measuring and monitoring systems and processes in organizations include all but whom of the following?
 a. Juran
 b. Crosby
 c. Deming
 d. Jeffreys

72. Individuals involved in quality improvement processes in a health care organization must determine all but which of the following?
 a. Who the customers are
 b. What the customers want
 c. What must be done to meet customers' expectations
 d. The gains for the health care organization

73. In 1985, QA standards were revised and resulted in a 10-step monitoring and evaluation process that focused on the important aspects of patient care and service. Who was responsible for this revision?
 a. TJC
 b. The Agency for Healthcare Research and Quality
 c. Institute of Medicine
 d. The Institute for Clinical Systems Improvement

74. Donabedian's quality assessment model is based on all of the following measures *except* _____ measures.
 a. structure
 b. data input
 c. process
 d. outcome

75. _____ defines quality as, "the degree to which health care services for individuals and populations increase the likelihood of desired health outcomes and are consistent with professional knowledge."
 a. Institute of Medicine (IOM)
 b. The Joint Commission (TJC)
 c. Agency for Healthcare Research and Quality (AHRQ)
 d. National Guideline Clearinghouse (NGC)

76. With regard to standards of clinical quality, four types of standards are relevant within the scope of clinical quality assessment. The following are all standards *except*:
 a. clinical practice guidelines and clinical protocols.
 b. accreditation standards.
 c. government regulations.
 d. filing and numbering standards.

77. *Computers, Communications, and Information* defines a(n) _____ as "a collection of related components that interact to perform a task in order to accomplish a goal."
 a. electronic health record
 b. information system
 c. computer
 d. network

78. All are components of an information system *except*:
 a. people.
 b. software.
 c. data warehouses.
 d. hardware.

79. The computer operating system is considered part of the:
- **a.** hardware.
- **b.** software.
- **c.** computer network.
- **d.** data warehouse.

80. Computers come in mainframe, minicomputer, and _____ sizes.
- **a.** microcomputer
- **b.** network computer
- **c.** industry computer
- **d.** workstation

81. A personal digital device is:
- **a.** designed for data retrieval.
- **b.** able to recognize spoken words.
- **c.** a handheld device used for computing, faxing, and networking.
- **d.** a minicomputer.

82. There are four major database models. They include all of the following *except*:
- **a.** relational model.
- **b.** object-oriented model.
- **c.** network model.
- **d.** systems model.

83. Information systems that provide information primarily to support managerial decisions are _____ systems.
- **a.** enterprise-wide
- **b.** operation-support
- **c.** expert
- **d.** management-support information

84. The four major phases of a systems development life cycle in chronological order are:
- **a.** planning, design, implementation, and testing.
- **b.** planning and analysis, design, implementation, and maintenance.
- **c.** system analysis, testing, implementation, and system upgrades.
- **d.** system design, planning and analysis, implementation, and testing.

85. In the development of information systems, questions about current health care business practices and users' needs are asked in what phase of the information system life cycle?
- **a.** Testing
- **b.** System upgrades
- **c.** Planning and analysis
- **d.** Design

86. The fastest and highest-capacity machines built today that are used in large-scale activities such as weather forecasting are called:
- **a.** mainframe systems.
- **b.** Web appliances.
- **c.** supercomputers.
- **d.** midrange systems.

87. A workstation is part of a powerful desktop computer used by a graphics specialist for multimedia production. It is classified as a:
- **a.** mainframe system.
- **b.** Web appliance.
- **c.** supercomputer.
- **d.** midrange system.

88. Backup processes, virus protection, and data recovery are part of the systems software that can be categorized as:
- **a.** utility programs.
- **b.** operating system.
- **c.** language translator.
- **d.** graphical user interface.

89. A patient appointment scheduling system at a primary care clinic has 10 computers connected to a server. This is an example of a(n) _____.
- **a.** wide area network (WAN)
- **b.** Ethernet
- **c.** local area network (LAN)
- **d.** systems area network (SAN)

90. WiFi-protected access is currently the most popular method of securing:
- **a.** computers.
- **b.** wireless networks.
- **c.** local area networks.
- **d.** system area networks.

91. The use of the medical information exchanged from one site to another through electronic communications for the health and education of the patient or health care provider and for the purpose of improving patient care is called:
   a. bandwidth.
   b. telemedicine.
   c. extranet.
   d. intranet.

92. All are considered administrative information systems *except*:
   a. patient registration system.
   b. financial information system.
   c. executive information system.
   d. materials management system.

93. The tracking of staff productivity, analysis of labor expenses by cost center, and monitoring of turnovers are functions of what administrative information system?
   a. Facilities management
   b. Executive information
   c. Financial information
   d. Human resource management

94. The expectation that information that an individual shares with a health care provider during the course of care will be used only for its intended purpose is referred to as:
   a. confidentiality.
   b. data privacy.
   c. data security.
   d. data integrity.

95. The protection and tools that safeguard information and information systems is referred to as:
   a. confidentiality.
   b. data privacy.
   c. data security.
   d. data integrity.

96. A descriptive list of data elements that are collected in an information system or database with the purpose of ensuring consistency in terminology is identified as a:
   a. data warehouse.
   b. data dictionary.
   c. data repository.
   d. data mart.

97. In the AHIMA data quality model, which component is described as the purpose for which the data are collected?
   a. Application
   b. Collection
   c. Warehousing
   d. Analysis

98. All are characteristics of data quality *except*:
   a. accessibility.
   b. reliability.
   c. accuracy.
   d. granularity.

99. Who is more likely to be part of the strategic information systems steering committee in a health care organization?
   a. Chief executive officer
   b. Chief of staff
   c. Chief of security
   d. Chief information officer

100. What position on the information systems technical staff is involved in database design, management, security, backup, and user access?
   a. Systems analyst
   b. Programmer
   c. Network administrator
   d. Database administrator

101. A barium enema may be used to diagnose:
   a. Crohn's disease.
   b. glaucoma.
   c. leukocytopenia.
   d. diarrhea.

102. A fluorescein angiography may be used to diagnose:
- **a.** Crohn's disease.
- **b.** glaucoma.
- **c.** leukocytopenia.
- **d.** diarrhea.

103. A white blood cell count may be used to diagnose:
- **a.** Crohn's disease.
- **b.** glaucoma.
- **c.** leukocytopenia.
- **d.** diarrhea.

104. Electrolyte studies may be used to diagnose:
- **a.** Crohn's disease.
- **b.** glaucoma.
- **c.** leukocytopenia.
- **d.** diarrhea.

105. For which diagnosis would the platelet aggregation test result in abnormality?
- **a.** Acute leukemia
- **b.** Cancer of the prostate
- **c.** Cancer of the breast
- **d.** Multiple sclerosis

106. Major changes in health care documentation and regulations began in 1910, primarily due to:
- **a.** the ACS Act.
- **b.** the Hill Burton Act.
- **c.** the Flexner report.
- **d.** the Anderson report.

107. An act to make insurance more portable and to address fraud and abuse as well as confidentiality issues is known by the acronym of:
- **a.** HCFA.
- **b.** CHIP.
- **c.** SCHIP.
- **d.** HIPAA.

108. A single patient record that maintains health care information throughout a patient's lifetime is known as a(n):
- **a.** traditional medical record.
- **b.** computerized medical record.
- **c.** longitudinal medical record.
- **d.** electronic health record.

109. Someone who is evaluated or treated but not admitted to the hospital and issued a room is defined as a(n):
- **a.** hospital outpatient.
- **b.** accredited patient.
- **c.** licensed patient.
- **d.** transfer patient.

110. The _____ requires one record for each patient; entries made by authorized persons; preoperative and final diagnoses; and thorough documentation of all procedures.
- **a.** American Osteopathic Association
- **b.** American Medical Association
- **c.** The Joint Commission
- **d.** Institute of Medicine

111. Registration, reason for visit, history, examination, labs and X-ray, initial diagnosis, and recommendations for treatment are all items given:
- **a.** at the first encounter.
- **b.** during lab visits.
- **c.** at each and every physician visit.
- **d.** at the second encounter.

112. Public health centers, neighborhood health centers, urgent care centers, private practice offices, and birth centers are all examples of _____ clinics.
- **a.** hospital ambulatory
- **b.** emergency ambulatory
- **c.** freestanding ambulatory
- **d.** hospital satellite

113. In _____ dialysis, the blood is filtered of wastes by means of a machine outside the body.
- **a.** peritoneal
- **b.** hemo-
- **c.** homostasis
- **d.** none of the above

114. To which regulatory standards is it most important and significant for dialysis units to comply?
- **a.** State regulations
- **b.** Federal regulations
- **c.** American Medical Association
- **d.** The Joint Commission

115. A minimum standard of living while incarcerated is guaranteed by:
  a. the 10th amendment to the U.S. Constitution.
  b. the 8th amendment of the U.S. Constitution.
  c. standard prison regulations.
  d. state mission, goals, and statements

116. Detention while awaiting trial, holding for federal, state, or mental facilities, and punishment for minor crimes are three major purposes for:
  a. jails.
  b. prisons.
  c. juvenile facilities.
  d. corporate detention.

117. HIPAA provides a greater degree of protection and confidentiality to mental health records than to:
  a. home health records.
  b. rehabilitation records.
  c. any other type of information.
  d. HIPAA provides same protection for all records.

118. Substance abuse records are protected by:
  a. state law.
  b. federal law.
  c. institutional policies.
  d. all the above.

119. Documentation of spiritual needs and responses is common for patients in:
  a. hospice care.
  b. home health care.
  c. ambulatory care.
  d. respite care.

120. A comprehensive initial assessment that includes not only basic assessment components but also the patient's legal, social, recreational, and vocational status is conducted with patients in _____ care.
  a. hospice
  b. home health
  c. behavioral health
  d. ambulatory

121. Medicare reimburses hospice at four different rates: routine home care, continuous home care, general inpatient care, and _____ care.
  a. emergency home
  b. family-support home
  c. inpatient respite
  d. outpatient respite

122. Jenny Jones is a patient at the Institute for Rehabilitation and Research. Jenny would have all the following documents in her record *except*:
  a. reports of assessment and individual program planning.
  b. follow-up for bereavement.
  c. individual's total program plan.
  d. plans from each service.

123. The interdisciplinary patient care plan is considered the central coordinating tool in which care environment?
  a. Home health care
  b. Behavioral health care
  c. Long-term care
  d. Ambulatory care

124. The service agreement would be found in the health record of a patient in _____ care.
  a. home health
  b. behavioral health
  c. long-term
  d. ambulatory

125. Long-term care is defined as a facility providing acute, specialized care for a length of stay averaging:
  a. 25 days or more.
  b. 30 days.
  c. 45 days or more.
  d. 60 days.

126. Physical therapy, nutrition input, respite care, and medical and social counseling are services:
  a. provided by home health.
  b. provided by hospice.
  c. that must be provided at a medical facility and not by home health.
  d. provided in correctional health.

127. Fees charged, services covered, services not covered, and payment expected are elements of:
    a. consulting contract.
    b. consulting laws and statutes.
    c. verbal agreement.
    d. conditions of consulting.

128. The defendant in a lawsuit is the:
    a. person being sued.
    b. person testifying.
    c. person suing.
    d. witness.

129. Depositions, interrogatories, and documented examinations are examples of:
    a. witness credentials.
    b. inadmissible evidence.
    c. discovery.
    d. licensure items.

130. Failure to do something a reasonable, prudent person would do in a similar situation is:
    a. breach of duty.
    b. medical abandonment.
    c. negligence.
    d. failure to warn.

131. A physician who fails to follow the standard of care, resulting in harm to a patient, may be charged with:
    a. malpractice.
    b. negligence.
    c. duty of care.
    d. abandonment.

132. Any health care provider disclosing health information must have:
    a. permission from treating physician.
    b. power of attorney.
    c. disclosure certification.
    d. authorization from patient.

133. Some elements of a valid release form are:
    a. name and identification, plus the information to be disclosed.
    b. signature and date of authorization.
    c. specific info and persons/organizations to receive info.
    d. all of the above.

134. The interests of biological parents and the interests of children seeking genetic information are two conflicting interests involved in releasing information relating to:
    a. minors.
    b. mental illness.
    c. inmates.
    d. adoption.

135. Two of the most significant developments in law and medicine in the 20th century are:
    a. reasonable patient and professional standards.
    b. advance directive and living will.
    c. doctrines of confidentiality and informed consent.
    d. common and civil law.

136. A subpoena commanding production of books, documents, and records is known as:
    a. subpoena duces tecum.
    b. subpoena ad testificandum.
    c. judicial notification.
    d. statuary notification.

137. Submitting a separate bill for procedures rather than using the code for the entire procedure for purposes of higher reimbursement is known as:
    a. malpractice.
    b. unbundling.
    c. upcoding.
    d. negligence.

138. The HIPAA privacy rule requires covered entities to:
   a. provide individuals with a notice of information practices.
   b. allow patients the right to view their health records.
   c. provide individuals with copies of their records gratis.
   d. refuse to treat noncompliant patients.

139. The privacy rule allows a hospital to disclose information to an employer when:
   a. the employer provides health care to the patient.
   b. the employee's injury affects his/her job performance.
   c. the employer suspects the employee of malingering.
   d. the employee has an infectious disease.

140. A public or private entity that processes or facilitates the processing of nonstandard data elements of health information into standard data elements is a:
   a. health care provider.
   b. health care clearinghouse.
   c. health care planner.
   d. service provider.

141. You have just been appointed Privacy Officer. Your duties will include which of the following?
   a. Release of information with authorization
   b. Risk management of potential lawsuits
   c. Handling privacy rule complaints
   d. Release of information training

142. Title II of HIPAA contains administrative simplification and:
   a. tax-related health provisions.
   b. group-health-plan requirements.
   c. health care access.
   d. security and privacy.

Code the following (questions 143–167) diagnoses and procedures.

143. Patient admitted for syncope due to taking a double dose of Verapamil (coronary vasodilator), which is being taken for hypertension.
   a. 780.2, 401.9
   b. 972.4, 780.2, 401.9, E858.
   c. 972.4, 780.2, 401.9, E942.4
   d. 780.2, E942.4

144. Patient admitted with ulcerative colitis of the entire large intestine. A total colectomy with an ileostomy was performed. The patient also developed a urinary tract infection due to pseudomonas and was given antibiotics.
   a. 558.9, 599.0, 45.8, 46.20
   b. 558.8, 599.0, 041.7, 45.8, 46.20
   c. 558.6, 599.0, 041.7, 45.8, 46.20
   d. 558.6, 599.0, 45.8, 46.20

145. Patient was admitted after a motor vehicle collision (driver) with another car. Patient sustained a pilon fracture (tibia and fibula-distal end) of the left leg. He also has a lung contusion, liver laceration, and three fractured ribs. His leg was treated with open reduction and internal and external fixators. The other injuries were treated conservatively.
   a. 823.82, 861.21, 807.03, 864.05, 78.17, 79.36, E812.0
   b. 823.92, 864.19, 807.13, 861.22, 78.17, 79.36, E812.9
   c. 823.82, 861.21, 807.03, E812.0, 79.17, 79.36
   d. 823.92, 861.21, 807.03, 864.05, 79.17, 79.365, E812.0

146. Patient was admitted with right lower quadrant abdominal pain. Patient was found to have choledocholithiasis of both the bile duct and gallbladder, with acute and chronic cholecystitis. Patient undergoes an ERCP with removal of stones and sphincterotomy. A laparoscopic cholecystectomy was performed the next day.
   a. 574.80, 51.85, 51.88, 51.22
   b. 574.40, 574.10, 51.88, 51.85, 51.23
   c. 574.80, 51.85, 51.88, 51.23
   d. 574.00, 574.10, 574.80, 51.85, 51.88, 51.23

147. Patient who had an anteroseptal myocardial infarction 2 weeks prior is admitted with continued unstable angina due to coronary artery disease. A PTCA with insertion of a drug-eluting stent was done on the RCA with infusion of REOPRO (platelet inhibitor).
   a. 410.11, 41401, 411.1, 36.01, 36.07, 99.20
   b. 414.01, 411.1, 410.12, 36.01, 36.07, 99.20
   c. 414.01, 410.12, 36.01, 36.07, 99.20
   d. 410.12, 414.01, 411.1, 36.01, 36.07, 99.10

148. A patient was admitted with gastrointestinal bleeding. A colonoscopy was performed and revealed bleeding AVMs (angiodysplasia). Epinephrine was injected and the bleeding stopped.
   a. 578.9, 569.85, 45.43
   b. 578.9, 569.85, 45.23, 45.43
   c. 569.85, 45.43
   d. 569.85, 45.23, 45.43

149. A female at 31 weeks gestation is admitted with preterm labor. Tocolysis was begun and the labor stopped. Patient also was noted to have bacterial vaginitis, which was treated with Flagyl.
   a. 644.03, 616.10, 041.9. 99.29
   b. 644.13, 646.63. 99.29
   c. 644.03, 646.63, 616.10. 99.29
   d. 644.03, 646.63, 616.10, 041.9, 99.29

150. A 10-year-old type 1-insulin dependent diabetic female was admitted in diabetic ketoacidosis, uncontrolled.
   a. 250.11
   b. 250.13
   c. 250.03
   d. 250.01, 250.11

151. A patient with a complete heart block is admitted for pacemaker insertion. A dual-chamber pacemaker is inserted in the atrium and ventricle without any complications.
   a. 426.0, 37.72, 37.83
   b. 426.0, 37.70, 37.80
   c. 426.0, 37.72, 37.82
   d. 426.0, 37.72, 37.81

152. A patient is admitted with a severe rash. A dermatology consult was obtained and patient was diagnosed with erythema nordosum. She also has ESRD due to hypertension and received hemodialysis before discharge.
   a. 695.2, 403.91, v45.1, 39.95
   b. 695.9, 403.91, 39.95
   c. 695.2, 585, 401.9, v45.1, 39.95
   d. 695.2, 403.91

153. A newborn boy is born in Houston Hospital with tetralogy of Fallot.
   a. V27.0, 745.2
   b. V30.00, 745.2
   c. V30.01, 745.2
   d. V30.00, 746.09

154. A full-term newborn born in the ambulance was brought to Houston Hospital.
   a. V30.00
   b. V30.10, V27.0
   c. V27.0
   d. V30.10

155. Bob was treated for BPH with bladder obstruction.
   a. 600.00, 596.0
   b. 600.00, 596.51
   c. 600.01, 596.0
   d. 600.01, 596.51

156. A 48-year-old female has acute and chronic cervicitis with subsequent vaginal hysterectomy.
 a. 622.0, 68.51
 b. 616.10, 68.51
 c. 616.11, 68.59
 d. 616.0, 68.59

157. Bob is diagnosed with dermatitis due to allergic reaction to penicillin tablets prescribed for strep throat.
 a. 960.0, 693.0, E856
 b. 960.0, 693.0, E930.0
 c. 693.0, E856
 d. 693.0, E930.0

158. Mrs. Jones, who is 98 years old and lives with her granddaughter, presented with decubitus ulcer of the sacral area with gangrene.
 a. 707.02, 440.24
 b. 707.02, 785.4
 c. 707.03, 785.4
 d. 707.8, 440.24

159. A lung mass is found on diagnostic bronchoscopy.
 a. 786.6, 33.23
 b. 611.72, 33.23
 c. 611.72, 33.24
 d. 680.2, 33.23

160. Girlfriend shot patient with revolver, and he received a moderate laceration to his liver.
 a. 864.13, E965.1
 b. 864.13, E965.0
 c. 864.01, E965.0
 d. 864.01, E965.1

161. Mr. Jones experienced urinary retention, which required the insertion of a Foley catheter.
 a. 788.20, 57.94
 b. 788.20, 57.93
 c. 788.21, 57.93
 d. 788.21, 57.94

162. Bob experienced a postoperative hemorrhage resulting in anemia from acute blood loss.
 a. 997.72, 280.0
 b. 998.11, 280.0
 c. 998.11, 285.1
 d. 998.11, 285.2

163. Bob is brought to the emergency room with a ruptured aortic aneurysm and is taken immediately into surgery for repair. Which code is assigned to demonstrate the anesthesia for the surgery will be affected by the emergency status of Bob?
 a. 99100
 b. 99116
 c. 99135
 d. 99140

164. Mrs. Jones is seen in the office for two subungual hematomas, one on the right middle finger and one on the right ring finger, with both evacuated. She receives no other service.
 a. 11740-F1, 11740-F2
 b. 11740-F3, 11740-F4
 c. 11740-F5, 11740-F6
 d. 11740-F7, 11740-F8

165. Removal of two lobes of the right lung.
 a. 32440
 b. 32482
 c. 32482-RT
 d. 32484-RT

166. Bob has otoplasty of protruding ears.
 a. 69300
 b. 69300-50
 c. 67800-50
 d. 67800

167. *Candida* skin test.
 a. 86485
 b. 86488
 c. 86470
 d. 86849

168. The principle that management should select, train, and develop workers scientifically so that the right person has the right job is a philosophy of which management theorist?
a. Max Weber
b. Frank Gilbreth
c. Henry Gantt
d. Frederick Taylor

169. The functions of management, planning, organizing, directing (leading), and controlling were contributed to administrative management by:
a. Henry Fayol.
b. Frank Gilbreth.
c. Henry Gantt.
d. Frederick Taylor.

170. Maslow's hierarchy of needs begins with physiological needs and ends with:
a. safety needs.
b. social belonging.
c. self-actualization or creativity.
d. self-esteem.

171. The person who has responsibilities has the right to give direction and expect obedience. This is known as:
a. assertion.
b. equity.
c. discipline.
d. authority.

172. All of the following are techniques of operations management *except*:
a. forecasting.
b. specialization of labor.
c. linear programming.
d. break-even analysis.

173. "Every employee receives direction and instruction from only one boss" is the management principle known as:
a. span of control.
b. espirit de corps.
c. authority.
d. unity of command.

174. Harmony, cohesiveness, and teamwork are expressed in the management principle of:
a. span of control.
b. espirit de corps.
c. authority.
d. unity of command.

175. Which is a scheduling tool that is a system of diagramming steps or component parts of a complex project?
a. Pert chart
b. Gantt chart
c. Process flow chart
d. Decision tree

176. A statement that describes the general purpose of an organization or group or how the organization or group expresses who they are is called a:
a. value statement.
b. vision statement.
c. long-term goal.
d. mission statement.

177. Managers who have subordinates who set individual objectives related to organizational goals is an element of:
a. TQM.
b. MBO.
c. administrative management.
d. operations management.

178. The standard at Thomas General for coders is an average of 30 records per day. If the hospital discharges an average of 310 patients per day, how many full time equivalents (FTE) coders does the department need?
a. 9.9
b. 10.1
c. 10.3
d. 11.0

179. What function of management deals with stimulating members of a work group to perform work in a manner such that the objectives are met?
a. Planning
b. Organizing
c. Directing/leading
d. Controlling

Use the following for questions 180–183.

This is your first week as the new director of health information. This new position is a 2-year-old facility that provides general acute care. Your employees are dependable but lack skills and knowledge about health information. They are eager to learn, yet sometimes they get very discouraged about what they do not know. To address the needs of your department you proceed as follows:

180. You begin to structure and assign tasks according to skill level and the department work flow. This management function is called:
a. planning.
b. organizing.
c. directing/leading.
d. controlling.

181. You conduct a meeting with your staff and inform them of the training program you will be implementing the following month. You solicit input from your staff as to the training needs, best days, and times they can participate that will not dramatically affect the workload. This is called:
a. planning.
b. organizing.
c. directing/leading.
d. controlling.

182. After the staff meeting, you meet with your assistant director and share with her your meeting schedule during the training period. You direct her to arrange to attend all meetings for you so that you may clear your schedule for the training. This is what function of management?
a. Planning
b. Organizing
c. Directing/leading
d. Controlling

183. Six months have passed. The training is complete. You now solicit feedback from your staff via surveys to determine if the training was beneficial. This is what function of management?
a. Planning
b. Organizing
c. Directing/leading
d. Controlling

184. Recently, numerous complaints have surfaced about the department's effectiveness. As the director of the HIM department, you choose to provide an in-service to assist department supervisors in improving productivity in their respective areas. Which of the following components is critical to achieving desired productivity outcomes?
a. Tailoring the training to each individual employee
b. Delegating employee training to the most efficient employee within the department
c. Determining productivity standards for each area and job function
d. Selecting the right person for the job

185. McGregor's theory, which characterized the managerial philosophy that employees will avoid work and have no ambition outside of their jobs, was labeled:
a. Theory W.
b. Theory X.
c. Theory Y.
d. Theory Z.

186. The director of health information wants to determine the usage of medical records stored offsite. There were 947 records retrieved from storage, which housed 22,400 records. What is the percentage of records retrieved from the offsite storage area?
    a. 4.2
    b. 5
    c. 23.6
    d. 23.7

187. Coder B codes consistently beneath the department's standard. Her supervisor has stated that she is not maximizing her time. The tool that would most accurately measure her production would be:
    a. work sampling.
    b. production time study.
    c. time log.
    d. standard time data.

188. William Esther, RHIT, informs his staff that he will begin to suspend individuals who are delinquent in meeting the required coding standard of 50 records per day. This reflects what power?
    a. Coercive
    b. Reward
    c. Referent
    d. Expert

189. The most important function of management, and the most neglected, is:
    a. planning.
    b. organizing.
    c. directing.
    d. controlling.

190. The power that is based on a follower's perception that an influencer has the capacity to administer some reward is:
    a. coercive.
    b. reward.
    c. referent.
    d. expert.

191. A narrative that presents the key responsibilities, activities, and working conditions of a job is called a:
    a. job announcement.
    b. job posting.
    c. job description.
    d. job opportunity.

192. The purchase of record folders, chart dividers, and out guide are what type of cost?
    a. Variable
    b. Semi-variable
    c. Fixed
    d. Rolling

193. _____ leadership refers to behaviors associated with more routine and continuing exchanges of effort and commitment between managers and employees.
    a. Transactional
    b. Transformational
    c. Translational
    d. Servant

194. The idea that leadership can be taught is part of the _____ leadership theory.
    a. trait
    b. genetic
    c. situational
    d. behavioral

195. A plan that is expressed with numerical values is called the:
    a. strategic plan.
    b. tactical plan.
    c. budget.
    d. operational plan.

196. All are suggestions to increase the accuracy of communication *except*:
    a. minimize noise that can distort the message.
    b. use active listening.
    c. have an answer already prepared.
    d. ask for feedback and listen to it without being judgmental.

197. The director of health information budgeted $350,550 for full-time salaries. The department actual spent $400,500 on full-time salaries. Overtime for full-time employees was $5000. What was the variance in full-time salary dollars?
  a. –$44,950
  b. $44,950
  c. –$49,950
  d. $49,950

198. The master budget is a consolidation of the:
  a. statistical, operating, cash, and capital budgets.
  b. department capital budgets.
  c. department operating budgets.
  d. department capital and operating budgets.

199. Identify the steps of the progressive discipline process in the correct sequence.
  a. Written warning, oral warning, written warning, and suspension
  b. Written warning, oral warning, suspension, and termination
  c. Oral warning, written warning, suspension, and oral warning
  d. Oral warning, written warning, suspension, and termination

200. You are the supervisor of the record-processing section at Houston Memorial Hospital. Your employees are exhibiting signs of boredom, tension, and lack of quality in their assigned tasks. You begin to incorporate some motivation techniques to inspire their assigned tasks. This would be considered the management function of:
  a. planning.
  b. organizing.
  c. directing.
  d. controlling.

References

Abdelhak, M., Grostick, S., Hanken, M. A., & Jacobs, E. B. (2007). *Health information: management of a strategic resource.* St. Louis: Saunders Elsevier.

American Health Information Management Association. (n.d.). *Analysis of final rule for FY 2008 revisions to the Medicare hospital inpatient prospective payment system.* Retrieved December 22, 2007, from http://www.ahima.org/dc/documents/MicrosoftWord-IP-PPSanalysis-FY08_000.pdf#page%3D1.

American Medical Association. (2007). *CPT 2008 professional edition.* Chicago: Author.

Bronnert, J., Edicott, M., Kostick, K., Hull, S., Scichilone, R., Stanfill, M., & Zeisset, A. (2007). *Clinical coding workout.* Chicago: American Health Information Management Association.

Brown, F., Leon-Chisen, N., & Rapier, A. (2007). *ICD-9-CM coding handbook 2008.* Atlanta: Health Forum, Inc.

Casto, A. B., & Layman, E. (2006). *Principles of healthcare reimbursement.* Chicago: American Health Information Management Association.

Department of Health and Human Services, Centers for Medicare and Medicaid Services. (2008). *Hospital quality initiative overview.* Retrieved July 24, 2008, from http://www.cms.hhs.gov/HospitalQualityInits/Downloads/Hospitaloverview.pdf.

Frazier, M., & Drzymkowski, J. W. (2000). *Essentials of human diseases and conditions.* St. Louis: Saunders Elsevier.

Green, M., & Bowie, M. J. (2005). *Essentials of health information management.* Clifton: Thompson Delmar Learning.

Horton, L. (2007). *Calculating and reporting healthcare statistics.* Chicago: American Health Information Management Association.

Joint Commission on the Accreditation of Healthcare Organizations. (2006). *Accreditation process guide for long term care.* Chicago: Author.

Joint Commission on the Accreditation of Healthcare Organizations. (2006). *Standards for ambulatory care.* Chicago: Author.

Joint Commission on the Accreditation of Healthcare Organizations (2006). *Standards for home health, personal care, support services, and hospice.* Chicago: Author.

Johns, M. (2007). *Health information management technology.* Chicago: American Health Information Management Association.

Johns, M. (2002). *Information management for health professions.* Albany: Delmar Thompson.

Kuehn, L. (2006). *CPT/HCPCS coding and reimbursement for physician services.* Chicago: American Health Information Management Association.

LaTour, K., & Eichenwald-Maki, S. (2006). *Health information management concepts, principles, and practice.* Chicago: American Health Information Management Association.

McWay, D. (2003). *Legal aspects of health information management.* Albany: Delmar Publishers.

Moisio, M., & Moisio, E. (1998). *Understanding laboratory and diagnostic tests.* Albany: Delmar Thompson.

Montana, P., & Charnov, B. (2000). *Management.* Hauppauge: Barrons.

National Center for Health Statistics. (2007, Oct. 1). *About the international classification of diseases, tenth revision, clinical modification (ICD-10-CM).* Retrieved April 9, 2008, from http://www.cdc.gov/nchs/about/otheract/icd9/abticd10.htm.

National Center for Health Statistics. (2007, Oct. 1). *International classification of diseases, ninth revision, clinical modification official guidelines for coding and reporting.* Retrieved April 9, 2008, from http://www.cdc.gov/nchs/datawh/ftpserv/ftpicd9/icdguide07.pdf.

National Committee for Quality Assurance. (2006–2007). *Disease management standards and guidelines.* Retrieved March 28, 2008, from: http://www.ncqa.org/tabid/381/Default.asp.

Osborn, C. E. (2006). *Statistical applications for health information management.* Sudbury, MA: Jones and Bartlett.

Peden, A. (2005). *Comparative health information management.* Albany: Delmar Thompson.

Puckett, C. (Ed.). (2007). *Annual hospital version the educational annotation of ICD-9-CM.* Reno: Channel Publishing.

Roach, S. (2005). *Pharmacology for health professionals.* Philadelphia: Lippincott, Williams, and Wilkins.

Safian, S. (2009). *The complete procedure coding book.* Boston: McGraw-Hill.

Shaw, P., Elliott, C., Isaacson, P., & Murphy, E. (2007). *Quality and performance improvement in health care.* Chicago: American Health Information Management Association.

Sultz, H., & Young, K. (2004). *Health care USA: understanding its organization delivery.* Sudbury, MA: Jones and Bartlett.

The Joint Commission. (2007). *Comprehensive accreditation manual for hospitals: the official handbook.* Chicago: Author.

Answer Key

CHAPTER 2

1. D Abdelhak 14, 49–50

2. C Abdelhak 475–476; Johns (2007) 401–402; LaTour 290–291

3. D Horton 14

$$\frac{10}{15} \times 100 = 66.6 = 67\%$$

4. B Abdelhak 107–109; Johns (2007) 54; Green 144

5. A Abdelhak 154–155; Johns (2007) 399–400

6. D Abdelhak 226–227; Johns (2007) 206

7. A Abdelhak 8–9

8. C Abdelhak 127

9. B Abdelhak 109

10. D Abdelhak 124; Johns (2007) 515; LaTour 195

11. C Abdelhak 223–226; Johns (2007) 769–770; LaTour 199

12. B Abdelhak 104–105; Johns (2007) 339; LaTour 176

13. D Abdelhak 126–127; Johns (2007) 351; LaTour 193–194

14. A Abdelhak 114; Johns (2007) 91; LaTour 186

15. C Abdelhak 237; Johns (2007) 349; LaTour 201–202

16. A LaTour 199

17. A Abdelhak 110; Johns (2007) 62; LaTour 182

18. B Abdelhak 110; Johns (2007) 62

19. C Abdelhak 109–110; Johns (2007) 68–69; LaTour 183

20. B Abdelhak 98–99; Johns (2007) 241

21. A Abdelhak 97–98; Johns (2007) 30, 32; LaTour 173–174

22. D Abdelhak 225–226; Johns (2007) 342; LaTour 200–201

23. B LaTour 183

24. D Abdelhak 20; Johns (2007) 618

25. D Abdelhak 109–110; Johns (2007) 68–69; LaTour 182

26. A Abdelhak 46; Johns (2007) 365–366; LaTour 104, 194–195

27. B Abdelhak 126–127; Johns (2007) 351; LaTour 193–194

28. C Abdelhak 475–476; Johns (2007) 400–401; LaTour 290–291

29. A Abdelhak 13

30. **C** Abdelhak 238–240; Johns (2007) 349–350
31. **D** Abdelhak 226; Johns (2007) 400; Green 230
32. **C** Abdelhak 238–240; Johns (2007) 349–350
33. **B** Horton 17–18

$$\frac{(134 \times 100)}{3489} = 3.84\%$$

34. **D** Abdelhak 643; Johns (2007) 345–346

$$517 \times 1.8 = 930.6 \qquad 36 \times 7 = 252 \qquad \frac{930.6}{252} = 3.69 = 4$$

Note: Since you cannot purchase 3.69 shelves, you must purchase 4.
35. **C** Abdelhak 33–36; Sultz 17
36. **B** Abdelhak 28–29; Johns (2007) 636; LaTour 185; Green 62–63
37. **A** Abdelhak 7; Sultz 68
38. **D** Abdelhak 11; Sultz 138
39. **D** Abdelhak 12; Sultz 51
40. **C** Abdelhak 13; Sultz 245–246
41. **C** Abdelhak 13; Sultz 241, 247–248
42. **C** Abdelhak 18–21; Green 13; Sultz 68–70
43. **A** Abdelhak 18; Sultz 131–134
44. **D** Abdelhak 19; Sultz 68
45. **B** Abdelhak 21
46. **D** Abdelhak 20; Johns (2007) 618
47. **B** Green 16
48. **A** Abdelhak 21–22; Johns (2007) 619
Note: All relevant TJC standards should be upheld.
49. **D** Johns (2007) 623–624
50. **D** Abdelhak 27–28; Johns (2007) 634–635

CHAPTER 3

1. **B** Abdelhak 509
2. **D** Abdelhak 515–518; LaTour 280–281
3. **B** Abdelhak 515–518; LaTour 280–281
4. **A** Abdelhak 507–508, 533
5. **A** Abdelhak 527–528; Johns (2007) 685
6. **C** Abdelhak 527–529; Johns (2007) 685
7. **D** Abdelhak 226–231; LaTour 282
8. **C** Abdelhak 512, 529–530
9. **B** Abdelhak 527; Johns (2007) 685
10. **A** Abdelhak 515, 517–518; LaTour 280–281
11. **B** Abdelhak 530
12. **D** Abdelhak 515, 517–518; LaTour 270, 273–274, 280–281
13. **D** Abdelhak 522; LaTour 249
14. **C** Abdelhak 516; LaTour 250
15. **A** Abdelhak 531
16. **C** Abdelhak 524
17. **C** Abdelhak 517
18. **D** Abdelhak 508
19. **A** Abdelhak 504; LaTour 241
20. **B** Abdelhak 514
21. **A** Abdelhak 504–505; LaTour 242

22. **A** Abdelhak 507; LaTour 243; Johns (2007) 690
23. **A** Abdelhak 504; LaTour 241, 244–247; Johns (2007) 691
24. **B** Abdelhak 517; LaTour 251–252; Johns (2007) 684
25. **C** Abdelhak 524–525; LaTour 252–260; Johns (2007) 700–701
26. **B** Abdelhak 515; LaTour 252; Johns (2007) 700
27. **C** Abdelhak 518, 524–525; LaTour 253; Johns (2007) 711
28. **A** Abdelhak 515–516; LaTour 253; Johns (2007) 711
29. **D** Abdelhak 515–516; Johns (2007) 710–711
30. **D** Abdelhak 526
31. **C** Johns (2007) 537
32. **D** Abdelhak 526
33. **A** LaTour 252–253
34. **B** LaTour 252–253
35. **B** Johns (2007) 722
36. **C** Johns (2007) 690
37. **C** Abdelhak 507; LaTour 243
38. **A** Abdelhak 515, 518–520
39. **A** Abdelhak 518, 525–526; LaTour 252
40. **A** Abdelhak 525–526; LaTour 252
41. **B** Johns (2007) 690
42. **D** Johns (2007) 690
43. **C** Abdelhak 517
44. **B** Abdelhak 517; LaTour 251; Johns (2007) 684
45. **D** Abdelhak 524
46. **D** Abdelhak 515–517
47. **C** Abdelhak 241; LaTour 206
48. **A** Abdelhak 524
49. **B** Abdelhak 524
50. **D** Abdelhak 517; Johns (2007) 684

CHAPTER 4

1. **C** Abdelhak 382; Horton 34–38; LaTour 404–405

$$\frac{6705}{31} = 218$$

2. **D** Abdelhak 382; Horton 34–38; LaTour 404–405

$$\frac{6750 + 7130 + 7470}{90} = 237$$

3. **B** Abdelhak 382–383; Horton 52–57

$$\frac{6615 + 6082 + 5668}{910 + 889 + 894} = 6.8$$

4. **C** Horton 42–44; Johns (2007) 457–459

$$\frac{(6750 + 7130 + 7470) \times 100}{(31 \times 250) + (28 \times 250) + (31 \times 300)} = 88.8\%$$

5. **D** Abdelhak 391–392; LaTour 434; Osborn 96–97
6. **A** Abdelhak 382; Horton 25–28; Johns (2007) 453–456; LaTour 404
7. **D** Abdelhak 374; Horton 64–65; Johns (2007) 462; LaTour 409

$$\frac{(7 + 1 + 1) \times 100}{237} = 3.79\%$$

8. B   Abdelhak 378–379; Horton 84–85; LaTour 411

$$\frac{(3+1+1)\times 100}{7+1+1} = 55.56\%$$

9. C   Abdelhak 378–379; Horton 85–86; LaTour 411

$$\frac{(3+1+1)\times 100}{7+1+1-1} = 62.50\%$$

10. A   Abdelhak 376; Horton 76–78; Johns (2007) 463; LaTour 409

$$\frac{2\times 100}{114+2} = 1.72\%$$

11. D   Abdelhak 378–379; Horton 89–90; Johns (2007) 465–468; LaTour 411–412

$$\frac{(3+1+1+1+3)\times 100}{7+1+1-1+1+3} = 75.00\%$$

12. C   Abdelhak 393; Osborn 143–145

13. A   Abdelhak 388–391; Johns (2007) 442–452; LaTour 430–434; Osborn 86–95

14. A   Abdelhak 394–395; Osborn 176–178

15. C   Abdelhak 376; Horton 76–78; Johns (2007) 463; LaTour 409

$$\frac{(5\times 100)}{(225+5)} = 2.17\%$$

16. A   Abdelhak 391–392; Latour 434; Osborn 96–97

$$15 - 5 - 5 - 5 = 0$$

17. B   Abdelhak 392–393, 406; Osborn 140–142

18. A   Abdelhak 375; Horton 68–70

$$\frac{(3\times 100)}{132} = 2.27\%$$

19. A   Abdelhak 376; Horton 76–78; Johns (2007) 463

$$\frac{(72\times 100)}{(980+72)} = 6.84\%$$

20. B   Abdelhak 378–379; Horton 84–85; LaTour 411–412

$$\frac{(10\times 100)}{52} = 19.23\%$$

21. A   Abdelhak 382; Horton 34–38; LaTour 404–405

$$\frac{(9901+331)}{30} = 341.06 = 341$$

22. A   Abdelhak 391–392; LaTour 434; Osborn 96–97

$$87 - 13 - 13 - 13 = 48$$

23. B   Abdelhak 388–391; Johns (2007) 442–452; LaTour 430–434; Osborn 86–95

$$\frac{(8+9)}{2} = 8.5$$

24. C   Abdelhak 382–383; Horton 52–57; Johns (2007) 459–461; LaTour 406–407

$$\frac{(1+3+3+4+5+7+8+9+10+11+13+17+21+25)}{14} = 9.78 = 9.8$$

25. C   Abdelhak 382–383; Horton 52–57; Johns (2007) 459–461; LaTour 406–407

$$\frac{(20+3+17+3+4+25+8+7+13+10+5+11+9+21+1)}{15} = 10.46 = 10.5$$

26. C Abdelhak 378–379; Horton 85–86; LaTour 411

$$\frac{(13 \times 100)}{(20 - 1)} = 68.42\%$$

27. B Abdelhak 374; Horton 64–65; Johns (2007) 462; LaTour 409

$$\frac{(20 \times 100)}{1244} = 1.607 = 1.61\%$$

28. D Abdelhak 382; Horton 34–38; LaTour 404–405

$$\frac{1113}{30} = 37.1 = 37$$

29. B Abdelhak 382–383; Horton 52–57; Johns (2007) 459–461; LaTour 406–407
30. D Johns (2007) 448
31. D Abdelhak 382–383; Horton 52–57; Johns (2007) 459–461; LaTour 406–407

$$(1 \times 105) + (209 \times 3) + (311 \times 2) = 1354; \quad \frac{1354}{(1 + 209 + 311)} = 2.59 = 2.6$$

32. D Osborn 141
33. B Abdelhak 382; Horton 34–38; LaTour 404–405

$$\frac{(498 + 606)}{365} = 3.03 = 3$$

34. C Abdelhak 382–383; Horton 52–57; Johns (2007) 459–461; LaTour 406–407

$$\frac{(4355 + 202 + 3998 + 300)}{(500 + 150) + (600 + 205)} = 6.08 = 6.1$$

35. D Abdelhak 382; Horton 34–38; LaTour 404–405

$$\frac{(4001 + 235 + 4500 + 268)}{365} = 24.6 = 25$$

36. A Abdelhak 376; Horton 76–78; LaTour 413

$$\frac{(1 + 2) \times 100}{(173 + 199)} = .806 = .81\%$$

37. B Abdelhak 382; Horton 42; Johns (2007) 457; LaTour 405

$$\frac{(4001 + 235 + 4500 + 268)}{(500 \times 151) + (512 \times 214)} \times 100 = 4.865 = 4.87\%$$

38. D Abdelhak 382; Horton 42; Johns (2007) 457; LaTour 405
39. C Abdelhak 376; Horton 76–78; Johns (2007) 463; LaTour 409

$$\frac{(3 + 5 + 1 + 3) \times 100}{(183 + 189)} = 3.225 = 3.23\%$$

40. A Abdelhak 376; Horton 76–78; Johns (2007) 463; LaTour 409

$$\frac{(72 \times 100)}{(980 + 72)} = 6.84\%$$

41. C Abdelhak 382; Horton 52–54; Johns (2007) 453–456; LaTour 404
(June 30 – June 28 = 2) + July 1, 2, 3, 4, 5, 6, 7, 8 = 2 + 8 = 10
42. C Abdelhak 382; Horton 25–28; Johns (2007) 453–456; LaTour 404
(June 28 + 29 + 30 = 3)
43. A Abdelhak 382; Horton 52–54; Johns (2007) 453–456; LaTour 404
Note: Patient was still in-house; thus, no discharge days.
44. B Abdelhak 382; Horton 25–28; Johns (2007) 453–456; LaTour 404
July 8 – July 1 = 7

45. A Abdelhak 382; Horton 34–38; LaTour 404–405

$$\frac{14,942}{31} = 482$$

46. B Abdelhak 391–392; Latour 434; Osborn 96–97

$98 + 6 + 3 = 107$

47. B Osborn 218

$.918506 \times .918506 = .84365 = .843$

48. C Osborn 253–256

$$\frac{16}{2} = 8$$

49. D Abdelhak 388–391; Johns (2007) 442–452; LaTour 430–434; Osborn 86–95

$$\frac{(79 + 82 + 78 + 81 + 87 + 92 + 99 + 79 + 80 + 84)}{10} = 84.1$$

50. B Abdelhak 393; Osborn 143–145

Note: Reject null hypothesis because the p-value (5.06887E − 08) is less than the alpha level, which was set at .05.

CHAPTER 5

1. C Abdelhak 7; Johns (2007) 240–241, 605
2. A Abdelhak 463; LaTour 491
3. C Abdelhak 463–464; LaTour 491
4. C Abdelhak 46, 76; LaTour 496–498
5. A Abdelhak 439
6. C Abdelhak 438
7. D Abdelhak 438, 440–441
8. D Abdelhak 407; LaTour 494
9. C Abdelhak 21–22; LaTour 504–505
10. D Abdelhak 441; LaTour 493
11. D LaTour 494
12. B LaTour 494
13. B LaTour 492
14. D LaTour 504
15. C Abdelhak 463–464; LaTour 509
16. D Abdelhak 438–439; LaTour 497–498, 496
17. A Abdelhak 438–439; LaTour 496–498
18. A Abdelhak 467–469; LaTour 505
19. D Abdelhak 7, 46, 76; LaTour 496–498
20. C Abdelhak 446–449; LaTour 505–507
21. C Abdelhak 446; LaTour 491
22. B Abdelhak 451–455
23. C Abdelhak 450–451; LaTour 669–670
24. B Abdelhak 444; LaTour 674–675
25. C Abdelhak 452; LaTour 424, 472–473
26. C Shaw 306–307
27. A Shaw 20
28. D LaTour 494
29. B Shaw 19–20
30. B LaTour 494
31. C LaTour 427–428, 674–675

32. A Shaw 363–364
33. A Shaw 108–110
34. C LaTour 509–510
35. D LaTour 503
36. A LaTour 509
37. A LaTour 511; Shaw 157
38. D Abdelhak 438–439
39. B Abdelhak 462–466
40. C Abdelhak 441
41. D Abdelhak 508
42. A Abdelhak 441
43. C Abdelhak 465–466
44. B Abdelhak 468
45. B Abdelhak 441
46. D Abdelhak 466–468; LaTour 504–505
47. D Abdelhak 441
48. C LaTour 509–510
49. B LaTour 509–510
50. A Department of Health and Human Services Web site

CHAPTER 6

1. B Abdelhak 494; Johns (2007) 801–803; Johns (2002) 66–72; La Tour 217
2. A Abdelhak 129; Johns (2007) 818–819; Johns (2002) 43, 91, 103; LaTour 130, 137
3. D Abdelhak 284; Johns (2007) 42–43; Johns (2002) 60–62; LaTour 557–558
4. A Abdelhak 287; LaTour 64–66
5. C Abdelhak 284; Johns (2007) 834–835; LaTour 577–582
6. C Abdelhak 299–301; Johns (2007) 577
7. C Abdelhak 255–256
8. D Abdelhak 295
9. B Abdelhak 315
10. C Abdelhak 243–246

$$\frac{(2500 \times 3072)}{1024} = 7500\text{k}$$

11. B Abdelhak 156, 215
12. B Abdelhak 285; LaTour 548
13. D Abdelhak 277
14. D Johns (2002) 135, 153
15. E Abdelhak 170–171
16. D Johns (2002) 219–220
17. B Johns (2007) 834
18. A Abdelhak 284–287; Johns (2007) 803
19. C Johns (2002) 226
20. A Johns (2007) 747; Johns (2002) 68
21. C Abdelhak 169
22. D Johns (2002) 273
23. C Abdelhak 284; Johns (2002) 33
24. B Abdelhak 169
25. B Johns (2002) 184
26. A Abdelhak 291
27. A Abdelhak 322; LaTour 113–114
28. C Abdelhak 284

29. B Abdelhak 284–286
30. D Abdelhak 165–169, 255
31. A Abdelhak 286; LaTour 214
32. C LaTour 205, 289
33. C Abdelhak 275
34. A LaTour 544–545
35. C Abdelhak 276–277; Johns (2002) 209–212
36. B Abdelhak 276–277; Johns (2002) 209–212
37. C Abdelhak 276–277; Johns (2002) 209–212
38. A LaTour 69
39. B Abdelhak 286–287
40. D Abdelhak 299–301; Johns (2002) 230–231
41. B Abdelhak 286–287; Johns (2002) 86–87
42. C Abdelhak 278
43. A Abdelhak 280
44. B Abdelhak 282
45. C Abdelhak 340
    Note: In year 3, changing to new system saves $1500.
46. A Abdelhak 339
47. C Abdelhak 341
48. D Johns (2007) 832
49. D Abdelhak 335–336
50. B Johns (2007) 831; Johns (2002) 36

CHAPTER 7

1. B Frazier 410–411
2. C Frazier 432–433
3. B Roach 222
4. A Roach 222
5. C Roach 147
6. D Roach 125
7. D Frazier 760–761
8. A Moisio 99–100
9. D Frazier 429; Roach 232
10. A Moisio 51–53
11. B Moisio 238
12. A Frazier 161
13. D Roach 349
14. A Moisio 100–101
15. C Roach 332
16. D Frazier 161
17. C Roach 45, 48
18. B Frazier 522
19. C Moisio 53–54
20. C Moisio 256
21. B Frazier 170
22. D Roach 396
23. A Frazier 439; Roach 232
24. C Frazier 775
25. B Roach 41
26. A Moisio 360–361

27. **D** Frazier 439; Roach 232
28. **B** Moisio 240
29. **C** Moisio 244–249
30. **A** Moisio 46–47, 50–51
31. **D** Moisio 32–40
32. **D** Roach 181
33. **B** Moisio 365
34. **C** Roach 7
35. **B** Roach 154
36. **B** Roach 45
37. **A** Moisio 98–99
38. **C** Frazier 504; Moisio 54
39. **D** Moisio 303–304
40. **D** Moisio 33
41. **D** Frazier 278
42. **C** Moisio 10
43. **A** Moisio 10
44. **C** Frazier 673; Roach 81
45. **B** Frazier 777
46. **B** Frazier 753
47. **B** Frazier 433
48. **D** Frazier 439
49. **A** Frazier 775
50. **C** Moisio 54–55

CHAPTER 8

1. **C** Brown 15
2. **D** Brown 43–44
3. **D** Brown 337–339
4. **C** Brown 49–50
5. **C** Brown 331–334
6. **D** Abdelhak 201–202
7. **A** Abdelhak 203
8. **B** Safian 296
9. **B** Brown 16
10. **B** Safian 36
11. **A** Brown 22–23
12. **C** Brown 64–66
13. **B** Brown 64
14. **D** Brown 207
15. **C** Brown 345
16. **D** Brown 63, 310
17. **D** Brown 289–290
18. **A** Brown 17
19. **B** Brown 263–264
20. **C** Brown 15
21. **A** Brown 64
22. **C** Brown 226
23. **B** Brown 310–311
24. **A** Abdelhak 203
25. **D** Safian 40

26. **A** Safian 108
27. **C** Kuehn 100
28. **A** Brown 83–84
29. **D** Brown 287–294
30. **C** Brown 101
31. **B** Brown 122
32. **A** Brown 109
33. **A** Brown 143
34. **D** Brown 161–162
35. **C** Brown 83
36. **A** Brown 207
37. **B** Brown 197
38. 574.80, 401.9, 51.23, 51.85, 51.88 (Brown 161–162)
    Patient admitted with gallstones and increased bilirubin. Has a history of hypertension and takes Zestril. Patient had an ERCP with ERS and stone extraction from the bile duct, preceded by a laparoscopic cholecystectomy. Final diagnosis is choledocholithiasis of gallbladder and bile duct with acute and chronic cholecystitis.
39. 654.53, 67.59 (Brown 211–212, 215)
    28-year-old G2P1 with cervical cerclage for incompetent cervix at 12 weeks.
40. 354.0, 04.43. 64721–LT (Brown 131)
    Patient admitted for median neuropathy. Carpal tunnel syndrome of the left hand for carpal tunnel release.
41. 836.0, 80.6, 29881–RT (Brown 322)
    Patient admitted with torn medial meniscus for arthroscopic partial medial meniscectomy of the right knee.
42. v25.2, 66.29, 58671 (Brown 219–221)
    Patient admitted for sterilization by scopeBTL.
43. 685.1, 244.9, 311, 86.21, 11770 (Brown 188–190)
    Patient admitted with pilonidal cyst for pilonidal cystectomy
44. 592.1, 401.9, 98.51, 50590–LT (Brown 173)
    Patient admitted with obstructing ureteral calculus. Has a history of HTN and takes atenolol 25 mg. daily. Admitted for ESWL.
45. 366.53, 13.64, 66821–RT (Brown 133–135)
    Patient has cloudy posterior capsule after cataract extraction, admitted for YAG laser posterior capsulotomy of the right eye.
46. 381.3, 20.01, 69436–50, 69990 (Brown 136–137)
    Patient with recurrent otitis media of both ears admitted for myringotomy with insertion of pressure–equalizing tubes in both ears.
47. 414.01, 413.9, 410.72, v45.82, 562.10, 401.9, 272.0, v17.3, v15.82, 37.22, 88.56, 88.53, 93510, 93543, 93545, 93555, 93556 (Brown 254–260)
    Patient (50 years old) with history of MI 6 weeks ago admitted for new onset angina. He is status post PTCA at time of MI, but admitted for preoperative workup for future repair of diverticular perforation of the large intestine. Left heart cath, selective coronary angiography, left ventriculogram.
48. 474.00, 478.1, 28.3, 42821 (Brown 141)
    A 12-year-old admitted with chronic tonsillitis and adenoid hypertrophy for tonsillectomy and possible adenoidectomy.
49. 752.51, 62.5, 62.5, 54640–50 (Brown 236)
    A 13-year-old admitted with undescended testicles for bilateral orchiopexy.
50. v76.51, v16.0, 211.3, 45.42, 45385 (Brown 157–158)
    If patient is admitted for screening colonoscopy, v76.51 should be principal followed by any findings.

CHAPTER 9

1. **D** Abdelhak 611
   98.3% – 92.4% = 5.9% production increase
2. **B** Abdelhak 611
   94% – 89% = 5% production decrease
3. **C** Abdelhak 611

   $$468 - 12 = \frac{456}{468} \times 100 = 97.4\%$$

4. **D** LaTour 624; Abdelhak 546–548
5. **C** Abdelhak 636; Johns (2007) 911–912; LaTour 692
6. **A** LaTour 660–662; Abdelhak 611–613
7. **B** Abdelhak 551; LaTour 608
8. **A** Johns (2007) 902–905
9. **D** Abdelhak 606
10. **B** Abdelhak 618, 637–638
11. **B** Abdelhak 556–565
12. **B** Johns (2007) 882; LaTour 602
13. **A** Abdelhak 668
14. **D** LaTour 614–615
15. **C** Abdelhak 636; Johns (2007) 911–912; LaTour 692
16. **A** LaTour 614–615
17. **B** Abdelhak 221
    24,000 – 40% (9600) = 14,400
18. **D** Abdelhak 598–600
19. **D** Abdelhak 567
20. **B** Abdelhak 611–614

    $$\frac{72}{27} = 2.66$$

    Note: The answer is 3 employees.
21. **B** LaTour 606
22. **D** LaTour 607
23. **A** LaTour 607
24. **B** LaTour 610
25. **D** LaTour 602
26. **C** LaTour 602
27. **A** Abdelhak 606
28. **C** Abdelhak 626
29. **D** LaTour 606
30. **B** Abdelhak 616
31. **B** Johns (2007) 897
32. **D** LaTour 606
33. **C** Johns (2007) 898
34. **A** Johns (2007) 905
35. **C** LaTour 608
36. **C** LaTour 607
37. **D** LaTour 612
38. **D** LaTour 608
39. **C** LaTour 608
40. **A** LaTour 686
41. **C** LaTour 669

42. A Abdelhak 645
43. D Abdelhak 620
44. C Abdelhak 613
45. C Abdelhak 594–595
46. A Abdelhak 575–576
47. B Abdelhak 546–548
48. B LaTour 606
49. A LaTour 605
50. B LaTour 603–604

CHAPTER 10

1. C Johns (2007) 26–29; Abdelhak 97–98
2. A Abdelhak 126–127; LaTour 193–195
3. B Abdelhak 126–127; LaTour 193–195
4. B Johns (2007) 345–347

$$\frac{2000 + 500}{36 \times 6} = 11.57$$

Note: Since you cannot purchase 11.57 shelves, you must purchase 12 new units.

5. B LaTour 201–202

$$\frac{2588 \times 100}{2694} = 96.06\%$$

6. C Abdelhak 143
7. D Abdelhak 123–124

$$\frac{1200(1873 - 673)}{1873} \times 10 = 64.1\%$$

Note: The generic formula for rates always is the number of times something happened *divided by* the number of times something could have happened *multiplied by* 100.

8. C Abdelhak 225–226

$$\frac{600 \times 6(3600)}{100} = 36 \text{ shelves}$$

9. B Abdelhak 234; LaTour 201
10. D Abdelhak 240
11. A Abdelhak 237
12. C LaTour 206
13. B Johns (2007) 27–29
14. B Johns (2007) 27–29
15. B Abdelhak 105–106; Johns (2007) 52–53
16. C LaTour 289; Abdelhak 400
17. A LaTour 289; Abdelhak 400
18. A Johns (2007) 72; Abdelhak 110
19. C Johns (2007) 403; Abdelhak 484
20. B Johns (2007) 375–376
21. D Johns (2007) 368–369
22. A Abdelhak 104–105
23. B Abdelhak 105
24. B Abdelhak 105
25. A Abdelhak 114–115

26. D Abdelhak 115

27. B LaTour 199

28. C LaTour 199–200

29. B LaTour 199

30. C LaTour 199

31. B LaTour 200

32. A Abdelhak 109

33. D Johns (2007) 105

34. C Abdelhak 117–119

35. C Abdelhak 114–115; LaTour 186

36. A LaTour 199

37. C Abdelhak 11

38. A Abdelhak 11

39. D Abdelhak 20

40. B Johns (2007) 402

41. D Abdelhak 392–393

42. A Abdelhak 392–393

43. D Abdelhak 391–392

44. B Abdelhak 406

45. C Abdelhak 393

46. C Abdelhak 396; Osborn 213–218
$(.76 \times .76) = .5776 = .58$

47. C Abdelhak 396; Osborn 210

48. B Abdelhak 406

49. B Abdelhak 393–395; Osborn 143–145

50. B Abdelhak 391–392; Osborn 96–97
$(67 - 3 - 3) = 61$

51. D Horton 70–72

$$\frac{(3 \times 100)}{203} = 1.477 = 1.48\%$$

52. B Horton 85

$$\frac{(10 \times 100)}{(52 - 2)} = 20\%$$

53. A Horton 35

$$\frac{(9901 + 331)}{30} = 341.06 = 341$$

54. C Horton 25–28
(March 31 – March 24) + (April 1st, 2nd, 3rd, 4th, 5th, 6th, 7th, 8th, 9th) = 16

55. C Horton 52–54

$$\frac{(20 + 3 + 17 + 3 + 4 + 25 + 8 + 7 + 13 + 10 + 5 + 11 + 9 + 21 + 1)}{15} = 10.46 = 10.5$$

56. C Horton 64–65

$$\frac{(225 \times 100)}{13,642} = 1.485 = 1.49\%$$

57. A Horton 87

$$\frac{(75 \times 100)}{(225 - 10)} = 34.883 = 34.88\%$$

58. D Horton 77

$$\frac{(5 \times 100)}{(225 + 5)} = 2.17\%$$

59. D Horton 42

$$\frac{(9173 \times 100)}{(410 \times 30)} = 74.57 = 74.6\%$$

60. B Horton 68–69

$$\frac{(3 \times 100)}{(58 - 4)} = 5.555 = 5.56\%$$

61. D Shaw 5–7; Johns (2007) 514–515; LaTour 492–493
62. C Shaw 306; Abdelhak 516; Johns (2007) 625–626
63. A Shaw 19–20
64. A Shaw 108, 110; Johns (2007) 504, 507
65. B LaTour 265
66. D Shaw 155; Abdelhak 459
67. C Shaw 13; Abdelhak 441
68. B Shaw 105–107; Abdelhak 462
69. A Shaw 277; Abdelhak 468
70. D Shaw 154; Abdelhak 461
71. D LaTour 490
72. D LaTour 491
73. A LaTour 491
74. B LaTour 496
75. A Johns (2007) 501
76. D Johns (2007) 503
77. B Johns (2007) 745
78. C Johns (2007) 745
79. B Abdelhak 275
80. A Abdelhak 274
81. C Abdelhak 274
82. D Abdelhak 276
83. D Johns (2007) 746–748
84. B Johns (2007) 750
85. C Johns (2007) 751
86. C Johns (2007) 756
87. D Johns (2007) 757
88. A Johns (2007) 757
89. C Abdelhak 277–278
90. B Abdelhak 278
91. B Abdelhak 292
92. C Johns (2007) 803–805
93. D Johns (2007) 803–804
94. A Johns (2007) 19
95. C Johns (2007) 19
96. B LaTour 115–116
97. A LaTour 107
98. B LaTour 105
99. D LaTour 130

100. D LaTour 138
101. A Moisio 235
102. B Moisio 244
103. C Moisio 9–13
104. D Moisio 30–40; Frazier 95–96
105. A Moisio 94–95; Frazier 483–484
106. C Peden 1
107. D Peden 6
108. C Peden 13
109. A Peden 26
110. C Peden 28
111. A Peden 66
112. C Peden 59
113. B Peden 137
114. B Peden 139
115. B Peden 164
116. A Peden 169
117. C Peden 231
118. D Peden 254
119. A Abdelhak 141–142
120. C Abdelhak 142–143
121. C Abdelhak 142
122. B Abdelhak 137
123. A Abdelhak 137–138
124. A Johns (2007) 84–85; Abdelhak 137–138
125. A Peden 327
126. A Peden 421
127. A Peden 570
128. A McWay 25
129. C McWay 27
130. C McWay 44
131. A McWay 44
132. D McWay 90
133. D McWay 97
134. D McWay 107
135. C McWay 129
136. A McWay 139
137. B McWay 139
138. A AHIMA 13; Abdelhak 515–516; Johns (2007) 702; LaTour 252
139. A Abdelhak 517; Johns (2007) 701–702; LaTour 258
140. B AHIMA 23; Abdelhak 516; LaTour 252
141. C Johns (2007) 733; LaTour 94
142. D Abdelhak 13–14; Johns (2007) 700
143. C Brown 337–343
144. C Brown 83, 157
145. D Brown 316–317
146. C Brown 161–162
147. B Brown 254–257
148. C Brown 157–161
149. D Brown 207–211

150. B Brown 95–99
151. A Brown 254–257
152. A Brown 187–189
153. B Brown 235–236
154. D Brown 242
155. C Brown 178–179
156. D Brown 179–180
157. D Brown 187
158. C Brown 188
159. A Brown 75–77
160. B Brown 309–312
161. A Brown 75–77
162. C Brown 350–351
163. D Kuehn 85–86
164. D Kuehn 108–109
165. C Kuehn 125–126
166. B Kuehn 180
167. A Kuehn 213
168. D LaTour 587–588
169. A LaTour 602
170. C LaTour 603
171. D LaTour 602
172. B LaTour 604
173. D LaTour 602
174. B LaTour 602
175. A Abdelhak 632–633
176. D Johns (2007) 886–889
177. B LaTour 604
178. C

$$\frac{310}{30} = 10.3$$

179. C LaTour 607–608
180. B LaTour 606
181. A LaTour 606
182. A LaTour 606
183. D LaTour 608
184. C Abdelhak 611
185. A LaTour 603
186. A

$$\frac{947}{22,400} \times 100 = 4.2\%$$

187. A Abdelhak 611–613
188. A LaTour 608
189. A LaTour 606
190. B LaTour 608
191. C Abdelhak 558
192. A Abdelhak 663
193. A Abdelhak 548–549
194. D LaTour 624
195. C Abdelhak 662–663

196. **C** LaTour 615
197. **C**

$350,000 - 400,500 = -49,950$
198. **C** Abdelhak 663
199. **D** Abdelhak 593
200. **C** LaTour 607

Index